DATE D

ACTIVELY SEEKING WORK?

DESMOND KING

THE UNIVERSITY OF CHICAGO PRESS

ACTIVELY SEEKING WORK?

THE POLITICS OF

UNEMPLOYMENT AND

WELFARE POLICY IN

THE UNITED STATES

AND GREAT BRITAIN

CHICAGO AND LONDON

R

St. John's College, Oxford.

The University of Chicago Press, Chicago 60637
The University of Chicago Press, Ltd., London
© 1995 by The University of Chicago
All rights reserved. Published 1995
Printed in the United States of America
04 03 02 01 00 99 98 97 96 95   1 2 3 4 5

ISBN: 0–226–43621–7 (cloth)
       0–226–43622–5 (paper)

Library of Congress Cataloging-in-Publication Data

King, Desmond S.
    Actively seeking work? : The politics of unemployment and welfare policy in the United States and Great Britain / Desmond King.
        p.   cm.
    Includes bibliographical references and index.
    1. Full employment policies—Great Britain.   2. Full employment policies—United States.   3. Welfare recipients—Employment—Great Britain.   4. Welfare recipients—Employment—United States.   5. Hard-core unemployed—Great Britain.   6. Hard-core unemployed—United States.   7. Public welfare—Great Britain.   8. Public welfare—United States.   I. Title.
HD5765.A6K557   1995   94-27883
333.13´7941—dc20   CIP

This book is printed on acid-free paper.

TO MY PARENTS

CONTENTS

Acknowledgments   ix

Introduction   xi

Chapter One   Work-Welfare in Great Britain and the United States   1

Chapter Two   "A Permanent Club for the Unemployed"?
                 Establishing Labor Exchanges in Great Britain
                 and the United States   19

Chapter Three   "Financial Succour for the Unemployed"?
                 The Institutionalization of British and
                 American Exchanges   65

Chapter Four   "A Cheap Pool of Forced Labor"?
                 Work-Welfare Training Policy   113

Chapter Five   Breaking the "Spider's Web of Dependency":
                 The Pyrrhic Triumph of Modern Work-Welfare   167

Chapter Six   Conclusion: The Politics of Institutions   203

                 Appendix: Comparative Tables on Work-Welfare   215

                 Notes   223
                 Bibliography   297
                 Index   317

ACKNOWLEDGMENTS

I owe a considerable debt to the many archivists who helped me acquire relevant documents in university and presidential libraries and in national archives in Britain and the United States. Second, I am grateful to a number of institutions for financial support to undertake research trips, principally to the United States: the Nuffield Foundation, the Staff Research Fund of the London School of Economics and Political Science, the Suntory-Toyota Centre for Research in Economics and Related Disciplines (STICERD), also at the London School of Economics and Political Science, and St. John's College, Oxford. Without the financial support of these institutions this work would have been impossible to undertake and I extend my thanks to them.

Robert Schaerfl, director of the U.S. Employment Service (USES), was kind enough to talk at length about the Service in 1991 and to give me the benefit of his knowledge. He also arranged for me to receive documents from the Service. David Robertson and Margaret Weir generously made available material from their own research. I am grateful to Alistair Cooke of the Conservative Party Research Department for permission to quote from the Party's papers deposited in the Bodleian Library and to the Comptroller of H.M.S.O. for permission to quote from Crown copyright material in the Public Record Office.

I am immensely grateful to the following colleagues who provided constructive comments upon an early draft of this manuscript: Nigel Bowles, Ross McKibbin, Alan Ware, and Vincent Wright. Nigel Bowles has been unwavering in his encouragement and support. John Stephens and an anonymous reviewer read the manuscript for the University of Chicago Press and offered valuable comments. John Tryneski at the University of Chicago Press was an outstanding editor. Both he and Randolph Petilos were unfailingly supportive. For comments on parts of the manuscript and other assistance, I am grateful to the following: Carolyn Cowey, David Finegold, Dan Finn, Michael Freeden, Mark Freedland, Peter Hall, the late Kieran Hickey, John Holmwood, Christopher Hood, Gary Mucciaroni, Robert Taylor, David Robertson, Bo Rothstein, David Soskice, Kathleen Thelen, Margaret Weir, Mark Wickham-Jones, and Joel Wolfe. Carolyn

Cowey provided intellectual and moral support throughout the project's research and drafting.

A penultimate draft of the manuscript received valuable readings by Michael Burleigh, Ross McKibbin, Jonas Pontusson, and John Stephens. I am especially grateful to Ross McKibbin for his generosity in reading the manuscript twice and for many discussions about labor exchanges.

Responsibility for any errors in the manuscript is mine.

INTRODUCTION

This book is an attempt to analyze the programs constitutive of "work-welfare" policy in Britain and the United States and to explain their politics. "Work-welfare" denotes three sorts of government policy for the unemployed: first, placement policies to marry jobseekers with vacancies; second, training schemes, intended to augment jobseekers' skills; and, third, workfare programs sometimes imposed upon job seekers as a condition of receiving benefits.

Welfare state programs are commonly studied as elements of a linear, generally benign, process progressing from selective policies to more universal ones. In my view, many of these programs are better conceived of as being cyclical and in which common elements reappear in policy choices. The potential for programs genuinely to progress is limited, in part because of choices made at their foundation, and because of the invidious fiscal and political pressures under which they operate. Many of the political arguments and programs salient in the 1980s were consistent with those in earlier decades of this century. The British work-test of "genuinely seeking work" applied in the interwar years has been succeeded in the 1980s by the injunction "actively seeking work." This commonality of response suggests the importance of a historical analysis of work-welfare programs and an appreciation of the persistence of the problems addressed, including the social fears created by those not participating in the labor market among those who do work.

Work-welfare programs acquire their importance from the centrality of employment in modern societies. It is an incontrovertible principle both of market and socialist societies[1] that those able to engage in productive work are expected to do so. Dressed up as an obligation consistent with a liberal conception of citizenship, this "work ethic" is an inescapable (and often grinding) necessity for survival. Doctrines of social citizenship[2] furnish a protective gloss and rationale for this dictate. A thinly camouflaged propensity exists to treat recipients of noncontributory benefits as lacking or giving up rights—in the words of an 1893 British report, "all persons receiving poor-law relief . . . *lose for the time their rights as citizen*"[3] including, until 1918, the vote. This view provides the logical base for insinuating the duties of beneficiaries and devising mandatory work-welfare schemes, such as have been popular in the 1980s and 1990s. The dissemination and absorption of this principle in Britain and the United States coincided with the establishment of market processes as the dominant system of economic organization, a not coincidental alignment. In Karl Polanyi's observation, "born as a mere penchant for non-bureaucratic methods, [economic liberalism] evolved into a veritable faith in man's secular's salvation through a self-regulating market . . . The liberal creed assumed its evangelical fervor only in response to the needs of a fully developed market economy."[4] The capitalist system of economic organization sanctified by liberalism did not meet the work needs of all job seekers.[5] This failure prompted the founding of public and private employment systems to increase information about vacancies and available workers' skills. The disparity also stimulated the creation of publicly funded and monitored training and apprenticeship programs to enhance the skills of those seeking employment.

The place of work in market societies is complicated by the fact that labor is a distinctive commodity. Labor is not separable from its owner. This feature has implications both for organizing and controlling workers and for relations between workers, employers, and the state. Governments cannot only provide facilities to enhance market efficiency but must regulate the use of their policies and ensure social order. This last requirement was vividly captured by Winston Churchill when he was president of the Board of Trade. He noted the need to establish an . . . "elaborate and effective system of testing willingness to work such as afforded by the system of labour exchanges."[6] The public employment system, designed to dissipate informational deficiencies, proved Janus-faced since it acquired, concurrently, responsibility for regulating labor. Monitoring workers was an objective driven by the place of workers within the economic and political order. Testing work availability or shyness to ensure they were 'actively seeking work' and imposing calibrations between categories of job seekers based on their worthiness muted solidarity amongst workers who occupied a similar location in the labor market. These measures also contributed to the dominance of liberal assumptions[7] about market organization.

Work-welfare programs have failed largely to serve the needs of many citizens in Great Britain and the United States, especially those at the margin of the labor market. This failure reflects the tenacious hold liberal principles enjoy on these programs.[8] In this book, I aim to demonstrate why liberal principles have dominated work-welfare programs in these two countries. I argue that the political origins of these programs and the way in which they were institutionalized explains the resilience of liberal tenets and the programs' inadequacies. I explain why American and British work-welfare programs emphasize the punitive experience of receiving public assistance while simultaneously failing to equip participants for effective labor-market entry.

In my view, public employment exchanges—that is, the government's network of publicly funded offices intended to increase labor market mobility and to distribute information about vacancies—offer a uniquely valuable account of how particular priorities about welfare and work have been realized in public policy. Labor exchanges process able-bodied workers, whether skilled or unskilled, seeking employment and penalize the so-called undeserving or idle workers. They epitomize the British and American approach to work-welfare, especially the priorities of excluding the undeserving from public assistance, distinguishing them from worthy recipients, and imposing work-requirements on beneficiaries.

The disappointing record of work-welfare programs is revealed in attitudes toward public labor exchanges. In Britain these were commonly termed "dole houses,"[9] and recourse to these for people in search of jobs was tantamount to personal failure. The social observer Pearl Jephcott reported that few girls leaving school considered exchanges places "where an enterprising person would be likely to find any particular help in getting the right kind of work. Certain of them regard it as the last resort of the lazy."[10] Exchanges were synonymous with unemployment, not employment. Similar attitudes prevailed in the United States. A 1964 congressional committee report recorded of the U.S. system: "the local employment office . . . is known as the 'unemployment office'. . . the worker views the public employment office as having on file chiefly the most unattractive, lowest-paid, hardest-to-fill jobs—while the employer . . . assumes that job-seekers registered . . . are . . . the least skilled [and] least reliable . . ."[11] Government work-welfare policy in both countries came to share and reify these perceptions by concentrating on unemployment instead of employment. The political origins of labor exchanges meant they were to enhance the position of jobseekers only by accommodating and maintaining the capitalist labor market.

The establishment of labor exchanges reflected the diffusion of the market economy, which modified the conditions of employment. In the absence of wage income, American and British workers and their families were destitute and made dependent upon public or private charity. At the close of the nineteenth century the phrase "hawking labor" was commonly invoked to describe the process whereby workers roamed from employer to employer seeking work. It was time-consuming, costly, and demoralizing. Unemployed Americans encountered similar degradation and problems during the Great Depression. Job seekers' access to information about vacancies was haphazard and often inaccurate. Charles Booth observed the system firsthand amongst casual London docks workers. When he addressed the 1892 Royal Commission on Labour, Booth advocated a public exchange system. He argued that irregularity in employment in the docks could be reduced with a system coordinating employers' needs:

> My view is that each department, having its list [of positions available] as is now the case, should communicate with some central department the evening before as to how many men they were short of or over on their list for the coming day, so that there might be a clearing between the departments that are short and the departments that are over . . . The information must be obtained by the men at the centre where their names are enrolled.[12]

The haphazardness of the labor market was less costly to employers since it guaranteed them a supply of cheap, unorganized workers. They had no difficulty recruiting additional workers, when needed, from the men hanging around their factory gates. That a role existed for some sort of market clearing labor institution was demonstrated by the development of private, fee-based, exchanges and the endeavors of unions and employers to create their own systems.[13] By the end of the nineteenth century, many unions and employers in Germany had established exchanges serving workers exclusively from their trade, a strategy imitated by some American and British trades unionists. Recognition of these needs, and of the social problems attendant upon unemployment, prompted municipalities in late nineteenth-century Germany and early twentieth-century Britain to establish networks of labor exchanges through which employers and employees communicated and in which information about job openings in neighboring districts was advertised.

In chapter 1, I review theoretical approaches to the formation of work-welfare programs and outline my framework. In common with other government schemes, work-welfare programs are the product of social and political forces which shape policy decisions. They differ across political systems on several criteria, including whether benefits are linked to work requirements; whether registration at labor exchanges is compulsory or voluntary; whether participation in training programs is required or optional; whether benefits are provided as cash or in-kind; and whether programs are designed to complement, supplant, or support market processes. The defining feature of British and American work-welfare programs is the integration of the receipt of benefits initially with placement and subsequently with the discharge of either work or training activities. I argue that this linkage derived from the priorities of the political coalitions (both to advance and oppose options) influencing work-welfare schemes in each society. This integration creates an organizational bias toward the monitoring of labor and away from the enhancement of work opportunities. In both countries, the institution through which this integration is formalized is the public employment exchange system. As I demonstrate, the way in which employment exchanges were used by British and American governments to manage the labor market institutionalized and consolidated these two polities' commitment to liberal work-welfare programs. Chapter 2 analyzes the establishment of labor exchanges in Great Britain and the United States. I explain how the decision to link placement and benefit distribution activities was taken in each polity, identifying the political interests informing this choice and outlining its consequences.

In chapter 3, I analyze the incentive structure created by a focus upon benefit over placement work within labor exchanges (exacerbated by tepid national regulation) and explain how this structure resulted in labor exchange administrators developing interests antagonistic to placement work. These failings were exposed in a series of official and external studies of the British and American labor exchanges conducted after 1945. Nationally, the American and British liberal approaches to work and training policy constrained attempts to reform the placement agencies. When attempts to broaden these policies were made in the 1960s and 1970s, documented in chapter 4, the weak placement system revealed itself as an encumbrance since it proved to be an inadequate institutional infrastructure through which to implement the initiatives. National reform was made innocuous by the limitations of local institutions.

The state's organization of labor is at present most salient when the level of unemployment or number receiving welfare is high. Government regulation of parts of the workforce is undiminished. As chapter 5 explains, work-welfare programs have come a full circle from the work-tests of the early twentieth century to the 'workfare' of the 1980s and 1990s. This resurgence illustrates the dominance and resilience of liberal values within these programs. Whereas early American work-welfare programs were built, in part, on laws and institutional arrangements transplanted from Britain, modern British work-welfare rests in part on programs whose design is borrowed directly and uncritically from the United States.[14]

This study focuses on a distinct set of programs which I term collectively "work-welfare."[15] I take an outcome common to two polities, liberal work-welfare programs, and explain it by reference both to factors common to each polity and to a number which differ. I argue that the combination of liberal principles advantaged in institutional arrangements is a characteristic of both British and American work-welfare programs. Although for different reasons, in neither case did political coalitions form which were sufficiently powerful to transform these programs into more generous schemes. I do not neglect the important differences between the two cases—most especially the differences in state organization and different political alignments—but I do maintain that the work-welfare outcomes are comparable. I use these theoretical precepts to guide my analysis. It is not my aim to use the case studies to produce a new theoretical framework.

The emphasis of this analysis is differentiated from much extant scholarship in the following ways.

First, whereas most scholarship in this area treats the whole welfare state—whether in aggregate or as disaggregated programs—as the question to be explained, my study is deliberately limited to the three work-welfare programs identified at the beginning of this Introduction. I advance no general claims about the "welfare state" and I eschew the use of typologies.

Second, my approach is intentionally focused on historical trajectories and upon two cases with important commonalities. I am sympathetic to much of the recent comparative work on welfare states and appreciate its theoretical sophistication. However, I believe much of this scholarship neglects the historical and political origins of programs unduly and that scholars are often overzealous in formulating typologies. Such approaches need to be complemented by studies historically sensitive to a small number of cases and to the functioning of particular institutions. That is my ambition in this study.

CHAPTER ONE

Work-Welfare in Great Britain and the United States

Reporting in 1893, the Government Committee, having studied ways of addressing unemployment, differentiated between those unemployed persons who had suffered "inward" from those who suffered merely "outward shipwreck."[1] Both categories of unemployed arose from the capriciousness of economic activity. Such economic uncertainty, together with its social and political consequences, explains why governments in Western democracies have uniformly been obliged to intervene to maintain the labor market. Although the character of this intervention has not been identical, there are significant similarities between Great Britain and the United States, and work-welfare programs share common principles which persist.[2] Explaining these principles and their tenacity requires an understanding of the politics of work-welfare programs and the institutional arrangements through which they are administered. In this chapter, I present the theoretical framework with which these two tasks are undertaken in subsequent chapters.

Political scientists have a rich set of theories with which to explain state actions and policy outcomes. The study of welfare policy has been especially extensive. Explanations based in political culture, the role of ideas, political dynamics—whether expressed through class pressures or articulated by political parties and interest groups or liberal reformers, industrialization, institutional arrangements, and civil servant initiatives—have been developed.[3] I draw upon two approaches, which can be schematically divided into the power resources or labor movement class analysis theory and the state centric explanations (based on state structures, policy legacies, and bureaucratic activity), including the new institutionalism. I argue that a cogent explanation of work-welfare policy requires a combination of factors emphasized by each perspective.

The Labor Movement or Power Resources Framework

The labor movement or power resources framework[4] is derivative of class analysis. In capitalist societies, location in the labor market is fundamental to the definition of power and interests. United action by employers can destroy workers' protests; effective collective organization by workers can bring industry to its knees. These class alignments also create the bases for electoral coalitions upon which parties can mobilize to effect policy through government. Neo-Marxist accounts of welfare state development emphasize such class patterns, and "labor movement" or power resources theorists explain cross-national variations in welfare programs through differences in class strength.

In the power resources perspective, constructing social democratic welfare systems has depended upon establishing universal programs which maximize solidarity between social groups, principally classes, and minimize hierarchical distinctions such as those between skilled and unskilled workers or between employed and unemployed. These political and social bases of solidarity translate electorally into social democratic or labor party control of government and the implementation of universal social rights of citizenship. Such measures consolidate the parties' electoral and political support and provide the basis for the parties' reinvigoration and perpetuation.[5] John Stephens presents a well-developed form of this thesis.[6] He argues that universalist policies depend upon three factors: the number of years of social democratic or labor party incumbency in government; the degree of centralization of unions; and within the union movement the dominance of industrial over craft unions. By implication, unions will be committed to achieving full employment and universal work-welfare programs because these enhance their leverage over wage bargaining and provide greater job control. These conditions cannot be applied easily to either Britain or the United States.[7] For countries approximating this model, the result has been a social democratic welfare state characterized by: a commitment to full employment, realized in part through an active labor market policy including a preference for training rather than simply unemployment benefits; an active state role in maintaining and expanding apprenticeship and training schemes for the unemployed and those seeking labor market entry; an emphasis upon universalism over means-testing in social programs; a limited use of discretionary payments over statutory rights; and a limited use of actuarial financing.[8]

In Britain and in the United States trades unions have been highly decentralized and craft union traditions have been more important than industrial union traditions. Decentralization and craft traditions have weakened British and American unions' commitment to full employment and to the expansion of national training programs. Highly differentiated unions have been more concerned to respect and maintain hierarchical divisions within the workforce than to ensure that those least skilled and holding the weakest market power have been incorporated into a national full-employment program. Decentralized craft unions have also prioritized apprenticeship programs based on small recruitment, generous remuneration, and skilled training. Unions have feared the erosion of their monopoly on training, a monopoly in which employers have colluded to minimize their costs.[9] In the United States unions have been reluctant also to extend training opportunities to black workers,[10] exacerbating instead of squashing an intra-class fissure. Although the creation of the Congress of Industrial Organization in 1936, and its subsequent merger with the American Federation of Labor,[11] signaled the power of industrial unions in addition to craft unions, many of the latter's traditions dominated the attitude of organized labor toward work-welfare programs, especially training measures.

The political and organizational strength of the workers (or potential workers) most affected by the work-welfare programs is limited, for two reasons. First, organizationally it is difficult for the most marginal citizens to organize,[12] at least independently of national political movements which rarely materialize. Second, the market power of such workers is the weakest of any group since they are unskilled or semiskilled, exist in large numbers and, for example, in the United States are readily replenished through immigrants prepared to take low-wage work. Therefore, for their interests to be addressed requires either the forging of an alliance with more powerful groups in the labor market or that the policies pursued by the organized labor movement indirectly benefit them.[13] Historically, both the British and American labor movements operated their own schemes to offset the hardship of their members, differentiating union members from nonunion workers and creating distinct interests for the two groups. This characteristic was documented in the British case by the 1893 report on the unemployed. The report's author, Hubert Llewellyn Smith, noted that unions ensured that nonmembers were excluded:

> . . . the financial interest of all its contributing members in husbanding its funds offers some stimulus to the members of the society both to endeavour to find situations for their unemployed fellow members, and to watch that the society is not being defrauded by idlers, who draw the out-of-work pay without genuinely seeking for employment.[14]

Labor movements which succeed in combining all members of the labor force into a purposeful and cohesive group to support social reforms are rare historically. This is especially true of British and American experience where divisions between workers (for example, between skilled and unskilled job seekers or between black workers and white workers) have militated against collective organization and exposed intraclass divisions as enduring as interclass cleavages. Work-welfare programs have several constituencies of whom, historically, three can be identified.[15]

Category A. This group consists of those normally in employment but made unemployed because of seasonal or cyclical trends or because of recession. During periods of economic growth, such as the years from 1945 to 1975 in Britain and the United States (and from 1982 to 1990 in the United States), this group is small. During a recession, the size of this group swells.

Category B.   This category includes the unskilled and long-term unemployed who have difficulty obtaining work even during periods of high employment. Historically this category originates in the casual labor market (though overlap with the first category existed).[16] Its members become a constituency for training programs intended to facilitate labor market entry. Early advocates of labor exchanges, such as William Beveridge, also argued for their linkage with training. Speaking in Ghent in 1913, Beveridge made much of the importance of "technical training of inefficient workmen."[17] In the modern period, category B includes the long-term unemployed, some of whom will never have worked.

Category C.   Welfare recipients who may or may not have worked previously, such as recipients of Aid to Families with Dependent Children (AFDC) in the United States, define this last group. This category originates with nineteenth-century paupers. Its existence stimulated the British New Poor Law of 1834 so as more sharply to distinguish able-bodied job seekers from the destitute who were incapable of acquiring employment. Welfare recipients have been increasingly incorporated into training or work programs as a condition of receiving their benefits.[18]

These three categories are inherently and ineluctably imprecise, especially historically. They often overlap. For instance, at times of high unemployment movement from the first to the second category is not uncommon (expressed programmatically by replacement of unemployment insurance with general assistance in the United States and of unemployment benefits with income support in Britain). In the United States, class and race overlap significantly[19]: black Americans have been disproportionately represented, relative to their population size, in categories B and C. Their position was also structured by the system of institutional segregation in public agencies and industries until the 1960s.

The close relationship between these categories of beneficiaries and the labor market is suggested by the efforts to ensure that work-welfare programs do not create disincentives to work. This concern is elemental to British and American work-welfare and its frequent invocation influences policies and reforms.[20] Arguments about disincentives have a lengthy genealogy. Criticisms of the abuse of relief occasioned the New Poor Law of 1834 in Britain. The law was a reaction in particular to the Speenhamland system, which made no distinction between different groups within the laboring poor and had in effect provided a "basic income."[21]

The 1834 reform established the principle of "less eligibility" for the receipt of assistance whereby the recipient's condition should be empirically worse than that of the poorest laborer. The new principle was administered by confinement within the workhouse. This "workhouse test" of genuine impoverishment is the precursor of the subsequent "work-test" administered through labor exchanges distributing unemployment compensation.

Two consequences of the diversity of the constituencies for work-welfare are significant. First, forging alliances between these different categories of unemployed persons is extremely difficult and, to succeed, must transcend other sources of division, such as the possession of skills or membership within a minority race or ethnic group. More often than not, alliances failed to form. Second, the programs formulated to address these groups must satisfy diverse and often competing needs: the requirements of a skilled worker made redundant after years of work differ from those of a young person with no labor market experience and from those of an unemployed single parent. Politically the incentive to enact programs meeting the lowest common denominator is considerable.

The power resources perspective correctly focuses analysis upon the political coalitions (and their formation) attempting to influence policy, but in the case of Britain and the United States it needs to be augmented with greater attention to reforms within the state and to the legacies of organizational routines. The balance of social forces does not itself explain the programs adopted or their persistence.

The State Centric Framework
Drawing on the state centric framework, I argue that, once established, the administrative arrangements organizing government intervention in the labor market proved enduring, thereby influencing subsequent initiatives, a thesis best advanced by historical institutionalists.[22] I combine elements of these two perspectives in a political-institutional framework. This thesis points to a number of crucial theoretical variables.

First, it is necessary to study the origins of the institutional arrangements to which I attach such significance. This I do by examining their political dynamics, a task for which power resources tenets are pertinent. Since work-welfare programs are directly related to the labor market, I focus particularly upon the interests and actions of employers, workers, political parties, and the state. Through a study of the founding of labor exchanges in chapter 2, I examine the constraints under which they operated, analyze how their interests were defined, and identify which ideas were privileged in implementation.

Second, I argue that labor exchanges, established as institutions to organize all members of the labor market, quickly became associated with those job seekers most marginal to the market. Their placement records were dismal. Employers and workers lost interest in public labor exchanges, an outcome reflecting institutional design and political origin. In both countries it occurred partly because employers' interests (for example, retention of the right to hire workers outside of employment offices) were integrated into the initial design of exchanges and labor was too weak to resist this. In Britain mass unemployment in the 1930s made exchanges politically important institutions but labor lacked the resources or power to modify them.[23]

Significant efforts to modify these institutional arrangements, to broaden the scope of work-welfare policy, were undertaken in each country. In the United States, the Great Society initiative in the 1960s aimed to achieve a work-welfare program of value to citizens most marginal to the labor market. In Britain in the 1970s, the push was toward establishing a social democratic style work-welfare framework. Both initiatives failed because the political coalition seeking the modification was insufficiently powerful. The weakness of these coalitions was forcefully demonstrated during the 1980s when, I argue, both the Republicans in the United States and the Conservatives in Britain succeeded in implementing punitive work-welfare programs. The way in which work-welfare programs were institutionalized through labor exchanges was important to both the success of the right-wing offensive and the failure of the more radical initiative.

Work-Welfare, Politics, and Institutions

I have identified the political origins of work-welfare policy and the programs' institutionalization as the two crucial developments for this study. Both processes are treated below. To examine my claim that institutional arrangements are powerful expressions of the work-welfare trajectories to which Britain and the United States are attached, I analyze, in later chapters, both the failure of reform initiatives attempting to establish social democratic work-welfare (in the 1960s and 1970s) and the success of initiatives sharpening features of the policy and institutional legacy (in the 1980s). I argue there that this latter policy success is a function of the proposals' compatibility with extant institutional expressions of political interests.

The Founding of Labor Exchanges. National labor exchange systems were established in Britain in 1909 and in the United States in 1933. In both countries, the linkage of placement work with the distribution of unemployment benefits defined work-welfare. This common outcome arose from nationally distinct political configurations, as chapter 2 makes clear, in which trades unionists, employers, political parties, and liberal reformers were involved.

Unions. British trades unionists and employers were greatly agitated about the establishment of a national labor exchange system. Unions feared that strikebreakers would be supplied through exchanges and that exchanges would fail to enforce agreed-upon union rates of pay. Trades unionists also perceived exchanges as institutions of relief rather than employment and made arrangements exclusively for their members.

The principal trade union organizations in Britain and the United States were selective in their membership. British unionists wanted no link with those at the margin of the labor market. This position was made clear in an intervention about labor exchanges by W. Mosses at the Trade Union Congress's (TUC) annual conference in 1911: "Everything that has been done to ameliorate the conditions of employment has been secured in the teeth of the opposing non-union elements, and yet these [non-union] men are to benefit by the Labour Exchanges equally with ourselves."[24]

Skilled workers were more likely to turn to their own trade society or union for assistance in searching for work (including traveling benefit) than to the labor bureaus, which they considered appropriate for the unskilled. That skilled workers looked askance upon exchanges reflects the powerful division between skilled and unskilled workers. As Stedman Jones writes, "Overriding all these finer distinctions of status, the cardinal distinction remained between the skilled and the unskilled, between the artisan who possessed a trade and the labourer who possessed none."[25] The salience of this distinction for work-welfare policy cannot be overstated. However, at their foundation labor exchanges were intended to serve skilled workers and other members of the labor market.

Other divisions amongst workers also influenced work-welfare policy. In Britain the earlier Poor Law system produced a dichotomy between those in work and those not. Some of those in the former category formed friendly societies and other organizations to offset their members' hardships.[26] These societies emphasized relieving distress during periods of illness (in effect, health insurance) and providing pensions ("a sum of money to be paid on the death of a member or his wife").[27] Many members of categories B and C identified above have been rhetorically treated as "undeserving" of assistance. The distinction between deserving and undeserving also originates in the Poor Law system, which emphasized willingness to work as a criterion of assistance and castigated malingerers as undeserving of public support.[28] An important aspect of the Elizabethan Poor Law tradition, which remained unreformed in Britain until the 1910s, was the cost of providing assistance to the unemployed. Destitution rather than unemployment was the threshold at which assistance became available, as described in 1893: "The present Poor-law aims at relieving destitution only, and though work may be imposed as a test, relief is not given in the shape of the payment of wages, but according to the necessities of each case."[29] The workhouse institutionalized the deserving/undeserving distinction and underscored the eleemosynary fate of its occupants.

American labor organizations have concentrated upon those in work and upon achieving rights in the workplace, an approach often characterized as "business unionism."[30] Organized workers in the manufacturing sector have benefitted.[31] Effective challenges to this strategy did not develop until the Great Depression, when the divergence between employers' and workers' interests was painfully exposed. The American Federation of Labor (AFL) was the dominant force in the first four decades of this century.[32] It was one of two major types of unions: those based in skilled craft unions who emphasized exclusive membership and, second, those industrial unions which attempted to organize all workers, including immigrants and blacks, ignored by the craft unions. The second culminated in the Congress of Industrial Organizations (CIO). This division between skilled (AFL) and semiskilled (CIO) organizations also coin- ·cided with ethnic and gender divisions. From the middle of the nineteenth century, immigrants (whose arrival provoked the nativist populism) were predominantly concentrated in the unskilled or semiskilled categories. Black Americans were excluded from most unions.[33] The shift from narrowly focused, self-interested, and elitist craft unions to a wide organization of workers through unions has consequently been slow and weak in the United States. Even within the AFL there was division between craft and industrial union traditions, the former exercising a majority on the Executive Council and opposing the organization of industrial workers. Both Presidents Samuel Gompers and, especially, William Green gave lukewarm support to militant rank-and-file members attempting to organize for collective rights. Green's rigid adherence to the decisions of the Executive Council was renowned, thereby prohibiting any deviation or alternative initiatives.[34]

Under the legendary Samuel Gompers, the AFL staunchly opposed receiving assistance from public funds to help its unemployed members. It preferred to achieve its members' aims through local agreements rather than government programs, a practice respected by Gompers's successor, William Green (AFL president from 1924 to 1952).[35] American trades unionists feared that involvement in government programs would be demeaning and politically weakening. Despite this position and modest membership levels,[36] the AFL did lobby for an exchange system, in part because of the profound unemployment crisis precipitated by the Great Depression.

The dichotomy between skilled and unskilled workers had a parallel in gender relations. As some scholars have argued, the movement toward highly organized craft unions was one for male wage-earners. This outcome was not inevitable, according to one influential account, but a pragmatic strategy in mid nineteenth-century Britain and the United States to effect a reduction in the working day.[37] In Brenner and Ramas's view, craft unions were determined to control entry into their trades and this ambition extended to the exclusion of women:

> The almost complete unanimity with which trade unions virulently opposed the entry of women into their crafts was part and parcel of a general attempt to limit potentially ruinous competition from labour willing to work at reduced rates. The "dishonourable trades," the euphemism for unapprenticed labor, were, even more than mechanization, the major threat to the privileged craft workers during the first two-thirds of the 19th century, and control of entry into the trade was the major weapon used by unionists to preserve their relatively privileged position in the labor markets . . . It is quite clear that when unions were unable to exclude women, a rapid depression of wages and general degradation of work resulted.[38]

Unions organizing on an industrial basis, such as the Knights of Labor in the United States, happily included women (and blacks) amongst their members. However, the AFL, which became the dominant organization, supported only protective legislation rather than the equality of women workers.[39] Household work, undertaken disproportionately by women, has remained outside of work-welfare programs.[40]

Labor exchanges were first organized, with trade union agreement, into separate offices for women workers, who were assumed to be seeking work as domestics or in the service sector and not in industry or manufacturing. This pattern broke down during the Second World War—when black Americans also had greater employment opportunities—but a tendency to categorize women differently from male job seekers persisted. Organized labor was a movement for skilled male workers and the interests of that group defined the movement's approach to exchanges.

In the United States, black workers faced formidable obstacles to overcome the discriminatory practices of white workers and of union organizations.[41] The extent of these, particularly of AFL affiliate unions (many CIO affiliates accepted black members), were apparent in the hearings held by President Franklin Roosevelt's Committee on Fair Employment Practice established in 1941.[42] This committee was responsible for monitoring discrimination in defense-related industries and in government agencies.[43] The barriers to building a cross-racial alliance between black workers and white unionists were also demonstrated in their opposing attitudes to segregation, with the latter determined that segregation should continue in government agencies and industry. The AFL's support for segregation had its origin in the nineteenth century when the AFL evolved into a union for highly skilled craft workers who were prepared to accept the prejudices of the white unionists. This evolution proved to be the most successful way of organizing effectively in an environment dominated by large numbers of unskilled workers who could be hired by employers. Craft unions opposed the entry of black workers into their coveted apprenticeships. Writing in 1960, the authors of an NAACP study concluded that "underlying the absence of Negroes in significant numbers from skilled-craft employment is their almost total exclusion from apprenticeship training programs. No matter what the causal factors involved, Negroes do not become apprentices."[44] These problems did not evaporate during the 1960s; indeed, most unions became virulently opposed to allowing blacks to enter apprenticeship programs.[45]

Employers. Employer organizations in both Britain and the United States are weak compared with other industrial democracies in which some sort of corporatist arrangement has been established. This has not prevented the frequent advantaging of employers' interests in public policy (and stronger associations might have resulted in even more limited programs). The organization of labor exchanges and the principles embedded in work-welfare programs were favorable to employers. British industrialists and large employers were transparently chilly about a national labor exchange system. As chapter 2 demonstrates, it was made clear to employer representatives that labor exchanges would not become institutions through which workers could organize. The president of the Board of Trade, Winston Churchill, stressed the limited consequences for worker organization of establishing exchanges. In the United States, large employers and industrialists, organized through the U.S. National Association of Manufacturers (NAM), have opposed substantial expansions in the federal government's role. Probably the period when this opposition was weakest occurred in the first years of the Roosevelt administration, when his mandate and the scale of the country's difficulties enabled government to assume new expenditure-based responsibilities.[46] It was during this period that the labor exchange act, the Wagner-Peyser Act of 1933, and the Social Security Act of 1935 were passed and the rights to collective bargaining established.[47] However, business opposition to the Full Employment Bill in 1946 (enacted as the Employment Act) significantly diluted its content and the government's role.[48] In the United States, business groups are advantaged, during most periods, because their values are widely shared. With the brief exception of the initiatives of the 1960s, most policymakers and voters prefer market to state approaches to policy questions.[49] Large American corporations were prepared to negotiate plant-level or sector-wide agreements with trades unions which included welfare components but were much less willing to support comparable initiatives for the whole workforce when these were to be achieved with federal legislation.[50]

Roosevelt's New Deal social programs marked a break in federal policy, but they did not amount to the creation of a universalist welfare system. Rather they were conceived of and administered in a framework distinguishing between contributory (insurance-based) and noncontributory (means-tested) programs. This actuarial and contributory framework minimized the costs to employers and placed limits on the growth of public welfare.

A similar emphasis upon actuarial principles was drawn in Britain by Churchill (in 1911) and Beveridge (in 1942), but the distinction between contributory and noncontributory programs was not inevitable. It arose from choices taken during the drafting of legislation and from the way in which welfare reforms were implemented. Speaking during the passage of the Old Age Pensions Act of 1908, David Lloyd George, then Chancellor of the Exchequer, berated the validity of this distinction:

> I demur altogether to the division of the schemes into contributory and non-contributory. So long as you have taxes imposed upon commodities which are consumed practically by every family in the country there is no such thing as a non-contributory scheme . . . A workman who has contributed health and strength, vigour and skill, to the creation of the wealth by which taxation is borne has made his contribution already to the fund which is to give him a pension when he is no longer fit to create that wealth. Therefore I object altogether to the general division of these schemes into contributory and non-contributory schemes.[51]

The administration of government programs institutionalized such a distinction, installing liberal political values.[52] A principal reason for this practice was the unanticipated cost of administering old-age pensions, which proved far greater than expected.

Parties.   The political parties most directly linked with workers and the unemployed, in class terms, were insufficiently powerful to establish work-welfare programs other than of a limited character. The electoral and political bases of the Democratic and Labour parties were fragile. Roosevelt's New Deal coalition was intrinsically precarious since it balanced support from potentially opposed racial and ethnic groups. The New Deal coalition, which engineered Roosevelt's election and Democratic control of the presidency, consisted of urban blue-collar voters in the Northeast and Midwest, Catholics, Jews, farmers in the Upper Midwest, Southern whites, and Northern blacks.[53] This combination provided a parlous foundation for policy innovation. Any advancement of black interests in conjunction with those of poor whites was resented and resisted by white Southerners.[54]

In Britain the Labour Party has been weaker electorally and organizationally than its Conservative rival: electoral outcomes have been crucial to the realization of policy and Labour has rarely enjoyed a sufficient incumbency to move beyond liberal work-welfare programs. On those occasions when its majority has been strong enough for social reform, Labour has not made it a priority. In both countries the forging of common ties between all workers, the unemployed, and beneficiaries of assistance has been rare. British workers were first mobilized electorally by parties other than Labour, making the latter's political task all the more daunting. Furthermore, trades unions were predominantly craft-based, a consequence of early British industrialization. The marriage of a centralized union movement and a Labour political party based in industrial unions and working-class support did not exist in Britain before 1914. Hence the divisions between workers within the labor market remained as salient as their commonalities.

Liberal reformers.   British work-welfare originated in the efforts of liberal administrations and reformers. Broadly, the liberal political tradition[55] respects individual freedom, privileges the market over government in the organization of economic activity, accepts a commitment to providing a safety-net for the least well-off and destitute though reserves a particular wrath for the able-bodied mendicant, promotes the claim of limited government and a narrow sense of self-sufficiency.[56] These political values set the framework for early work-welfare decisions, though legislation did not replicate them exactly.

Rather than Labour Party activists or trades unionists pursuing policy it was Liberal politicians, such as Lloyd George and Winston Churchill, influenced by social reformers, notably Beveridge and the Webbs, and suffused with "new liberal" principles, who effected the Labour Exchanges Act of 1909 and the insurance program in 1911. One of the principal reformers in both the time periods of 1909 to 1911 and 1944 to 1945, William Beveridge, was especially enamored of these ideas, an influence reflected in the legislation. Michael Freeden characterizes the movement for social reform stimulated under the rubric of new liberalism as the attempt to "establish an ethical framework to prescribe and evaluate human behaviour and, where necessary, to re-create social institutions."[57] This doctrine allowed for a synthesis of collective solutions (that is, government policies) within an individualist, liberal ideology. Freeden argues that this doctrine was absorbed widely into British political culture. Writing about the legacy of the 1906–11 reforming Liberal administration of Herbert Asquith he argues:

> The liberal heritage could not be contained in a single demonstrative act
> . . . the success of that heritage was a generalized one. By the end of
> the [inter-war] period . . . most progressive intellectuals, political activists,

and reformers no longer recognized their principles as explicitly liberal. Liberalism had transcended its distinct institutional and ideological shape and thus, paradoxically, ensured its survival.[58]

This ideology imbued all those influential in work-welfare policy formulation.

In the United States, Roosevelt's New Deal reforms were also imbued with liberal ideas. Although his reforms required a significantly expanded federal role, this expansion and its institutionalization in work-welfare reflected liberal assumptions about responsibility and arguments about the desirability of an actuarial basis to public welfare. Roosevelt warned against welfare as a "narcotic, a subtle destroyer of the human spirit" when advocating his New Deal reforms. Both the President and the Congress supported policies constructed upon a distinction between contributory and noncontributory programs, with the exclusion of certain occupations initially from the former.

The State.　Federalism has had a profound impact on the development of work-welfare programs in the United States. Most programs have been formulated and implemented as federal-state ones, with fiscal and administrative responsibilities divided between Washington and state capitols. This arrangement has resulted in significant variations between states in the standards of the programs provided, eligibility and degree of inclusivity, and in components where a number of options have been permitted in federal regulation. Writing during the Carter presidency, Senator Daniel Patrick Moynihan summarized the arrangements thus:

> The New Deal made the basic policy decision—some have bemoaned it, others not—to leave the administration of programs such as Aid to Dependent Children (as it then was) and Unemployment Insurance with the individual states, allowing them to set their own levels of payments in accordance with Federal matching formulas. This meant, from the outset, that Southern states had low payment levels.[59]

Federalism was intimately related to the New Deal electoral coalition, itself shaped by race relations in the South. The combination of political forces within the Congress during the 1930s ensured that the legislation did not harm Southern (white) Democratic party interests. Southern Democrats chaired the committees enacting Roosevelt's New Deal programs and were wholly resistant to federal intervention if it affected the position of blacks in their states. The old-age assistance component of the 1935 act was designed for local administration to ensure maximum control by local politicians, a guarantee that conditions of eligibility and rates of benefit would vary between white recipients and black recipients. The Social Security Act of 1935 defined the occupations covered by unemployment insurance in such a way as to permit the exclusion of most black American workers. This arrangement assisted the maintenance of exploitative relations between white landlords and black tenant farmers. As Quadagno argues:

> Social policy was shaped by the ability of the southern planter class to wield a disproportionate share of political power in the broader nation-state. Southern planters gained political power through the establishment of a one-party South, which effectively stifled opposition to the dominant planter class, and through the structure of the committee system in Congress, which allowed southern representatives to exercise a controlling negative influence on national legislation.[60]

The same political elements insisted that the American public employment system be organized as a federal-state decentralized system, which included local offices whose senior officials were gubernatorial appointees.

The Institutionalization of Work-Welfare

The original work-welfare legislation and the institutional arrangements for administering these programs are the two aspects of the institutionalization of work-welfare that have been crucial to the persistence of their liberal character.

The institutional choices made at the foundation of national labor exchange systems in Britain and the United States, or soon thereafter, determined the system's placement capacity. The administrative decision to link the placement work of labor exchanges with the distribution of unemployment compensation produced an institutional bias within exchanges toward the latter (though this policing role may not have been the primary concern of policymakers). This bias was more developed in Britain and the United States than in other countries whose governments were also concerned about the abuse of benefits by claimants,[61] a feature reflecting the emphases of other aspects of work-welfare programs.

The bias proved remarkably resistant to change because of how it structured the incentives of officials working in exchanges and because of weak national regulation, themselves reflections of political choices. It is crucial to explaining the failure of government attempts during the 1960s to broaden work-welfare in Britain and the United States. Administration articulates and defines political values and priorities and, because of the absence of powerful political reformers, locked work-welfare institutions into trajectories from which subsequent policy was unable to wrest them. Powerful institutional and policy legacies were created. In both countries, the failure of exchanges to operate effectively in the labor market diluted employer hostility while unions concentrated upon the needs of their members who, for the most part, did not use exchanges.

As I document in chapter 2, the integration of placement and benefit work in the United States occurred after a bureaucratic struggle, in contrast to Britain where it was a consequence of the founding legislation. In both countries the linkage was prompted by the desire to administer a work-test to ensure the efficiency of government policy. Although institutionalization rested upon different factors in the two countries, the outcome was shared.[62]

Federalism and the distinct race relations of the South contributed to the persistence of the American public employment system's indifferent placement record. Attempts to federalize the service after World War II were thwarted by a combination of congressional power (principally Southern senators and representatives) and gubernatorial pressure. The Interstate Conference on Employment Security Agencies (ICESA), founded in 1937, proved a resolute defender of the status quo, lobbying for a speedy return of the employment service to the states after the period of federal control and attacking critics of the service. The ICESA reflected the view of employment service officials whose loyalty was principally toward employers and state politicians. They did not want to alienate the former by expanding their work for the least easily placed members of the labor market. Opponents of defederalization—such as the NAACP and sections of labor—proved unable to prevent the Service's return to the states.

In Britain high levels of employment after 1945 reduced the labor exchanges' role considerably. The Labour Party used its striking electoral success in 1945 to implement the NHS and other general welfare state measures and to advance its nationalization program. Its greatly reduced majority in 1950 precluded further significant reforms. Exchanges were perceived by both employers and unions as responsible for the most marginal sections of the workforce only. The state compounded this attitude by accepting a voluntarist approach to training, which further limited their role in labor market policy.

In sum, the decision to integrate the activities of job placement with the administration of unemployment insurance through labor exchanges resulted in institutional patterns harmful to placement. Integration limited placement capacity and reinforced the focus upon excluding undeserving supplicants. This priority undermined other aspirations, notably job placement and training. Through their modest role in promoting employment, labor exchanges reveal accurately the liberal roots of British and American labor market policy, including the low emphasis upon training policy, the assumption that markets are largely self-clearing (an assumption which assumes government intervention only in response to unemployment crises), the preparedness of government, employers, and unions to organize training (principally apprenticeships) to satisfy their own interests, and the institutionalization of a distinction between contributory and noncontributory welfare benefits. Public employment exchanges in Britain and the United States not only failed effectively to place many of those seeking work but institutionalized the systematic exclusion and political weakness of the most disadvantaged job seekers and welfare recipients, particularly in the United States, where it had special implications for black Americans.

Although unintentional in both countries, welfare legislation had the effect of institutionalizing the distinction between benefits received from contributory programs as an entitlement and those received from noncontributory means-tested programs as an alm. While policy during the 1945–75 period pushed British work-welfare programs toward the social democratic welfare trajectory, they did not fundamentally break the distinction between universal contributory-based programs and those allocated through means-testing. This distinction was advanced by Beveridge in his 1942 report. Fortuitously, high employment made the second category—national assistance—insignificant until the mid-1970s.

These institutional arrangements remain in place. In Britain at present there are contributory benefits based upon weekly payments into a national insurance fund while the payee is in work. Payees are entitled to unemployment benefit after three days out of work, if contributory conditions are satisfied, a benefit exhausted after fifty-two weeks. A further thirteen weeks of work is required to requalify. For those not in work a national assistance scheme was established in 1948 providing noncontributory-based benefits. In the 1980s this latter was replaced by income support distributed on means-tested criteria (for the most recent changes, see chapter 5). In the United States, the Social Security Act of 1935 institutionalized a distinction between contributory programs such as social security, and unemployment insurance and selective noncontributory means-tested public assistance and welfare programs—now principally Aid to Families with Dependent Children (originally ADC), food stamps, and general assistance (all programs were controlled by the states). This institutional dichotomy contributed to a popular distinction about legitimate public assistance to the deserving and benefits for the unworthy.

In the United States a tension arose from the 1935 Social Security Act's division between insurance- and noninsurance-based programs. The inclusion of women and children in the latter category under the ADC program appeared unproblematic at the time. However, the transformation of ADC into AFDC in the 1960s and its expansion in the ensuing twenty years provided a programmatic object for conservative critiques of work-welfare in the 1980s and 1990s.

These British and American patterns have resulted in work-welfare programs which emphasize divisions within the workforce and hierarchies based on power in the labor market derived from skills (possessed disproportionately by white males) and being in work. Unions and political parties have collaborated in distinguishing between deserving and undeserving beneficiaries and in conceiving of benefits in insurance terms.

Conclusion

In sum, my argument emphasizes the political origins of work-welfare programs, the institutionalization of those programs, and the political coalitions seeking to modify or defend them. As Stephens points out, countries which satisfy his three conditions have, as a consequence of class solidarity, implemented active labor market policy.[63] In the cases of Great Britain and the United States, I maintain in this book, few factors favorable to universalism have been historically available. Instead, my argument explains how the combination of political forces in Britain and the United States (for instance, the organizational weakness of labor and the dominance of craft and decentralized trades unions), party political alignments, government structures, and the interplay of these factors (for instance, American federalism, the Southern agricultural system, race, and the power of Southern members on congressional committees) resulted in early work-welfare programs (in 1909 and 1933, respectively) of a liberal character. Work-welfare programs have reflected far more the influence of liberal politicians and reformers wedded to limiting the state's role and not labor-supported social democratic politicians. The subsequent institutional arrangements (linking training and work testing) and the policy legacies of such schemes maintained the programs' initial character, despite their evident failure to place job seekers. These arrangements and legacies proved more powerful than the attempts of Labour and Democratic party reformers to ameliorate each polity's work-welfare system. Measures to reinforce the status quo, however, were easily accommodated.

My argument about the political origins and institutionalization of work-welfare programs makes it unsurprising that Britain and the United States continue to lack the institutional framework conducive to adequate training systems.[64] This inadequacy arises from two factors. First, training has been distorted by its linkage with anti-unemployment schemes and its integration into work-welfare. Second, and more fundamentally, work-welfare programs (and other government measures) have failed to dislodge the institutional structure within which training occurs. That structure produces incentives geared to minimizing short-term costs rather than accepting long-term payoffs. This incentive structure is shared by individuals, firms, trades unions, and the state.[65] Each actor lacks the incentive to modify his or her behavior, the institutional infrastructure for a comprehensive training program is absent, and the state lacks the political capacity to effect change. Finegold and Soskice term this institutional configuration a "low-skills equilibrium."[66] It is a self-reinforcing system and attempts to reform the framework confront formidable institutional and policy legacies, themselves rooted in political and social interests. The fate of the Manpower Service Commission in Britain and of American manpower programs in the 1960s are analyzed in chapter 4 to illustrate these claims. The political will and comprehensive institutional reorganization necessary to establish effective programs (including new incentives for participation by the crucial social actors) have yet to materialize in either country.

CHAPTER TWO

"A Permanent Club for the Unemployed"? Establishing Labor Exchanges in Great Britain and the United States

Introducing the Labour Exchanges Bill to the House of Commons in 1909, the president of the Board of Trade, Winston Churchill, observed that

> it is not possible to make the distinction between the vagrant and the loafer on the one hand and the *bona fide* workman on the other, except in conjunction with some elaborate and effective system of testing willingness to work such as is afforded by the system of labor exchanges.[1]

This precept dominated the development of British and American public employment exchange systems. The linkage between the placement of job seekers and the distribution of benefits became a defining feature of work-welfare programs in both countries. The foundation of exchanges was vitiated by the dual, often contradictory, purposes of increasing labor market efficiency and applying work-tests. Labor exchanges became mechanisms through which American and British governments could enforce a division between worthy and unworthy supplicants for assistance. Such a view was expressly stated by Churchill during parliamentary discussion of the enabling legislation. And, increasingly after the 1920s, the operation of labor exchanges socialized officials into a particular routine and definition of their role after the First World War.

In this chapter, the political and institutional origin of the linkage between benefit and placement is analyzed through an examination of the establishment of the British and American national labor exchange systems under the Labour Exchanges Act of 1909 and the Wagner-Peyser Act of 1933 respectively.[2] Although a similar linkage was created in each country, the route to it differed. In Britain this linkage itself stimulated the establishment of an employment service. It was promoted as a prerequisite to unemployment insurance, constituting a mechanism for testing willingness to work. In the United States the employment service acquired this latter function only under a redefinition of functions necessitated by the Social Security Act of 1935. In both countries, distributing unemployment compensation dwarfed placement work fiscally and administratively, and dominated public perceptions of the employment service.

This chapter analyzes how liberal claims about efficiency and work-test mechanisms influenced British and American exchanges' formative years. I demonstrate that these terms dominated decisions about the founding and implementation of labor exchanges. I analyze the role of employers' and workers' organizations at the founding of exchanges and turn finally to the protracted negotiations which rendered the U.S. Employment Service the administrator of unemployment benefits.

Market Efficiency and Work-tests

In Britain, the Labour Exchanges Act of 1909 issued quickly upon, though independently of, the work of the Royal Commission on the Poor Laws which convened during the years from 1905 to 1909. The authors recommended the urgent founding of "a Labour Exchange, established and maintained by the Board of Trade, to provide efficient machinery for putting those requiring work and those requiring workers into prompt communication."[3] This recommendation was anticipated in the work of the Board of Trade. David Lloyd George was the board's president until 1908. He was fiercely committed to social reform, and is commonly identified as the principal liberal architect of the British welfare state.

The political circumstances were unpropitious for social reform. The Liberal government of Sir Henry Campbell-Bannerman, replaced by H. H. Asquith as prime minister in 1908, enjoyed a powerful electoral mandate from 1906 but had failed consistently to receive agreement from the House of Lords for much of its legislative program. However, in 1908 the National Pensions Act, formulated by David Lloyd George, was enacted and Lloyd George's successor as president of the Board of Trade, Winston Churchill, promised a comprehensive national insurance scheme and reform of the labor market. As Chancellor of the Exchequer, Lloyd George was in a powerful position to aid these ambitions. The Labour Exchanges Act of 1909 addressed labor market organization. The National Insurance Act took until 1911, coming after the two elections of 1910. These were conducted as clashes between the two chambers, the "peers versus the people" conflict. That the Labour Exchanges bill succeeded, passing through a Conservative-dominated House of Lords whose behavior earned the sobriquet, "Mr. Balfour's poodle,"[4] reflects the government's fortitude, the success of the scheme's principal advocates and the reluctance of the House of Lords to defeat "labor" issues.

The Majority and Minority Poor Law Commissioners' reports concurred in recommending labor exchanges.[5] According to the commissioners, neither workers nor employers had a satisfactory system of pooling and distributing information about jobs. As Joseph Painter noted in the Commons, "If Labour Exchanges do nothing else, they will at any rate put an end to those demoralising influences [that is, hawking labor around] and they will allow a man to seek employment in a way not fraught with the terrible amount of demoralisation which follows upon the present method."[6] Some contemporaries were unconvinced about the efficiency claim. When the 1909 bill was introduced in the Commons for its first reading, Havelock Wilson M.P., the bill's principal opponent, boasting his "considerable skill," maintained that the "Labour Exchange for seamen, as now managed by the Board of Trade, is an absolute failure."[7] He alleged further expenditure would be extravagant. At the second reading, Alfred Hutton argued that focusing upon school-leavers would be a better strategy for preventing unemployment. Facilities for juveniles were incorporated in the bill. The cost of the proposed scheme, necessitating new buildings in central positions in large cities and new appointments, excited hostility: "Apparently one of [the Government's] great desires is to provide berths for officials. That is the most fatal policy that can be adopted. It tends to great extravagance."[8]

The Poor Law Commissioners believed that labor mobility was trammeled by the absence of information about job vacancies: "The community has provided no public machinery for helping the unemployed workman to find work which may be waiting for him."[9] Beveridge's strong advocacy of labor exchanges was premised upon their contribution to clearing the labor market. This influential liberal reformer acquired his expertise about exchanges both from research into unemployment and its causes, particularly in the London docks, and from his experience as chairman of the Employment Exchanges Committee of the Central (Unemployed) Body of London, which, with powers granted in the 1905 Unemployed Workmen Act, established exchanges in London.[10] He argued that unemployment wasted valuable resources and skilled labor. Exchanges had the potential to avoid this waste: "The spread of information is a matter that cries out for organized rather than for individual action. The need for markets and the wastefulness of not having them are recognized in every other branch of economic life."[11] He contrasted the absence of exchanges in Britain with their presence in most European countries. Beveridge's liberal justification of the exchange system was utilitarian and economic. His rationale for government intervention to rectify inefficiency was consistent with the "new liberalism."[12]

The Poor Law Commissioners singled out exchanges' association with relief as one major factor accounting for the failure of exchanges established prior to 1909 (under the 1905 Unemployed Workmen Act). In 1909 the commonest view of these institutions was as agents of relief and charity and not as centers of employment. The commissioners reported that

> there is a tendency to confuse the exchanges with the Distress Committees, which repels many employers who object to a system of "State-created work." On the other hand their association with an authority administering assistance to the lower type of unskilled and casual labourers has led to their

> being looked upon with suspicion by the Trade Unions, who have in some
> cases unhappily regarded them as "blacklegging" organizations.[13]

This extract reveals the centrality of the distinction between deserving and
undeserving beneficiaries in British work-welfare programs. The Board of
Trade wished to improve the image of exchanges. Ameliorating their image
was supported by the Parliamentary Committee of the TUC: "You have got
to remove this prejudice against labor bureaux in establishing your new
scheme."[14] Churchill, the president of the Board of Trade, proposed that
unions make the exchanges one center of their work, modifying gradually
workers' perception of these institutions and implanting a positive image of
exchanges with "respectable" workers:

> My idea is that these rooms could also be utilised by arrangements for a
> small rent by trade unions who wish to have their benefit meetings and so
> forth there . . . Then we can arrange that the Labour Exchanges will put
> itself in touch with all the people in the trade unions. The people we want to
> get there are trade unionists, first of all. We do not want to have only the
> poor people who are at the tail end of employment, because they will dis-
> credit our business and we shall get mixed up with distress; we are not dis-
> tress, we are organization.[15]

Beveridge also emphasized the separation of relief and exchanges as a precondition for labor exchanges to succeed: the system "is industrial in as much
as it deals with the problem solely from the point of view of industry and is in
no way connected with the question of relief or of charity . . . The only thing
to be obtained at a Labour Exchange is ordinary employment and there is no
inducement for those to come who seek relief and are not capable of employment."[16] To illustrate the potential value of a national exchange system, the
Commissioners' Report alluded positively to the London exchanges and to
the system in operation in Germany about which they had received testimony
from Beveridge.

The drafters of the 1909 bill had two priorities of equal importance: to
place the unemployed and to exclude the alleged undeserving from benefits.
Placement and insurance were jointly conceived. Labor exchanges provided a
mechanism with which to distinguish the loafer from the able-bodied unemployed. This feature of the German system was cited enthusiastically by the
Commissioners: "We have been informed that it was one of the objects of the
German labor exchanges to 'get a perfect test for unemployment as a means
of knowing if a man is really unemployed against his will' . . . You can only
do this if you can see the whole labor market and all the jobs that are on
offer."[17] This aspect of the exchanges was endorsed and stressed by the president of the Board of Trade, Winston Churchill, when he introduced the 1909

bill in the Commons: "Labour exchanges are indispensable to any system of unemployment insurance, or, indeed, I think to any other honourable method of relieving unemployment."[18] Churchill continued: "I am quite sure that those who know the sort of humiliation to which the genuine working man is subject, by being very often indistinguishable from one of the class of mere loafers and vagrants, will recognise as of great importance any steps which can sharply and irretrievably divide the two classes in our society."[19] This view was shared by Beveridge. Speaking in 1913 he observed that, "Labour Exchanges and Unemployment Insurance were interdependent to a very great degree. It would indeed be impossible to work the scheme of Unemployment Insurance except in connection with some apparatus for finding work and testing willingness to work like Labour Exchanges. It is therefore proposed that the machinery of administering Unemployment Insurance will be the Labour Exchanges with certain additions."[20]

For Churchill, the labor exchanges were the "necessary preliminary"[21] to the implementation of the unemployment insurance scheme, since they allowed a work-test to be established prior to this program: "We have got to get the apparatus of the Labour Exchanges into working order before this system of insurance can effectually be established or worked." The liberal values informing labor exchanges and subsequent welfare reforms suffuses this administrative arrangement. At the bill's second reading, Churchill stressed again this interrelationship: "I hope the House will realise that we propose to work this system of Labour Exchanges in conjunction with a system . . . of unemployment insurance. We do not wish to organise only the mobility of labour, but also the stability of labour."[22] In all of his interventions, Churchill stressed the efficiency arguments for exchanges. His view was complemented by Beveridge,[23] who emphasized equally their work-test role in public welfare provision: "This is a function of an efficient Labour Exchange in affording a direct test of unemployment. The central problem of the Poor Law is to relieve without relieving unnecessarily."[24] In place of the crude Poor Law principle of deterrence, labor exchanges provided a substitute: "If all the jobs offering in a trade or a district are registered at a single office, then it is clear that any man who cannot get work through that office is unemployed against his will. He may be relieved without deterrence, yet without any fear that he is being relieved when he could work, or is being drawn needlessly from industry to pauperism."[25] The pivotal role of exchanges in applying work tests is expressed here.

Beveridge prepared a detailed confidential memorandum about the 1909 bill (not dissimilar to the memorandum prepared by Senator Robert Wagner in 1933 for his senatorial colleagues). Beveridge explained each clause of the short bill and anticipated criticisms of the proposed legislation identifying and dismissing eleven likely charges.[26]

Speaking in Parliament, the president of the Board of Trade reported that both the Majority and Minority Report Commissioners advocated a system of labor exchanges as "the first step which should be taken in coping with the problem of poverty and unemployment."[27] Churchill cited the support of trades unionists, the Central (Unemployed) Body, economists, delegates from a trip to study the German system, and the Opposition. Labor exchanges were the best response, according to Churchill, to two problems of efficiency singled out by the commissioners: "the lack of mobility of labour and the lack of information about all these questions of unemployment. For both of these defects the policy of labour exchanges is calculated to afford a remedy."[28] Increasing the mobility of labor was necessary because "modern industry is national."[29] Consequently, a system of communicating employment opportunities throughout the country was required. Through the collection and analysis of statistics, labor exchanges could "afford as accurate contemporary information about the demand for labour, both as to the quantity and quality for that demand, as between one trade and another, as between one district and another, and as between one season and one cycle and another."[30] As a side benefit, the regularization of labor, based upon accurate information, would eradicate casual employment.

The short bill was enacted on 20 September 1909.[31] The act empowered the Board of Trade to establish labor exchanges where it judged appropriate. The exchanges were empowered to "collect and furnish information as to employers requiring workpeople and workpeople seeking engagement or employment."[32] The act superseded existing legislation for exchanges.[33] The Board of Trade was empowered to issue regulations for managing the exchanges. It prohibited exchanges discriminating against workers who refused to accept employment "where the ground of refusal is that a trade dispute which affects his trade exists, or that the wages offered are lower than those current in the trade in the district where the employment is found."[34] Both industrial disputes and wage levels featured extensively in the pre-act negotiations conducted by the Board of Trade. The Board of Trade was empowered to establish advisory boards, "in such cases as they think fit . . . for the purpose of giving the Board advice and assistance in connexion with the management of any labour exchange."[35] Finally, the board was empowered to make appropriate recruitments and expenditures for the administration of the new service.

Churchill addressed in detail unemployment insurance. He declared its immediate establishment impracticable because "it would be risking the policy to cast one's net so wide,"[36] an opaque and uninformative explanation. The hostility of the House of Lords to Asquith's Liberal administration certainly made innovative lawmaking difficult. Churchill outlined the role of labor exchanges in the new insurance scheme as follows:

> For as soon as a man in an insured trade is without employment, if he has
> kept to the rules of the system, all he will have to do is to take his card to
> the nearest Labour Exchange, which will be responsible, in conjunction
> with the insurance office, either for finding him a job or for paying him his
> benefits.[37]

This arrangement became the familiar "dole system."

Despite some criticisms of the Labour Exchanges Bill there was wide support for the measure in the House. The Leader of the Opposition, Arthur
Balfour, promised no "severe" criticisms of the bill,[38] a notable promise
given the Conservatives' hostility toward liberal legislation during this
Parliament. The bill's aims made opposition difficult. The bill was successfully read for the third time on 29 July. The Labour Exchanges Bill had its
second reading in the Lords on 3 August. The debate paralleled that in the
House as did the breadth of support for the bill.[39] In his speech to the House
of Commons about the Poor Laws Commissioners' Reports the night before
introducing the Labour Exchanges Bill, Churchill reported that a joint departmental committee supervised by the Board of Trade was examining the proposed scheme; the "details are now very far advanced."[40] The costing and
implementation of the proposed labor exchange scheme was undertaken by a
committee established within the Board of Trade in January reporting in
March 1909,[41] whose membership included Beveridge and Chairman George
Fry. The committee recommended purpose-built buildings, despite the additional expense, rather than the modification of existing accommodation.[42]
The recruitment of staff was to be overseen by the Board of Trade but the
committee emphasized the value of local knowledge: "Superintendents of
Exchanges should preferably be chosen, as far as practical, from the
Divisions in which they are to serve, as knowledge of the local conditions of
labour matters is desirable in their case."[43]

The desire to emphasize labor exchanges as institutions for those in work,
and not just the unemployed, led to some calls for a different name for the
new institutions. In one letter from the South Central Metropolitan
Employment Exchanges to the president of the Board of Trade in 1909, the
district manager of the SCMEE's wrote, at the request of his Local Advisory
Committee, that

> my Committee are of opinion that this title will tend to restrict the use of the
> proposed Exchanges to Manual Workers, other class's of Workpeople
> assuming from the title that they are not intended for them. My Committee
> therefore suggest that as the Metropolitan system of "Employment
> Exchanges" have already done good work and are steadily growing, that if it
> is not possible at this stage to alter the title of the whole system to
> "Employment Exchange" the London system might retain the title they have

been known by for the last three years. This will prevent the misconception that will follow from the term "Labour Exchanges."[44]

In reply, the South Central's district manager was assured that his committee's suggestions would "receive consideration," though evidently not adoption, until some years later.[45] The district manager's letter reflected a widespread perception of the exchanges, particularly in their pre-1909 form, as adjuncts of distress committees providing relief work. His predictions about labor exchanges' constituency proved well founded. In his survey of bureaus established after 1905, Lowry noted that the "best employers and the best workmen have been inclined to hold aloof, under the impression that the Bureau is intended to meet the needs of the inferior workman, while those whom it is fashionable to call the unemployable have flocked to the Bureau in the hope of gaining a few shillings by devoting a short time to work more than nominal." Consequently a "prejudice" had formed against labor bureaus which Lowry believed could be ended only "by restricting the operations of the Bureaux."[46] Some practitioners believed that in addition to modifying its work, the exchanges should alter their name, a proposal indicative of how the needs of semiskilled and unskilled workers were perceived.

In the United States the Great Depression stimulated arguments for improving the efficiency of the labor market, if necessary, through government initiative. Such a view was promulgated by politicians and experts, principally economists. It was summarized in a National League of Women Voters' pamphlet: "Since 1914, there has been a steady flow of recommendations from diverse sources for a federal employment service which should collect information as to employment opportunities in all parts of the country, act as a clearing-house for labor between the states, and co-ordinate state (and through them, their subsidiary) agencies with a view to the development of standard practices and the exchange of employment services across state borders."[47] In November 1932 Franklin D. Roosevelt was elected president on the promise of a "new deal" for Americans, displacing Herbert Hoover's tepid administration and hostility to federal activism. Despite a Democratic majority in the Congress the new president faced opposition to the new role for the federal government which his legislative program implied.[48]

The Wagner-Peyser Act was the product of congressional initiative supported by Secretary of Labor Frances Perkins and pressure from organized labor represented by the American Federation of Labor (AFL). Bills to establish a national employment service were introduced sequentially to the Senate (S.510 on 20 March 1933) and to the House (H.R.4559 on 3 April 1933) and assigned respectively to the Senate Committee on Education and Labor and to the House Committee on Labor. They were almost identical to the bill passed by the 72d Congress but vetoed by President Hoover, and to the legislation examined favorably by the joint committee of the 69th Congress.[49] The bill was signed into law by President Roosevelt on 6 June 1933.

The service was proposed as part of a comprehensive approach to the United States's exceptionally high unemployment but also as an institution appropriate to periods of normal economic activity. The inadequacies of the existing federal system were uppermost in the minds of many legislators during the House debate. Congressman Welch noted:

> The main reason for this legislation is that the present United States Employment Service is most unsatisfactory. . . . The Federal service not only does not coordinate with the State service, but, in most instances, is actively competing with the State service and running an independent office in the State when there was already in the same State or the same city a State employment service. Also, there is actual friction between the employment services.[50]

Secretary Perkins stressed how America lagged behind other countries in developing a labor market placement system: "As a consequence, the organization of the labor market in this country has been left quite largely to private initiative."[51]

Although the United States Employment Services (USES) was created in 1933, the struggle for its establishment stretched over the previous decade.[52] Congressional hearings about a national employment system were held in 1919 (accompanying the Kenyon-Nolan bill[53]), 1928, 1929 and 1930, and a bill was passed by the Congress in 1931 but vetoed by President Hoover. From the late 1920s, the principal congressional activist was Senator Robert F. Wagner from New York, the liberal reformer.[54] He campaigned for a national employment service as part of a framework for dealing with unemployment. Wagner introduced his 1931 bill (S.3060) on 9 January.[55] With two other bills, Wagner characterized his proposals as constituting a "single program of legislation to deal with the unemployment problem."[56]

To accompany S.3060 Wagner prepared an explanatory memorandum about the role of exchanges in unemployment policy. It was circulated to his senatorial colleagues. Wagner had first to convince many of them that unemployment was a federal responsibility. He contended that "the problem of unemployment is . . . a national problem because some of the remedies which need to be applied can only be applied through national government" and were beyond the resources of state or local governments.[57] Unemployment challenged the national administrative capacities of the United States polity, which were traditionally limited, and the states' rights tradition.[58]

Five elements of the bill were discussed. First, the object of the bill was defined as the provision of a nationwide employment exchange system which would be administered locally but according to federal standards. Second, the bill proposed creating "federal instrumentality" by establishing the

Employment Service as a Bureau in the Department of Labor. Third, the Service's "method of operation" would consist of a federal grant to the states empowering them to establish placement offices. The bill provided for the creation of federal offices in those states whose governors declined to cooperate with the national system. Fourth, effective state cooperation was to be gained by requiring participation in the system before receiving federal assistance. Fifth, industrial cooperation was to be achieved with the creation of federal and state advisory councils composed of representatives from among both employers and employees; and "by adhering to a policy of neutrality in labor disputes, impartiality and freedom from politics; applicants for work must be given notices of strikes or lockouts, if any, in the work places to which they are referred."[59]

Wagner's arguments for a federal role in addressing unemployment were challenged by Southern politicians in Congress.[60] Despite his detailed memorandum, one senator from Washington immediately denied the legitimacy of federal action: "Should it be enacted into law it would embark the National Government upon an activity into which it ought not to enter, and one which is not necessary."[61] Resistance centered on the creation of a new federal agency. When Wagner requested an appropriation of $4 million on 12 May he faced complaints from his senatorial colleagues about the cost to taxpayers. Responding to such a charge from Senator Overman, Wagner restated efficiency arguments for exchanges:

> If we want to solve this subject of unemployment, if the Government is to do anything toward its solution, it has to create the machinery and select the personnel to perform that work . . . if, as a result of this legislation, a million men can be brought to the job one day sooner—and that is an exceedingly conservative estimate—assuming that the average earning per day of $4, a million men brought one day earlier to a job would save the Nation $4,000,000 directly in salaries, besides the wealth which these employees create during that particular day.[62]

Wagner's scheme envisaged an expansion of the federal government's role. He posited this new role in language designed to appeal to politicians wedded to classical economic beliefs (and not without parallels with the "new liberalism" influencing Wagner's earlier British counterparts). Wagner's rationale for employment exchanges was twofold: first, they would enhance labor market efficiency by providing a clearing mechanism; and, second, by reducing demands upon public benefits they were fiscally attractive. Advancing such tenets explains, in part, how labor exchanges contributed to the institutionalization of liberalism. Wagner placated a sufficient number of his colleagues for the passage of S.3060, but President Hoover's pocket veto delayed the reformer's work.

On 11 May 1933 the Senate Committee on Education and Labor issued a brief report about S.510 based on its deliberations. The committee's members concluded that a "national system of employment service, a Federal-State system, with real cooperation and real coordination by the Federal Government, is essential for the reconstruction period ahead, as it is also for the present period of the depression."[63] The committee also supported a strong federal role in the new system, believing it a prerequisite to a successfully coordinated employment service: "By taking the leadership, the Federal Government can set up standards, statistical control plans, give the necessary study, circulate the necessary information, and assist in bringing all of these offices into one general system."[64] The bill was read and passed quickly on the Senate floor on 29 May, with Senator Wagner observing that "the Senate on two occasions has approved this legislation."[65]

The House Committee on Labor held hearings on H.R. 4559 on 17 and 18 May 1933. It began with the insertion of a letter from Secretary of Labor Perkins strongly supporting the proposal. The bill's sponsor, Representative Peyser, introduced into the record letters of support from the National Women's Trade Union League of America, the National League of Women Voters and the American Association for Labor Legislation.[66] To justify the bill, Peyser castigated the existing system: "In many cases . . . the State bureaus compete with the Federal bureaus."[67] Federal appropriation would act as an incentive for state cooperation, with the federal agency centralizing and distributing information about employment patterns. One target of the bill noted by Representative Dunn was the "private employment agencies racket"; "one thing that it [the bill] is going to do will be to stop these parasites and bloodsuckers, like the man who gets a fellow a job and takes twelve or fifteen dollars out of his salary."[68]

The Wagner-Peyser Act abolished the existing employment service and established the new United States Employment Service (USES) as a bureau within the Department of Labor headed by a director appointed by the Labor Secretary. The act's brief was to establish a national system of employment offices through which men, women, juveniles, and veterans could acquire information about employment and to maintain a farm placement service. Section 3 of the Wagner-Peyser Act provided that

> the bureau shall also assist in coordinating the public employment offices throughout the country and in increasing their usefulness by: developing and prescribing minimum standards of efficiency; assisting them in meeting problems peculiar to their localities; promoting uniformity in their administrative and statistical procedures; furnishing and publishing information as to opportunities for employment and other information of value in the operation of the system; and maintaining a system for clearing labor between the several States.

It was a federal-state program with the cost divided between the two governments.

To receive assistance, each state had to enact legislation founding a state agency charged with establishing and maintaining employment offices in cooperation with the USES and according to the latter's specifications. In effect, each state (by act of either the legislature or the governor) was required to establish an agency which worked with the USES (and by November 1934, twenty-two of the state employment services had affiliated with the new USES).[69] The act implied a decentralized service: a national employment system created by the federal government would assist the states to legislate and establish a service in their jurisdiction. According to Palmer, this local emphasis "recognizes the principle that the organization and conduct of employment offices is best done by state and municipal governments."[70] But it also created the potential for a weak federal regulatory role. Furthermore, the directors of each state employment service were appointed by the governor, making this office a gubernatorial gift, which affected the loyalty of appointees. A federal-state division was also a device to dilute congressional hostility toward an active national role. This hostility was based on a profound commitment to limiting federal activism and privileging the states at the core of the United States polity. Other New Deal reforms confronted comparable palisades.

The act accorded considerable power to the USES's director in overseeing the state agencies and making annual appropriations. The director was also responsible for appointing the members of a Federal Advisory Council composed of an equal number of representatives from business, labor, and the public.[71] The council's responsibility was to assist in the formulation of policy and to ensure political neutrality and impartiality in the USES's work. Each state was also to appoint its own council in cooperation with the USES with representation of business, workers, and the general public. This advisory system was similar to that established in Britain after the 1909 act.

Before the passage of the Wagner-Peyser Act, Secretary of Labor Frances Perkins established the National Re-employment Service in early 1933. In her own words, this Service "was really the beginnings of the USES when we should get the statutory authorization for it."[72] Under the executive order the Department of Labor founded employment offices throughout the United States.[73] Perkins appointed Frank Persons as director of the service, "always knowing that if we got the Wagner-Peyser Act through, I would appoint him head of the USES, which I did."[74] Once in place, the early years of the USES were used by the new director as an occasion to define, publicize, and reiterate the agency's mission as he understood the congressional mandate. Persons's primary concern was to differentiate the ES's work from any association with relief, an affiliation pronounced and exaggerated by the agency's birth during the Great Depression.

The National Re-employment Service continued to function after the passage of the Wagner-Peyser Act, supplementing placement work. Its role in administering Roosevelt's New Deal public works programs made Persons especially conscious of the danger of a public association between employment service offices and relief. At a conference of the Civil Works Administration in November 1933, the new director observed that "this recruiting of labor must be so conducted that the avenue to the job is not through the relief offices, because if you have to go to the relief office to get a passport for a job you are going to have more applications for relief than you can accommodate on jobs, and the net result would be to increase your relief burdens."[75] Neither the self-sustaining nor the relief-based unemployed were to be favored:

> We must not take either exclusively from self-sustaining unemployed nor exclusively from the dependent unemployed. The clear indication is that we must place these men on Public Works on the basis of qualification for the job and without regard to relief status. Then we have the wholesome incentive of having an employee being and remaining fit for workmanship.[76]

Although the Reemployment Service was responsible for administering the Public Works Board's labor market policy, Persons reminded his audience that the building of a permanent placement system was the primary objective: "The State Director of Reemployment Service who permits even the suspicion that in any state he is trying to build up something that is to remain distinct and separate from the State's effort is rendering, unintentionally, of course, some measure of disservice to the future program. We regard Reemployment Service as a necessity. We regard it under that name, obviously, as a transitory thing."[77] Through its 3,320 local offices the National Reemployment Service registered, in a period of ten weeks, 9 million applicants.[78] Perkins judged an effective public employment system fundamental if the New Deal public works schemes were to succeed.[79] Subsequently the federal government merged the Reemployment Service offices with the new state USES offices.

In his talks Persons emphasized the undesirability of relief projects as a substitute to employment. He restated often the USES's priority to job placement. Addressing a conference of Work Projects Administrators in June 1935 he noted:

> It seems to me to be taken for granted that an employment service which can encourage the desire for self-support on the part of the unemployed by giving them a permanent agency for the seeking of employment, which can prevent people from coming on to public relief rolls by getting them into private jobs, and which can encourage those that get Works Projects jobs to look at that agency for chances for permanent private employment, is the

agency that we should both accept, you and I, as something that has to be
built up, developed, and used.[80]

Both Persons and Secretary Perkins gave innumerable speeches between
1933 and 1935 to explain the USES's role and to enhance its visibility. Their
target was the image of the ES as a temporary agency mobilized to address
short-term contingencies. They stressed its importance as a permanent agency
tackling unemployment. Conceding that the ES did not create jobs, Persons
argued that it nonetheless constituted an "indispensable link in the chain of
any organized attack on unemployment or any program for social security . . .
In its performance of the placement function, the public employment service
provides an employment exchange for bringing together applicants and jobs
in private industry."[81] He emphasized the uneconomical waste of resources
caused by the absence of a national exchange mechanism.

The processing of applicants at each exchange followed a common pattern. It was labor intensive and resulted in the compilation of information
about workers and employers. Upon visiting an Employment Service office, a
worker was interviewed by a person from that division within the office most
appropriate to her or his skills. This interview registered details about the
applicants, forming a permanent record of their work experience and skills or
qualifications. The applicants were then listed on the active registration file
under those occupations for which they were suitable. When employers
sought workers, the ES officials selected and forwarded them names from
this active registration file. A similar process was followed when an employer visited the ES office seeking workers. The active registration file was consulted and, if suitable applicants were registered, then these were reinter-
viewed in the office. If no appropriate applicants were listed, the ES office
contacted employment offices in other districts.

Under the terms of the Wagner-Peyser Act, each state employment service
established an advisory council to facilitate lay participation. Affiliation of a
state employment service with the national system was to be dependent upon
the existence of such a council. This clause was not enforced.[82] Under USES
organization, state advisory councils were to consist of no fewer than nine
members (they averaged eleven), with membership approved by the USES
director to ensure equal representation of employers and employees. The
councils were required to meet at least twice a year and to forward a copy of
each meeting's minutes to the USES. There was considerable state variation.
In the majority of the states the ES director recommended appointees whom
the governor ratified.[83] Apart from assisting in propagating the service and in
arranging introductions with some employers, the advisory councils assumed
a marginal role in the administration and life of state employment offices.
These were dominated by career officials. Meetings were infrequent. The

councils were not called upon to resolve conflicts between capital and labor. They were regarded as "advisory" bodies and for advice many state employment offices found more valuable sources. The record of local advisory councils was even less distinguished.[84]

Employers, Unionists, and the Unemployed

The efficiency arguments for employment exchanges demonstrate how they were perceived by the state as a mechanism with which to organize the labor market of expanding capitalist societies to foster efficiency, to remove the vagrancy problem, and as a palliative in contracting societies as well as those in recovery. Such organization and intervention affects both the state's role and the interests of workers, employers, and the unemployed. Particularly in Britain where an organized labor movement existed by the time of the Labour Exchanges Bill, the government anticipated a mixed response from the trades unions. It also expected employers to be uncooperative with any institution enhancing the organizational capacity of the working class. Effective organization of the workforce gave trades unionists the power to advance their demands about wages and working conditions. Control of the workforce through exchanges could provide employers with a mechanism to exclude union members or troublemakers. Subdivisions within each social grouping could also occur as skilled workers wanted exchanges to exclude the unskilled or immigrants while groups of employers could organize on an occupational basis. The experience from Germany, where Beveridge had identified seven different ways of organizing exchanges, revealed that these alternatives were recognized and acted upon. Establishing exchanges was part of the Trades Union Congress's (TUC) demand for a Minister of Labour, first expressed at their 1904 annual conference.[85] In the United States the American Federation of Labor (AFL) lobbied for a national employment exchange system.

Keir Hardie welcomed the "labour registries and exchanges" provided for in the 1905 Unemployed Workmen's Act. But he urged vesting "the control for them in the Labour Department of the Board of Trade . . . Were this done a uniform system of Registries and Exchanges would be set up for the Country as a whole. Workmen and employers in search of each other, could, however far apart, be put in instant communication . . . The advantages of this suggestion are so obvious as not to require elaboration."[86] Before 1909 British employers were slow—arguably unwilling—to use exchanges as institutions through which to hire labor and reluctant to notify exchanges of vacancies.[87] This reluctance did not decline. Employers feared that the exchanges might impose conditions and terms of contract for workers hired through them.

The attitude of British trades unionists toward exchanges was summarized in a letter prepared in October 1906 by the Joint Board representing the

TUC's Parliamentary Committee, the General Federation of Trade Unions, and the Labour Party. It was prompted by the numerous requests from distress committees to establish labor exchanges. Before it would support exchanges the Joint Board identified three necessary conditions. First, exchanges should not discriminate against union members in favor of nonunion workmen, supply labor during industrial disputes, or provide labor to firms paying below the "recognized rate of wages or under conditions of employment other than those obtaining in each particular trade in the district."[88] Second, the letter stipulated that trades unions should be entitled to maintain their own Vacant Book at each exchange and "with the exception of the place of Registration, shall be allowed to continue their present methods."[89] Third, the board requested that "where an organized system of Registration is already in existence, covering any trade, such Registration shall be accepted by the Distress Committee in the locality as sufficient for the purposes of that trade, and the members of such Unions shall participate in the operations of the Exchange in the same manner as those who register directly."[90] Neither the second nor the third condition was fully satisfied in the 1909 act.

At the 1909 Trades Union Congress Conference, J. Sexton, representing the Liverpool Dockers, moved that the exchanges' boards (which became the "advisory committees") should be composed equally of union and employer representatives chaired by a neutral official; that the exchanges should not supply labor to those employers who paid below the standard trade union rates; that workers should not be sent to firms with industrial disputes; that a separate room for trade union activity should be made available; and that women workers' needs should be adequately addressed by the exchanges.[91]

Sexton was unwilling to endorse the compulsory registration of unemployed persons because it equalized union and nonunion workers: "The moment the Government made it compulsory for all unemployed workmen to go through the Labour Exchanges they would have the unskilled labourer up against them."[92] Seconding the resolution, C. Hickin of the Sheet Metal Workers urged trades unionists to "get inside them [labor exchanges] to obtain most of the administrative power in order that they might shape the destinies of the Exchanges."[93] Though supporting the motion, J. N. Bell of National Labor defended the exchanges against Sexton and Hickin. He urged the removal of the "attitude of suspicion towards these Exchanges . . . otherwise it would be reflected in the attitude of the rank and file, who in the end would be driven into the hands of the employers."[94] Will Thorne of the Gasworkers attributed unionists' suspicions to the activities of existing exchanges; these were "used by employers as blackleg agencies."[95]

These deliberations illustrate how exchanges were perceived by organized workers. Exchanges were feared because of their potential to favor nonunion over union workers and to supply workers during industrial disputes.

Overcoming fears about the exchanges' bias toward employers and their negative image amongst workers explain the TUC's guarded endorsement of their national enactment. They foreshadow the issues dominating negotiations between the Board of Trade and the Parliamentary Committee of the TUC. Churchill's meetings with the Parliamentary Committee began on 17 June 1909. A second meeting was held in July. On 18 June 1909, the president of the Board of Trade, supported by eight advisors, met a twenty-three strong delegation from the Federation of Engineering and Ship-Building Trades. In these trades labor organization was extremely high, the workers skilled, and the federation's main concern was to protect their interests. In August, Churchill held meetings with employers represented through the Engineering Employers' Association and the Ship-Building Employers' Federation.

Churchill dominated the meetings with trades unionists. He conducted most of the discussion himself. He began the meeting on 17 June by characterizing the conference as a "private informal talk about the details of the Labour Exchanges Bill."[96] Shackleton replied: "It is necessary for us to get to know what is in the minds of the Government and yourself in regard to the regulations, because there is really nothing to talk about in the Bill."[97] The brevity of the bill meant that much government policy would rest upon the regulations administered by the Board of Trade. For the trades unionists this procedure excluded too many important decisions from parliamentary scrutiny. For Churchill, parliamentary approval of the bill's general principles provided an opportunity to discuss the regulations with "the different parties interested"; the president noted that, "of course, either side, employers or workmen, can bring the scheme to its knees by standing aloof at any moment."[98] Churchill held that the exchanges' implementation rested upon partnership between labor and capital aided by the state. He evidently feared losing the cooperation of either side.

Both the trades unionists and the employers had general principles to protect and also wanted to win assurances for particular issues. For the unionists, equalizing nonunion members with union members in the labor market was highly undesirable. The Federation of Engineering and Ship-Building Trades' greatest concern was the advantaging of nonunion members in the exchanges. They did not wish to "see non-union men put upon the same footing through these labour exchanges as the society men are" and had no wish to assist unemployed workers.[99] The federation feared that the exchanges would open up to nonunion members the advantages and contacts available to unionists.[100] Churchill agreed that such information be regarded as confidential. The federation delegates were further concerned that unions' collective bargaining power could be eroded if the exchanges supplied nonunion workers: "If the non-unionist is to have equal facilities for getting into the Works, then down goes our supremacy and under modern conditions down goes the conditions we have helped to build in past years."[101] Churchill adopted a similar response to the one used in the conferences with the TUC. He argued that exchanges were in the union interest, yet declined to give any assurance that they could be used to enforce union conditions and wages. Such a strategy "would really be not keeping to the impartial view at all; it would be going down and using a tremendous arm and a tremendous machinery in a matter in which it is vital for us to keep impartial."[102] Abandoning impartiality would encourage employers to hire workers outside of the exchanges. Churchill sketched his vision:

> The right thing is to have all the transactions done in the exchanges, so that the worker should have the opportunity of obtaining full information of what he is going to get, and so that he should know what the standard rates are exactly, what the trade union view is, and the conditions of the job. He should be in a position to choose between jobs all over the country if neces- sary, and he should not be held up by one particular employer in one partic- ular place. That is my idea, and I am sure it is the only one.[103]

Such a system had, he maintained, strengthened and stimulated, not weak- ened, unionism in Germany and he anticipated a similar outcome for British unions. He argued that if the exchange was impartial, employers seeking to undercut wage agreements would be exposed because that would come to light in the exchange—the "men who are waiting in the exchange will have an opportunity of knowing what the standard rate is and what is the differ- ence between that and what is being offered."[104]

Churchill concluded his conference with the Engineering Federation in similar style, emphasizing the historic importance of the exchange system. It constituted the first major government intervention in the labor market. Exchanges constituted a mechanism for organizing the market for labor, facilitating efficient employer-employee exchanges, and unemployment insurance. He also stressed the importance of excluding the idle. Future ini- tiatives would address the problems of the residual unemployed—through "curing processes and helping processes—farm colonies and those kind of things—for people who won't work, who are not very good, who are weak in character and so on"—and improving information about labor market trends respectively.[105] The last would offer a basis for a selective public works pro- gram invigorated during recessions. Churchill was animated about his initia- tives. Together they represented the "full proposition, and in fighting for it, we really are fighting for the social future of the working-classes of this country. It is a great risk, it is full of perils, it is full of difficult questions, and it will be the permanent glory of trade unionism if they come forward and fearlessly encounter those things and carry it all through with safety."[106] The delegates left the conference in a positive mood believing that Churchill understood and was sympathetic to their interests.[107]

In August 1909, the president of the Board of Trade, accompanied by his advisers, met representatives of the Engineering and Ship-Building employers' organizations. There were three representatives each from the engineers and shipbuilders. Each delegate was from a different company.

The delegates were not sanguine about exchanges. They believed "that the evils attendant upon the suggested Exchanges will far outweigh any advantages which may be expected to accrue from them. . . . It is feared . . . that the Exchanges may be centers for the spread of discontent and will increase instead of alleviate the misfortunes of those they are intended to benefit."[108] Beveridge dismissed the threat of class conflict or industrial disruption posed by exchanges. The employers' delegation believed further that exchanges would devalue jobs by reducing the effort required by workers to obtain them. This outcome in turn weakened "personal character." Neither federation had received any demand for exchanges from their workers. Finally, the federations believed the exchanges were unsuited to the hiring methods operating in their industries, which were "at present employed with success:

> First, the foremen have usually in their possession a list of men out of work with whose capacity and character they are acquainted. Second, recommendations of other workmen on whose opinions the foremen can rely. Third, trade union and other organizations. And, fourth, the public press.[109]

These procedures were precisely those which the Labour Exchanges Bill was designed to end.

The employers were further concerned that exchanges would offer a mechanism through which trades unions could impose their preferences about work conditions or create a mechanism for distinguishing between union and nonunion members: "The selection and engagement of a workman should rest exclusively with the employer . . . [and] Employers should be free to employ workmen on whatever terms are mutually agreed."[110] The employers also wanted agreed restrictions upon the powers and responsibilities of local advisory councils to the extent that they enjoyed "no *locus standi* in any matters appertaining to the Exchanges and neither directly nor indirectly be permitted to influence the conduct or control of them."[111] The employers' expectations about the work of exchanges during disputes did not differ sharply from trades unionists. The registrar should be instructed, "(a) to continue operations on the usual lines without reference to circumstances obtaining, or (b) a notice should be posted in the Exchange announcing the fact of a strike without comment."[112]

These general points were made by Alexander Siemens of Siemens Brothers and Company, who was supported by Fred Henderson of D & W Henderson and Company. In engineering and shipbuilding, Henderson argued, the exchanges "will do us no good at all . . . we have our own Labour Exchanges every morning." Both Henderson and Siemens stressed the importance of employing impartial officers in the exchanges; they should "absolutely have nothing whatever to do with either any employers' or any men's organizations, and never had anything to do with them, because there is no doubt a man once a trade unionist is always a trade unionist."[113] The president of the Board of Trade responded by emphasizing the voluntary character of the proposed exchanges. He noted the absence of any compulsion upon workers to register at them. He urged employers to use the exchanges, though that was a matter of individual choice: "I would like to make that clear at the outset: there is absolutely no sort of interference at all."[114]

Adopting a different stance to that deployed in discussions with trades unionists, Churchill stressed the exchanges' punitive role in dealing with vagrancy and tramps: "There is no reason at all why people should wander about in a loafing and idle manner; if they are not earning their living they ought to be put under some control."[115] The exchanges' role in promoting liberal values in British work-welfare program is perspicuous here. The exchanges would organize the commodity market for labor and monitor workers' efforts to find jobs. Any potential for disorder was to be avoided by ensuring that unemployed persons returned home after registering at the exchange: "They will be there purely for business purposes, and there will no sort of loafing about at all . . . it is not intended that it shall be *a sort of permanent club for the unemployed*."[116] Churchill denied that the incentives to look for work would be eradicated by the existence of exchanges since there was little but hardship in the existing arrangements: "Merely to wait in stagnant misery in your home without any wages and so forth is such a pressure and such an incentive, it is the pressure almost of starvation, or certainly the poor law, that it would force him to get work if he can. The difficulty now is that so many people do not know where to turn."[117] For the president, this lacuna constituted a powerful defense of exchanges and one which did not contradict the self-help principles championed by Siemens and Henderson.

Three major issues dominated the president of the Board of Trade's meetings with worker and employer organizations: the bases of local representation on advisory boards, the exchanges' role in industrial disputes, and the exchanges' position on wage rates.

Representation of Interests

The TUC delegation sought assurance that the representation of interests in each exchange (on the advisory committees) would not be confined to representatives from the local trades councils or Chambers of Commerce since neither group was entirely representative: "So far as the Parliamentary Committee is concerned they agree that no trade should be left out . . . but all the trades should be represented, large and small."[118] Churchill was opposed to any fixed ruling about union representation: "I think it would be a mistake if we were to say formally once and for all that no one but a trade unionist should sit upon these boards. I think the employers would very likely to be prejudiced by that."[119] However, Churchill conceded the principle of asymmetrical representation for resolving disputes: "When we come to test questions, issues between capital and labour . . . then it will be only labour and the employers' representatives in strictly equal numbers, with an impartial chairman," the German model.[120] TUC delegate Steadman's request for a "unionists only" rule failed, a decision supported by the civil servant Llewellyn Smith: "Speaking in this room, I should think probably it would turn out to be ten out of ten; but still it is quite a different thing to putting it into an Act of Parliament."[121] To which observation Churchill remarked, "I think I should not like to have it put in."[122] A nascent tripartite arrangement structured representation on the exchanges' advisory committees. Churchill promised that this body would be composed of "the parity principle and with a certain portion of impartial people."[123] Discretion about the final format remained with the board. The delegation's efforts to achieve a binding commitment to exclusive union representation was rebuffed. Obviously, if the board disregarded the views of the parliamentary committee, the labor exchange system would suffer; as Churchill observed, "aloofness" by either the unions or employers would disable the system. Power had to be balanced, but the board held the upper hand.

The issue of representation remained unresolved after the implementation of the Labour Exchanges Act. In a meeting in March in 1910 between the Board of Trade and the parliamentary committee, J. Sexton requested that

> as soon as possible Advisory Boards should be appointed consisting of an equal number from both sides. And I would urge that no dual representation should be allowed. There is a possibility—in fact, I believe there is a suggestion—that associations, if I may say so, masquerading as workmen's organizations, but subsidised by employers, will lay claim to be represented on the Advisory Boards.[124]

The function of advisory boards was to inhibit the exchanges from sending men to jobs which paid below union rates and to firms with industrial disputes. Sexton requested a regulation requiring employers to register disputes with the exchanges. In response, the new president of the Board Trade, Sydney Buxton, reiterated the promises of his predecessor: "Our full intention . . . is to have the Advisory Committees consist of representatives of the employers on the one side and of employees on the other, with an impartial chairman, who, in the event of matters arising will not have to cast a vote, but refer the subject to the Board of Trade."[125] He promised also to grant representation to genuine unionists.

At a second conference with the Board of Trade on 8 July 1909, Shackleton returned to the issue of local advisory committees. He expressed the delegation's desire to learn who would be eligible for nomination as representatives of workers and who would act as nominators. The parliamentary committee feared relegation to a "permanent minority" on the committee.[126] Churchill assured the delegates that "when it comes to the committee in relation to any disputed matter between employers and labour, then there will be an absolutely even number of combatants on each side."[127] Churchill indicated a willingness to permit representation of unions in each district on a proportional basis. Although the Board of Trade conceded parity of representation for industrial disputes, Churchill still sought to dominate: "I want to have the power to appoint others on the local committee, and I do not want to be tied down rigidly to absolute parity . . . between the combatant parties."[128] Thus two committees were envisaged for each exchange. First a subcommittee composed equally of representatives from capital and labor—in Churchill's phrase the "absolutely equal committee"—and, second, the full committee dealing with the management of the exchanges.[129] In addition, Churchill proposed constituting a national advisory committee upon which the TUC sought representation. This request was accepted.

The federation's president, Mr. Jack, was positive about the exchange scheme—a "great workable scheme"—but shared some of the parliamentary committee's reservations.[130] He sought union representation upon local advisory committees: "We want, if at all possible, that these advisory committees which are formed will have trade unionists on them the same as there will be employers. . . . [and] we do not want . . . benevolent parties at all to be on. What we want is men who have come through the thick of the battle. . . . not . . . these slipper people."[131] Churchill easily accepted this request. He promised that, "in the vast majority of cases" worker representatives would be union members since "it is no good our putting on a committee men who are not representatives . . . who have not got authority . . . and whom the workmen will not recognise."[132] As in the conference with the Parliamentary Committee of the Trades Union Congress, Churchill distinguished the managerial work of the advisory committee from its role in employer-worker disputes. During disputes "I do not propose to have any outsiders in at all."[133] He again proposed a subcommittee for this latter work "consisting of absolutely equal numbers of workmen's and employers' representatives and one impartial chairman."[134] Later in the conference Churchill resisted declaring this arrangement formally: "Between making that [equal representation] very clear and absolutely saying that we will not recognise any man but a trade unionist as a workman, there is a gulf. I should get into trouble in all sorts of other quarters if I were to go as far as that, and make a formal statement."[135]

Exchanges and Industrial Disputes

One of the most contentious issues in the operation of the new exchange system was how to respond to strikes and lockouts. Both the registrar of the earliest exchange, in Egham,[136] and Beveridge had practiced neutrality toward industrial disputes. In his capacity as chairman of the Employment Exchanges Committee of the Central (Unemployed) Body of London between 1906 and 1909, Beveridge kept the exchanges impartial in industrial disputes. In December 1906 Beveridge recommended that exchanges be "impartial as between employers and employed, upon whose voluntary co-operation they depend, and in order to be impartial must avoid the responsibility for decisions of questions in which the interests of the two parties are opposed."[137] The exchanges were at that stage operating the German "strike clause," neither registering vacancies nor unemployed men from disputes. In Beveridge's vivid phrase, exchanges "are market places for labour in time of peace not time of war."[138] Impartiality also precluded the exchanges from reaching decisions about the wage levels offered in firms since this action would exceed its brief as a marketplace and not as employer.[139] This position was adopted by Churchill in the bill. Speaking in Parliament, he was unequivocal about the exchanges' role in the incidence of strikes:[140] "The whole principle of the Labour Exchanges is to be absolutely neutral between capital and labour. It depends for its success upon the co-operation of employers and workmen. We must have both or the scheme cannot be a success. And we cannot get both unless we give confidence to both parties, that neither will be aided in any struggle with the other by any action or operation of the Labour Exchange."[141]

Speaking on behalf of the delegation, Shackleton (himself a future permanent head of the Ministry of Labor) reiterated that the issue of most concern to trades unionists was the exchanges' role during strikes. He outlined the parliamentary committee's preferred role:

> There should be an understanding that when hostilities are on in a particular trade in a particular district, the exchange itself is absolutely out of gear so far as finding work is concerned. If the exchange is used to find work during a strike or a lockout, it appears to me that it will mean . . . that it would be closed by the absence of our representatives on these advisory boards . . . they would simply withdraw from representation.[142]

As a model for his proposals, Shackleton cited German practice.

Addressing the unionists the president of the Board of Trade was unequivocal in specifying an impartial role for the exchanges. He disallowed the holding of union meetings at the exchanges to discuss trade disputes "because the Exchange is neutral."[143] In response to Shackleton's request, he proposed the following rule: "to let each side post up a clear statement what the conditions are, and so forth; let them be clearly known, and let the people have an opportunity of choosing, wisely or unwisely, only with full knowledge."[144] To avoid Shackleton's prediction that partiality would place the exchanges "out of gear," Churchill was willing to establish his rule by "regulation," though not by inclusion in an act. He rejected the need totally to disrupt the labor exchange—throwing it "out of gear"—while a dispute continued, the action which Shackleton maintained would make workers more favorable to the new exchange system. The president was less accommodating about the presence of union officials in the exchanges to notify workers about each dispute.

Churchill reminded the delegates that if an exchange were thrown "out of gear" by its withdrawal from supplying labor to firms with strikes, by the same token it would be unable to register the strikers. Despite the president's assurances, the parliamentary committee delegates persisted with this question. The M.P. Alex Wilkie, cited the precedent of the distress committees:

> The great objection when we are meeting the local representatives is that the present distress committees have been used to supply labour when a dispute is on, in other words, to supply blacklegs. We want to be able to say that the new exchanges are not to do so.[145]

Wilkie and his colleague Steadman (who noted similar problems with the Central [Unemployed] Body Committee in London) accepted Churchill's assurance that the system to be enacted by the Labour Exchanges Act would be "entirely new."[146] The president proclaimed that "we are not at all bound by the practice in the past. We want to set up a complete national system under principles which have been agreed on. What we are trying to get at today is the general principles. I do not think you need worry about the past; let us look ahead."[147] "My feeling," he said enthusiastically, "is that if you get a lot of men in a room together, trade unionists and non-unionists, and they stay waiting there for a few hours, perhaps for two or three days in succession, they will realise the solidarity of their class interest in a way which they do not now . . ."[148] It is not clear that the TUC delegates shared Churchill's enthusiasm.

At the second conference, D. J. Shackleton reported that, upon reflection, the parliamentary committee accepted that exchanges should work during strikes, provided that "there must be conditions which we think are absolutely essential in the case of non-suspension, such as that there should be the publication of the fact that there is a dispute at a place."[149] This requirement did not differ greatly from Churchill's proposals during the first conference.

This issue was also addressed in Churchill's meeting with employer representatives. As in the consultations with the trades unionists, it was pivotal to the conference. Siemens reported employer opposition to any demand that the "exchanges should stop when there was any dispute on."[150] Churchill stressed the importance of carrying "both parties with me to [make] this thing a success."[151] He proposed that a notice be posted in the exchange agreed with an authorized person from both sides of the dispute. The decision whether to work there would be an individual one. The president advanced this scheme as advantageous to employers:

> There will be a notification that there is a strike or a lock out, otherwise the thing will go on as before. I do not think, if anybody had said a year ago that the trade unions would have agreed to a Government Labour Exchange sending 50 or 100 men to an employer whose men are out on strike, that anybody would have believed it at all. I confess I did not think it would go.[152]

Workers recruited to sites of industrial disputes might come from exchanges "some hundred of miles away and arrive by motor cars or railway."[153] Not surprisingly, this version was not the one presented to the trades unionists. Again, when discussing the composition of the advisory committees Churchill noted that representatives of workmen need not necessarily be trades unionists. This also contradicted his assurance to the TUC delegation.

Exchanges and Wages

Churchill was uncompromising about the use of the exchanges to enforce "standard rates"[154] in wages. The president of the Board of Trade was prepared for wage rates to be advertised in the labor exchanges, but he rejected any effort to establish appropriate rates:

> The general principle is that you should post up your rates, and that should be known—everything should be stated quite clearly—and your members should have opportunity of being advised and guided by their own leaders; but, broadly speaking, the exchange has no views at all. It is meant to be a perfectly neutral system, and if a man, knowing what the trade union rate is, chooses to accept work below that rate, that is a matter for the trade unions to deal with ordinary methods.[155]

Churchill believed wage undercutting inevitable. He contended that wider union organization, not the enforcement of standard rates, was the solution of this problem.

The parliamentary committee delegates' dissatisfaction with this proposal reflected their observations in Germany. According to the M.P. Bowerman, a member of the visiting group, the wage differentials "are religiously protected by the exchange."[156] Bowerman contended that, in the absence of agreed rates for each trade, the exchanges would degenerate into bartering centers. But the union representatives won no concessions from Churchill. He restated his view that labor exchanges could assume responsibility only to post stan-

dard rates, themselves arbitrated, a practice which "I should have thought . . .
a much greater buttressing up of the standard rates." He rejected any more
forceful policy:

> I am quite sure it would be a very serious thing to say no engagement will
> be made through the labour exchange except at the standard rate, in fact I
> am quite certain it would lead to the other party not coming in at all.[157]

Churchill expressed his personal support for the standard rate[158] but declined
to give the exchanges a role in its establishment or maintenance. This reluctance, he indicated, arose from the attitude of employers:

> I have to think of the other party, whose co-operation is as necessary to the
> success of this scheme as yours. Both sides are vital: without it there is no
> way forward. I do see this difficulty: Are you going to say, "We will only
> deal with business at the union rate in the Exchanges?"—because if so, it
> means that all business outside that rate is to go on outside the Exchange.[159]

In replying, Shackleton acknowledged Churchill's difficulty but suggested that he too faced a choice: to be associated with maintaining current
inequities or recognized as the architect of their destruction.[160] Bowerman
argued that unions and employer representatives had reached agreement on
standard wage rates in several parts of the country. He suggested that "personally, I believe that the success of the exchange will depend upon your
decision on that point," to which Churchill retorted: "it would be absolutely
fatal in my opinion to the whole thing."[161] He resolutely opposed using the
exchanges to advance sectional interests: "What we do not want to have to
do is to make this very powerful machinery of labour exchanges definitely
take sides in favor of the standard rate. We want it to be used just like the
Post Office is used for all sorts of matters."[162] In the unionists' eyes,
employers' interests were being advantaged. This statement still did not satisfy the parliamentary committee, one of whose members alluded to "a good
deal of suspicion throughout the country already in reference to these labour
bureaus."[163] Steadman argued that adverse economic conditions facilitated
employer exploitation by undercutting standard wages. Churchill judged this
scenario improbable since "my idea is that the employers would not come
into the waiting-room where all the workers were waiting for their employment."[164] Furthermore, "if the employer says he is giving the standard conditions, and he is not doing it, that is a fraudulent statement, and so far from
the men being penalized for throwing up the job, it would be the employer
who would be penalized for having made a false statement to the
Exchange."[165] This view, while apparently reasonable, underestimated how
difficult it was for a unionist to demonstrate employer deceit. The president
then requested the delegates to "keep an open mind" about the issue, con-

tending that the absence of an enforced standard is "really on your side and to your advantage."[166]

At the second TUC-Board of Trade conference, the TUC delegation pressed for a public statement of wages and conditions from employers seeking workers. They noted that a workman did not learn his wage "until the end of the work."[167] Shackleton proposed a significant concession to Churchill. He indicated the committee's willingness to waive the demand that only employers offering trade union rates should use the exchanges in exchange for acknowledgment that "the workpeople should know what the conditions are if they are the trade union rate. We think that is an important point. If the employer is not prepared to pay the recognized rate of the district, we must know what he is going to pay."[168] Churchill was slow to accede. Shackleton persisted: "We want to secure the exception. Where a man deliberately goes to the Exchange for the purpose of getting men at less than the rates, he ought to state that—not that he should take the men and then leave us the trouble afterwards."[169] Llewellyn Smith was more sympathetic to the union position:

When you come to the Labour Exchange supplying men, they must know the normal local rate. The object of the exchange is not to supply men, but to notify vacancies. The moment you get to promoting it, to advancing money, or to sending people, of course you must ask the rate. I do not think there is any question about that, the moment you take any responsibility.[170]

The president of the Board of Trade suggested that by making two or three positions available to workers, employers would be forced to advertise the wages they were paying. The board member, G. R. Askwith, argued that it was unions who should establish wage rates with employers by withdrawing labor and refusing to grant this role to the exchange: "It seems to me very important in these Labour Exchanges to make the officer in charge as free as possible from any interference between employer and employed, or perhaps from having to judge questions of difficult fact."[171] In partial response, Churchill stressed the definition of the exchange as an institution at which to notify vacancies and not one which supplied labor. Shackleton was unmoved: "We think if an employer is determined to take men on and not pay the rate, he ought to say so in advance; I do not think we ought to allow the fellows to go and then have the trouble afterwards."[172]

Beveridge, a member of the Board of Trade, opposed publication of the wages offered. On the basis of the Berlin case, he concluded that to know all of the wages of all of the vacancies would be too great a task: "Any man before he takes a job can insist on knowing the wages, but if the superintendent and all the other people there are to know it, it is perfectly certain the employers, who do not want too much publicity, would keep away."[173] Beveridge believed that employers would not use the exchanges if conditions, such as publishing their wage levels, were attached to the registration of vacancies. Churchill stressed the danger of losing either employers or organized labor from the exchanges. Shackleton was unconvinced. His colleague Cooper supported him: "Where there is a distinct trade union rate, and an employer wants to go behind that rate and use the Exchange for that purpose, all that we are saying is that he should be compelled to make a statement as to the amount that he intends to pay for the labour supplied. There is nothing at all objectionable about that."[174]

Hubert Llewellyn Smith correctly noted that the level of organization in Shackleton's trade was sufficient for wage levels to be agreed on universally. Such organization was absent in most trades and this made wage agreements haphazard and localized. Churchill accepted the necessity of full information as an operating principle but he did not wish to "make it a sort of pillory for putting an employer in. . . . It would be fatal to the Exchanges to use them as places for pillorying bad employers, . . . [though adding] Just as it will be fatal to use them for pillorying any workmen—because you can use them either way."[175] Employers' interests prevailed over those of workers. Llewellyn Smith finally conceded that the board "should be able to make a regulation that will meet the substantial point, and yet not throw out the employers."[176] Churchill was less pliant.

Meeting with employers, Churchill allayed their fears that exchanges would advantage trades unionists and provide a site for union recruitment. His assurance was at variance with the view expressed in conference with the parliamentary committee. He also confirmed the right of employers to reach agreement on "any terms with a man you like."[177] This right would obviously include wage rates. He and Llewellyn Smith agreed with the absence of any *locus standi* right for unionists or employers.

Employer preferences were also assisted by the decision to make the labor exchanges a centralized rather than a locally controlled system (a choice adhered to in subsequent work-welfare programs). Decentralization would most likely have increased the power of unions in the functioning of exchanges. Craft unions valued local control more highly than they did the realization of national policy. When presented with a choice between centralized direction or local control during the formulation of the 1909 bill, and despite knowledge of the decentralized character of the German system, where control rested with municipal or other local authorities, the Board of Trade opted for the former. Beveridge evaluated national and local options (the latter based on his study of the German system): "I put, as more or less evenly balanced alternatives, a national system directly under the Board of Trade and local authority exchanges encouraged and coordinated by the Board of Trade with grants in aid. The Government, without hesitation, decided for the first alternative: for national Labour Exchanges under central control."[178]

Disagreement between the Board of Trade president and trade union representatives was fundamental. Few concessions were made by the Board of Trade. When the parliamentary committee became insistent, the president cited the need for fairness toward employers' interests. The negotiations were important to the Board of Trade for two reasons. First, to implement the labor exchanges system successfully they required the cooperation of both the trade union movement and of employers and so were obliged to take both groups' interests into account. Second, labor exchanges were already perceived unfavorably by workers. Consequently, early and ardent union support of the new system was essential to overcome this hostility. Unions also feared that labor exchanges would tend to equalize the status of skilled and unskilled workers, and this helps to explain why labor exchanges quickly became the province of the least skilled and most marginal job seekers.

When the labor exchanges were debated at the TUC conference in 1910, some delegates were critical of their role in industrial disputes. Mosses, of the Patternmakers, argued that "the Labour Exchanges as at present managed are proving prejudicial to the Trade Union movement."[179] To end this, he moved that a recognized trade union official receive information about wage rates at workplaces to which the exchanges forwarded workers and that it be stipulated in the exchanges' administration rules that "under no circumstances shall the divisional superintendent or the superintendent of any exchange cause to be exhibited any notice, or entertain in any way whatever, applications from firms who may have a dispute with their workpeople, after such dispute has been officially notified by the Trade Union concerned."[180] Exchanges, Mosses suggested, increased the problem of blacklegging, an outcome obviously contrary to the expectations of labor and of the Board of Trade. The resolution was seconded by J. G. Gordon of the Sheet Metal Workers, who charged that workers were being directed from the exchanges to different districts in order to undercut wages. Similar complaints were aired by seven other unionists representing different trades.[181]

It fell to David Shackleton M.P. to defend the parliamentary committee's support of the exchanges. First, he rejected the claim that organized labor had not advocated a national labor exchange system. He referred Mosses to earlier conference reports and to the TUC's Unemployed Bill: "We have always had a clause dealing with and calling for the formation of Labour Exchanges. Every one of these points has been before the Congress and the Labour Party, and it is therefore incorrect to say that the Labour movement has never asked for Labour Exchanges."[182] Shackleton rejected the call for the trades unions to administer the exchanges. He noted that the TUC could claim only a membership of 2 million from a workforce of 11 million. He rejected the criticism of exchanges' role during disputes. He reminded the congress that in their negotiations with the Board of Trade they decided "after careful and deliberate discussion . . . against closing the exchanges in cases of dispute." He observed: "I quite admit there may be complaints which ought to be carefully inquired into; but on the point as to the use of exchanges in times of strike, we have agreed that they shall remain open." Curiously, despite his defense of the arrangement, he conceded that it "may have been unwise in deciding to have the exchanges open during disputes."[183] He urged the delegates to vote against the resolution. Feelings amongst the delegates were especially incensed by a circular from Julia Thornton of the Board of Trade to labor exchange managers reported by Yorkshire delegates. This circular referred to the shortage of women workers in Bradford and Hull and "suggested that the Labour Exchanges might sometimes be able to find places for widows, and daughters from 13 years of age and upwards, in receipt of Poor Law relief, either temporarily or permanently."[184] The circular was too damaging for Shackleton's plea for support to succeed and the resolution was supported by a majority of 875,000 (1,147,000 for and 272,000 against).[185]

This debate at the 1910 TUC conference reveals both the persistence of "suspicion" of the exchanges amongst delegates and predictable teething problems in establishing them. The exchanges' potentially damaging role for trades unionists most concerned the delegates: industrial disputes, wage rates, and union recruitment. The trades unions' limited recruitment of their potential membership impressed the vulnerability of the TUC upon its members; it explains their fear about the potential damage to union interests by exchanges if these latter precluded the need for organization. These issues were raised in March 1910 between a meeting of the parliamentary committee and the president of the Board of Trade. At this meeting the new president repeated the board's position during negotiations before the bill's passage. Buxton rejected again the proposal that exchanges should be "thrown out of gear" by disputes. In anticipation of unemployment insurance, he noted that "after all, there are many others besides Trade Unionists to be considered"—exactly the TUC's concern.[186]

In 1911 Mosses again moved a resolution[187] on the exchanges, supporting them now but on condition that they better promoted the interests of unionists: "We certainly are asking that special treatment shall be accorded to Trade Unions." He continued: "After all, the Labour Exchange is an industrial institution, and all the benefits which have been secured by the workers of this country have come by and through the Trade Unions, often at cost of great sacrifice in money and effort: and we have never yet heard of anything being done by non-society men to uplift the class to which they belong."[188] Like all unionists, Mosses understood the problem of free riding later immortalized by Mancur Olson.[189] His ideal—and one shared by other unionists— was that the exchanges should be administered wholly by trades unionists for their members' benefits. The improbability of such an arrangement being accepted by the Liberals made the presence of union representatives on advisory committees vital. Mosses also conveys trade union hostility toward nonunion members and the weakness of solidarity amongst the working class more generally.

The unemployment crisis following World War I produced changes in the exchanges' potential role amongst officials at its central office.[190] In a confidential C.O. Circular in 1918, titled "Supply of Information by the Managers of Employment Exchanges with regard to Actual or Threatened Labour Disputes," the Acting Assistant director instructed managers in future to "furnish the C.O. and the Divisional Offices simultaneously with narrative reports respecting threatened or existing disputes or strikes unless they are confined to one establishment and are unimportant in character." The acting assistant director sought information obtained by each manager "through any channel which he feels he can rely," a broad definition of sources: alternatively information should be furnished which the manager "can easily obtain without appearing to concern himself directly or indirectly with the disputes"—ensuring the semblance of impartiality on the exchanges' part.[191]

Representatives of both workers and employers were closely involved in the establishment of labor exchanges. The detailed and, by the standards of the period, lengthy negotiations testify to each side's apprehensions about the new system. This close attention did not last. The combination of labor exchanges' marginalization as sources of employment (though not of benefit distribution) and their concentration upon those least skilled enabled unions and employers to marginalize them as well.

For over a decade before the enactment of the 1933 Wagner-Peyser Act, the American Federation of Labor (AFL) had lobbied for the establishment of a labor exchange system. The AFL's monthly publication, the *American Federationist,* regularly carried editorials and articles calling for the founding of an employment service.[192] In February 1930 the journal argued that "obviously there should be municipal employment services which clear through a central Federal agency. Work toward this end can begin with two courses: local efforts to secure better municipal employment services and the enactment of Federal legislation."[193] The impetus to the AFL's endorsement of a federal employment service was the mounting unemployment from 1929. In October 1930 an editorial in the *American Federationist* titled "Unemployment" argued that "our nation has two major responsibilities for the unemployment problem: Employment exchanges so that the unemployed may at least be informed where jobs are available without payment of fees and relief for those who can not find work."[194]

The AFL's annual conferences regularly carried motions for the establishment of an employment service and as regularly excoriated the practices of private, fee-based, employment agencies. As a component of the AFL's 1930 program to address unemployment, it advocated a federal employment service: "Such a service would be equally useful to employers informing them where to get the kind of employees they need . . . The Government is now furnishing information and advisory services to other economic groups; the interests of wage earners are equally important to national advancement."[195] The creation of a "nationwide system of employment exchanges" was the fourth of ten priorities included in the AFL's unemployment program.[196] The employment service was not offered as a panacea for mass unemployment but as a necessary element of any strategy: "The public employment office cannot of itself lessen unemployment. But it is an instrument of service essential to the development and execution of any program of mitigating the shocks of unemployment and of regularizing industry for the increased stability of employment."[197] Again in 1931, a system of employment exchanges was incorporated in the AFL's emergency unemployment program for the winter of 1931–32; they were to be linked to a public works project. According to the AFL, "Official employment bureaus will be essential to make any of this work-providing program possible."[198] AFL President Green mobilized local unions and state federations in support of a national employment service. They responded by sending hundreds of telegrams to Congress urging enactment of the 1931 bill. For the long term, an employment service was linked by the AFL to economic development: "Every industrial community ought to have a public employment agency so efficient as to command the respect of employers and employees. This office should have its contacts with industries and all employing groups and have at hand that specialized information of job requirements necessary to render satisfactory service."[199] Thus, the AFL considered a labor exchange system important both to alleviating the current crisis and to organizing the labor market during periods of normal economic activity. Their capacity to promote this view was, however, restricted. First, union membership was low and, like its British counterpart, the dominant tradition in the AFL was localist, though the founding of the CIO in the mid 1930s marked a slow movement away from that tradition. Second, organized labor had little support in the Congress before the 1930s, and it was only the National Labor Relations Act of 1936 that legitimized their presence in the labor market.[200]

The Hoover Veto

The AFL's support for an employment service is well illustrated by its outrage at President Hoover's pocket veto of the 1931 bill initiated by Senator Wagner to establish a national employment service (ES).[201] Wagner represented labor's interests and engaged in heated debate with Hoover's Secretary of Labor William Doak about the veto. The president argued that the Wagner bill would create a new bureaucracy, result in no service for a transition period and violate states' rights. According to Secretary Doak, the bill would breach states' rights by, for example, the "insistence [that each state] set up another bureaucracy to supervise state machinery and coerce the states into joining an employment system which would be wholly inadequate to meet the needs, either of the present situation or the future."[202] Doak argued that the bill would force those twenty-seven states without an employment service to join the new system or else to forego federal aid. He concluded that the bill created a conflict between voluntary federal-state cooperation and arrangements under which "the states are to be coerced into establishing a system which would be inflexible and which would provide no machinery for bringing the unemployed in one state or section to jobs which might be available in other states or sections."[203]

Bizarrely, President Hoover maintained that passage of the bill would be a "serious blow to labor during this crisis." Despite having "repeatedly urged" the extension of the employment service, Hoover concluded that the Wagner bill "unfortunately, abolished the whole of the present well-developed Federal Employment Service," replacing it with a new system.[204] Hoover's principal objection hinged upon the alleged delay between abolition of the existing system and the effective operation of its successor. His veto was based on advice from both Doak and Attorney General William Mitchell. Mitchell maintained that "it is obvious that months must elapse before substantial progress could be made in setting up the new service."[205]

Hoover's controversial veto reversed the advice of his own Presidential Emergency Committee for Employment. One labor commentator, George Trafton, believed it exposed "an opposition which had been quietly exerted through Administration leaders in the House for many months."[206] The same author queried the credibility of the reasons given for the veto. He observed that the administration's worries had not been communicated to the House during the committee or floor debates. The president of the AFL, William Green, a staunch supporter of the Wagner bill, declared that the "reasons offered for the exercise of the Presidential veto are unconvincing and unacceptable. [The veto is] . . . a direct and severe blow to working people in the industrial sections of our country who are unemployed and are forced to seek work."[207] The *American Federationist* concurred: "His veto has placed upon him personally full responsibility for seeing to it that the labor market is organized and that those who invest their personal capacities in industry as producing workmen gave information and advice in helping them find employment."[208] The claim that placement services would be completely suspended during a transition period was widely dismissed. The economist Sumner Slichter observed that "practically all of the placements are being made by state employment offices, which are Federal in name only and whose operations would not have ceased for one second if the Wagner bill had become law."[209]

Wagner himself provided a detailed critique of the administration's grounds for vetoing his bill. First, he dismissed the Hoover charge that his bill delivered a "blow to labor." He cited the strong support for the legislation from organized labor, including Green of the AFL and Sidney Hillman of the American Association of Clothing Workers.[210] Wagner noted that support for his bill was not confined to labor but included business, bankers and economists, and the administrators of state employment services. The senator then delivered a stinging rebuke to Doak, mindful of the Labor Secretary's contribution to the drafting of the Nolan-Kenyon bill in 1919: "I cannot forget and the public in passing upon this issue will not forget that Mr. Doak himself, as representative of the Brotherhood of Railroad Trainmen, privately and publicly advocated the passage of the Employment Service Bill. His opposition began only after he became a member of Mr. Hoover's cabinet."[211] This Brotherhood was not an affiliate of the AFL. AFL President Green had been disappointed at Doak's appointment in 1930, writing to Hoover to express his opposition.[212]

Hoover's veto reflected both institutional and ideological motives. Institutionally, Hoover and Wagner took alternative approaches to the proper role of the national government. Wagner's efforts to enlist national officials in the struggle against unemployment through the establishment of a nationally coordinated, funded, and regulated employment placement system clashed with Hoover's preferences for state over federal government and his instinctive aversion to active government.[213] It would require the election of Roosevelt to expand the federal government's role. This difference about the role of government masked a difference in definition of interests. Hoover's reluctance to mobilize federal government and his championing of states' rights reflected his free-market principles.[214] His appointment of Doak was also a deliberately divisive choice. In pursuing a new federal employment system Wagner received the support of progressive economists, state administrators, and interest groups such as the AFL. Wagner's interests were those of the unemployed. His preferred solution required a novel active government policy.

American business leaders were less interested in labor exchanges than British ones principally because they were established during the mass unemployment of the 1930s. Large employers and industrialists—principally those represented through the U.S. National Association of Manufacturers (NAM)—were far from enthusiastic about any expansion of the federal government's role. James Emery worked as NAM's counsel and appeared before congressional committees during the 1920s to oppose federal intervention in the labor market, including the creation of a national labor exchange system.[215] Representing the interests of small businesses, the U.S. Chamber of Commerce was less resistant to a national labor exchange system and supported the bills introduced to establish a national service. Business attention was most concentrated upon other aspects of Roosevelt's New Deal, particularly public works schemes to which they did object.[216] As Piven and Cloward observe, such work programs "appeared to threaten the private enterprise system itself . . . and Civil Works Administration minimum-wage scales raised the specter of government interference in the conduct of private enterprise."[217] The American Liberty League was founded in 1933 by large employers to oppose New Deal legislation but enjoyed marginal success, failing to prevent the passage of the key National Labor Relations Act which formalized collective bargaining rights.[218] Until 1936 the Supreme Court, therefore, was the most important defender, if indirectly, of business interests. Roosevelt's policies did encounter greater resistance from business in the second half of the 1930s. The persistence of unemployment encouraged popular perceptions of unemployed persons as unworthy. Leuchtenburg reports an observation to this effect from Hopkins: "Americans, Harry Hopkins wrote in 1937, had become 'bored with the poor, the unemployed and the insecure.'"[219]

The birth of the American employment exchange system during the Great Depression in response to the exceptional levels of unemployment obviously carried with it the danger that the system would be associated with relief and not jobs. This danger was increased by the service's early role in administering positions for the New Deal public works programs. However, unlike Britain, exchanges were not directly linked to the distribution of compensation or benefits, though the public works schemes may have approximated this role in some supplicants' eyes. Such perceptions were magnified by the decision, taken in 1938, to integrate placement work with unemployment compensation distribution.

USES and Unemployment Compensation

This chapter has already demonstrated the importance of implementing a work-test through labor exchanges as a condition of establishing unemployment insurance in Britain. The two measures were launched almost concomitantly and unquestionably were conceived of concurrently. In the United States integration of placement and compensation work occurred subsequent to, and independently of, the national employment service's establishment. It was a controversial decision. Section 903 (a) of the Social Security Act of 1935 stipulated that "all compensation is to be paid through public employment offices in the State or such other agencies as the Board may approve."[220] In March 1937, an agreement was reached between the Secretary of Labor and the Social Security Board resolving that a "state employment service shall be regarded as a single unified service comprised of activities financed by Federal and State funds in accordance with the provisions of the Wagner-Peyser Act and of activities financed through funds granted by the Social Security Board in accordance with the Social Security Act."[221] It was the intention embodied in this Agreement that the employment and compensation services be "coordinate divisions" within a single state administrative agency, a plan which stimulated the fears of USES officers who strenuously opposed the merger. Within the USES, anxiety was generated by the agreement's final resolution. This stated that the agencies "shall act as if they were a single agency, jointly and concurrently, with respect to all matters affecting a state employment service."[222] Both anxiety and opposition were personified by ES's Director Frank Persons.[223] He conducted a campaign against the merger because of the likely damage to the ES's placement work. No doubt personal vanity also fueled his hostility.

On 21 February 1939 a short news item in the *Washington Post* reported the resignation of Frank Persons as director of USES. Behind this announcement lay three years of intense controversy and friction between the ES and the Social Security Board about the integration of placement and compensation work. These conflicts reveal a great deal about the USES, especially about the institutional bases of its lamentable placement record after 1938. Why were Persons and his colleagues so reluctant to consent to integration and what was the position of Secretary of Labor Perkins? Did resistance to integration reflect bureaucratic turf-defending or a genuine concern about the best system? While some turf-defending occurred, the primary motive, I will suggest, arose from the belief (later vindicated) that the USES's placement work would be irretrievably distorted. While the virtues of administrative convenience arising from a merger were pronounced at the time, the ES quickly shifted into a policing role, as predicted, with a limited placement record. This should have not surprised Arthur Altmeyer, chairman of the Social Security Board,[224] since in 1934 he observed that having to determine whether an applicant was actively seeking work placed the Service "in the position of perverting its main purpose."[225]

The separation of placement and compensation became increasingly problematic after 1936 as the implementation of the Social Security Act began. In October 1938 Arthur Altmeyer observed to a conference on state unemployment compensation agencies, "I know that one of the big problems that has confronted you is the proper integration of placement functions and insurance functions." He continued: "I am now of the opinion that complete coordination and integration at the Federal level which is so vital to successful operation at the State and local levels, will not be achieved until the two Federal agencies are united."[226] The Social Security Board sought cooperation first, between the board and the Department of Labor at the national level; and, second, at the state level cooperation between the state unemployment compensation agency and the State Employment Service—a single agency was deemed necessary with authority over these two functions.

In a speech in May 1937, Altmeyer made clear his determination to integrate: "The basic problem confronting all of us whether we are Federal officials or state officials is the integration of the placement function and the benefit function without the loss of integrity of either." He maintained that the "objectives of one function are in no way inimical to the interests of the other." Consequently, "the state employment service must be regarded as a single unified service, comprised of activities financed by Federal and state funds in accordance with the provisions of the Wagner-Peyser Act, and of activities financed through funds granted by the Social Security Board in accordance with the provisions of the Social Security Act."[227]

The basis of Persons's hostility to merger was explained in a series of memoranda to Secretary Perkins beginning in 1936.[228] In April 1937, he submitted a twenty-page memorandum. In support of his position he cited the reservations of the USES's Federal Advisory Council articulated at their meeting in January of that year. According to Persons, merging the ES with the Social Security Board would reduce the Service to a "minor sub-division" of the Unemployment Compensation Bureau. He argued that the language of both the Wagner-Peyser and Social Security Acts did not necessitate a merger: "The Social Security Act seems only to offer the opportunity (and a most desirable opportunity) for cooperation between the State Employment Service and the State administration of Unemployment Compensation":

> Certainly it must be held that the duties and responsibilities of the United States Employment Service as expressed in the Wagner-Peyser Act are not changed by the Social Security Act. It follows that the United States Department of Labor and the United States Employment Service must endeavor to retain the authority and the means (conferred by the Wagner-Peyser Act) to discharge those duties and responsibilities.[229]

Persons argued that these "duties and responsibilities" were distinct from those of the unemployment compensation bureau. To discharge them required ensuring the independence and integrity of the USES. Persons stressed the responsibility of the USES as a regulator of the state employment services "to make certain that each is conducted in accordance with the uniform rules, regulations, and standards of efficiency prescribed in accordance with the provisions of the Act."[230] Each state ES established a distinctive relationship with the USES. This arrangement created administrative responsibilities: "A State Employment Service has assumed obligations of an administrative character and a relationship of cooperation with the United States Employment Service with respect thereto, which are broader than and different from obligations which it may assume in cooperation with the administration of unemployment compensation."[231] Persons maintained that these obligations and responsibilities were not modified in any way by the Social Security Act. He argued that, in most states, the state ES had been rendered a subordinate part of the unemployment compensation administration.[232] In most states, the Commissioner of Labor appointed one individual with responsibility for administering the placement and compensation functions, though that administrator was aided by two staff charged to maintain the integrity of each function.[233]

In another lengthy memorandum to Perkins in January 1939, a month before his forced departure, Persons responded to complaints about poor relations between the two agencies. He identified the Social Security Board's efforts to ensure that state ES's "are merged" with the unemployment compensation administration as the cause: the "USES holds that the State ES's must retain their identity and administrative responsibility in order to be able to practice and protect the uniform standards and procedures which are required under the terms of the Wagner-Peyser Act."[234] By this date merger was ineluctable. Some USES staff had abandoned their initial opposition to integration,[235] and a special Senate committee recommended integrating the two functions in a single agency: "There should be one office where the worker can register in order to qualify for his unemployment compensation and where, at the same time, he can talk with officials charged with the duty of assisting in securing employment for him."[236] Employment offices were receiving funds from the Federal USES, state governments, and the Social Security Board, the latter by far the largest contributor, an arrangement strongly criticized by the report. The report's authors correctly identified the Social Security Board's fiscal preponderance as a factor advantaging the board at the USES's expense.

Secretary Perkins was ambivalent about the merger. In a letter purporting to summarize her view, Altmeyer wrote: "My understanding from my conversation with you is that you believe that there should be a single bureau but you are not prepared to state at this time what the organization of that single bureau should be."[237] Speaking to the Federal Advisory Council of the USES in 1937 Perkins denied that the payment of compensation would "swamp the placement function of the public employment office." She added: "The bringing of these two agencies into one office will have the effect of stimulating the whole idea that the great problem is to find work for them, not to give them compensation and forget about it, but to find them work, letting them use the compensation as a tide-over."[238] Referring to Altmeyer's proposals, Perkins argued that "all we have agreed upon is that on the Federal level we will cooperate; we must cooperate; we have no choice."[239] It is revealing that Perkins felt it necessary to counter the criticisms about the swamping of placement work. She gave an unwavering commitment to the USES:

> I shall never allow it to be submerged. Neither will Dr. Altmeyer. The fact is that 44 States have passed laws and appropriations, providing that the placement work and the unemployment compensation work will be under one unified direction. What we have to do on the Federal level is to find a way of dealing with that situation. The Government of the U.S. has to perform a gigantic task in administering the Social Security Act. At the same

time it must maintain an ES. These functions must be related otherwise effort and knowledge in the field is duplicated and expense increased to an unjustifiable degree.[240]

Speaking privately, Perkins's attitude was ambiguous. Her concerns became apparent during the Brownlow reorganization of the Executive Office of the President,[241] which recommended that the ES be made part of the Federal Security Agency. Harold Smith, from 1939 director of the Bureau of the Budget, records his conversations with Perkins around this time. Writing in his diary on 27 April, Smith reports a phone call from Perkins in which she "lectured me for an hour on the historical and philosophical conception of the Labor Department."[242] The lecture had been prompted by Perkins's concern about the USES:

> Madame Perkins made it clear that she was greatly disturbed about the transfer of the Employment Offices to the new Federal Security agency. She told me that she had not been consulted in any way—that this was contrary to the report of the President's Committee on Administrative Management—and would lead to the ruination of the Employment Offices which would be submerged, gobbled up and what not by Unemployment Compensation.[243]

Smith was privy to information that the Brownlow Committee had "deliberately reversed itself after careful consideration," but could not divulge this change to Perkins. Perkins's concerns reappear in Smith's diary in another conversation on 6 May: "In this lengthy conversation I could only politely listen. On the whole it was rather embarrassing. She did not know, of course, that the President had asked me not to discuss the moving of the ES with her."[244] Plainly there was a political battle in which both Perkins's and the ES's future were entangled: "[Perkins] also said that the removal of the ES she considered a slap at her and that she wondered how many more slaps she would be justified in taking."[245]

Roosevelt became involved in the controversy early in 1939. On 16 January, Marshall E. Dimock, the second Assistant Secretary of Labor prepared a long memorandum for Perkins about the coordination of the USES and unemployment compensation bureau. The memorandum was the basis for a meeting between Roosevelt, Dimock, and Altmeyer. Dimock considered the situation "acute" for four reasons. First, the differences between the Murray bill (transferring the ES to the Social Security Board) and the Ramspeck bill (proposing to appropriate extra funds to the ES in order that it would continue to operate separately). Second, the "emotional-psychological situation" was harming the work of the ES and undermining collaboration between the two agencies (a view supported by evidence above). Third, "because of the existing confusion, the interests outside of the Department of

Labor are encouraged to foster state legislation whose result [but not object] is to weaken state departments of labor by diffusing their organization and responsibility."[246] Fourth, the political implications of the confusion were undesirable: "Unless clear-cut steps are taken to protect the autonomy of the Employment Service and its secure position in the Department of Labor, then various pressure groups, among them the veterans and the trade unions, may be expected to raise a public protest which may have embarrassing political repercussions."[247] Dimock characterized the USES's role in addressing unemployment as "perhaps unequalled in importance among the total responsibilities of the U.S. Department of Labor."[248] He also believed that merger would reduce the ES to a subordinate position: "I deduce this conclusion from the general proposition that each part of a total program tends to take on the intrinsic nature of the social organism as a whole."[249] He proposed substituting the phrase "act as if they were a single agency" in the March 1937 agreement between Altmeyer and Perkins with "coordination"; the problem was no longer "merely a quibble over words":

> If I understand correctly, the Social Security Board is advocating a plan in which there would be a complete unity of line organization with advisors on unemployment compensation and employment offices acting merely in a staff or an advisory capacity to the top executive . . . Complete unification inevitably means that the job-getting function will not be aggressively pushed.[250]

He advocated lobbying Congress and mobilizing organized labor to resist the merger. AFL President William Green was a supporter of the USES. Green wrote to Roosevelt: "The employment service is designed to serve labor and to help working men and women find suitable employment. We cannot conceive of any service set up by the Federal Government designed to serve labor in a special way better than the United States Employment Service. Surely such a serviceable organization ought to be included in the administrative authority of the Department of Labor."[251] Senator James Mead sent a memorandum on 21 June 1940 to the president outlining his opposition to the transfer and citing the interests of organized labor. Mead highlighted the disappointing placement record of the ES since the merger and urged its return to the Labor Department: "While it is true that the actual placement work in the States is done through State offices and State personnel, nevertheless the integration at the Federal level even to the extent of abandoning the title 'U.S. Employment Service' has apparently resulted in subordinating employment functions to insurance payment functions."[252]

Linking the work of the unemployment compensation bureau of the Social Security Board with the Employment Offices of the Department of Labor proved protracted and acrimonious. Competing definitions of the ES's functions clashed. The original agreement, in March 1937, for an integrated system between Perkins and Altmeyer did not materialize until the second half of 1939. By then the merger had been supported by the Senate Committee's report on Unemployment and Relief and the influential Brownlow Committee and at the local level integration was de facto. Harold Smith records a conversation with the Social Security Board's Director, Oscar Powell, on 19 July 1939 about the merger's progress: "Powell seemed to feel, and this is confirmed by what I have heard, that the bringing together of the Employment Office with Unemployment Compensation is now moving along rather smoothly in view of the tension and emotionalism that has been inherent in the reorganization since the passage of the orders."[253]

The merger controversy was also affected by the politicization of the ES. Most of the institutions established by the Roosevelt administration as part of the New Deal program were political. The officials appointed as administrators of state- and county-level works programs were frequently accused of political bias and there were persistent rumors and charges about pressure placed upon participants in public works programs to vote Democrat. The USES was not immune to these problems. Wagner's attempt to make ES employees federal civil servants (an aim which failed) was precisely that they would then be responsive to federal regulations and not local fiats.[254] Furthermore, the record of the pre-1933 employment service was tainted by charges of political bias and patronage in appointment decisions. In her study Ruth Kellogg concludes of the post-Doak reorganized service that "it seems certain that politics and the spoils system have had much to do not only with the determination of cities in which offices were to be located but also in the matter of selection and appointment of the staff."[255] The decentralized structure of the USES exacerbated these processes. During the hearings for his bill S.2687 in March 1932, Wagner challenged the ES director about the suitability and experience of state appointees. As Kellogg concludes, the reorganized USES was "handicapped from the start just as is any organization that attempts to operate under the control of the spoils system . . . It means almost inevitably that persons are appointed to the positions primarily for other reasons than fitness for the specific duties of the office."[256] This practice left a dismal legacy for the Employment System after 1945 when its wartime status as a federal agency was ended and it was returned to state control.

Officials appointed to state employment service offices were sometimes accused of being political appointees lacking the relevant skill, though Persons reported that most of these appointees did in fact have experience of working with organized labor. However, the employees of the employment service offices were not part of the Federal civil service. This non-civil service status undoubtedly influenced perceptions of the ES offices and their officials. The post-1945 ES was criticized frequently for its lack of professionalism, poor placement service and segregated structure. The system was reorganized in the 1960s (though this did not end the criticisms).

The integration of the placement and compensation functions was unacceptable to Frank Persons. He resigned in February 1939. His vigorous opposition to integration of placement and compensation made his removal a necessity for Roosevelt and Perkins.[257] Members of the Roosevelt administration worked to find Persons an alternative position. In a confidential letter to the President dated January 20, Robert Fechner, Director of the Civilian Conservation Corps expressed some resistance to employing Persons: "At the request of Secretary Marvin McIntyre I have thoroughly discussed the possibility of finding a suitable position with the Civilian Conservation Corps for Mr. W. Frank Persons, with the Madam Secretary of Labor and the Second Assistant Secretary of Labor. I explained . . . the difficulties that I saw in setting up a new position at a high salary in my small organization."[258] In fact, Fechner did find a position for Persons. This was fortunate for the USES director, since Roosevelt was prepared to sack him and signed a letter to that effect on 15 February 1939. In a phone conversation with the White House, Fechner reports that "I have just learned this morning from Mr. Persons that he had not known anything about the situation, and I suddenly learned that he must submit his resignation today or the President will dismiss him."[259] Persons's difficulties within the USES were thus considerable and his resignation unavoidable.

The USES defined its objective as fundamentally the placement of the unemployed through the establishment of state offices and the regulation of those offices. This put the USES at the center of the Roosevelt attack upon unemployment. Legislation subsequent to the 1933 executive order and Wagner-Peyser Act pulled the Service in alternative directions. The public works and employment programs gave the USES (and the National Reemployment Service) a pivotal role in the massive federal employment boosting effort. The later Social Security Act's implementation of unemployment insurance gave the ES a second role as dispenser of benefits. Both roles were tied to the relief of the problem of unemployment but the USES defined itself principally as a labor market institution and not as a bureau for distributing unemployment compensation and evaluating the merit of claimants for that compensation. This tension in the USES's roles has persisted since the 1930s, recurring, tellingly, at different stages in United States work-welfare policy. The USES had difficulty in reconciling these competing claims, even after its integration with the compensation function.

Conclusion

Reformers in Britain, influenced by the ideas of "new liberalism" played a crucial role in founding labor exchanges. Working tirelessly as an advocate of greater governmental responsibility for unemployment and labor market organization, William Beveridge pressed his labor exchanges proposal with the Liberal administration. Beveridge's experience in London provided the stimulus to his favoring exchanges. At the Board of Trade, Beveridge's proposals found a receptive listener in President Winston Churchill. Both Beveridge and Churchill were moved by the plight of the unemployed but sought solutions compatible with market processes.

The principal representative of organized labor, the Parliamentary Committee of the TUC, on balance supported labor exchanges, but with reservations. First, it feared that the exchanges would be used to weaken workers in their relationship with employers. Some of these concerns were assuaged during negotiations with the Board of Trade. Second, trades unionists resented any potential privileging of nonunion members through the organization of exchanges. They did not want those workers who either failed to join a union or lacked market power skills to enjoy the same benefits as usually skilled unionists. In 1909, the TUC's membership extended to only 2 million in a workforce of 11 million. This second factor has important implications for the political support of work-welfare programs. It suggests that, in the presence of decentralized craft unions, the fear of assisting nonunion members is a more powerful force than advancing the collective interests of all workers. This fear was reified in reformers' rhetoric and in administrative arrangements distinguishing between worthy and unworthy beneficiaries.

The use of such language helped liberal reformers overcome employers' resistance to founding labor exchanges. Churchill's insistence that the idle should work, that exchanges would not assume the character of workers' clubs and assurances to employers that they could forge their own contracts of employment diluted the possible threats posed by exchanges to their power. For Churchill, both workers and employers constituted important supporters or opponents of his reform. His negotiations with them illuminate the politics of government intervention in the labor market. To unionists he stressed the improvement in employment likely to result, while employers were persuaded of the more efficient monitoring of workers anticipated. These dual concerns were institutionalized in the organization and operation of labor exchanges. They disclose the political priorities exchanges expressed.

In the United States, liberal reformers also drove the 1933 legislation establishing labor exchanges. The reformers' task was greater. They had to convince opponents that federal government intervention itself was appropriate. In this task they were assisted incalculably by the election of Franklin Roosevelt. Roosevelt's victory heralded a new approach to the problem of unemployment. Resistance to Roosevelt's plans remained in Congress, especially amongst Southerners and conservative Republicans. The principle of labor exchanges, formulated by Senator Wagner, was placed within a general anti-unemployment program. His efforts were well assisted by Roosevelt's

Secretary of Labor Frances Perkins, also committed to increased federal action in behalf of workers. The language of reform adopted by these activists was not dissimilar to that derived from "new liberalism" in Britain: enhancement of, and compatibility with, market processes through the improved organization of information about vacancies. Initially, this motive was not linked with a concern to monitor the unemployed. Monitoring became a priority only after the introduction of a federal unemployment insurance program in 1935. It speedily resulted in the integration of placement and benefit work (or organization and monitoring). This resulted in a public employment institution whose values mirrored those of its British counterpart. The arguments advanced for this integration were largely those of efficiency but included claims about the necessity of preventing any abuse by benefit claimants. The language of worthy and unworthy recipients was quickly articulated.

Organized labor, despite representing a small proportion of the U.S. workforce (11.3 percent of nonagricultural workers in 1933[260]) was less worried about advantaging nonunion members through exchanges.[261] The AFL was a consistent supporter of a national labor exchange system, its support growing in parallel to mass unemployment after 1929.

Opposition to the new exchange program in the United States emanated principally from fiscally conservative Republicans supported by employers. Both succeeded in preventing reform before 1933, but the Roosevelt election and Democratic Congress undercut these impediments. Opposition also came from Southern Democrats, opposed to any empowering of black Americans. At the state level, of course, these opponents could be more effective in delaying passage of legislation and ensuring half-hearted implementation; but even here the momentum of Roosevelt's New Deal was powerful. The integration of placement work with benefit distribution sat comfortably with these opponents. The principal advocate of merger, Altmeyer, marshalled efficiency arguments to support the linkage.

Opponents of the ES derived some solace from federalism. The weak national American state and strong centrifugal federalist forces resulted in the creation of a federal-state system under the Wagner-Peyser Act. This arrangement advantaged the local over the national, permitting wide variation and, subsequently, deterioration in many state services. Furthermore, the weak national role precluded active federal intervention to ensure that placement work was not disregarded to the extent predicted by opponents of integration. The USES was to prove most successful during the Second World War when it was "federalized," the federal-state partnership was terminated, and the work of state ES's was directed by the War Manpower Commission. Despite the support of President Truman, lobbying to maintain the federal control of the USES after 1945 was unsuccessful.

American work-welfare programs originated during the 1930s under the impetus of Roosevelt's New Deal. The Wagner-Peyser Act of 1933 belongs to this era. The priorities of complementing rather than subverting market processes and of excluding undeserving beneficiaries find their expression both in the work-test role assigned the Employment Service from 1938 and in the flagship Social Security Act of 1935 which created the dichotomy between contributory and noncontributory programs. It is to these legislative sources and their resultant institutional arrangements that the scholar must look for understanding of the values dominant in American work-welfare, rather than simply to assertions about the U.S. political culture or to worthy but uninfluential alternative schemes.

In sum, efficiency claims drove the establishment of labor exchanges as mechanisms for organizing the British and American labor markets and laid the foundations for subsequent work-welfare programs. Attempts by representatives of organized labor to harness labor exchanges to improve their members' power in the labor market failed. Once unemployment compensation was enacted the organization of the labor market competed with the rival aim of regulating the distribution of benefits. The pernicious consequences of this pattern for placement work are the subject of the next chapter.

The most significant effect of this early organization arose from the political determination to exclude the undeserving from the receipt of public benefits. This aim overrode the commitment to improving labor market placement and information. The costs of this priority were recognized by the architects of integration in each country, Beveridge and Altmeyer.[262] Writing in 1930 about the 1909 Act, Beveridge observed that "in the shadow of the companion scheme of insurance their [namely, employment exchanges] growth has been stunted and the thoughts and energy needed for their development as placing agencies has been devoted to the lesser service of paying benefit; atrophy rather than hypertrophy has been their danger."[263] He claimed also that even if the commitment to unemployment insurance had not been concomitant with exchanges, these would have been established anyway since the Royal Commission listed them as their first priority for reform. It is improbable that Churchill would have concurred, given his opposition to creating a "permanent club for the unemployed." One year after the passage of the Wagner-Peyser Act, Arthur Altmeyer realized that the USES's work would be affected significantly if Congress enacted an unemployment insurance scheme since the ES would be made responsible for administering a "work test" to those seeking compensation.[264] He acknowledged the difficulty of imposing such a role upon the USES: "If the Employment Service . . . undertakes to refer a suspected malingerer to a job in order to determine whether that person is voluntarily unemployed, it places itself in the position of perverting its main purpose and of destroying confidence on the part of employers in using the service."[265] After his appointment as chairman of the Social Security Board, Altmeyer appears to have forgotten these reservations.

His worries were even more justified by the pressure placed on the USES immediately after it assumed responsibility for unemployment compensation on 1 January 1938 by the 1937–38 recession. More than 1.5 million applicants for work registered in USES offices during January 1938. Over 2.5 million original claims and 2.5 million continued claims for unemployment compensation were filed in public employment offices.[266]

CHAPTER THREE

"Financial Succour for the Unemployed"? The Institutionalization of British and American Exchanges

Speaking in 1936 Arthur Altmeyer, chairman of the Social Security Board, explained why integrating responsibility for placement with the distribution of unemployment benefits was inexpedient:

> If you have the same personnel in a local office helping in insurance
> . . . that help in . . . placement, the paper work and the necessity of the
> personnel interviews with persons relative to their benefit rights may
> swamp them to the extent that they have no time and energy to think
> about efficient placement work. With the best of intentions to maintain
> the two separate functions, if there is not adequate staff to take care of
> the placement function, that function will become subordinated. . . .
> [Work tests] . . . [are] of the nature of a *police function*, whereas the
> Employment Service ought to be a *service function*.[1]

This chapter examines how British and American labor exchange institutions developed after their establishment in 1909 and 1933 respectively. I analyze the emasculation of each country's system, measured by their unimpressive placement record. I argue that these undistinguished records stemmed from decisions about exchanges' institutional design. In Britain the relief image and work-test legacy of the 1930s was not eroded by wartime success. In the United States, the combination of a poor image with weak and inactive federal regulation fundamentally harmed the system's capacity to play an effective placement role in the postwar American economy, despite its inclusion in the War Manpower Commission between 1942 and 1945. Both systems consistently failed in their central responsibility: to place job seekers in employment. Federal oversight and national regulation of the systems were ineffectual, an outcome concealed by propitious economic conditions. During the first two postwar decades, economic prosperity, a tight labor market, and lack of interest in training programs marginalized the USES's placement role despite a consensus about achieving full employment. During the 1950s and 1960s several highly critical reports failed to goad the employment service into a successful discharge of its role. Critical reports were also produced about the British service.

Despite the postwar commitment to full employment, in Britain neither employers nor trades unionists nor the state were perturbed by the labor exchanges' concentration upon regulating unemployment compensation and serving the least-skilled members of the labor force. In the United States, the decision to return the Employment Service to the states after 1945 effectively removed it from national economic policy. This decision was engineered by a coalition of conservative Democrats and Republicans in Congress, the states, the Interstate Conference of Employment Security Agencies (ICESA, representing local employment offices) and employers. The interests of those served by exchanges were far weaker and were mostly based in sections of organized labor, the National Association for the Advancement of Colored People (NAACP), and other pressure groups who opposed decentralization.

The chapter ends with the decisions in both countries to separate placement and benefit work, decisions which were responses to each service's poor placement record and which reflected the ambition to include exchanges' within national labor market policies. This aspiration was to collapse too.

The Placement Record

The placement record of the British exchanges for the postwar decades is unimpressive. Placement numbers declined from the 1940s. After placing 4,045,000 adults in 1949, the service placed 2,644,000 in 1955 and 1,291,000 in 1962.[2] The expansion of the workforce during these years meant that the stable placement figures constituted a decline proportionately. The service's penetration rate—that is, proportion of all job placements in a given year obtained through the labor exchanges—was no more than 20 percent and probably closer to 15 percent in the postwar decades.[3] Table 3.1 provides a summary of postwar placement figures by the labor exchanges.

The British employment service was principally the preserve of unemployed persons. In 1970 90 percent of its registrants were unemployed. This characteristic shaped its public profile as being chiefly a "placing service for the unemployed."[4] Employers were selective in notifying the employment service offices of vacancies, in part because of previously unsatisfactory experience with the choice of applicants provided. As a result, the employment service was "always short of vacancies—in 1969 there were nearly 4.5 million adult registrations, but only some 2 million adult vacancies were notified."[5] Workers seeking nonmanual employment used the exchanges sparingly, if at all. Since manual workers formed a declining proportion of the workforce, this trend was ominous for the service's future.

Table 3.1 **Adult Placing by British Employment Exchanges ('000s)**

Year	Numbers Placed
1947	2,609
1948	4,234
1949	4,045
1950	2,531
1955	2,644
1960	1,621
1965	1,561
1970	1,442
1974	1,557

Source: Derived from B. Showler, *The Public Employment Service* (London: Longman, 1976), p. 43.

In 1955, the director of the Bureau of Employment Security (which combined the USES and unemployment insurance), Robert Goodwin, spoke glowingly about the nation's public employment system:

> From a simple labor-exchange in a relatively few cities and a number of States, we now have a nation-wide service with about 1700 local employment offices and about 2400 branch offices. In 1953, we made 6 million non-agricultural and 9 million agricultural placements. Over 750,000 were given employment counseling and over 920,000 were given aptitude tests. Local employment offices were participating in community employment planning in many areas.[6]

Goodwin confidently predicted that the USES would "become increasingly an instrument for developing and carrying out social and economic policy."[7] In the same year, Assistant Secretary of Labor Rocco C. Siciliano praised the employment security program's capacity to respond positively to reform proposals.[8]

Just two years later, in 1958, a major study of the USES's record during the first postwar decade unequivocally indicted its placement performance, standards, and implementation of policy. Later reports were equally caustic. The report, prepared by Robert Thomas of the Office of Research and Development, began ominously: the ES "seems to be in serious trouble."[9] The report's central motif was the long-term decline in the USES's placement record. Contrary to Goodwin's boastful claims, the ES made *fewer* placements in 1957 than it had eleven years earlier in 1947. In 1947, 4,564,643 nonagricultural placements were made com-

pared with 4,506,431 in 1957; in the same period, nonagricultural employment grew by 20 percent from 43,300,000 to 52,500,000.[10] In 1947, 17
percent of the ES's work concerned "short-time" placements (jobs of less
than three days duration); in 1957 the comparable figure was 30 percent,
an increase of 86 percent:

> These 'short-time' placements largely consist of the repeated dispatch
> of a very few individuals, over and over, to jobs of limited economic
> value . . . They are of limited value both to the workers involved and
> to the unemployment insurance program which must depend on the
> employment service for an effective work test.[11]

In the same period, nonagricultural placements, excluding short-time jobs,
declined by 8.6 percent, and within this category service and unskilled
labor placements accounted for 65 percent in both 1947 and 1957.[12]
Thomas argued that the stability in the USES's placement record was not
simply a function of high employment: "In an expanding economy it
amounts to a condition of continuous retrogression"; and

> unless the significance of this situation is understood and unless sub-
> stantial and effective action is taken fairly soon this trend will inevitably
> continue. In fact it may very well continue to the point where the pub-
> lic employment service will affect so small a segment of the labor mar-
> ket that it will not be worth the administrative effort and the money
> required to maintain it.[13]

In an accompanying memorandum, Charles Stewart spelled out the report's
serious implications for the USES. Of greatest concern, the dwarfing of
placement by compensation persisted: "In view of its low penetration of
the labor market, one could conclude that it survives at all only to provide a job-availability test for the unemployment insurance system, and
does this none too well in view of the small proportion of jobs to which
it exposes workers." The ES had "lost sight of the central fact that the
placement function is the essential function of an employment service,"
symbolized by "eleven years of stalemate if not progressive decline in
the placement function."[14] In 1955, Assistant Secretary of Labor Siciliano
was contrite about the employment service's placement failure. He said
the ES aimed to "insure that placement program, methods, and facilities
are suitable for meeting worker and employer needs in all occupational
categories, including professional, technical, clerical, and highly skilled
occupations, and to achieve needed balance in serving all occupational
groups."[15] As Siciliano acknowledged, the ES had a skewed placement
pattern: 40.5 percent of ES placements were of unskilled workers who
constituted only 7.6 percent of the workforce. Skilled and professional

workers constituted only 7.0 percent of ES placements, yet they composed 31.7 percent of the workforce. And although professional and skilled workers were most in demand, "in terms of placement service, it is often thought that the Employment Service system had little to offer."[16] Siciliano believed a reversal of this pattern would increase the satisfaction of ES staff and win employers' confidence. The ES's failure to offer a service to skilled and professional workers was an outcome consistent with the Service's early bias, a bias created from the ES's role in administering benefits.

As a consequence of these trends, the ES had failed to displace alternative channels of job search. Thomas painted an appalling picture from an employment office in a large Eastern city:

> All of the records were of the "self application" variety, prepared by hand by the applicants themselves, most of whom had no skill in accurately describing the component elements of their past jobs. Many of the cards were illegible. In theory after the applicant finished his card as best he can he sees a skilled employment service interviewer whose task it is to add . . . to the record . . . Sixty-five percent of the cards in the active files of the office did not contain evidence that a single occupationally significant item of information had been added by the employment service staff. At least half the cards were inadequate for selection purposes.[17]

These failures of the basic interviewing process intrinsically limited the service's capacity. The ES offices were failing to refer workers to potential employers:

> during the 11 years 1947–57, an average of less than 25 percent of *all* job applicants were selected for referral to employer openings from the application files in the offices. Instead the selection offered to the great majority of employers was restricted to the applicants who happened by chance to appear in person in the office on the day or two while the order was still open.[18]

Both employers and applicants were underserviced. Despite assurances that all relevant job notices would be forwarded, Thomas concluded that, after registration, "by and large [the applicant] will never hear from the office again unless he happens to drop by in person."[19] Repeated registration of applicants visiting their local employment office needlessly diverted staff time from placement work. As a consequence, "it is estimated that between 1947–57 the ES offices, on the average, failed to fill between 35 percent to 45 percent of the *permanent* type job orders given to them by their local employer-customers."[20] This last statistic provides a partial explanation for employers' lack of interest in ES offices. In visiting employers in the local labor market, ES staff misjudged the use of their time. Rather than visiting the major employers (those 15 percent controlling 75 percent of the jobs), the "public employment offices, between 1947 and 1957 diverted over half of their employer visits or 'sales' time to small employers."[21] Thomas criticized the internal management of local employment offices, a serious problem given the complexity of unemployment insurance and variety of employment service programs.

The USES's unfavorable image and low placement record outlived Thomas's indictment. A report by the General Accounting Office to Congress in May 1963 criticized on economic grounds many practices within the Bureau of Employment Security. These practices included failure adequately to evaluate the necessity of relocating local offices, the use of funds appropriate for personnel purposes to buy equipment and the bureau's failure to monitor stringently state agencies' control over equipment purchased with federal grant funds.[22] A congressional committee report, issued in 1964, singled out for criticism the number of short-term, unattractive positions filled through the Service and the high percentage of domestic servants it placed. It concluded that the "service has not yet managed to make a real breakthrough toward the goal of participating in a fairly representative cross section of the Nation's hiring transactions."[23] A Task Force established by the Secretary of Labor in 1965 to study the ES reached similar conclusions. It reported that the linkage of placement and compensation functions "created a public image of the Employment Service that obscures other, more positive elements of its overall program. This 'image' has influenced the attitudes of potential clients on both the supply and demand sides of the labor market."[24]

The USES was defensive and brittle about its placement record. In 1962, Robert Goodwin told Secretary of Labor Arthur Goldberg that "the overall average penetration rate for fiscal 1960 was 15 percent. In manufacturing the rate was 21 percent."[25] At the end of the 1960s, President Nixon's Secretary of Labor James Hodgson expressed his dissatisfaction with the placement record of the USES. He noted the "low proportion of job vacancies listed with local ES offices . . . Some employers find the ES of little use to them . . . Unless we can make gains here, much of our effort to combat discrimination in hiring, to find jobs for the disadvantaged, and to attain our goal of providing comprehensive service to employers will be blunted."[26] Table 3.2 reports the statistical trends provoking Hodgson's comments. Between 1950 and 1970 the number of job openings available through ES offices fell at a steady rate from 1966. Thus, nonagricultural placements in 1970 were a million lower (at 4.6) than in 1950. The number of nonagricultural employer visits undertaken by ES officials dropped by 66 percent from over two million in 1950 to 751,000 in 1970. The Service's placement success was disproportionately concentrated among unskilled and clerical job seekers. The cost of placement work increased while the performance record declined. The ES's placement to skilled positions was risible: "Measuring ES funding against placements, the cost per non-agricultural placement has roughly tripled since 1965 from $33 to $100 . . . The ES is handling a large number of high turnover jobs that present little opportunity for advancement, and in some cases, little likelihood of permanence."[27]

Table 3.3 expresses these figures as ratios. They confirm the dismal assessment of the USES's record. Although new applications have grown proportionately—a likely consequence of the Service's administration of programs for the disadvantaged discussed above—percentages for placement are unimpressive. Unemployment and the size of the civilian labor force increased during the 1960s, but the number of job openings, referrals, employer contacts, and placements undertaken through the offices of the USES did not. Employers' failure to use the ES reflected both employers' low opinion of workers sent to them by employment offices and ES officials' failure to stimulate job vacancy listings in their offices. Both factors were problematic. In 1970, 11.5 percent of the workforce sought assistance at one of the USES's 2,000 local offices and only 5.3

Table 3.2 USES Placement, 1950–70 ('000s)

| Year | New Applications | Nonagricultural Job Openings | | | | Placements Nonagric. | Nonagric. Employer Visits |
		Active File	Available	Referrals	Total		
1950	7,752.4	2,238.1	7,283.9	9,767.6	13,409.3	5,624.7	2,186.3
1955	7,983.2	2,231.3	7,827.0	10,194.0	14,958.0	6,051.8	1,265.0
1960	10,117.3	3,764.0	7,297.3	10,224.0	15,272.6	5,818.2	1,117.2
1961	10,502.3	3,676.6	7,465.4	10,783.4	14,708.2	5,902.1	1,645.6
1962	10,792.4	3,443.9	8,541.9	12,478.9	15,191.0	6,724.8	1,563.9
1963	10,980.3	3,342.3	8,419.4	12,414.8	13,817.5	6,581.1	1,444.4
1964	10,754.3	3,054.4	8,358.6	12,618.8	12,732.7	6,281.4	1,188.6
1965	10,900.1	2,648.1	8,358.6	13,348.1	11,174.3	6,473.4	1,094.9
1966	10,532.2	2,433.8	9,423.0	13,750.3	10,659.8	6,493.1	877.1
1967	10,866.0	2,543.3	8,417.3	12,902.0	10,174.4	5,817.3	879.0
1968	10,366.7	2,428.0	8,374.2	12,954.1	10,338.4	5,733.2	864.3
1969	9,853.5	2,615.1	7,760.5	11,985.6	9,889.9	5,153.0	750.4
1970	9,957.1	NA	7,131.8	NA	9,143.5	4,603.1	751.5
[1984	14,793.1	NA	7,529.9	7,025.5	5,081.6	4,675.7	NA]

Source: "Employment Service Placement Activities," in *Research and Education,* Bulletin No. 82 (Washington, DC: Employment Security, 15 December 1970), p. 3.

Table 3.3 USES Placement Ratios, 1950–70

Year	New Applications as a Multiple of:		Total Placements as a % of:		Nonagricultural Placements as a % of:	
	Total Un-employed	Nonagricul-tural Jobs Available	Average Labor Force	New Applications	Openings Available	Total Referrals
1950	2.4	1.1	21.6%	72.6%	77.2%	57.6%
1955	2.8	1.0	23.0	75.8	77.3	59.4
1960	2.6	1.3	21.9	57.5	68.8	56.9
1961	2.2	1.4	20.9	56.2	79.1	54.7
1962	2.8	1.3	21.5	62.3	78.7	53.9
1963	2.7	1.3	19.2	59.9	78.2	53.0
1964	2.8	1.3	17.4	58.4	75.5	49.0
1965	3.2	1.2	15.0	59.4	72.8	48.5
1966	3.7	1.1	14.1	61.6	68.1	47.2
1967	3.6	1.3	13.2	53.5	69.1	45.1
1968	3.7	1.2	13.1	55.3	68.5	44.3
1969	3.5	1.3	12.3	52.3	66.4	43.0
1970	3.3	1.4	11.2	46.2	64.5	N/A
[1984	1.8	2.0	4.4	31.6	62.1	66.4]

Source: "Employment Service Placement Activities," in *Research and Education*, Bulletin No. 82 (Washington, DC: Employment Security, 15 December 1970), p. 4.

percent of the workforce obtained their position as a result of ES placement. Employers evidently did not turn immediately to the local employment service office when filling a vacancy. By 1986, a United States General Accounting Office report was urging greater referral by ES offices of job seekers to *private employment agencies!*[28]

Placement Attained: The Second World War

A respite from the American and British labor exchanges' bleak placement records occurred during wartime. Each system was integrated into national planning to mobilize workers into key industries and made responsible for classifying occupations according to importance. Placement was more successful and there were several reasons for this improvement.

First, in the United States the system was federalized. This limited the discretion of local offices, many of whose officers were biased toward compensation work. During the Second World War, the USES became the War Manpower Commission's "principal operating arm."[29] The War Manpower Commission (WMC) was subsequently described as "little more than a superstructure of policy-making officials directing the activities and handling the inter-agency relationships for the USES."[30] The dominance of the USES within the WMC is suggested by personnel numbers. Of a total WMC staff of 25,021 in 1945, 22,161 were employment service staff.[31] There were 1,500 USES offices throughout the country. Despite the prominence of the ES network within the WMC, its local offices remained tainted by association with the relief activities they administered during the 1930s: "This low esteem (shared by many old-line government agencies) and the implications of the job ahead served to reinforce the somewhat inferior(ity) complex which affected many parts of the organization."[32] The same authors suggest that the ES's success during the war as an arm of the WMC erased the Service's low profile. The USES's placement work grew substantially. In 1937, the ES made 3,640,934 placements and in 1939 4,500,399. By 1943 this figure had almost tripled to 12,253,224 placements.[33]

Second, in both countries the integration of placement agencies into national planning systems gave them a prestige and bureaucratic prominence wanting during peacetime. In 1939, the British employment service took responsibility for ensuring that the labor needs of essential industries were satisfied. The employment service became the "principal agent of the Government in the compulsory direction of manpower, 32 million registrations being carried out for national service and 22 million vacancies being filled in industry during this period."[34] The employment service created a central register before the outbreak of war to facilitate the direction of specialized workers to priorities identified by the government, industry, and armed services. After 1945, the employment services processed the demobilization of 15 million men and women and coordinated their return to civilian occupations.

Wartime broadened the responsibilities of the USES and some of its officers judged this a positive development. Speaking to the Federal Advisory Council in 1942, Altmeyer anticipated the "conversion of the USES from a labor exchange, pretty largely, to more and more a labor rationing instrument."[35] In addition to all the special wartime work of the USES, it continued to act as a labor market placing institution, a fact also acknowledged at the Federal Advisory Council meeting. WMC Director Paul McNutt stated: "while I stress the manpower responsibilities of the Employment Service, I am keenly appreciative of the fact that the USES must operate as the referral agency for State unemployment compensation administrations."[36] It spent much less time on distributing unemployment compensation because employment was high in these years. The WMC's historian gives qualified praise to the USES, attaching two caveats. First, shifting the USES to the control of the WMC encouraged many staff to leave or, in the case of those who remained, to give more loyalty to state capitols than to Washington; this problem persisted throughout the USES's history. Second, the staffing difficulties limited the extent to which a nationwide integrated employment service developed in practice: "Integration of the 48 State systems into a relatively effective national Employment Service required constant attention and direction from the Washington headquarters and never actually achieved the coherence and flexibility that a national system implies." Despite these problems the same writer concludes that the USES came "through the testing period of the war with considerably enhanced prestige."[37] Given its low status, the ES's image could hardly have declined.

Third, in both the United States and Britain that factor most damaging to the employment exchange systems during peace—unemployment—was minimal, giving them the opportunity to develop their other skills. Consequently, the exchange officials were not driven by the need to respond to unemployment benefit requests and to organize their administrative work around this task. Since unemployment was also low in the postwar decades, this factor is insufficient to account for the decline of the public employment systems.

Fourth, the national labor exchange systems were accorded positive roles in postwar national economic proposals. These were Keynesian in character and, while focused upon macroeconomic measures, paid at least lipservice to exchanges' roles in information gathering and placement. For instance, Donald Kingsley, an adviser to the USES's director, identified four features of the postwar employment market likely to affect the employment service's work:[38] first, the new public responsibility to assist the realization of full employment; second, a recognition by private employers that good personnel were crucial to production, an appreciation which would encourage them to improve and enlarge their recruitment and selection processes; third, increased trade union activity in the hiring and placing of their members, including a greater use of closed shops; and fourth, an enlarged public role in the utilization and employment of persons with handicaps and minority groups.[39] These aims were laudable, but their achievement was problematic.

In Britain, the 1944 White Paper on Employment Policy consigned these labor market tasks to the labor exchange system. Observing that in a dynamic economy "numbers of people will . . . be registered as unemployed at Employment Exchanges on any particular date," exchanges were made responsible for collecting data on the "manpower position."[40] More positive roles for the employment service were outlined in 1948 in the Employment and Training Act, which superseded the Labour Exchanges Act of 1909.[41] In the 1948 act, the exchanges' placement work was conceived of as central to achieving full employment:

> By the substitution of rational and scientific methods of labour engagement for the haphazard and unregulated methods which previously existed the employment service has made a contribution of the first importance towards the more efficient organisation of industry and commerce . . .

It is today an integral part of the economic and industrial life of the country, playing—by means of its machinery of local offices covering the whole county and the sources of information at its command—an indispensable role both in planning and implementing the policy of full employment.[42]

In the mid-1960s, the employment service received more frequent reference in statements of general economic and employment policy. In 1966, the Ministry of Labour referred to the trend in industrialized countries to develop "active employment market policy which goes far beyond the relief services in which most Ministries of Labour had their origin many years ago."[43] The Ministry envisaged an employment service transformed "from being an institution which is largely about unemployment benefits to being an economic agency which is predominantly about employment."[44] Though frequently invoked, this aspiration was unrealized in Britain. The report referred to the employment service's new occupational guidance scheme and new system of area management (coordinating the work of several employment exchanges under a single area manager). Together with other measures, these were collectively designed to result in a new understanding of a public employment exchange: instead of focusing principally upon unemployment benefit, assisting job seekers in finding work was the intended priority. Computerization was an important part of this modernizing process.

Programmatically, the USES's postwar tasks appeared considerable and included responsibility for reconversion. The context for this was the haunting memory of prewar unemployment: "There was a great fear on the part of many people that we were going to have high unemployment. Their rationale was simply that we had had 10 or 12 million in service and that industry just could not absorb the veterans fast enough to avoid widespread unemployment."[45] This worry prompted the Employment Act of 1946, under which, according to one observer, the USES would be the "keystone."[46] Writing to Goodwin, Donald Kingsley envisaged a greatly expanded postwar role for the ES deriving from a national commitment to achieving full employment:

> The post-war employment situation will present a challenge and an opportunity to the Employment Service beyond anything we have previously experienced. Despite the absence thus far of any integrated governmental programs for insuring high level employment, it seems increasingly clear that the principle of public responsibility for something approaching full employment has been accepted. *A broadly conceived public employment service should be a major instrumentality in any program designed to insure [sic] high level employment.*[47]

Within the War Manpower Commission it was believed a new sort of

ES was required for its postwar role. A document prepared in August 1945 accepted that the postwar ES would undertake work of a different character to that of the 1930s: "Its job in the reconversion and postwar periods will call for something quite different from a simple return to a pre-war basis of operations. Its location in the past has been influenced by temporary conditions which are not similar to those which will exist in the years ahead."[48] The report's author believed the ES's wartime activities—in measuring worker skills, placing workers in manufacturing industry, cooperating with industry and labor through its national, regional, and local management-labor advisory committees—would enable the ES to "serve as a major instrument of national policy in dealing with labor market conditions and the relationship of workers to their jobs."[49] Such a role would best be achieved by retaining the national character of the USES (a preference unrealized).

The USES's own major policy statement about its future, issued in August 1945,[50] assumed that full employment was the overarching objective of postwar policy. The ES expected a disruptive transition to peace:

> Millions of men will be released from the armed forces. Some will have had their career and intended life pursuits interrupted by military service. All will have matured while in the armed forces and many will have new skills and vocational interests. Handicapped workers who found employment during the war will encounter obstacles in their search for employment. Older workers will have difficulty finding and holding jobs. Millions of women workers recruited for war work will meet with keen competition for jobs in a labor market dominated by males. Youths who during the war left school either to work or enter the armed forces may find themselves at a serious disadvantage because of the lack of adequate education or vocational training.[51]

Anticipating substantial postwar unemployment, the report's authors advocated positive programs by industry and government to stimulate economic activity and jobs. They stressed the ES's role in this process, through the prediction of labor market trends, counseling, and placement. The report's authors judged a return to the mass unemployment of the 1930s politically unacceptable: "Wartime developments have brought new horizons . . . [requiring] . . . a National economy in which haunting job uncertainty and the miseries of mass unemployment are eliminated."[52] Reminiscent of the prewar period, the document's authors asserted that to realize these aims a "method for bringing jobs and workers together promptly and in an orderly manner is a basic requirement in any program to achieve maximum employment."[53] This task fell obviously within the placement remit of the Employment Service.

The report identified the USES's counseling role as crucial to these

aims: counseling for individual job seekers at USES offices and counseling provided in schools.[54] The discussion of the ES's placement service repeated many of the themes of the 1930s. The document concluded
in a style reminiscent of prewar USES memoranda:

> Thus, the activities, experience, and information of the Employment
> Service, when coordinated with the programs of other government agen-
> cies, become important not only in attaining full employment and employ-
> ment stability, but also in bringing about a higher level of national income
> and production. In this way the national system of local employment
> exchanges serves as an instrumentality of government to achieve nation-
> al objectives and to carry out public policy.[55]

A similar view informed the section about the USES in drafts of the annual economic report prepared by the Council of Economic Advisers.[56] One
WMC author believed, rejecting or perhaps wishfully disregarding memories of the 1930s, that an entirely new sort of agency would be developed after the war:

> I am now convinced that there is very little future for an employment
> service of the type we have had in the past, and that we are not going
> to be able to build the sort of Nation-wide support the agency demands
> unless we embark upon a broad and imaginative program in the devel-
> opment of which we enlist the assistance of management and labor groups
> throughout the country.[57]

Regretfully, the political and administrative support for such a program
did not exist. The decision to return the ES to state control effectively
excluded it from federal policy until the 1960s when the integration of
the employment service into national economic policy became a prominent theme and when training policy, combined with attempts under the
Great Society program to improve the economic positions of black
Americans, stimulated a commitment to manpower policy. Predating the
Great Society, the Manpower Development and Training Act of 1962
nonetheless anticipated it. The USES was expected to have a central role
in these initiatives. Thus a report to the Secretary of Labor prepared by
the U.S. Employment Service Task Force believed that if the USES could
"become a more effective center for manpower services in the community, it can contribute much more significantly toward the full and efficient implementation of the public programs dealing with manpower
development and utilization . . . [which was] . . . especially important for
members of minority groups."[58]

Explaining the Poor Placement Records

This section examines the factors contributing to the institutionalization of British and American exchanges as organizations principally concerned with benefits, not placement.

Work Tests

The most enduring aspect of the founding of the British exchange system and the early experience of the American one was the decision to integrate placement work with the administration of unemployment benefits. How damaging a linkage this proved for placement work is suggested by the statistics cited above.

During the 1920s and 1930s, the British exchanges' responsibility for administering a work-test indelibly and detrimentally shaped their public image among both those who did and did not use the exchanges. The relationship between placement and benefits, however, acquired none of the bureaucratic drama as it did in the United States. Rather, it resulted principally from the institutional design of the exchanges enacted in the 1909 act, when the two activities were conceived of as linked by their principal architect, the president of the Board of Trade. In the first scholarly study of the British exchanges, the authors dismiss as unproblematic the relationship between these two functions, despite conceding that placement work was dwarfed by benefit payments: "It is not necessary to discuss . . . which is the more important of the functions with which the Exchange system is concerned. In point of volume circumstances have decreed that the insurance work should bulk the more largely."[59] The same authors nevertheless later observe that it is by their placement work that the exchanges should be evaluated.

Unemployment insurance was introduced in the National Insurance Act (Part II) of 1911, and it fell to the exchanges to administer the new system. The scheme operated from 1912 and was administered by the Employment and Insurance Department in the Ministry of Labour (at its inception[60]), which also controlled the labor exchanges. In 1929 the two functions were divided administratively with the creation of the Employment and Training Department and the Unemployment Insurance Department. Each section was under a Principal Assistant Secretary. During the 1920s there was at least one additional act each year amending or modifying the unemployment insurance scheme, such was the complexity of this program and the magnitude of the economic problems it addressed. Most amendments widened the scheme's eligibility and increased the seemingly voracious appetite for benefit work which remained at the core of exchange work.

The 1911 act covered two million workers, a number which had grown to three and a half million by 1916. By December 1913, the exchanges had processed 1,041,755 claims and had authorized the payment of 1.5 million benefits to 650,000 persons, a low figure reflecting a tight labor market. Legislation enacted in 1920 extended the national insurance scheme to the entire industrial population within the terms of the compulsory program. This extension had major implications for the labor exchanges. They were the "only agency by which the Act as a whole [could] be put into operation."[61] Legislation in 1921 established a distinction between two types of benefit: those to persons on the basis of a sufficient number of contributions paid while in employment; and those to individuals who had insufficient time in full employment to meet the contribution criterion of thirty payments (and who gave evidence of genuinely seeking work).[62]

From 1921 the exchanges were required to establish whether claimants were "genuinely seeking work but unable to obtain suitable employment."[63] This clause accompanied the extension of unemployment benefits in 1921 to recipients who had not yet contributed sufficiently to the unemployment insurance fund to qualify for payments. The clause had a devastating effect for exchanges since it undermined their placement rationale and politicized their role: "between March 1921 and March 1932 nearly three million claims for benefit were refused because the claimant had failed to meet this condition."[64] Between 1919 and 1925 alone the Ministry undertook nine inquiries into alleged malingering, each of which discovered that this group constituted less than 2 percent of all claimants.[65] Exchanges were established to assist unemployed persons in finding work; but in administering unemployment benefits they could only dispense funds to those persons who had in effect hawked their labor between alternative potential jobs. The exchanges were thus emasculated in two ways: they were punitive in granting benefits and they failed to provide jobs.

The 1930 Unemployment Insurance Act further expanded the numbers eligible for assistance. Under this legislation, "the liability for the benefit paid to those who cannot satisfy the first statutory condition, that thirty contributions have been paid in respect of them in the preceding two years, was transferred from the Unemployment Fund to the Exchequer."[66] Benefits were now provided as both covenanted benefit (as a contractual right) and uncovenanted benefit (as a discretion to those who had exhausted benefits).

The 1920 Committee of Inquiry into Exchanges[67] concluded that the pressure upon labor exchanges to administer unemployment insurance had precluded the development of an effective placement program. This pattern did not diminish during the 1920s or 1930s when the steady and serious deterioration in economic activity and employment resulted in mass unemployment and greater demand upon the exchanges. Writing in 1928, Seymour singled out the burden of administering unemployment insurance to explain low placement.[68] As Showler observes, "There is no doubt that the severity of the depression in the 1920s and 1930s forced a further emphasis upon insurance work by the exchanges, and had a severe effect upon their original employment and placing functions."[69]

Reporting in 1932, the Royal Commission on Unemployment Insurance found that between 40 and 60 percent of the exchanges' administrative work was undertaken by staff hired temporarily to address the inflated claims for benefits resulting from mass unemployment.[70] Contemporary publications by the trades union movement make only fleeting reference to the role of labor exchanges in addressing unemployment or as components of anti-unemployment strategies.[71] The Trades Union Congress (TUC) promoted the notion of "work or maintenance" and fiercely rejected benefit schemes which distinguished recipients on a contributory and noncontributory basis. In their response to the 1932 Royal Commission, the TUC endorsed the commissioners' proposal to create specialized exchanges and to make notifications of vacancies by employers mandatory.[72] The latter proposal was ardently resisted by employers and successive governments were disinclined to make this arrangement.

The eligibility test was abrogated, after much protest, in March 1930, though it was succeeded by another means-testing program also administered by the exchanges. The memory of the exchanges' role in administering these tests was powerful and lingered long after the 1930s. Alan Deacon observes that the test constituted a "sledgehammer used to crack a relatively small . . . nut."[73] The Ministry of Labor officers, charged with ascertaining how much effort a claimant expended on the work search in order to exclude alleged malingerers, undertook this work intrusively and sometimes malevolently. Consequently, the exchanges became, in Ross McKibbin's view, the "theatre of their [the unemployed] politics . . . [and] were regarded by the unemployed as enemy territory."[74]

McKibbin identifies two pernicious legacies of the exchanges from this period. Both stemmed from their role in determining applicants' work search exertion. First, he emphasizes the ineluctably investigative and furtive attitude of the clerks staffing the exchanges and charged with identifying abuses: "However well-intentioned the supervisors and means test officers, however fair the courts of referees, they were all servants of 'them,' all trying to do down the unemployed."[75] Second, the exchanges' failure in their purported aim—to place unemployed persons in jobs— irked their clients: "Throughout the 1930s only about one-fifth of adult vacancies were filled through them. There seems little doubt that the unemployed lacked faith in the exchanges as places to find work; a skepticism shared by those many employers who made no attempt to use them." As a consequence of these failings and impositions, for unemployed persons the exchanges were "simply instruments for state handouts . . . The attitude of the unemployed to the exchanges was, therefore, almost wholly negative."[76]

The wider public perception of labor exchanges was also unfavorable. Those using them to find work or to receive benefits were frustrated in the first quest and brutalized in the second. As Rodney Lowe concludes, in the interwar period, the Ministry became "obsessed with the eradication of abuse to the detriment of more constructive objectives, such as counselling claimants and canvassing for jobs."[77] Labor exchange officials were compelled into limpetlike practices. The political necessity during the 1930s of not appearing to give state handouts to the lazy forced upon the exchange officials an ever more differentiated system of grades and entitlements which they had to administer. In McKibbin's assessment, it was the "exchanges themselves, the size of the dole, and the manner of its payment [which] became . . . the appropriate focus of politics" in the 1930s.[78] Employers frequented the exchanges erratically, much less often than had been envisaged by those promoting their establishment in 1909. Indeed, the crisis presented by the 1930s was exactly the circumstance under which exchanges were intended to flourish. The combined hostility of unemployed and employers toward labor exchanges could only weaken their public reputation. They were infelicitous antecedents for an expanded role in postwar labor market policy. Lowe argues that it was these benefit responsibilities which ensured the survival of the Ministry of Labor as a Ministry in the 1920s when the Treasury sought its abolition.[79] Treasury hostility to the Ministry seriously limited its capacity to formulate its own policies for unemployment beyond those of a narrow character and required Labour officials regularly to conduct studies of claimant abuse of benefits.

After the Second World War, the employment exchanges continued to administer monies under both the national assistance and the national insurance schemes. Both types of benefits assumed an "availability to work" on the part of claimants. Consequently, the "employment and benefit sections of the Ministry of Labour's local offices worked closely together."[80] The office assessed the claimant's status in a way not dissimilar to the interwar period:

> If the placing officer considers that a claimant has imposed such conditions on his registration for employment as to make him not "available for employment," or if the claimant refuses to accept employment which is considered suitable, he refers the case to the statutory authorities set up under the National Insurance Act for them to decide whether the applicant's claim for benefit is valid. Similarly, the placing officer

informs the National Assistance Board if any applicants for national assistance seem unreasonably to be failing to take advantage of employment opportunities.[81]

The authors of the International Labour Organization's (ILO) report took an upbeat view of these tasks. They noted that the employment office's principal aim was to place registrants in work as quickly as possible, an objective which explained the simultaneous registration for work and benefit. The employment offices were also responsible for assessing benefit claims under the National Insurance Act of 1946, which authorized payment to claimants who had exhausted their right to it.[82] The decision to give such payments was made by a local tribunal established under the 1946 act. The tribunal reported directly to the employment exchange officers, who were required to submit a detailed report about the claimant:

> In order that the tribunal may be fully informed about the circumstances of the applicant and the industrial conditions in the district an individual report is furnished by the Ministry of Labour local office showing the employment history of each applicant for 'extended benefit' and each local office furnishes regularly to the local tribunal a report on the employment situation in the area.[83]

The ILO Report depicted a busy and active employment service in Britain.

An otherwise buoyant account of the British employment exchanges to the Organization for Economic Cooperation and Development (OECD) in 1965 conceded that the system was still defined by its benefit work: "Because of the agency function of the employment exchanges in relation to the administration of unemployment benefit and national assistance, a substantial proportion of the workers using the system tend to be those who can less easily obtain employment." The report assessed the implications of this association:

> In the public mind, this situation helps to protect an image of the local employment exchange as a centre more closely associated with the financial succour of the unemployed than with the placement of those who are seeking opportunities for useful and productive work. However superficial this picture may be today it is unfortunately based on the widespread use of the employment exchanges for this purpose in the inter-war years and lives in the personal experience of many of those now in middle age. Moreover, in spite of the substantial expenditure of public funds on the construction of new premises and the strenuous efforts which have been made to improve those which date from before the second world war, there is no doubt that a number of employment exchanges still provide a depressing atmosphere.[84]

Revealing a striking complacency, the same report judged a separation of placement and benefit work impossible, since it is "difficult to see how these two complementary duties could be efficiently and economically conducted in offices which were separated physically."[85] Such a separation was recommended by the end of the decade, only five years later.

By the late 1940s, memories of the integration conflict had subsided in the United States, though echoes of the dissension were manifest periodically. Indeed, USES Director Robert Goodwin favored the institutional linkage of placement and compensation. In his view, "one of the Employment Service's functions [is] to administer the work test for unemployment insurance. People are offered work and if they refuse then they are not eligible for unemployment insurance. It is desirable to have those two things operating together."[86] Goodwin was remarkably impervious to the effects of this role on the USES's participation in postwar employment aims. Thus, the Director of War Mobilization and Reconversion feared that the placement record established by the ES during the war and its other new activities—skill testing and measurement, counseling, special programs—would be harmed by the historic linkage with unemployment compensation. He argued that in a "postwar economy which seeks to achieve full employment this function [that is, the work-test] is less important than the functions of serving as a labor exchange, offering vocational direction, and assisting in national and community employment planning."[87] He warned against the submersion of placement work, stating that the Employment Service

> can contribute greatly to the achievement and maintenance of a high level of employment. In our postwar program, this function is so important that it would be unwise to subordinate the Employment Service to an unemployment insurance program designed to serve workers who do not have jobs. . . . [C]onsolidation of the two programs would almost inevitably tend towards too much emphasis on the role of the Employment Service as a source of unemployment benefits.[88]

The director argued that a constructive program could be developed to integrate the two functions without damaging the ES's new "positive" role in employment policy principally through its placement work. Such aspirations were unattained.

The same report also recognized how attending to benefit work fostered particular skills on the part of ES staff at the expense of those appropriate to placement. These alternative skills were implied by Altmeyer's distinction between service and police functions:

> Different personnel skills are required to operate a manpower services center as contrasted to the administration of the unemployment compensation laws. The latter essentially involve personnel well versed in the specific state Unemployment Compensation Law . . . [T]he provision of manpower services requires personnel who are expert in labor market organization and trends and who have considerable skill in aiding job seekers to develop their full occupational capabilities . . . To the extent that the Unemployment Compensation functions demand the attention of the Employment Service personnel they will tend to inhibit the development of satisfactory manpower services.[89]

The fiscal and administrative dominance of compensation work in employment offices created a value system biased against placement activities and an incentive structure which rewarded compensation, not placement activity. The situation had not improved twenty years later.

Similar fears about the linkage of placement and compensation were expressed by the Labor Committee (composed principally of trades unionists) of the National Planning Association.[90] The committee noted that "experience has shown that domination by unemployment compensation agencies seriously impairs the Employment Service program." It argued that the two services could cooperate without the "subjugation of the USES to the state agencies." Again this ambition was unrealized. The association maintained that the unemployment compensation agencies would require the employment offices to administer an unduly harsh work-test regime by imposing a strict referral system: unemployment compensation agencies "could require local employment offices to report a worker who refuses to take a job that is unsuitable when compared with his experience and income requirements. Then they could deny his benefits. This amounts to using the Employment Service to force down the worker's standard of living by driving labor into cheap jobs."[91] Advocates of the latter were dominant among the pressures (especially from the states) to transfer the ES from federal to state control after 1945. These undesirable practices could be avoided, the National Planning Association believed, by maintaining federal control of the service and enforcing national placement standards.[92] The association stressed the importance of the employment offices to applicants other than those seeking benefits, including minority workers whose exposure to discrimination was anticipated to rise after the war ended. However, the Interstate Conference of Employment Security Agencies was active and, ultimately, successful in lobbying for the ES's defederalization.

The USES's own postwar statement acknowledged its work-test responsibility. Predating Goodwin's appointment as director, the report's authors were sensitive to the crisis provoked by integration. They rejected the view that the ES was overshadowed. Because the State Unemployment

Compensation laws required that beneficiaries register for work at a public employment office, "close cooperation between the Employment Service and the Unemployment Compensation Agencies is essential and need not involve the subordination of either program to the other." And, they continued,

> The employment office staff must not only apply the work test to benefit claimants, it must also be familiar with the standards relating to suitable work and the procedures involved in taking claims. *Aggressive placement activity* by the Employment Office is very important in shortening the duration of unemployment for individual workers and thereby reducing the social and monetary costs of joblessness.[93]

During the full employment which ensued from 1946, this agreeable relationship between placement and compensation was not severely tested. The report's authors were correct to formulate the relationship as a comfortable one, since the wartime activity of the USES had broadened its functions and widened considerably the number of workers affected by its offices: "Millions of workers who had never before utilized the service were . . . brought into local employment offices which were encouraged thereby to expand their services to industrial and commercial employers."[94] This wartime experience was contrasted with the negative legacy of the New Deal period: the USES's "early history qualified its acceptance and use by employers and skilled labor . . . It continued to be regarded as part of a relief system, concerned overwhelmingly with registering and placing unskilled casual or domestic service workers."[95] The USES ended the wartime period with a somewhat improved public reputation. It won "recognition by management and labor to a degree hereto considered visionary because of its responsiveness to local conditions and its willingness to cooperate with their representatives in administering voluntary manpower programs with a minimum of bureaucratic authority."[96]

Weak National Control

In both countries national regulation of the labor exchange systems was weak. This was especially the case in the United States.

By 1970, most British employment exchanges had deteriorated into physically run-down and poorly administered offices unattractive to job seekers. Their usage was dominated by claimants for benefits. Exchanges were located in buildings constructed in the interwar years (or sometimes even earlier) when dispensing benefits was the principal activity. In the 1940s and 1950s, the exchanges also had responsibility for distributing assistance to applicants to the National Assistance Board.[97] These applicants were able-bodied and available for work, "for whom registration for employment at a local office is consequently a condition for the receipt of a national assistance grant."[98] Employed persons wishing to change jobs rarely availed of them. Employers used them as sources of short-term unskilled labor.

High employment in the postwar years made British governments uninterested in the exchanges. Nevertheless, this did not dissipate a concern with malingerers and abusers of the system, as the chairman of the National Assistance Board told the Conservative Party in 1954:

> There was some abuse but on the whole this problem was not very serious, though the psychological effect was bad. He intended to strengthen slightly the area officers so that they would be in a position to investigate cases which local officers had reported as appearing doubtful. If one or two cases of fraud were exposed and given due publicity, many others contemplating similar tactics would be deterred from so doing.[99]

Consequently, they weakly monitored employment exchanges' performance. This neglect allowed the bias among exchange officers toward benefit rather than placement work to persist. No pressure groups, such as unions, monitored the exchanges' work to press for modifications.[100]

A 1970 review by the Department of Employment and Productivity (DEP) of the employment service identified basic failings. These included weak national regulation and inadequate placement.[101] By 1970 the service was placing 1.5 million adult workers a year. The report's authors argued that if the "employment service did not exist, the level of unemployment would be substantially larger at a cost greatly exceeding the cost of the service," a problematic conclusion given the service's own failings.[102] The service's record and activities still had the potential to improve. Only one-fifth of all adult placements occurred through the service—a figure consistent with the 1930s. As in the 1920s, 1930, 1940s and 1950s, these placements were "predominantly in manual work."[103] A 1967 survey of employer recruitment patterns revealed that although the majority of skilled (78 percent), clerical and commercial (89 percent), and managerial, executive and technical (96 percent) employees were recruited outside of the employment service, employers would have preferred an effective public service. The service had a greater role in dealing with redundancies and unemployment. Employers were required under the Redundancy Payments Act of 1965 to give two to three weeks notice of large redundancies to employment exchanges, and in some cases the employment service responded by establishing on-site employment offices. Its principal role in redundancies was to assess redundancy pay entitlements.

In contrast to the United States, there were no parliamentary committees nominally responsible for monitoring the exchanges' work. While employment was high, the trade union movement did not investigate their workings. Those using employment exchanges were judged marginal to the mainstream of organized labor's interests, a shortsighted and debilitating attitude. The Conservatives, elected to government in 1951 (though with a small majority and a lower vote than Labour received), were eager to maintain the commitment to full employment,[104] but economic conditions did not deteriorate sufficiently to require them to initiate new policies for this end. They were under no pressure to address the needs of unemployed persons in categories B and C—the long-term unemployed, the unskilled, or welfare recipients—the exchanges' principal users.

In his 1958 report Thomas maintained that the division of responsibilities between the federal government and the states in the administration of the public employment service was inherently problematic: "One reason the Public Employment Service has failed so badly to keep pace with the expanding economy, is that the Federal Bureau has seriously misunderstood its basic mission"[105]; it failed to acquire appropriate information about the operation of the ES in local offices. Consequently, it was "unable to make its influence felt effectively in the administration of the State agencies."[106] The federal government was given the role in the employment service, despite the fact that each state agency is a part of state government accountable to the governor, of ensuring that a similar placement and compensation system operated everywhere. To give the federal office such authority, "Congress endowed it with the power of the pursestrings."[107]

Applying four criteria of federal responsibility—"minimum standards of efficiency," dissemination of standards, annual review for appropriations, and assessment of technical needs—Thomas judged the federal bureau's performance of all four tasks "seriously inadequate." This defect arose especially from the failure to perform the fourth criterion, the "regular and competent appraisal of State agency operations, program quality and achievement."[108] Between 1947 and 1955 the federal overseers undertook no regular assessment of any aspect of the employment service. It therefore lacked the basis for allocating techniques. Its decisions about annual appropriations were a "slipshod business, since such determination cannot be made in the absence of objective and accurate information as to the adequacy of State operations in terms of program status and quality."[109] The laxity of federal officials was extraordinary: "even the elemental step of ascertaining the validity of the reported activities of the several State agencies was not taken"; as a result, the grants process was "seriously corrupted."[110] Overall, the original intent of Congress expressed in the Wagner-Peyser Act of 1933—to ensure the presence of a federal bureau overseeing and coordinating the activities of state employment agencies—had failed:

> There is . . . a kind of authority . . . derived from superior knowledge, techniques and "know-how." The Congress clearly did contemplate that the Federal partner would establish and use this kind of authority in order to carry out its mission. It endowed the Federal partner with money power in order to reinforce this special kind of authority contemplated for it. This leadership and authority has not developed, and a basic reason for this fundamental failure has been the inability or unwillingness of the Bureau to inform itself adequately with respect to the State operations.[111]

The consistent failure of the federal bureau to learn about the system of local employment offices is Thomas's most reiterated and severe criticism. In 1957, a modest evaluation program was introduced by Robert Goodwin. Each regional office in the ES was required to submit an evaluation of each of its states' work every two years. Even this scheme was subject to detailed criticism by Thomas. He concluded that the "Bureau has been guilty of serious misrepresentation:

> for example, 85 percent of the biennial evaluation reports submitted by the Regional Offices contain no useable evaluation of placement achievement. Ninety-three percent of the reports provides no useable information with respect to the quality of the basic work products involved in the placement program. None of the reports touch upon the quality of the matching process (a key item in placement service).[112]

Thomas also criticized the failure to assess the validity of claims about placement rates or to train regional office staff in evaluation techniques.

The USES did not allocate its staff to achieve "optimum effectiveness."[113] By assigning half of its staff to the regional offices, the federal bureau left its headquarters "too stripped to be effective. The half assigned to the Regional offices has in turn been spread too thin among 11 widely separated locations to be effective in terms of the Bureau's basic functions."[114] Thomas explained this "illogical disposition of its limited staff resources" by the bureau's failure to pursue its placement objective and to the system of administration established during World War II.[115] Under this system, "regional centers were given wide grants of delegated authority for making the host of day-to-day administrative decisions necessary to the administration of the huge 1800 local office system if it was to function with any degree of effectiveness."[116]

Thomas interpreted Congress's intent in 1933 to be that—in its relations with local employment service offices—the federal bureau should be activist, not laissez-faire. Washington had, however, adopted a laissez-faire approach.[117] The two most important congressional defenders of this style were Representatives Wilbur Mills, the powerful chairman of the House Ways and Means Committee, and John Fogarty, chairman of the Labor-HEW Appropriations Subcommittee. Thomas did not hesitate to identify this weak federal role as largely responsible for the decline of the employment service. Part of the decline in employment office staff "resulted from Bureau reluctance to impose even the simplest expenditure controls to protect against diversion of employment service staff to meet UI peak loads."[118] To confound this problem, in 1948 the Service began decentralizing the unemployment insurance (UI) program to local offices. The bureau took no "effective action to protect the Employment Service from its effects."[119]

Another example of poor federal supervision was the approval of new offices. Approval for each such office was supposed to be preceded by a survey of demand for it. Yet Thomas found that of 118 new offices opened between February 1956 and March 1958, "the required justification (or prior survey in the case of metropolitan areas) was submitted to the Bureau in only 10 cases! Nevertheless the Bureau has underwritten all costs despite its announced standards and justification requirements."[120] Improper reporting of work by state offices was similarly ignored by the federal bureau. The bureau failed, in Thomas's judgment, to "create a climate of accountability in its relationships with the 53 State agencies . . . [which] . . . left the Federal-State system without standards and without the comparable current information on the relative performance of the several State agencies that is essential in establishing a sense of accountability."[121] It was the incompetence and indifference of the federal bureau which especially accounted for the incoherence and confusion about the employment service's purpose.

Thomas also noted other ways in which weak national control led to the ES's unimpressive placement record. First, there was a decline in the number of staff in local employment offices (despite a growth in the USES's annual budgetary allocation). Second, the distribution of the Employment Service's offices was illogical. This involved, principally, an overservicing of rural areas and serious underservicing of the largest metropolitan centers "where the need for an organizing middleman in the labor market is so apparent."[122] Historically, the ES had played a role in shifting workers from rural areas to urban industries, and this legacy bequeathed it an excess of rurally located offices. Third, oversight by the federal gov-

ernment was inadequate: "the Federal partner which has no direct responsibility for administration provides by grant 100 percent of the administrative budget of the Employment Service agencies of the State
governments."[123] Consequently, responsibility and accountability were
diffuse.

Fifth, Thomas revealingly argued that the ES was unclear about its
central purpose, a "confusion of mission as to what was wanted of the
Public Employment Offices . . . [T]he dissipation of energy, inability to
plan and execute effectively and the turmoil of an organization at cross
purposes, which is engendered by serious confusion of purpose, would
create substantial barriers to achievement in any enterprise."[124] In explanation, Thomas pinpointed the relief-giving origins of the ES prior to its
wartime absorption by the War Manpower Commission. This development undercut the emerging "relatively clear-cut concept of where it wanted to go and what it wanted to do. In its simplest form, it hoped to become
a significant factor in the placement activities of private industry in the
community labor markets where public employment offices were located."[125] The ghost of Frank Persons stalked the Service!

To restore the lost sense of purpose, the Bureau of Employment Security
had adopted a six-point program: a placement service; an employment
counseling service; special services to veterans; personnel management
services; labor market analysis and information services; and community services and participation. Other activities were added later, including:
a selective placement for the handicapped person; an older worker program; a youth program and a school program; and a minority groups program. Unfortunately, "this hectic uncontrolled push for more and more
new programs far exceeded the absorptive capacity of most of the State
and local offices, with the result that for the most part these 'special services' didn't 'take' too well and are either low in quality or extremely
limited in quantity"; it has, Thomas cryptically observed, "apparently
seemed easier and more attractive to adopt new programs than to make
existing ones effective."[126] This strategy had, however, been endorsed by
the 1954 Department of Labor policy review.[127]

In the absence of a strong placement service "which is accepted and
used substantially by a significant and representative segment of the
employing community," Thomas argued, special programs could not flourish.[128] Special programs were inadequately staffed. In the local employment offices, staff were responsible for both placement work and
unemployment insurance: "since 70% of these offices have staff numbering between 1 and 15 for both activities (with between 5 and 6 employment service staff including clerks) the personnel resources available for
special programs are severely restricted," but these schemes have "expanded in great abundance."[129] Again, resources were badly allocated:

In the relatively few larger cities the counter-parts of all or part of these full-time specialists can also be found in the local offices where they have specialized performance duties. The local office "specialist" jobs were assigned generally higher classifications and pay than the placement interviewers. As a result many of the more able placement people moved out into these new better paying jobs. Since no extra staff was given, over-all, this simply meant that the placement staff lost strength in the large urban areas.[130]

In those offices lacking specialist staff, administration of these programs was a burden added to the ordinary workload of employment office staff. That the ES was placing fewer workers in 1957 than 1947, in a period when nonagricultural employment grew by 21.2 percent, did not surprise Thomas given these resource allocations and program priorities: "the wonder is that the deterioration wasn't even worse."[131]

Thomas's scathing report exposes an inept federal bureau failing to oversee, regulate, and coordinate a national employment service, the roles accorded it by Congress in 1933, or to define clearly its aim. It demonstrates also the ability of powerful members of Congress to protect the ES from public scrutiny. Thomas recommended the urgent reorganization of the federal bureau's resources to ensure effective control of the national employment system. He urged the

Bureau to move as expeditiously as possible to centralize and consolidate its limited staff resources . . . The Regional Director would maintain liaison for the Bureau with the State agencies, coordinate the timing of entry of Bureau staff into State agencies, and carry out his present mobilization and civil defense duties.[132]

Without such a change the bureau would, Thomas predicted, remain "relatively powerless" to discharge its responsibilities.[133] The federal bureau's work needed to change from a concentration upon data collection and bookkeeping to a focus upon its two key programs—employment service and unemployment insurance (though this latter seems not to have suffered). The major reform within the employment service had to be a renewed emphasis upon its placement program: "The present and augmented resources should be deployed so as to put prime organizational emphasis on the central program of Placement (including employer promotion)."[134] The combination of congressional support for the USES and the intense lobbying of the ICESA ensured that the likelihood of such modifications was slim.

The Politics of Institutionalization

Britain: Employers, Unions, and Exchanges

Why did not economic prosperity prove an opportunity for improving British labor exchange performance instead of reinforcing prevailing patterns? First, neither unionists nor employers nor government officials was attentive to the economy's training needs or interested in broadening economic policy to include micromeasures (see chapter 4). None of these groups was particularly exercised by the needs of the comparatively small, though persistent, minority failing to participate in the labor market.

Second, no institution existed to raise these sorts of policy issues. It was only after 1973 and the founding of the Manpower Services Commission (MSC) that an obvious institutional mechanism was established through which training and placement could be analyzed and proposals formulated. And indeed the MSC conducted comparative studies of labor market policy, particularly of Sweden, as models for British policy. The 1944 White Paper on Employment Policy,[135] Keynesian in tone, treats cursorily the role of employment exchanges, charging them only with collecting data about the "manpower position."[136] A 1952 ILO study of the employment service confirmed the role anticipated in the White Paper:

> The role of the employment service in the formulation of employment policy is to assess the probable effect of proposed economic policies on the employment situation and to ensure that the Government's economic plans, including the program of industrial production, are not beyond and equally are not too small for the manpower resources of the nation. To this end the employment service prepares forecasts of manpower resources for several years ahead.[137]

Lacking a positive and well-defined role in macroeconomic policy, the employment service was unable to exchange its prewar image for a self-assured and confident one. Job seekers were unlikely to view the employment service's statistical collection role as an improvement upon its placement responsibility despite the ILO's characterization of such activity as "a major role in the Government's policy for maintaining a high and stable level of employment."[138]

Its minor role was criticized by Beveridge in 1960.[139] He advocated compulsory notification of vacancies by employers, a proposal partially realized in the Notification of Vacancies Order of 1952. But this measure reflected the pressures of a tight labor market, not a desire to raise the service's profile.

The ILO report included a bland statement about placement work and underestimated the Service's debilitating work-test legacy. While assigning placement as the employment service's "primary object" or "first duty," its characterization of this process suggested conditions of high employment.[140] It assumed that in a "modern society enough jobs for all can be maintained only if people are willing and able, when necessary, to change their type of work and sometimes their place of work."[141]

Throughout the postwar decades the advisory committees established under the 1909 Labour Exchanges Act were operative, if inactive and inaudible. These consisted of a National Joint Advisory Council composed of representatives from the CBI (until 1965 the FBI), the Trades Union Congress, and the nationalized industries and was chaired by the Minister of Labor. Locally each exchange was directed by a local employment committee, of which there were 400 by 1965, with local representatives from employers and workers.

In sum, representatives of neither business nor labor were greatly interested in labor exchanges after their establishment. This lack of interest was exacerbated by the labor exchanges' concentration upon the most marginal, often unskilled and unorganized, members of the labor market—though the causal relationship between these processes (lack of interest and exchanges' concentration of the most marginal) was undoubtedly interactive. It was fostered by the high employment of the 1950s and 1960s when involuntary unemployment was widely judged a small problem. High employment provided apparent proof that government commitment to full employment was succeeding. The Conservatives, in office from 1951 to 1964, were disinclined to pursue the needs of the long-term unemployed, whom they did not perceive as part of their electoral coalition. Economic policy was focused on macromeasures and the defense of sterling.[142] Thus, although the British state concentrated power in the political executive, enabling them to implement significant reforms, the Conservatives were unwilling to exercise this resource to improve labor exchanges during their thirteen years in office. The one exception to this pattern came at the end of their period in office, when the inadequacies of British training stimulated the creation of industrial training boards. As I explain in chapter 4, the stimulus to this initiative was Britain's poor comparative economic performance, of which training was identified as a major cause.

The United States: Congress, the ICESA, and Segregation

The conflict over the USES's return to the states after the war reveals the political interests mobilized around the United States's national employment system and demonstrates the strength of Southern advocates in Congress, supported by the states and ICESA, and the weakness of opponents such as organized labor, the NAACP, and the National Planning Association.[143] In 1959 the Secretary to the Ohio State Advisory Council on Unemployment Compensation recalled the antagonism created by the federalization of the Service during the war.[144] Federal and state officials received different pay. They were subject to different working routines: employment exchange officials were not recipients of federal pay agreements or subject to federal civil service regulations, both characteristics likely to influence their work. He spoke of "battle royals" between state and federal agencies.

This conflict echoed many of the issues of the 1930s; the segregated nature of the service was also addressed.[145] Proponents of federalization attempted a write-in campaign to "keep USES Federalized," urging newspaper readers and others to send prepared slips to President Truman. They implored the president to resist pressures to return the Service to the states.[146] Although the president supported state control, he pocket vetoed a bill in 1945—H.R.4407—intended to transfer the Service to the states within a hundred days.[147] Truman issued a memorandum of disapproval explaining his decision. The president stated that:

> while I believe such a transfer should be made at the proper time, I am
> convinced that this bill requires that it be made at the wrong time, and
> in the wrong way. . . . Our local public employment offices are now,
> and will be during the next several months, in the midst of the peak
> work load in their history. This is because the offices are now engaged
> in counseling and placing millions of applicants who require individu-
> alized service.[148]

Truman maintained that organizing the reemployment of the USES's 23,000 staff from the federal government to the states would be disruptive and would deflect the Service from its role in postwar reconversion, as "an effective job-counseling and placement service."[149]

After the war the ICESA,[150] the principal representative of the states and, despite federal funding, effectively an interest lobby, unsurprisingly sought the Service's return to the states.[151] It was opposed by the International Association of Personnel in Employment Security (IAPES), which reflected "substantial sentiment among former state employees still federalized,"[152] the NAACP, some officials in the national ES, and organized labor.[153] Federalization was also supported by the WMC. The IAPES believed that the future role of the ES in national employment policy required a unified national service.[154] In Goodwin's view, the national character of the United States economy required a national employment service: "a Federal system can be more efficient. I think it can be adjusted to the local differences that do exist."[155] The distribution of power between the federal and state governments limited the former's capacity to influence organization or personnel in the ES: "the states were responsible for administration. They hired the people and fired them. We required that they do that through a merit system, but we could not substitute our judgment for theirs in the selection of people or getting rid of people. In those areas they had full control."[156] Local control undoubtedly assisted the persistence of the Service's segregated practices.

The states and ICESA won. Two bills were introduced in 1946: H.R. 4437, known as the Dirksen bill, and S.R. 1848, the Murray-Wagner bill.[157] The former, which was successful, returned the USES to the states and, significantly, allowed for the Service's financing exclusively by the federal government without state matching funds. The states were required to maintain federal employees but were empowered to dismiss them when they failed to satisfy state merit systems. The alternative bill was essentially a social democratic one, which posited the ES as part of a national full-employment strategy, centralizing the Service and the establishment of a National Advisory Service Policy Council. Contrasting these bills, Ira Katznelson and Bruce Pietrykowski correctly note that, "the decentralizers were keen to see state unemployment compensation administrators deny benefits to those who would not work in low-paid jobs, while the centralizers sought a very active manpower policy directed at egalitarian social goals."[158] By 1950, the bulk of the USES's budget was transferred directly to the states—$176 million from a budget of $184 million.[159]

Consequently, the two staffs separately responsible for placement and unemployment compensation were again integrated in each state. Business representatives, such as the United States Chamber of Commerce, also favored returning the ES to the states. They "feared the nationalization of unemployment compensation, but also . . . because they [did] not care what happens to the Employment Service."[160] Additional support for maintaining federal control over the USES in the postwar period came from the trade union-dominated Labor Committee of the National Planning Association. The committee noted that in every employment crisis—during both world wars and the Great Depression—the federal government had had to assume control of the employment system. They anticipated comparable problems during postwar reconversion: "experience will prove that the public employment service cannot handle the employment and labor market questions that face it today unless it is run by the federal government as a single, nation-wide service."[161] Subsequent placement records vindicated this prediction. The association believed the principal impetus for devolution to the states arose from the need to administer unemployment compensation. Given prewar experience, this dynamic had regrettable implications: "It is claimed that these laws cannot be administered efficiently unless the local employment offices at which the unemployed register for work are run by the same agency that is responsible for unemployment compensation."[162] The association believed cooperation without integration was sufficient.

One formidable source of support for a return of ES to the states came from Southern Democrats who wanted a return to the prewar status quo—states' rights and segregation—as quickly as possible. This group exercised control generally on federal policy, subverting federal intervention in the states.[163] The director of USES between 1945 and 1948, Robert Goodwin, remembered: "One of the things that Congress wanted to do immediately was to turn the E.S. over to the states. The President was in favor of keeping it in the Federal system. We fought this battle out with the Congress and we lost; they returned the E.S. to the states and set it up on much the same basis as it had been before the war."[164] Members of the Congress were vigorously lobbied by the ICESA and state employment administrators. On the key committees (Ways and Means in the House, Labor and Education and Finance in the Senate, and appropriations committees[165]), there was strong support from senior members for state control, a preference disproportionately reflecting Southern interests, though it also received strong support from Representative Everett M. Dirksen (a conservative Republican from Illinois).[166] The Senate was less committed to defederalization, but House supporters of the USES succeeded in this aim by attaching an amendment to a bill which did not face a conference committee.[167] Returning the USES to the states was supported by almost all Republicans in the House and 74 of 100 Southern Democrats; of 108 non-Southern Democrats 95 voted against it.[168]

A congressional committee review of the USES in 1964 was reluctant to attribute importance to federalizing the service. This reluctance was unsurprising given the local orientations of members of Congress:

> Strong arguments have been, and will continue to be, advanced in favor of establishing an entirely Federal service. Nevertheless, the present Federal-State system has been in existence for 30 years, *it is firmly institutionalized,* and it has developed strong support for its continuation. Moreover, federalizing the service would not prove to be a panacea for all the problems confronting it.

That the ES was "firmly institutionalized" was a major cause of its dismal record and not a characteristic to be celebrated. The committee was, however, prepared to recommend stronger mechanisms for interstate clearance and accepted that the existence of fifty individual state agencies had militated against an efficient system. This work should be "a responsibility of the Federal agency, the U.S. Employment Service."[169] The committee recognized also that since salaries were set by states, many of them were inadequate to attract the most capable recruits.

Fiscally the USES was dominated by the funds it received for administering the unemployment compensation system. This arrangement underpinned its political support. The consequences of this dominance were corrosive for its placement work, as the 1965 Task Force recognized:

> The close relationship between the Employment Service and
> Unemployment Compensation has created certain limitations on the sup-
> porting financial arrangements. A basic deficiency is that the present
> reliance on financing through the Federal Unemployment Tax does not
> reflect the much broader functions and responsibilities that have been
> assigned to the Employment Service in recent years. This has meant that
> the availability of funds has not been directly responsive to the chang-
> ing requirements of the Employment Service. Serious questions are also
> raised by the fact that a tax levied on employers' payrolls to finance the
> system of Unemployment Compensation is used to support other and
> broader activities as well.[170]

Returning the ES to state control shaped the system's character for the
next four decades. It allowed the reassertion of the prewar patterns and
practices and confirmed the weak managerial control exercised by the
Department of Labor over the state employment security agencies, and
indeed consolidated it. Neither the federal nor the individual state advisory councils proved efficacious regulators or overseers of the labor
exchange system. They concentrated on unemployment insurance and,
at the state level, instead of counteracting the political influences exercised over the state employment security agencies became part of their
exercise.

Combined with congressional committees and the Department of Labor,
the ICESA, representing local ES offices, constituted an iron triangle
impervious to external pressures. The ICESA assumed a pivotal position
in ending federal control in 1946 and defusing criticism of the USES.
This included any pressures to improve placement practices or to coordinate placement with training needs, to rescind the segregationist arrangements commonplace throughout the Southern states or to open up the
apprenticeship system. A glimpse of the ICESA-congressional linkage is
provided by a congressional conference committee report in 1949, in
which the Managers of the House and the Senate state that they would
not "disturb the cooperative working relationship existing among the State
agencies and between the Conference and the Federal agencies concerned
as regards problems of administration of this Federal-State program"; the
committees committed themselves to "review periodically the practical
application of the arrangement," a tractable qualification.[171] The ICESA's
activities were criticized by the AFL, who accused the organization of
using public funds to lobby Congress. Responding to a letter from AFL
President William Green, in 1950, the Secretary of Labor Lewis
Schwellenbach denied any wrong doing by the ICESA: "I want to assure
you that the Department has never granted funds to the States or to the
ICESA for lobbying purposes." The same letter did concede that the

Department does not consider that expenditure of granted funds incurred by State employment security officials are prohibited for purposes of furnishing information or views directly to their own Congressmen or to an appropriate committee of Congress, if there is an indication that such information or views are desired. Therefore, the Department does not question expenditures for the purpose of providing such information or appearing before appropriate committees of Congress, even in the absence of formal advance request as long as there is evidence that the information is desired or the committee requests that the officials be present.[172]

One powerful motive driving Southern Democrats and Southern state governors to reestablish state control of the ES rested in American race relations. Southern and border states operated systems of segregation (as did the District of Columbia) that extended into state employment services and this was a source of the USES's negative image among black Americans. Another source was the failure in many offices to categorize black job seekers for any positions other than menial and custodial ones. The brief abandoning of such practices during the Second World War in response to national labor needs quickly ended after 1946 as prewar practices revived. The National Association for the Advancement of Colored People engaged in lengthy correspondence with the Social Security Board and Department of Labor about discrimination in the USES. It argued that it was illegal for a federally funded service to discriminate by race. A NAACP memorandum from 1949 provides a vivid portrait of this system:

In Southern and border states many employment services are presently operated on a segregated basis, i.e., separate offices are maintained for white and Negro job seekers and employers are permitted to specify in their job orders whether they wish to have white or Negro employees. In other states where Negro and white applicants are served by the same offices, discriminatory job orders are accepted and filled. In general, these segregated offices notify each other of orders in which an employer indicates willingness to take either white or colored employees. In the St. Louis employment service, at least, the Negro office makes a practice of checking with the white office to see whether a sufficient number of white workers have been sent out to fill a job on which whites or Negroes will be accepted before sending any Negro workers. A comparable check is not made by the white office before referring white job applicants. In general, the white offices are larger and more centrally located and it may be expected that employers more readily place their orders at the white office.[173]

Similar practices were reported in many states by the NAACP. As a memorandum recording a meeting between Walter White and the USES reports:

> The Secretary cited as an example . . . a situation in Nashville, Tennessee, where there are two employment offices, one labelled for "skilled workers" and the other for "unskilled and domestic workers." All whites are registered at the former and all Negroes at the latter. Even at the Jim Crow office in Nashville, Negroes, whatever their training or experience, are registered as unskilled workers and obtain a second classification on the basis of their skill only when the individual Negro worker knows his rights and insists upon them. Even then no requests for skilled workers are ever referred to the Negro office until every available man has been employed from the white office.[174]

The USES state system reflected local politics, and local officials were unwilling to relinquish the power they derived from this segregated system. The Federal Security Agency reflected these local pressures: "those in that agency are very much opposed to any plan for abandoning discriminatory orders or wiping out segregation in southern states."[175]

The NAACP fought for many years with the Bureau of Employment Security about discrimination in the USES state offices. It compiled documentation about local policies as the basis for a sustained campaign to reform discriminatory practices. Responding to one NAACP letter in 1940 about practices in Tennessee, the chief of the Employment Service acknowledged that "at present there are no Negro personnel in the Tennessee employment service divisions serving Negro workers." He provided a standard explanation: "There are no qualified eligible Negro applicants on the existing civil-service registers for that State and from which applicants must be selected to fill openings in the local offices."[176] This latter system of civil service recruitment was subsequently severely criticized by representatives of black Americans.[177]

The NAACP cared greatly about the inadequacies of the USES and its discriminatory record but lacked the resources to effect change. Not surprisingly, the NAACP opposed the return of the USES to the states after 1946. It argued that unless a state promulgated procedures which outlawed discriminatory job orders, ensured that black job seekers were referred to positions for which they were qualified, and that separate offices for white job seekers and black job seekers were abolished, control by the states would result in discrimination and inadequate service for black Americans.[178] The NAACP wrote to all of the state governors in October 1946 requesting their assurance and support that USES offices would practice nondiscrimination once returned from federal control.[179] A coalition under the National Citizens' Political Action Committee documented the need to retain federal control of the USES to reduce discrimination. Amongst other concerns, the committee predicted that "return of the Employment Service to the states will automatically remove any responsibility on the part of the federal government for a continuation of a policy of non-discrimination and will automatically make it possible for local employment services to revert to prewar practices of discrimination."[180] Within a year of the USES being returned to the states, NAACP Labor Secretary Clarence Mitchell reported discrimination to the Congress: "More than a thousand NAACP branches throughout the country have almost had first hand experience with state employment service discrimination against colored job applicants."[181]

Although the NAACP and AFL shared similar views about the importance of federal control and regulation of the ES, their divergent positions on segregation made the formation of an alliance problematic. For instance, AFL representatives in Washington opposed efforts by the Department of Labor to desegregate ES offices in the District of Columbia. In a disheartening memorandum for the Secretary of Labor in 1946, Goodwin reports meeting two AFL members on this issue:

> We stated that we felt now that the USES, if anything, was "behind the times" in DC by practising a policy less liberal than the community as a whole. . . . Mr. Howard and Mr. Conaty strongly defended the policy of segregation in the local DC office on the basis that that was what this community wanted overwhelmingly.[182]

This attitude demonstrates the nationally distinctive dimensions informing political cleavages in the United States and the difficulty of forging a social democratic coalition based on labor market location. The CIO was much more sympathetic to and supportive of antisegregation, including the abolition of separate ES offices in the District of Columbia[183] (they organized pickets of the DC USES office), but it had far less influence than the AFL affiliates with the Department of Labor.

The same question posed about Britain—why did economic buoyancy not stimulate instead of constrain successful placement activity?—can be posed for the United States. The USES was dominated by local and state politics. ES officers were not federal but state employees loyal to local politicians and to local employers, little interested in national economic aims. The return of the Service to the states also meant a weakening of standards both in appointments and performance. Goodwin himself identified this problem in October 1945:

> Administrative standards in effect prior to the federalization of the USES were wholly inadequate for the needs of a public employment office system. Since the federal government is financing the ES, it should be able to prescribe policies and minimum standards for operations, and if any state is unwilling to carry out these policies and standards, the fed-

eral government should be enabled to maintain adequate public employment facilities by withdrawing funds from the state and using the funds withdrawn to provide and maintain necessary facilities.[184]

Such measures did not materialize.[185]

The USES featured in proposals to reorganize the Department of Labor during and after the Second World War. The transfer of the USES to the Social Security Board was unpopular with many organizations. The AFL argued that this transfer, together with the removal of other functions under Roosevelt's reorganization of the executive, eroded the Department of Labor's prestige. As a result, the "spirit and procedures of the Department . . . have not been in accord with the understanding of organized workers nor even in promotion of their interests."[186] Within the Department of Labor, officials were committed to expanding the DOL to assist workers in achieving assured incomes and jobs: "The war has . . . demonstrated that our national welfare requires provision of opportunity to our manpower and full use of our productive capacities."[187] Because the USES could speed the "waiting time of workers in search of jobs and of employers looking for men, it is a key instrument in the promotion of full employment."[188] Despite the prewar experience, the postwar planning committee stressed placement over compensation: "The certification of eligibility or of ineligibility for unemployment insurance should not be permitted to overshadow its primary placement function."[189]

USES's transfer to the Department of Labor was the subject of memoranda to Gerhard Colm in the summer of 1945. R. C. Atkinson argued that the ES's data collection work could be continued whether or not the service was based in the Department of Labor, while the effectiveness of its placement and counseling work "would not be increased by inclusion in the Labor Department."[190] This view was disputed on behalf of the USES by Robert Clark, in part because of the failure of prewar integration: "The stresses and strains which accompanied these mergers were not inconsiderable and the effectiveness of the field organization was seriously hampered. Many of the wounds had not healed by the time the State Employment Services and State Unemployment compensation organizations were pulled apart again by the nationalization of the Employment Service in January 1942."[191] He argued that the DOL's key role in implementing the full-employment program necessitated retaining USES within this executive department and expanding its remit: "No concept of the function of the employment exchange system can be accepted therefore which limits its service to the marginal worker and the marginal industry . . . the whole Nation must be included and not merely those places where there are heavy concentrations of Industry."[192] To realize these objectives required locating the USES, Clark maintained, in a department centrally engaged in formulating and implementing the postwar full-employment program. These objectives would fail "if the Service is returned to the Federal Security Agency where it would be auxiliary to the unemployment insurance system."[193]

As in Britain, no obvious agency existed to force issues of skill, training, and placement onto the political agenda. Having opposed defederalization, organized labor was concerned that the ES should remain an independent organization at the state level but the administrative pressures pushing local offices away from placement to benefit work were considerable. Writing in 1946 about efforts by the Federal Security Agency and the Bureau of Employment Security to merge the two activities, Goodwin reported to the Secretary of Labor that

> the CIO and AFL are concerned lest the Employment Service becomes, again, a mere claims-taking adjunct to the Unemployment Compensation program in the States. They are especially concerned over the possibilities that too close an integration of the Unemployment Compensation and ES programs in the states will result in the undermining of labor standards. They fear that by controlling the ES machinery, the Unemployment Compensation agencies can further reduce the tax rates of employers under experience rating by forcing workers to accept substandard jobs on the threat of denying them Unemployment Compensation benefits if they refuse to do so.[194]

Despite the ES's positive role in facilitating wartime mobilization and manpower utilization, it still shouldered a negative image among employers. One WMC official argued to Goodwin that the "prestige of the U.S. Employment Service as a placement agency is relatively low . . . Such low prestige underlies the failure of organized management groups to rally to a federalized employment service."[195] The perception from the 1930s of employment offices as sources of relief for the unemployed confirmed business's lack of interest in them. Any concern employers might have had about employment offices becoming centers of labor organization and protest against them were alleviated by the ES's disproportionate work for those most marginal to the labor market. The losers in this configuration were black and poor Americans who failed to acquire the skills or information necessary to enter the labor market independently and who were, therefore, obliged to fall back on the USES.

Separating Placement and Benefit Work

From the 1960s onward, active labor market policy rapidly achieved popularity among policymakers and economists in industrial democracies. As a component of national economic planning, governments were urged to direct and coordinate the labor market, to facilitate the improvement of skills apposite to a modern economy. Fundamental to such labor market interventions was an effective institutional infrastructure, epitomized by labor exchange networks. This view was promoted by the Organization for Economic Cooperation and Development (OECD) in 1965: "the public employment agency is a central body for the implementation of an active manpower agency"; and while no national system satisfied this role fully the "most outstanding is the Swedish system."[196]

In contrast to the United States and Britain, the Swedish labor exchanges were positively perceived and, thus, constituted a mechanism for postwar labor market policies—initially various public works schemes and ultimately an extensive training program. In the United States, a 1964 congressional committee concluded that "there are compelling reasons for the Congress to take steps to give the Federal-State employment service a new charter which is fully commensurate with the responsibilities that the service now bears. Such a charter is needed as a positive statement of the central place of the employment service in an active national manpower policy." The committee added that a new charter would act as "a final, definitive answer to the unwarranted claims that the employment service had no legitimate function other than assisting the currently unemployed."[197] Both the British and American public employment systems aspired to this sort of role as their respective governments pursued training programs from the 1960s. Separating placement and benefit work was judged a prerequisite to the discharge of these responsibilities. Ultimately, the reforms of labor exchanges occurred too late to implement labor policy successfully (see chapter 4). While the stimulus to the new roles included the perceived skill problems of the American and British workforces, this dynamic was quickly replaced with the need to improve the opportunities and abilities of the most disadvantaged members (and potential members) of the labor force.

From the late 1940s until the 1970s, the British employment service stagnated. In a reversion to the interwar pattern, it was relegated to distributing unemployment benefit rather than serving as an agent of employment. Despite replacing the 1909 Labour Exchanges Act with the Employment and Training Act in 1948, neither the powers nor the responsibilities of the employment service was significantly altered. Too few staff, inadequate buildings,[198] and a national economic buoyancy permitted the public employment service to slip into a marginal position in the labor market. The employment service poorly served disadvantaged groups in the labor market such as older workers or the long-term unemployed. These criticisms were made in an OECD report about British manpower policy and by an internal departmental review, both published in 1970.[199]

The departmental review began with an all too familiar assessment:

"The context within which the service has operated since the war has been very different from the inter-war period with its mass unemployment. But in the employment exchanges unemployment benefit work still predominates over the tasks appropriate to an effective employment service."[200] Technological developments in the economy, skill shortages, and labor market imbalances strengthened the authors' "view that the employment service ought in the years to come to have an increasingly significant role as a flexible and serviceable instrument in the manpower field." This required more "radical changes than have previously been envisaged . . ."[201] The 1970 report analyzed what the role of an employment service ought to be and listed recommendations for its enactment. Its proposal affected both the subsequent development of the Service and anticipated the founding of the Manpower Services Commission (MSC) in 1973.

The reasons advanced for an effective employment service rehearsed many of the factors identified sixty-one years earlier when the Labour Exchanges Act of 1909 was passed. They demonstrate the tenacity of the liberal values at the heart of British work-welfare. The report's authors were in the happy position of assuming full employment, but they recognized that "unemployment in some areas remains high" and that greater selectivity by workers between jobs, technological developments, and increased need for retraining necessitated a mechanism for efficiently redeploying labor.[202] Policies to satisfy these demands needed to be "supported by an effective national manpower service" able to satisfy all job seekers' needs.[203] Predictably, the employment service was judged unsuccessful in meeting these needs. The DEP report's authors held high hopes for such a comprehensive and reformed service:

> Encouragement to the individual to develop his potential, access to vocational guidance and advice and to careers and occupational information, the availability of particulars of unfilled vacancies, assistance in making contact with employers and special help for the socially disadvantaged and the longer-term unemployed . . .[204]

The report's authors recommended separating the benefit and placement functions within the employment service as an "essential precondition of the new service." In the authors' judgment, the "integration of benefit administration with the public employment service is a fundamental obstacle to its development into an effective manpower service. This is because the service grew up against a background of mass unemployment with which it became firmly associated in the public mind." This image had still to evaporate; such a change would not occur without a separation of benefit and placement activities. The report's authors recommended undertaking steps "progressively to separate benefit from employment work both physically, with different premises for each, and organizationally, with a separate chain of management for each. It should be pressed forward with all possible speed . . ."[205] The employment service should no longer administer benefit work; staff should specialize in one or the other activity and "dual training covering both functions would be eliminated as far as possible."[206] A "crucial factor" was improved training of staff, since the "present basis of staffing dates from the days of mass unemployment, when almost the sole function of the adult service was to match benefit claimants with notified vacancies."[207] A modern employment service required staff competent in interviewing and advising applicants.

Other secondary recommendations followed. As in the United States, the British employment service was criticized in this 1970 DEP report for inappropriate resource allocation. The service was urged to relocate in central-city areas and to acquire modern offices.

These proposals reflected the government's belief that "an effective manpower service is both desirable on human and social grounds and likely to yield economic benefits much exceeding the costs involved."[208] Two of their features are striking. First, the recurrence of problems identified in earlier periods. The integration of benefit and placement had damaged the employment service and inhibited its development as an effective national system. Second, these proposals are products of their buoyant economic times. They reflect the need for a national placement system within a tight labor market despite the economy's postwar success without such a service. The proposals are remarkably removed from microeconomic labor market policies such as training programs.

The criticisms developed by the DEP report were echoed a few years later by an academic study of the public employment service.[209] In his Fabian pamphlet, Brian Showler chided the Conservative and Labour parties for neglecting the service. For Labour, he suggested that an effective employment service could play an important role in achieving other social ends such as reducing poverty:

> The problem of poverty is very closely linked with types and levels of employment, and whilst quite clearly the PES cannot be expected to reverse the deficiencies in the education service suffered by many unskilled workers, nor be able to correct deficiencies of demand in a high unemployment situation, a great deal more effort could be put into its advisory guidance, retraining and placing services for disadvantaged workers . . . no systematic policy has been pursued addressed specifically to the disadvantaged in the labor force, and specialist counselling personnel are virtually non existent.[210]

The service's work had been biased, according to Showler, toward providing income maintenance assistance instead of directing applicants toward new jobs. Showler also recommended separating benefit from placement work. He argued that the "involvement of exchange officials with the rating of benefit and the enforcement of social security regulations leads to a distrustful and antagonistic attitude towards the exchange amongst job seekers that makes it very difficult to fulfil the positive placement and employment functions."[211] He recommended establishing special services, and establishing purpose-built offices (later called Jobcentres). He also advocated limiting the work of private employment agencies and introducing compulsory vacancy notification. Historically, it was when the compulsory notification order was in place that the service was most successful.

The far-reaching criticisms of the USES made by the Thomas report in 1958 were also accompanied by proposals for improvement. Thomas recommended that the federal bureau impose three changes upon the states. First, the bureau "should move to assert the prime importance and the central nature of the placement program. The air badly needs clearing on program emphasis."[212] Second, the bureau should set placement targets and ensure that the state agencies realized them. Third, though no less important, Thomas argued—unsurprisingly—that the state agencies should concentrate their service in large metropolitan areas, those with populations of 250,000 and above where the potential to place was greatest. This latter objective required the redeployment of staff in urban areas. Thomas urged the federal bureau to formulate a strategy to reverse the long-term decline in employment staff numbers and to evaluate the relationship between placement and compensation:

> These plans should include a careful analysis and a re-evaluation of the number and complexity of the combined ES and UI functions which have been imposed on local management staff in decentralized States. It should be determined whether from a practical standpoint they do not exceed the capacities possessed by civil servants available at the levels of compensation which are possible in State placement services. If they do exceed these capacities, avenues of relief must be explored through reorganization, realignment of functions, or by other means.[213]

The historic problem of integrating placement and compensation work had evidently not yet been resolved, or at least, efforts at its resolution had resulted in the predicted damage to the ES's placement activity. Thomas's report documented how the dual tasks had resulted, for whatever reason, in a concentration upon compensation by ES officials.

Thomas's recommendation that the ES concentrate and use its resources more effectively in large cities touched upon an issue dealt with by a report to the ES's Federal Advisory Council in 1957.[214] This report was prompted by the decision taken in Newark to divide work between the city office (where claimants had to register for work) and the suburbs (where claims for benefits were filed). The committee concluded that it was preferable to combine the functions in a single office, but in certain areas geographic spread dictated a division of labor: "The committee is convinced that if it results in no more than minor inconvenience to the worker, it is preferable that he be directed to register for work at the occupational or industrial office that can best serve his needs."[215]

No significant restructuring occurred, principally because of ICESA lobbying and congressional support for the ES. Similar criticisms were repeated within a few years. In October 1959 a working paper prepared for the ES's Federal Advisory Council called for a fresh assessment of the employment service's role. The confusion of purpose which concerned Thomas had not abated: "Shifts in program emphasis and misconceptions in the public mind of the basic purposes of the Employment Service have tended over the years to obscure its objectives and services and to create an unclear image of the role the Employment Service should play in the national economy."[216] The staff paper distinguished between two roles: that of an employment exchange or of an institution with broad responsibilities defined by national manpower utilization policy. The most interesting suggestions concerned the ES's service to workers. The report suggested that the principle of offering a placement service to all workers had overtaxed the ES's resources and resulted in a concentration upon the most disadvantaged and least employable (which in turn shaped the service's external image). This emphasis "tends to create the impression of a service devoted primarily to the disadvantaged applicants in the community. This can have unfortunate results in gaining employer acceptance and obtaining a large share of job openings."[217] Again this problem derives from the decision taken in the 1930s to integrate placement and compensation work. As then predicted by many opponents of the merger, compensation work had overshadowed the former and defined the Service's administrative structure.

Two groups received disproportionate attention from the employment service—claimants and veterans—and the Service had developed in a skewed fashion to respond to these groups' needs. Many claimants were, it was argued, not genuine applicants for work because they expected to receive such notification either from an employer or through a trade union which traditionally took responsibility for their placement:

> In either case, unless the claimant desires assistance in finding work outside of the employer or union attachment, it serves no purpose to register the applicant; indeed, if intensive efforts were made to place

such claimants it would be a disruptive influence on the work force.
Many State agencies continue to require the Employment Service to register all claimants despite these considerations, basing their decision
upon rigid interpretation of State Laws or Registration.[218]

The paper recommended a change to state laws to allow the employment
offices greater opportunity fully to engage in placement work for those
claimants not connected with an employer or union.

The power of the states in these programs is considerable since they
set the rates of benefits and their duration. Only in the 1950s did most
states begin to give benefits for the period of twenty-six weeks recommended by the federal government and by President Eisenhower in his
Economic Reports. Secretary of Labor James Mitchell argued in 1954
that "there appears no reason to believe that a maximum duration of benefits of 26 weeks in all States would not be generally adequate to meet
the objectives for which unemployment insurance was established."[219]
Under both the Servicemen's Readjustment Act of 1944 and the Veterans'
Readjustment Assistance Act of 1952 the employment service offices were
required to give priority to veterans over nonveterans in job referrals. The
working paper noted that a broader role for the employment service—
beyond the basic function of "matching men and jobs"[220]—was implied
in developing proposals for national manpower policy but judged it pre-
mature to specify any new role. Initiatives to separate placement and benefit work gathered pace from the early 1960s and the election of the
Kennedy administration. The Manpower Demonstration and Training Act
of 1962 marked a new approach to manpower policy, and reforming the
USES was deemed a prerequisite to this new program. Separation began
from fiscal year 1962. By 1964 "this separation [had] been generally
accomplished in about 50 of the 55 areas, either by actually placing
employment services and unemployment insurance activities in different
locations, or by using separate entrances, internal partitions, or separate
floors to insulate one activity from the other at a common location." This
reform was judged the "single major organizational step" undertaken to
improve the Service's image and finally to rescind the relief image.[221]
    In fact, in 1960 the Department of Labor issued a statement,
"Manpower—Challenge of the 1960s,"[222] which did envisage a role for
the employment service in national policy. In a conference organized by
the Employment Service designed to discuss the Service and to forge better links between it and the universities, this 1960 Manpower document
framed the discussion.[223] In introducing the conference, the ES representative observed that changes in the nature of employment and in the
characteristics of the unemployed presented challenges to the Service's
fundamental purposes. For instance,

the basic function of unemployment insurance is no longer as clear as it once was. The requirements of the '60s may be different from what was needed in the '30s when the unemployment insurance system was started. Should it remain geared to meet recession needs or should it be revised to meet the impact of persistent unemployment, technological displacement etc.? What should be the benefit duration, benefit amount and who should be protected?[224]

The university consultants reported continued confusion about the Service's purpose and persistence of its poor image. According to working group "B," the ES's limited placement activity "resulted from the unfortunately poor 'public image' that the Service has. Virtually all of the text books and research studies tell us that employers list the least desirable jobs with the Employment Service and that the least desirable employees apply there for jobs."[225] The group's discussion emphasized the poor quality of the ES's placement work in addition to its modest quantity. Group B's spokesperson concluded with familiar injunctions: "The difficulty is not so much knowing what the ES ought to do, but rather, convincing the community of the necessity of providing adequate funds for doing what we know ought to be done."[226]

The 1965 Task Force study of the USES engaged in the customary call for a better definition of the ES's mission through an integration with national manpower policy. The authors wrote: "The public Employment Service can no longer be considered a simple labor exchange bringing together job seekers and employers. Rather, it must be established as a comprehensive manpower services agency whose activities provide vital support for a variety of government programs."[227] The same report was unequivocal about the need to separate placement from compensation:

> Separate administrative arrangements should be established for Unemployment Compensation and the manpower functions of the Employment Service at the federal, state and local levels. Some measures already have been adopted to achieve this end, but they should be strengthened and extended. There should be different executives for the two activities and each should have his own staff and line of authority.

In addition to separating placement work, the ES should also "be financed independently of the Federal Unemployment Tax Act."[228]

Conclusion

This chapter has documented the failure of the British and American public employment exchanges to provide effective placement services from their establishment to the end of the 1960s. This failure, I have argued, stemmed from institutional arrangements which coalesced to bias exchanges against placement work. The political support for these arrangements thwarted modifications or improvements. Both systems, but especially the United States Employment Service, were remarkably impervious to criticisms of their practices or placement records, and this was fostered by full employment and weak national political control. Resistance to reform was the more powerful in the American system because of an institutional organization which enhances the independence of local and state governments from federal control. This advantage was financially institutionalized in the federal funding but state control of the USES, and judicious and extensive lobbying of Congress by the ICESA confirmed the state advantage.

The decision in 1945 to return the USES to the states and to reduce federal control to a minimum, despite maintaining 100 percent federal funding, enabled old practices rapidly to revive, including segregation, and the problems associated with principal-agent relations to persist.[229] The state unemployment compensation agencies quickly became the major influence in employment offices and accountability to state rather than federal government prevailed. This problem was compounded by the reluctance of the federal bureau to assume a strong role in defining the mission of the USES, which might have precluded the rapid dominance of unemployment insurance.

I have argued that the antecedents of these patterns lie in the administrative origins of the USES in the 1930s and the choices made during that decade. The decisions then to build a federal-state system and subsequently to integrate placement and compensation activities laid the framework for the problems identified by Robert Thomas in 1958. Institutional origins and developments are crucial to policy implementation. The important caveat to this judgment concerns the decision to return the Service to the states: had President Truman and the Congress acted differently and had high unemployment become a postwar reality, a different sort of Service might have resulted.

Although labor exchanges were established to assist all participants in the labor market in finding work, their dual responsibility for work-tests and placement pushed them into a concentration on the most disadvantaged workers, a focus reinforced by the perception among employers and unions that exchanges served principally unskilled and unorganized job seekers. In the United States this tendency was increased by the determination of Southern representatives, aided by the ICESA, to defederalize the ES—a determination against which opponents such as the NAACP and CIO locals were powerless. Consequently, in both countries—though for different reasons—the labor exchange infrastructure inherited in the 1960s was one focused upon work-tests and routine placement work.

Although each national system dealt with the most disadvantaged part of the workforce, these were still nominally members of the workforce. Each system was about to be assigned broader responsibilities for job seekers with no linkage to the labor market.

One implication of the ES's persistently negative image and its association with relief and unemployment benefit was the proposal in the 1960s to make it an institution especially for such disadvantaged groups. In his oral history, Robert Goodwin discusses the dispute within the ES during the 1960s as to its appropriate clients: should it provide a general employment service or confine its activities to the most disadvantaged? He attributed this debate to sources within the antipoverty bureaucracy:

> It . . . got to the point where one large state sent out an instruction that unemployment insurance claimants would not be registered with the Employment Service because they were job-ready and they could take care of themselves. Well, that was really the turning point. Employers got on their ear because they said we're financing the Employment Service, and we have to be permitted to use it. One of the results of that philosophy was that the number of placements performed by the Employment Service went down because employers lost confidence in it.[230]

This debate about the appropriate clients for American and British labor exchange systems is the subject of the next chapter, in which I analyze the decisions in both polities to formulate training programs targeted to the disadvantaged and administered through the exchanges. Unfortunately, as this chapter strongly implies, neither the British nor the American exchanges were the appropriate instruments to implement such programs.

CHAPTER FOUR

"A Cheap Pool of Forced Labor"?
Work-Welfare Training Policy

In the decades after 1945, "modern capitalism" was born in Western states.[1] It rested upon full employment and national economic growth. The achievement of these goods depended in part on institutional arrangements distinct to each polity. Among Western states, a distinction lay between those countries in which priority was given to training as a component of national economic success and those in which training was neglected. Britain and the United States both fell into the second group. They were also judged least successful in economic management. This point was noted by Shonfield in 1965: "There is indeed an element of paradox in the fact that the two nations which had earliest and most readily absorbed the Keynesian message—Britain and the United States— were also the least successful among the Western capitalist countries in managing their economies after the Second World War."[2] Shonfield's observation was common currency amongst British and American[3] politicians and policymakers in the 1960s, and this was the context in which efforts to improve each country's training system were undertaken.

In this chapter, I examine these initiatives (beginning in the United States, with the Manpower Development and Training Act of 1962 and, in Britain, with the Industrial Training Act of 1964) and argue that training programs designed to address the needs of those experiencing short-term unemployment were diverted into assisting those at the margins of the labor market. As a consequence, training policy is better understood as anti-unemployment policy. I analyze the reasons for this outcome. Both initiatives defined the problem as one of a poorly skilled workforce damaging to their respective economy's international competitiveness and likely in the long-run to result in large numbers of redundant workers.

Economic growth, judged unacceptably low and the target of government policy, required improved skills, and training was thus made a priority in Western countries in the 1960s. The role envisaged for public employment services in this was foreseen at a major OECD conference in 1965. In his introduction to the published proceeding, Solomon Barkin summarized the new role:

> The public employment agency is a central body for the implementa-
> tion of an active manpower agency . . . The older concept of the Public
> Employment Service as a passive institution designed primarily to enroll
> the unemployed and to determine their eligibility for benefits is giving
> way to a more dynamic concept of its function as the primary institu-
> tion through which we can seek to assure the optimum utilisation of
> manpower.

This shift to an active labor market policy required a "new formulation"
of the old labor exchange's functions: "It is to be a community manpower
centre which helps co-ordinate activities and provides services for all
groups in the community in order to promote national, local and personal aspirations."[4] These views were manifest in both Britain and the United
States during the 1960s.

The sudden interest in training reflected its absence in British and
American macroeconomic policy. The United States and Britain both made
major commitments to Keynesian principles in macroeconomic policy in
the 1940s, but despite this, however, both had adopted strikingly few
Keynesian microeconomic measures. They pursued full employment through
national macroeconomic policy, which did not necessarily imply the neglect
of microeconomic programs but in practice had this effect.[5] In Shonfield's
judgment, the "success of the continental Europeans was so glaring that
by the early 1960s it had become a significant factor in both British and
American domestic politics."[6]

Until the late 1960s, British macroeconomic policy focused on full
employment and economic growth.[7] The priority of full employment originated in the 1944 White Paper on Employment Policy and it committed
the government to maintaining high and stable levels of employment.[8]
The Conservative and Labour parties agreed about the importance of the
White Paper and the commitment to full employment. A paper prepared
by the Conservative Research Department in 1948 characterized it as a
"most admirable document." Labour's leading intellectual and theorist,
Anthony Crosland, published his seminal book, The Future of Socialism,
in 1956, which also affirmed the Party's commitment to full employment.[9] There was a universal fear of high unemployment. The human suffering and misery of the 1930s loomed over government policymakers at
the end of the war, and election of a Labour government in 1945 epitomized a general determination to avoid a return to this misery. The sense
of building a new policy is apparent throughout the White Paper. Its
authors describe themselves as "pioneers," resolved to "learn from experience, to invent and improve the instruments of our new policy as we
move forward to its goals."[10] This enthusiasm did not extend to training.
The 1944 White Paper dealt cursorily with employment exchanges. The

Ministry of Labour and National Service was charged with the responsibility of assembling accurate and current statistics about employment and unemployment, or the "manpower position."[11] The White Paper did not propose a positive role for the employment service as an integrated component of a full-employment policy. In a comparative perspective, this absence was unremarkable.[12] Upon establishment (in 1973), the Manpower Services Commission (MSC) commissioned a comparative study of labor market policy.[13] The study recommended developing training and work programs for young people which required an expanded role for labor exchanges. The Employment and Training Act of 1948 repealed the earlier Labor Exchanges Act of 1909. It set out the responsibilities of the Ministry of Labour for training and employment policy. The act's brief implied that the public employment service would be, through its placement service, an instrument for the achievement of full employment. In practice, the employment service was confined to administering unemployment benefit. Insufficient staff, inadequate buildings, and low unemployment quickly marginalized the public employment service, as it had before the war. Nor did it have programs designed for the needs of disadvantaged groups in the labor market such as the long-term unemployed or older workers.

Between the end of the war and the early 1960s, British Keynesian policy meant principally the application of monetary and fiscal instruments in demand-management. This strategy was linked frequently to other government aims, in particular the defense of sterling's position as a reserve currency, as Hall argues:

> To an unusual extent . . . budgetary policy in Britain came to be dictated by incipient balance of payments crises. While expansionary policy was still undertaken largely in response to rising levels of unemployment, deflationary policy was pursued whenever a serious balance of payments crisis arose; and such crises struck the British economy frequently in the 1950s and 1960s.[14]

To shift from defending sterling to generating economic growth in the 1960s required modifying the Keynesian nuances of national policy. This included a renewed emphasis on micromeasures such as training.

In the United States, macro-Keynesianism begins legislatively with the Employment Act of 1946. This act established the government's three priorities as maintaining employment, pursuing economic growth, and seeking price stability.[15] It committed the federal government to demand-management through monetary and fiscal policy, well illustrated by the Kennedy/Johnson 1964 tax cut. The momentum for the 1946 Act developed during the Second World War[16] as the federal government's intervention demonstrated the capacity of public policy to realize economic security.[17] In Keynesian terms, the legislation identified government's role as one of responding to the absence of demand.

In a letter to Senator Robert Wagner in 1945, the Office of War Mobilization and Reconversion concluded that the "war has demonstrated that our economic system can provide jobs when demand for its product exists."[18] Later in the same year, President Truman urged John McCormack of the Executive Expenditures Committee to speed the implementation of the employment bill: "It is time that the people be reassured by the Congress that the Government stands for full employment, full production and prosperity, not unemployment and relief."[19] Robert Goodwin (then director of the ES) recalls that "there was a great fear on the part of many people that we were going to have high unemployment. Their rationale was simply that we had had 10 or 12 million in service and that industry just could not absorb the veterans fast enough to avoid widespread unemployment."[20] For Goodwin, the 1946 Act marked a shift in the "philosophy of government": "I guess the main thing it did was to affect attitudes toward other specific legislation from time to time."[21] Leon Keyserling (a founding member of the Council of Economic Advisers created by the 1946 Act and later the Council's chairman) argued that whereas the New Deal had demonstrated the ability of the federal government to intervene in the economy, the Second World War revealed how such intervention could systematically be coordinated and what could be achieved under "a really unified, mature, comprehensive economic program . . . based . . . on the major activities in the Government, and this was the idea of the act."[22] Of the CEA's three original members (Edwin Nourse, Leon Keyserling, and John C. Davis), it was Davis who assumed responsibility for labor statistics and the labor market. Davis identified training as a priority:

> That training programs are inadequate is known but it is difficult at present to answer questions such as, where are they inadequate, why inadequate and what can be done to make them more adequate? The whole area of counseling, training and proper placement offers a fertile field for reform which, if successful, would result in a better utilization of our labor force. . . . Work done in this area must be correlated with efforts now being made to make the USES more effective as a labor-exchange.[23]

However, when the CEA was most influential upon policy—during the Kennedy and Johnson years—it was staffed by economists wedded to fiscal and monetary Keynesianism and not to active labor market policy, a legacy in large part of its first chairman, Edwin Nourse, who conceived of the council's role narrowly.[24] The agency which might have advanced

labor market programs, the National Resources Planning Board, was terminated six years after its creation in 1939, having no support—not surprisingly—among Southern Democrats or conservative Republicans in
Congress.[25] The CEA had little influence on labor market proposals. These
came from labor market economists working either in the Department of
Labor or as congressional staff.[26] As such they were identified, in the
former case, as advocates of a partisan constituency—organized labor.[27]
By the late 1950s, the capacity of the American workforce to adapt to
new skill requirements and to retrain workers to take account of technological developments was widely discussed. A 1959 congressional committee established to study this problem detected widespread consternation
about the United States's training system.[28] The AFL-CIO and American
Vocational Association urged a greater federal role in training and retraining the American workforce, influences felt in the Department of Labor,
the White House, and among congressional committees. A report on the
USES, also in 1959, prepared by outside consultants, outlined an expanded role for the agency leading a comprehensive manpower policy:

> Since national policy on full employment was formally stated in the
> Employment Act of 1946, other Federal agencies have developed pro-
> grams to implement this policy. The Legislative branch has its Joint
> Committee on the Economic Report and the Executive branch has its
> Council of Economic Advisors. To establish a similarly appropriate,
> positive program for State and local areas seems essential if unem-
> ployment is to be minimized. The Federal-State public employment ser-
> vice could provide both leadership and services to implement this policy.
> The need for such a positive program is apparent and may be expect-
> ed to persist.[29]

The consultants' report stressed the different problems confronting policymakers after 1945 compared with those prompting the ES's foundation
in 1933, when unemployment was substantial and geographically widespread. By 1959 the aim of the ES was to contribute to full employment:
"Effective service to employers and employees alike must do more than
simply find jobs for the unemployed who apply for unemployment benefits. The public should understand the waste and social costs of 'less
than full' employment. The man-job matching and related assistance in
career planning should be recognized as services of great social and economic importance to every citizen."[30] The report outlined a series of
familiar reform priorities: improved labor market information, eradicat-
ing the relief-agency image by defining lucidly the ES's aims, and establishing clear standards of performance.

In both Britain and the United States, labor exchanges, in their transmogrified forms, were deployed as mechanisms with which to implement and refine these training programs. Using exchanges required separating placement and training counseling from the business of administering unemployment benefits. The chapter begins with this development. In the case of the U.S. Employment Services, it also necessitated terminating the segregationist practices and institutions quotidian throughout the American South.

From Benefits to Placement

By the late 1960s, any positive role for the British employment service in government economic policy was nullified by the Service's concentration upon administering unemployment benefit. This conclusion was acknowledged by the Department of Employment in 1971: "Much of the Service's emphasis has been on the administration of unemployment benefit and the problems of the long-term unemployed. Many employment exchange premises and other facilities were indeed designed primarily for this work."[31] To use exchanges for implementing training programs therefore required separating placement and benefit work.

Reform of exchanges was initiated with the department's report, issued in 1971, "People and Jobs: A Modern Employment Service." The department emphasized the need for several job-finding mechanisms. It took the view that "the Service can carry out its many existing economic and social functions more effectively than any alternative machinery provided it is organized efficiently . . ."[32] Four objectives were identified as defining the Service's rationale: encouraging employers to provide increased notification of vacancies; encouraging job seekers to use the service when changing positions; broadening the Service's clientele from the unemployed and low-skilled to professional workers; and improving the Service's knowledge of labor market trends. These objectives required a new management structure, an enlarged network of employment offices, better training of employment office staff, "greater concentration in local offices on identifying and meeting employers' needs," a service for professional and technical workers, and the removal of benefit work from those responsible for placement.[33] Historically, it was the last which was most significant and upon which all of the other measures turned. The existing managerial structure was fragmented and deficient.[34] The report proposed making the Employment Service a "departmental agency" holding powers of self-management within the Department of Employment under the authority of a chief executive.

The pursuit of these objectives was outlined in a 1972 publication, *Into Action: Plan for a Modern Employment Service.*[35] The *Into Action* plan proposed the establishment of a network of "Jobcentres" located in city centers in purpose-built premises. In contrast to the old employment premises, Jobcentres were to have a "distinctive new look, with new standards for siting, design and furnishing; situated in good central sites to attract business and provide services; having job self-service sections and open-plan lay-outs."[36] Each Jobcentre would provide a single location at which job seekers could acquire information about vacancies or training.[37] A subsequent report noted the contrast between modern Jobcentre buildings and their predecessors which were "old" and "were neither designed nor sited to encourage job seekers not claiming unemployment benefit to make use of them."[38]

The 1971 *People and Jobs* report focused on the relationship between placement and benefit work. By the early 1970s, the pressure to separate placement and compensation functions in the British employment exchange had mounted sufficiently to achieve this outcome. Based on eighteen months of preparation, the report's authors concluded that the "development of an effective employment service—that is, of finding suitable jobs for people and people for jobs—is seriously handicapped by its present close association with the payment of unemployment benefits."[39] The image of the dole queue overshadowed public perceptions of the employment offices. The report's[40] next sentence drew the obvious inference: "the administration is therefore to be separated." The combination of these tasks, the movement of staff between placement and benefit work and their shared location collectively had had "thoroughly undesirable consequences." The outcome was not dissimilar to that recorded during the interwar period:

> The Employment Service has come to be regarded by many workers and employers as catering primarily for the *unemployed* and as having a poor selection of jobs and of workers seeking them. Thus if the Service is to improve its quality and reputation for satisfying a wide variety of needs its "dole image" must be removed.[41]

The report continued by stressing the incongruous character and requirements of placement and benefit work:

> Even more important, the two functions, which are so different in character, call for substantially different qualities, aptitudes and interests from the staff; different styles of staff training; and different kinds of managers. They also call for wholly different types of office in different locations.[42]

Separation meant distinct management structures and staff for the two tasks and, in most places, a physical separation to two sites. The new management team was charged with achieving the "rapid separation of the work of placing people in jobs and paying unemployment benefit and for relating the management structure more closely to the structure of local labour markets."[43] The Employment Service retained its policing role in the administration of unemployment benefits. It was charged with "protecting the National Insurance Fund against abuse by reporting prima-facie cases of refusal of, or failure to apply for, suitable employment and of any restrictions on availability for work of people drawing benefit."[44] To receive unemployment benefit, unemployed persons were required still to register with the appropriate Employment Service office. The Department of Employment promised that "arrangements will be made to ensure that satisfactory liaison between the employment and unemployment benefit services continues."[45] This liaison had encumbered earlier administrators.

Into Action, based on trials in selected offices, committed the Department of Employment to separating placement and benefit work by July 1974. The document anticipated 11,000 staff in the benefit branch organized into seventy-five area commands, divided into smaller regional units. It promised improvements to benefit offices and the implementation of a computerized payment system.

The establishment of the Manpower Services Commission (MSC) in 1973 changed the status of the Employment Service.[46] It became the Employment Service Agency (ESA), a statutory body accountable to the Manpower Services Commission. The new agency issued a policy state-ment in October 1974.[47] By then, the separation of placement and bene-fit work had been completed, the new management structure established, and the Jobcentre network developed. This paper defined the ESA's work progressively as a labor market institution whose rationale was to facil-itate job placements within a market economy. According to *The Employment Service,* the ESA "operates as a catalyst in the market place. It is not directly concerned with the production process nor can it take the deci-sions reserved to buyer and seller."[48] The agency was charged with pro-viding a nondiscriminatory service to all job seekers and to employers. It had "an equal responsibility" to employers and job seekers, and "it can as a rule only give satisfactory service in practice if it caters for the needs of both in a balanced way."[49] The ESA's work was divided into four pro-grams: meeting labor market needs; developing a professional and exec-utive recruitment service; meeting the rehabilitation needs of individuals; and administering the agency, tasks compatible with the functions of an employment placement service.

As a part of the MSC, the Employment Service Agency's priorities were dovetailed with the commission's general remit to address unem-ployment. Unemployment in the wake of the 1973–74 oil price crisis quickly gave the MSC an unexpected prominence. In 1976, the MSC launched the Work Experience Programme, which funded employer-spon-sored projects for the long-term unemployed. The MSC's concern with unemployment among young people resulted in the creation in 1975 of the Job Creation Programme. Both sorts of program grew after 1981 in parallel with unemployment. The ESA was exposed to the twofold pressures on the commission: providing training or a placement service for those in employment and programs designed to control and rehabilitate the unemployed. This conflict set the context for a historic reversal to integrate placement assistance (and the modern outgrowth, training) with the receipt of benefits.

The first Jobcentre (administered by the Employment Services Agency of the MSC) was opened in Reading in 1973. There were 555 functioning by March 1979. Jobcentres were the government's institutional response to the criticism that placement and compensation work should be separated: "the concept of the Jobcentre was developed with a view to meeting the needs of the labor market more effectively by bringing together all the local facilities of the Employment Service in a way which was administratively practical, operationally efficient and publicly visible and convenient."[50] The Jobcentres provided information about training, job vacancies, and counseling. They were not initially responsible for benefits.[51]

A 1978 report by the Department of Employment found that the new centers processed and successfully filled more vacancies than their predecessors. Employers were more willing to notify vacancies to the Jobcentres than to the old employment service offices.[52] The placement rate of the new offices was also higher. Surveys of Jobcentres found they placed "50 percent more people than the employment offices they replaced."[53] Jobcentres succeeded in their core rationale of dissociating the image of unemployment from the employment service. Their self-service facilities were popular and heavily used. In 1988–89, for instance, the Jobcentres made 1.9 million placings of whom 81,000 were of people with disabilities.[54] By 1989 about twenty-five percent of annual employment engagements were made through the Jobcentres. The majority of users of Jobcentres, 80 percent, were still unemployed. They were satisfied with the service provided: "A recent survey of nearly 6,000 claimants found that 83% used Jobcentres, 72% visited a Jobcentre at least once a fortnight and 41% visited weekly or more. The majority of those responding were satisfied with the layout and accessibility of the Jobcentre and found the staff helpful and sympathetic."[55]

Ironically, when the federal government came to formulate a national labor market policy that would require a broader role for the USES, it characterized this institution as concerned "almost exclusively with placement activities," even though its placement record was derisory.[56] Such a misreading of the Service's record boded ill for the expansion in its role sought by both Presidents John Kennedy and Lyndon Johnson. This new role, of course, necessitated a separation of placement and compensation work if the Service's activities were to increase. Its record during the 1960s as federal manpower policy developed was to leave many national officials doubtful about the long-term value of the USES.

In 1949, the funding system for the U.S. Employment Service was amended to provide 100 percent federal financing from the unemployment trust fund. This was supported by the U.S. National Association of Manufacturers, but opposed by the AFL-CIO. They maintained that it "wipes out the present federal-state relationship in a program designed to meet the national problem of unemployment . . . and it remove[s] the Federal Government from any effective control over standards applicable to state unemployment compensation laws."[57] The AFL believed the reform weakened federal labor standards. The federal government had complete financial control of the ES, but state employment agency officials considered employers—who paid into the unemployment trust fund—to be their paymasters. They developed programs to respond to employers' needs (even though their subsequent placement record was risible and placement offices were little used by employers). Although the Employment Service was intended under the Wagner-Peyser Act (1933) to be financed by federal grants-in-aid on a matching basis with states (each level contributing 50 percent of the cost), the ES was actually funded by the unemployment insurance tax levied on employers. Both state officials and Southern Democrats in Congress, naturally, strongly supported this reform since it gave the former increased federal largesse and furthered the latter's aim of limiting federal interference in their states. Consequently, state ES offices received funds from a federal tax paid by employers in their state, whom they subsequently identified as their core constituency. Given that employers also supplied the job vacancies ES officials needed, employers' influence on the Service was considerable. The political bases of work-welfare were biased toward employers, a bias buttressed by the ICESA's congressional lobbying. No lobbyists for the interests of marginal workers achieved equal influence with exchanges.

A further consequence of this financial arrangement was the independence from the annual federal budget appropriation process granted the ES.[58] This autonomy was one powerful factor explaining the ICESA and ES officials' determination to end federal control after 1945. In this aim they received congressional support through the ICESA's successful lobbying of the House of Representatives HEW-Labor Appropriations Subcommittee and of the Department of Labor. It was only with the death of Congressman John Fogarty in 1967—chairman of this subcommittee and an indefatigable defender of the ES (he dismissed the criticism of the Service in the 1950s such as the Thomas Report)—that the independence of ES could be breached, though not ended. During the 1950s and early

1960s, it was not uncommon for members of House and Senate appropriations subcommittees to complain about the large budget consumed by the ICESA: for instance, a House Report of 8 March 1949 observed of the ICESA that

> the committee believe . . . too many meetings are being held and that the costs involved are excessive. It would appear that an appreciable amount of conference activity duplicates the duties and responsibilities assigned by the Congress to the Bureau of Employment Security and that this duplication should be eliminated . . . The committee wishes to emphasize that as long as the activities of the Interstate Conference are financed from funds made available by the Congress for the administration of the employment security program the activities of the conference should be conducted at all times in such a manner as to assure the Congress that it is concerning itself solely with problems connected with the administration of the program.[59]

The regularity of this complaint did not result in closer scrutiny of ICESA or in a reduction of its annual appropriation (see chapter 3). Fogarty's death reduced Congress's benign tolerance of the ES's appalling placement record. The chairman of the House Ways and Means Committee, Wilbur Mills, continued to act as a defender of the ES but grew increasingly critical of its performance and progressively sympathetic to Bureau of Employment Security requests for reform.[60]

States viewed the trust fund monies as "theirs," although it was collected and distributed by the federal government. They rebuffed any right of the federal government to use it as a mechanism of oversight or control. During the 1950s, federal control of the service was very weak. Both the dominance of the states and the Federal Bureau of Employment Security's poor regulation were subsequently excoriated in the 1958 Thomas report. The institutional arrangements for the administration of the ES created incentives biased toward local (state) control and a negligent national oversight. The ES officials perceived themselves as principally administering unemployment compensation and serving the short-term unemployed, to whom only a small section of employers looked for workers. Because employers were their paymasters, ES officials were reluctant to supply job applicants lacking appropriate qualifications and experience. This reluctance did not subside after the ES was integrated into work-welfare programs for those with no work experience. This pattern was exaggerated by the buoyant economic conditions of the 1950s, and the ES had no incentive—or directive—to address the needs of those unqualified to apply for unemployment insurance, or who had exhausted benefits, or who had never entered the labor force. These groups became the focus of national labor market policy in the 1960s. But by then the

ES was routinized into a low-placement pattern responsive only to unemployment insurance claimants whose applications were systematically, though unimaginatively and nonchalantly, processed.

In a 1967 memorandum to Director of the Bureau of Budget Charles Schultze, Special Assistant to the President Joseph A. Califano[61] was still urging relieving the ES of "all responsibility for administering unemployment compensation and charging it with new responsibilities in the manpower field . . . ; and making it the main operating manpower organization with more effective interstate and local offices capable of serving as comprehensive manpower centers." Califano wanted the ES organized on a regional basis. A role was envisaged also for private agencies: "authorize the Employment Service to contract with private agencies to place disadvantaged youth in white collar jobs in high prestige institutions (banks, investment houses, corporations)," institutions with whom the USES had no relationship.[62]

The separation of placement and compensation functions was not completed until 1969. In that year, the Employment Service was combined with the Bureau of Work Training Programs to form the U.S. Training and Employment Service, a division of the Manpower Administration within the Department of Labor. A 1967 initiative to separate placement and compensation was opposed by the state governors, under the orchestration of the ICESA. This coalition failed to win congressional support.[63] The 1965 Task Force on the Employment Service emphasized the urgent need to separate placement and compensation.[64]

A powerful national motive for reforming the USES was to end its tarnished reputation for segregated employment practices—its maintenance of separate facilities for black job seekers and white job seekers—and to ameliorate opportunities for black Americans and other minorities. The elections of Democratic Presidents Kennedy and Johnson gave this motive an added impetus. The 1965 Task Force observed that "it is not sufficient . . . merely to reaffirm existing laws and policies as they relate to this agency. Instead, Employment Service personnel at every level must make a positive effort to understand and cope with the special problems that confront members of racial minorities in the labor market."[65] Indicative of the USES's record is a memorandum from Robert Goodwin in 1948. This recommended *against* the adoption of an explicit regulation opposing discrimination in the ES's regulations for two reasons[66]: the differences between the states in their Wagner-Peyser legislation; and, second, "the practical and political effect of incorporating in the USES Regulations, a prohibition against discrimination will do much more *damage to the USES and its program than it can possibly accomplish by way of benefit to minority groups.*"[67] Goodwin recommended a weaker statement.

Discrimination had featured in policy debates at the end of the Eisenhower administration. In June 1959, Eisenhower's Secretary of Labor James P. Mitchell was advised to announce publicly "a non-segregation policy for all public employment facilities and begin action to achieve this objective with all deliberate speed." Three measures were proposed by his staff:

> Negotiations in many areas of the South should be able to bring about at least token compliance in many areas, such as single entrances to offices. Certainly, if public parks, playgrounds, pools, transportation waiting rooms etc have been ordered integrated by the Supreme Court, we have little reason to ignore the segregation of the public employment service. Examine closely the legality and wisdom of refusing Federal funds or interstate clearance services to public employment offices which practice segregation. Reaffirm in a public statement of policy the Department's regulations prohibiting the acceptance of discriminatory job orders, both intra- and inter-state.[68]

The problem of the U.S. Employment Service was brought by Mitchell to the Cabinet at the end of 1959. He reported that in the "solid South there are still four or five states where USES has not been able to eliminate the segregation of its offices. Persuasion may be our only resource since otherwise it might mean a complete abandonment of the USES in the areas involved."[69]

Discrimination within the USES remained in the mid-1960s. The Bureau of Employment Security circulated all state employment agencies in 1964. The circular highlighted the implications of discrimination for placing black Americans and exposing the prevailing assumptions:

> Minority group applicants who meet the performance requirements for nontraditional jobs may not be found in the local office active file because: (1) they may have been classified only for "traditional" jobs, even though qualified for other jobs; or (2) they may not have registered at the local office because they felt the nontraditional jobs were not open to them.[70]

President Kennedy instructed his Secretary of Labor, Willard Wirtz, to eliminate racially discriminatory practices in state employment service offices. In an interim report to Lyndon Johnson at the beginning of 1964, Wirtz reported "good progress" toward this end but identified three cases in which an impasse had been reached: Alabama, Louisiana, and North Carolina. Of Alabama, Wirtz reported that "there clearly is racial discrimination in the hiring and promotional practices of the Alabama employment service." A "long series of conferences" with state officials made it "clear that the State offices are [unchanged] and officials are not going to change their position in response to the kind of Federal

efforts exerted so far."[71] Wirtz sought presidential assistance. He identified three alternative strategies: "(a) White House or Cabinet level discussions with the Governors of these three states; (b) the issuance of
specific and meaningful notice that funds will be cut off from these states
if they do not comply with the standards which have been established;
or (c) instructions to Federal personnel to continue discussion of this situation with the State officers with whom they work."[72] The second strategy was the most powerful, but not one the White House was prepared
to countenance.

Guaranteeing equality for minority Americans became a federal design
after the passage of the Civil Rights Act of 1964. Title VI required government intervention by each agency, not the mere promulgation of regulations. At the Department of Labor, the Office of Equal Opportunity in
Manpower Programs[73] was established to monitor Title VI nondiscrimination regulations in the department's manpower programs, including
those under MDTA and the USES. This office discovered instances of
discrimination persisting in 80 percent of 131 cities studied:

> Sometimes it was found in physical facilities; other instances were more
> subtle, such as the undercoding of applicants, and in referrals of minor-
> ity applicants only to jobs traditionally reserved for their racial groups
> . . . It was almost a common occurrence to find the applications of minor-
> ity workers coded far below their capacity. For example, the applica-
> tion of a Negro girl with a college degree was discovered in the files of
> one agency coded as a domestic.[74]

The apprenticeship programs were also contaminated by discriminatory practices, with information withheld from minority applicants and
selection standards not identical for whites and blacks. Workplace sites
were frequently segregated. The Bureau of Apprenticeship and Training
(BAT) certified apprenticeships, principally those of the AFL-CIO building trades unions. The apprenticeships were financed through funds from
collective bargaining agreements undertaken between management and
unions. The historic tension between craft unions of skilled workmen
(linked through the AFL) and industrial unions (the embryo of the CIO)
inhibited the formulation of an agreed position toward apprenticeship
schemes, since each feared the other would lose under any arrangement.
From the New Deal and the later merger of the AFL-CIO onward, trades
unionists supported apprenticeships as long as they could control them,
a pattern not dissimilar to the British one.

BAT administered no apprenticeships of its own. As in Britain, apprenticeships were a dominant mode of industrial training outside of state
administration in the United States, but the proportion of the working
population engaged in them was low. By the late 1980s, only 0.16 per-

cent of the U.S. workforce participated in an apprenticeship system, despite the growth of the U.S. workforce by 20 percent in the previous two decades. The number of apprentices remained constant at around 300,000 a year from the late 1970s onwards.[75]

The state employment service offices were given significant responsibilities by the Office of Equal Opportunity to expand labor market participation by minorities despite their record of segregation. Among personnel working in state employment agencies, the percentage of minorities grew, though in 1967 they were still disproportionately concentrated in custodial-service categories.[76] After 1 August 1967, claimants at state employment security agency offices were to be recorded by race, color, and national origin, but only for statistical purposes and not for placement decisions (a fine distinction). The Employment Service was also supposed to monitor the discriminatory practices of employers, revising its operating procedures to prohibit referrals to positions in companies operating recruitment choices contrary to federal, state, or local law. Title VI of the Civil Rights Act extended this ruling, outlawing any referral to an employer known to practice discrimination. Since the employment services offices were federally funded, this was a further violation of the act. Local employment service offices were supposed to monitor those employers practicing discrimination and to deny them referrals if the prejudice continued. The Manpower Administration within the Department of Labor was charged with monitoring the proper implementation of Title VI of the Civil Rights Act. These compliance reviews revealed widespread discriminatory practices in state employment offices throughout the United States. The most prevalent problems were the miscategorization of minority applicants to jobs for which they were absurdly overqualified and the failure to refer other minority applicants to the ES's counseling services. Each state employment service was required to appoint Minority Group Representatives to liaise with national officials. Section 1294 of the Employment Security Manual, strengthened in 1967, prohibited ES cooperation with employers practicing discrimination during hiring and elaborated procedures for countering it.[77]

After 1967, the ES adopted an "individualistic" approach to the employment opportunities for minorities. Rather than serving only those applicants obviously qualified for employment, the ES was supposed to assist all job seekers, including those without requisite skills. The testing methods used for categorizing applicants were revised under this approach with a new employability plan approach. This entailed abandoning traditional assessment tests, which required certain abilities, and assessing an applicant's potential rather than his or her limitations. These employability plans are pivotal to modern work-welfare programs in Britain and the United States.

Between the passage of the MDTA in 1962 and 1970, the federal government spent over $3 billion in training programs—job training, training allowances, and related support services. However, the ES's record in serving minority Americans did not improve. According to one study in 1971, instead of striving to eradicate prejudice among employers, the ES reified it:

> The chief weakness of the ES with regard to minorities is that it mirrors the attitudes of employers in the community. The ES should provide a model of vigilance and aggressiveness toward affirmative action for equal employment opportunity. Instead, it is frequently a passive accessory to discriminatory employment practices; it is widely viewed in that light by the minority community.[78]

The post–Civil Rights Act of 1965 period certainly created the instruments through which discriminatory practices could be monitored. The same report accepted that "some offices have . . . taken noteworthy steps to eliminate all forms of racial discrimination"; however, more commonly, "the majority of the services have given this goal a low priority."[79] ES staff were disproportionately white: only between 5 and 7 percent of managerial-supervisory positions were held by minorities. The 1971 National Urban Coalition study believed that subtle and not so subtle racism occurred in many ES offices despite laws and regulations outlawing such practices. It cited many incidents to verify this charge: many state agencies, for example, continued to use written testing to determine job classification, a practice contrary to a Department of Labor directive.

From Training Policy to Work-Welfare

Until 1963, voluntarism prevailed in British training policy. Training policy assumed little political or economic prominence, and the national institutions established to improve arrangements were moribund.[80] Whether through government policy or general economic prosperity, high employment was achieved in the postwar decades. This fostered a neglect of training, to which Shonfield drew attention:

> In most West European countries the ground was well prepared for a major effort to train more people to a higher level of skill. There is no doubt that the success in doing so has contributed something to the high rates of economic growth which have been maintained. . . . [I]n all the countries . . . the state has played an active role in the organization of industrial training . . . In Britain for nearly two decades following the war this lesson was ignored; there was fierce resistance to any intrusion by the state into the sphere of industrial training.[81]

High employment enabled both employers and unions to define and protect their own priorities for training and to solidify the historical and institutional reasons for Britain's poor training framework.[82] This strategy was consistent with the 1944 White Paper.[83] The trades unions' priority was to protect highly skilled positions in manufacturing apprenticeships.[84] Under the apprenticeship system, a small number of workers gained, and its industry-based nature militated against nationally coordinated policy. A Conservative Party research department paper described the system very well in 1947, a description which remained accurate for the next several decades:

> Apprenticeship is the only traditional form of organized training in industry, and dates from the Middle Ages. The problems which arise in connection with it to-day are largely those which result from the comparatively small size of a large proportion of the firms of this country. While some small firms can and do provide a full craft training for their apprentices, others are unable to do so owing to the limited range or specialised nature of their production processes. Where this is the case, the problem can only be solved by some form of cooperative arrangement between firms, with or without the aid of the local education authority. There are still far too many abuses of the apprenticeship system at the present time. It is an essential duty of Government to ensure that apprentices are properly bound and that they receive adequate treatment and supervision. They should be paid a standard wage rate, determined on an industrial basis. Here again, the general practice requires raising to the level of the best. The training problems of the small firm can only be solved by cooperation.[85]

Such cooperation failed to develop and the state failed to address the problem.

These characteristics were subsequently contrasted unfavorably with German practice.[86] Apprenticeships give workers the right to perform defined tasks which come to define the workers' skills and "job territory," the modification of which arrangements unions naturally resisted.[87] The high wages achieved by unions for apprentices to skilled trades reduced the incentive for employers to expand training. The one actor capable of overcoming voluntarism and broadening the definition of training, the state, withdrew from policy in the years from 1945 to 1964; during that period of time, it was closing Government Training Centers and reducing the number of training places available annually.

Criticism of Britain's comparative economic performance became common in the 1960s and was particularly directed at the voluntarist ethos of industrial training.[88] In response, policymakers examined ways to improve economic growth by developing national economic planning[89] and by establishing tripartite institutional arrangements (though employers and unions were unenthusiastic about the latter). The National Economic

Development Council (NEDC),[90] established in 1962 (and only abolished after the Conservatives' fourth successive electoral victory in 1992), identified an expanded training program as a necessary element for faster economic growth. NEDC argued that the improvement of training required government action: "it will be necessary for the Ministry of Labour to play a bigger role in providing adult training facilities for redundant workers or other workers who want to change their jobs."[91] The Labour Party's new leader, Harold Wilson, stressed the importance of science and education for Britain's future.[92]

Under the Industrial Training Act of 1964, twenty-four Industrial Training Boards (ITBs) were set up to reform the postwar voluntarist approach to training. Concurring with NEDC, the government maintained in the White Paper that the rate of economic expansion was restricted by the shortage of skilled workers: "This means that the rate of industrial training must be increased."[93] The 1964 act's innovation was to impose order upon industrial training by creating statutory ITBs organized on an industrywide basis. ITBs had the right to impose a levy on the firms within their industry and to distribute the funds so collected as grants to firms administering training according to prescribed standards. Theoretically, the levy gave the new ITBs a power which broke with the staple voluntarism. The establishment of the ITBs signified a change in the state's role and the government's acceptance that voluntarism was an insufficient policy response to British training needs. By placing a fiscal cost on employer responsibility for training, the levy system appeared an important innovation.[94] The ITBs were organized on a tripartite basis.[95] This quasi-corporatism was precarious since the national tripartite body, the Central Training Council, was restricted to an advisory role. The TUC regretted this limited role and subsequently criticized the Council's record: "[I]t had not performed some of the functions that were envisaged when it was established. It had not kept the performance of training boards under review."[96]

These measures were greatly influenced by the prevailing voluntarist framework. The apprenticeship system was unaffected by the ITBs. Indeed, the boards played a crucial role in *maintaining* the framework of British training policy as one rooted in apprenticeships, reflected in the ITBs' industry and sector-based structure.[97] ITBs were criticized on several counts. The levy was designed as an incentive for the expansion of industrial training, but according to the MSC it did not produce "any sustained growth in the number of people trained beyond the needs of individual firms."[98] In its first report, the MSC concluded that the industry-based character of the ITBs was problematic. It provided limited training for occupations common to several industries and provided no information about local labor market trends.[99] The tripartite Central Training Council established by the 1964 act had limited powers over the individual training boards. It was reduced to exhortation rather than direction.[100] The levy system was criticized by smaller firms who felt their financial contribution in the training system was inequitable and that they could not afford to meet ITB regulations (such as those recommending off-the-job training for workers). Downturns in the economy harmed small firms and many gained exemption from the levy during these periods. Finally, the ITB system reinforced the tendency toward firm specialization in training yet failed to rationalize such training across industries within the same sector. The ITB system encouraged firms to confine their efforts to their own, often short-term, requirements.

Tripartite organization had the potential for employer-union collaboration but included no incentive for developing or enforcing new programs, thereby limiting initiatives to a lowest common denominator acceptable to the state, employers, and unions, which often proved to be inaction. The boards consolidated the system in a way agreeable to both employers and unions and failed significantly to "challenge the position of skilled workers or the short term horizons of the average employer."[101]

The founding of the Manpower Services Commission (MSC) in 1973 was intended to impose a national framework for formulating training policy.[102] The Employment Secretary told Parliament: "The Commission and the Training Services Agency will be able to take a national view of training needs, which no industrial training board can do . . . and will be able to promote training in sectors which are not covered by training boards."[103] The establishment of the commission reflected continued anxiety about the long-term skill needs of the British economy and immediate government-employer-union relations.[104] In 1972, the Department of Employment issued a consultative paper entitled, "Training for the Future."[105] After discussions with employers and unions,[106] it was agreed to establish the MSC. The decision reflected also academic[107] and international influence upon British policymakers.[108] The key motive was short-term. It arose from negotiation about pay in 1972–73: "Nothing might have happened had Ministers not wished to conciliate the trade union movement as part of their attempt to reach an understanding on pay during 1972–73" and to compensate for the effect of the Industrial Relations Act of 1971.[109]

The corporatist ambitions informing the MSC were embodied in its tripartite membership. On the commission there were three members each from employers and trades unions nominated by the CBI and TUC respectively, two local authority representatives and an academic, together with a government appointed Chairman.[110] By giving the unions and employers equal positions in a national executive body, the MSC represented the

strongest form of tripartitism in British postwar training policy.[111] Trade
union representation on the MSC gave unions a role in national policy
coordination advantaging labor's interests.[112] But in a move favorable to
industry, the 1973 act also weakened the ITB levy arrangement, thereby
enabling firms to win exemption from payment.[113] Thus, the new tripartite institution had advantages for both trades unions and employers.

Unemployment in the wake of the 1973–74 oil price crisis rapidly ele-
vated the MSC's profile despite its modest origins. Both political parties
referred positively to the MSC in their manifestoes for the October 1974
election. Labour promised to "transform the existing MSC into a powerful body, responsible for the development and execution of a comprehensive manpower policy. Redundant workers must have an automatic
right to retraining."[114] But when Labour Chancellor of the Exchequer
Denis Healey allocated additional funds to the MSC in 1975, it was to
expand training for unemployed persons and redundant workers and not
to develop a "comprehensive manpower policy."[115] The MSC was compelled to address the needs of long-term and youth unemployment, and
in 1976, it launched the Work Experience Program and, in 1975, the Job
Creation Program for these two groups respectively.[116]

The MSC's tripartite institutions resulted in the protection of those
arrangements which had failed previously to generate sufficient training.
This outcome reflected, in turn, their imposition on a set of liberal institutions. The commission had only a marginal impact on the extant training framework, thus allowing the ITBs to carry on much as before. They
remained "important and influential bodies, particularly those for
Engineering, Construction and Road Transport"[117]; the MSC rapidly
focused on rising unemployment among young people leaving the ITBs
to their own devices.[118] Thus, in a 1977 publication about skills, the MSC
judged it unnecessary "at this time to seek new institutions to carry out
what needs to be done although steps should be taken to ensure that sectors of industry, commerce and the public services not covered by ITBs
participate fully."[119] This attitude enabled the unions to maintain their
dominance of skilled apprenticeships. It was only after 1981 that the
apprenticeship system was weakened and the ITBs terminated.[120] Thus
the tripartite institutions intended to improve training were weak and facilitated the maintenance of existing priorities among employers and trades
unions.

Between 1981 and 1988, using the vehicle of the MSC, the Conservatives
expanded their budgetary commitment to training and broadened the activities included under this rubric. The commission's budget grew from
£727.1 million in 1979/80 to £3232.0 in 1987/88. The traditional definition of training as apprenticeships was of diminishing utility in the face
of both mass unemployment and a declining manufacturing sector. This

context enabled the government to weaken the collectivist institutions established between 1973 and 1979 that had protected employers' and unions' preferences, thereby attacking both groups' interests. Training programs, designed for nonmanufacturing sectors, were initiated particularly for young people. The results, however, fermented controversy. Criticisms of Britain's skills level persisted,[121] as the priority of containing unemployment overshadowed training for those in employment.[122] Training became associated with programs for the *unemployed* rather than with *skill enhancement*.

In 1981, Mrs. Thatcher appointed David (now Lord) Young as chairman of the MSC, an appointment which increased the commission's profile since Young was closely associated with the prime minister's policies.[123] Young's tenure as chairman was active. He introduced new training programs for the young, the long-term unemployed, and middle-aged displaced workers (see table 4.1), making the MSC's programs the central platform of government anti-unemployment policies (see table 4.2). In September of 1988, the Conservatives introduced their major training program, titled Employment Training (ET), based on proposals outlined in its February 1988 White Paper.[124] The program is similar to those introduced in the United States in the 1980s to assist welfare recipients in acquiring the skills needed to work. ET purported to be a coherent government intervention in the labor market to direct and coordinate training most appropriate to labor market needs. ET, Youth Training, and their predecessors are best understood in terms of the liberal framework influencing Conservative intervention in training policy and are addressed at length in the next chapter.

In the United States, the development of training programs stemmed directly from a concern about the workforce's skills. Throughout the Kennedy administration, economic problems caused anxiety. While their problems appear modest historically, especially after the experience of the 1970s and 1980s, at the time, increases in unemployment or inflation provoked an immediate response from the president's policymakers. Early in 1961 the Secretary of Labor[125] attached a note, in his regular memorandum about unemployment claims, that the figure for February 4th— 3,358,400—was the "highest weekly figure ever recorded. It surpasses the previous peak reached in April 1958, in the recession of that year."[126] Unemployment for the same period was 8.3 percent. These problems led eventually to the set of Keynesian fiscal measures commonly recognized as an important innovation of the Kennedy presidency. In effect, Kennedy's policy realized the Keynesian potential of the Employment Act of 1946.[127] It resulted also in the decision to formulate a "manpower" and training program as part of the federal government's remit[128] (focused on the

Table 4.1 MSC Training Programs (Selected)

Program and Purpose	Date Established
1. Incentive Training Grants	pre-1974
2. TOPS for young people (introductory courses)	pre-1974
3. Work Experience Program (wide range but emphasized craft/apprenticeships). Renamed Work Experience on Employers' Premises (1978)	10/1976–04/1978
4. Job Creation Program (TSA training programs; computer/office skills; work for community benefit; temporary work for people who would otherwise be unemployed)	10/1975–12/1977
5. Youth Opportunities Program (replaces Job Creation Program and Work Experience Program; for 16–18-year-olds who have been continuously unemployed for six weeks)	04/1978
6. Special Temporary Employment Program (replaces Job Creation Program and Work Experience Program for 19–24-year-olds unemployed for six months and for those 25+ unemployed for twelve months)	04/1978
7. Training for Skills Program (administered by ITBs)	1978
8. Voluntary Projects Program (voluntary activities for the unemployed with no affect on their benefits)	08/1982
9. Community Enterprise Program (replaces Special Temporary Employment Program; work off benefit to the community, for those 18–24 and 25+ years of age)	04/1981
10. Enterprise Allowance Scheme (allowance for unemployed setting up own business)	1981
11. Youth Training Scheme (for those under 18 years old; consolidated programs for young people; one year training and work experience with thirteen weeks minimum off from the job training/education component)	04/1983
12. The New Job Training Scheme (long-term unemployed, especially 18–25-year-olds who did not participate in YTS)	1987
13. The Community Program (work experience in areas where there was a social benefit)	1982

Table 4.2 **Number of Participants in MSC Programs (Selected)**

Years	Work Experience	YOP*	YTS**	Community Program	JTP†
1978/79	128,200	162,000			
1979/80	182,100	216,000			
1980/81	304,500	360,000			
1981/82		553,000			
1982/83		543,000		39,527	56,900
1983/84			354,000	112,886	58,200
1984/85			389,400	132,755	58,200
1985/86			398,700	199,919	54,800
1986/87			360,000	243,444	68,800
1987/88	50,300††			222,731	

Source: *Manpower Services Commission Annual Reports,* 1978–1988.

*Youth Opportunity Program

**Youth Training Scheme

†Job Training Program

††In 1986/87 the new job training scheme was introduced with 2,700 participants and 100,100 in 1987/88.

unemployed defined by categories A—the temporarily unemployed—and B—the long-term unemployed with few skills—in chapter 1). Thus two imperatives characterized the Kennedy presidency's economic programs: fiscal policy for macroeconomic problems and manpower policy to address technological changes and workforce needs. The training theme was spelled out early by the president in his 1961 Labor Day address:

> Old skills are rapidly outmoded. The demand for new skills outreaches the supply. It is clear that the maintenance of a fully competitive labor force requires constant reinvestment in skills so that greater job opportunity, resulting from an expanded economic life, can be capitalized upon.[129]

Similar themes had been anticipated in the 1959 consultants' report on the ES, whose authors conceived of the Service as complementing federal efforts to achieve full employment:

> Although we may be optimistic about the effectiveness of built-in stabilizers in restricting cyclical unemployment, several other types of unemployment appear likely to continue to create serious problems. Seasonal unemployment continues to cause individual and family hard-

ship and extensive economic waste. Technological change, including automation, results in an apparently never-ending displacement problem that requires the discovery both of new sources of specialized skills and new jobs, perhaps in different industries, occupations, and localities. "Spot" unemployment persistently strikes particular industries and localities. An extension of job-finding, counseling, and financial assistance may be necessary to aid in the relocation of unemployed workers.[130]

Kennedy's Secretary of Labor Arthur Goldberg emphasized manpower policy throughout his tenure, as did his successor Willard Wirtz.[131] Early in his appointment, Goldberg's office drafted a proposal for a Youth Conservation Corps and a local public service work program. He described the latter as an "integral and important part of the manpower development job facing the nation."[132] Goldberg's department also proposed a "Full Employment Act of 1961" which included training initiatives with other expenditure and taxation proposals. Such schemes were supported by the AFL-CIO, who feared the growth of unemployment which directly affected their members. Business and employer interests articulated by the United States Chamber of Commerce and United States National Association of Manufacturers were well disposed toward such initiatives.[133]

This agenda was subsumed in the 1960s by the twin pressures of high unemployment, especially among minorities, and of civil rights. These propensities combined and underpinned Johnson's War on Poverty. While manpower policy was stimulated initially by a perceived skills crisis, succession to the presidency of Johnson, who identified the eradication of poverty as a distinct aspect of his administration[134] but then responded to the social turmoil of the 1960s by prodding policy away from skills enhancement to the provision of basic skills to the disadvantaged, many of whom had little or no labor market experience. This transition proved fundamental to the character of United States labor market policy. The flavor of these dynamics is conveyed in a 1966 memorandum from the secretary of labor to the president. At a time when the national unemployment rate was 3.7 percent, the Labor Department concluded that, "there are today, in most large cities in the United States, identifiable areas in which the sub-employment rate . . . is approximately thirty-five percent."[135] Wirtz wanted the War on Poverty, and federal training and education programs, focused directly on this urban problem:

It is a feasible objective, relying only on available and reasonably prospective resources, to get at least 100,000 to 150,000 of the hardest-core unemployed in the city slum areas into self-supporting (and family supporting) employment each year for the next three years. This won't win

the war on poverty. But it will turn the tide of battle. And it will defuse
the most dangerous social dynamite in the country today.[136]

This statement provides the context for both the formulation of federal
training programs and their targeting on the most disadvantaged members of the labor market. Similar points are made by Stanley Ruttenberg
in his recollections of the 1960s. By the time MDTA was operative, "it
was quite clear that automation and technology weren't the real problem.
The real problem were the hard core, disadvantaged individuals, the individuals with low levels of education and training."[137]

Johnson's Great Society

The switch in emphasis to the "hard core, disadvantaged individuals"
signaled the beginning of President Lyndon Johnson's Great Society and
War on Poverty programs.[138] Table 4.3 lists some of the main programs,
particularly those relating to work-welfare. The philosophy and target of
the programs initiated under the auspices of the Economic Opportunity
Act was different to that of manpower training. This difference was
important since it is the former which has been the most lasting: "The
programs and delivery systems created by the Economic Opportunity Act
added a new dimension to the manpower effort. Unlike the MDTA, which
stressed retraining so that labor could follow the demands of industry,
the EOA focused on helping the individual overcome his disadvantaged
status and fulfill his personal potential."[139] From the late 1960s onwards,
the Office of Economic Opportunity (OEO) relinquished control of most
of its programs to the Department of Labor. The latter's acceptance
implied that implementation through local employment service offices
was practicable. The ES was also made the key delivery agency of the
Model Cities Program established in 1967. OEO-DOL delegation agreements were signed to formalize these transfers. The National Urban
Coalition study in 1971 reports considerable ambivalence among OEO
officials who feared their programs would suffer from the change of control.[140] A similar judgement was reached about reforms in the early
1970s:

> The overall impression is that Labor Department planners have developed impressive concepts of modernization, but they have failed to commit the substantial resources needed to achieve institutional change. They
> have been unwilling to accept the political battles that would inevitably
> result from an imposition of meaningful federal controls over the state
> agencies. The result: much superficial activity but little lasting reform.[141]

Several reforms were undertaken to refocus the Department of Labor

Table 4.3 The Manpower Development and Training Act 1962 and Subsequent Changes

Year	Program or Amendment	Key Federal Agency	Key Local Agency	Programmatic Objective
1962	MDTA	DOL & HEW	State ES and local contractors for on-the-job training	Formal institutional-based and on-the-job training for identified jobs
1964	Economic Opportunity Act	OEO DOL HEW	Community action agencies	Job training and support services for the disadvantaged
1964	Job Corps	OEO DOL (from 1969)	Officials at camps	Skill and counseling special training programs for disadvantaged youth
1964	Neighborhood Youth Corps	DOL	Local community groups working with regional manpower administrator	Vacation and part-time employment for disadvantaged youth
1964 –68	Adult Work Experience	HEW	Local welfare offices	Training for some welfare recipients
1964	New Careers	OEO DOL (from 1967)	Contractors and community agencies	Training as paraprofessionals for the disadvantaged
1967	Concentrated Employment Program	OEO DOL (from 1968)	Local ES offices and community action agencies	Job training and support services to disadvantaged persons in areas of high poverty
1967	Job Opportunities in the Business Sector	DOL	National Alliance of Businessmen created and linked to state ES to develop training contracts with local businesses	Private-sector based on-the-job training supposed to include a commitment to hiring the trainees on completion
1967	Work Incentive Program (WIN)	HEW DOL	Local welfare agency and local ES office coordinate referrals and assessments	Job training and support services, including education for AFDC welfare recipients to enter workforce

through its national USES network to the needs of disadvantaged job seekers.

First, the Human Resources Development program was allocated an additional 3,264 staff and a circular issued to all state employment agencies directing them to give it priority. There were few signs that ES offices did so, and one reason for this was the attitude of ES state officials. They continued to see themselves as principally responsive to employers and were too inflexible to switch to addressing the needs of the disadvantaged.

Second, there was an "employability development teams" program. This program consisted of specialist teams numbering three to five members, with skills comprehensive enough to meet each individual's needs. The team focused on a group of two hundred job seekers. In practice, the team approach had little impact within ES offices: "Even though some teams were found to be effective in relating to their disadvantaged clients, many were insensitive to the special needs of the poor. *The biggest shortcoming of the new program, however, was its failure to develop jobs for the participants and to achieve permanent placements—its primary purpose.*"[142]

Third, the 1970 "Conceptual Model" (COMO) approach subdivided ES staff into three groups dealing, respectively, with open listings of vacancies for skilled job seekers, employability assessment for the hard to place, and employability development for the disadvantaged. Again, this initiative was not an obvious success. It was treated skeptically by many ES state and regional officials. They continued to prefer those job applicants who were most easily placed in positions, a preference improved through computerization.[143]

Under Johnson's Economic Opportunity Act, several job creation schemes were inaugurated, including the Neighborhood Youth Corps, Operation Mainstream, Public Service Careers and programs to persuade large employers to recruit and then train inner-city disadvantaged job seekers. Historically, these programs constituted a framework for state work-welfare schemes in the 1980s. The Neighborhood Youth Corps developed public service work projects for teenagers both still at school and for those who had not graduated or who had dropped out. Title V of the Economic Opportunity Act was targeted toward welfare recipients to provide them with work-experience for vocational rehabilitation. It created a Welfare Administration as an agency of the Office of Economic Opportunity through which were developed programs for welfare recipients; they were to be more extensive than earlier ones. Responsibility for Title V programs was given to the Department of Labor from 30 June 1967 with the clear implication that the department's federal training services should be coordinated with addressing the rehabilitation needs of welfare beneficiaries.

Revealed here are the antecedents for subsequent federal work-welfare programs, culminating in the Family Support Act of 1988. Since the 1960s federal officials have recognized the need to coordinate welfare benefits with exposure to and participation in training programs. While the origins of these programs in the 1960s are social democratic, by the 1980s the dominant liberal motifs of earlier work-welfare programs had revived sufficiently to destroy this progressive component. Furthermore, the Republicans controlled the White House. A shift in ideological emphasis occurred: in the 1960s, poverty was blamed on structural factors; in the 1980s, on the reluctance of welfare recipients to seek work.[144] The linkage between welfare and training persisted, but its specification was tighter, and the training component increasingly diluted.

The implications of Title V for the Department of Labor and the USES were significant. It implied a primary focus on the needs of welfare recipients. It included an injunction to "realign the manpower services to meet the rehabilitation needs of the welfare client." The results were not promising. Few families achieved independence.[145] This assessment signaled the death of work experience programs and Johnson's ensuing budget proposals reduced the appropriation request (the growing American involvement in Asia also limited domestic spending). In its place the Work Incentive Program (WIN) was established, under which job training fell completely to the Department of Labor.[146] Between 1966 and 1968, 130,000 persons and 828,000 dependents were assisted by being provided with work experience and training opportunities under Title V. These groups covered two categories: those entitled to receive benefits under states' approved public assistance plans and those not entitled under state AFDC regulations. Technically, all participants had to be needy parents with dependent children and over twenty-one years of age. Most participants were on the margins of the labor market, with little experience of work; they lacked the education and skills requisite to employment.[147] Title V programs were coordinated with Employment Service offices.

The Work Incentive Program (WIN) was consolidated under the 1967 Amendments to the Social Security Act. The aim of rehabilitation rather than simply long-term maintenance on public assistance was made explicit. In theory this arrangement created a powerful and comprehensive manpower rehabilitation initiative. All states were required to participate by 1 July 1969. Its target was the long-term or hardcore unemployed, including those in receipt of AFDC benefits. The law required the referral of all such recipients for employment or training. In fact, lack of resources ensured that few were so directed. Formally, "an individual referred to the program and refusing to participate without good cause may have his or her welfare payments cut off, though the family may continue to receive them. This action will be taken only after hearings by an impartial body."[148] Thus the mandatory element associated with contemporary work-welfare (or workfare) programs was established under this WIN scheme. Implementation of this element was dilatory and it was rare for clients to have their benefits cut off by caseworkers. Work-experience activities were broadly drawn to include on-the-job training, special works projects operated by public agencies, or private nonprofit organizations and funded by the Department of Labor with recipients' welfare grants.

The USES and the Great Society

The Great Society initiatives were complemented by a study of the USES which urged its transformation into an agency administering and refining a federal active labor market policy, of a type associated with European social democratic regimes. The Schultz Task Force on the USES declared in 1965 that "the public Employment Service can no longer be considered a simple labor exchange bringing together job seekers and employers. Rather, it must be established as a comprehensive manpower service agency whose activities provide vital support for a variety of government programs." Both the needs of the economy and new legislation gave this proposal its urgency: "Congress has enacted an amalgam of legislation dealing with manpower, education, and civil rights which is designed to improve the quality of American life and to broaden the distribution of the benefits of economic progress. Clearly, the Employment Service must adjust to these new circumstances in order to retain and enhance its effectiveness."[149] Similar views were expressed at the 1963 annual meeting of the ICESA, a group of whose members had undertaken a field trip to continental European countries explicitly to study their manpower programs and reported favorably upon them. One delegate, Mr. Bernstein, declared that the group "returned home with a hope that our country might be able to import some of the very practical and proved techniques employed abroad aimed at better utilization of their labor forces, programs which aided these countries to reduce unemployment to amazingly low levels."[150] This view sat infelicitously with the ES's previous record and ICESA's own activities.

For the Schultz Task Force, placement was to be the principal activity of the ES, an aim consistent with the 1933 enabling legislation:

> In this framework, the placement function remains as the key objective in the operations of the Employment Service. But now it will be part of a systematic effort at manpower development rather than the primary concern of a labor exchange. The development of a comprehensive manpower services center can provide a powerful antidote to the casual,

"one-shot" placement psychology that has frequently characterized the
Employment Service in the past.[151]

The Task Force urged the ES to maintain an active placement service,
collect and disseminate labor market data, improve its counseling services, and assist other agencies such as the Office of Economic Opportunity,
Council of Economic Advisers, the Bureau of Apprenticeship and Training,
and public welfare agencies.

Many operators of private fee-paying employment agencies opposed
expansion of the ES's scope and activities. They wrote frequently to
Presidents Kennedy and Johnson about their fears. In one response in
1964, the director of the Bureau of Employment Security explained why
there was ample opportunity for USES expansion without harming private agencies: "The number of private agencies reporting under State
Unemployment Insurance laws grew from 810 in 1953 to the current total
of 2,347—an increase of 190 percent. . . . Since both private and public
employment services account for only 20 percent of the total job openings filled in the national job market, there appears to be ample room for
expansion on the part of both of these agencies."[152] In a letter prepared
in 1964 by the Department of Labor for the Special Assistant to the
President Ralph Dungan, to send to another private agency—Lee
Associates—the Department unwittingly disclosed the Service's limited
success and decrepit condition: "The high percent of *unemployed* persons
placed by the public employment service (98%, according to the latest
survey in April) as compared to the also high percent of *employed* persons placed by the private employment agencies (85% to 90%) indicates
that little or no common ground for competition exists." Dungan's letter
then observed the problems unaddressed by private agencies: "Private
agencies cannot be required to organize effective assistance to youth who
'drop-out' from schools before graduation. They cannot be required to
conduct skill surveys, identify training needs, and make provision for
meeting those needs."[153] Comparable responses were made to Senators
Daniel Brewster and Glenn Beall and Congressman George Fallon by
Secretary of Labor Wirtz, each of whom contacted the White House in
behalf of Lee Associates.

Improving the quality of appointees in the ES and ensuring that they
acquired skills appropriate to specialist placement work were accented by
the Schultz Task Force. The local control of the fifty state employment
services had ensured both that standards of appointment could be low and
that appointees might be advanced on political grounds. The task force
recommended making ES officials' salaries comparable with professional jobs elsewhere in the public sector. The training available for new
recruits needed to be improved greatly.[154] Lastly, the task force urged a

reorganization of the ES's finances, by distinguishing between the funds necessary to administer work-tests, to be deducted from the Federal Unemployment Tax Fund, and separate congressional appropriation for placement work financed from general tax revenues. "By adopting this approach, Congress would be in a better position to determine the needs of the Employment Service and to evaluate the efficiency of its operations in the manpower field on a regular basis."[155] Lacking an independent financial base, the ES's placement work was always vulnerable to the greater priority accorded compensation work, as indeed occurred.

The 1965 Employment Service Task Force's recommendations appeared at an opportune moment for policy reformers. Not only did the passage of the Manpower Development and Training Act in 1962 signal a shift toward a national labor market policy framework,[156] but by 1964 President Johnson had embarked upon his ambitious War on Poverty, pivotal elements of which were those programs to expand equal opportunities for minorities, youth, and the long-term unemployed. Johnson's focus was on the unemployed in categories B and C, namely, the long-term unemployed with little work experience and welfare recipients with no work experience, with the latter's importance enhanced by the civil rights mobilization and empowerment of black Americans effected by the 1964 Civil Rights Act. The MDTA emphasized the training of those unemployed over employed persons and young people, but it provided the potential to be applied to persons falling into categories B and C. The act identified heads of households as deserving particular attention. This referred to males made redundant, not to the single, female heads of households who subsequently dominated this category.

The USES seemed destined to lead these initiatives since the Department of Labor was accorded administrative responsibility for MDTA (notionally in coordination, but practically in competition, with the Department of Health, Education and Welfare).[157] The task force's recommendations were never fully implemented.[158] The Department of Labor was still thrust into a new manpower policy role under the MDTA regime which presupposed a national network of local offices capable of performing tasks more complex than the humdrum processing of benefit claims and lethargic placement listing. In its manpower work, the ES offices faced competition from the community action agencies (CAAs) established under the Office of Economic Opportunity (OEO) program as alternative channels for political and community participation, producing wasteful overlap and conflict. More traditional competition arose from existing vocational education agencies. These conducted the training under MDTA while the employment agencies screened applicants and placed graduates. Under MDTA, trainees received free vocational education and a cash allotment for subsistence.

Both Presidents Kennedy and Johnson singled out the Employment Service as capable of much better serving the needs of citizens on the margins of the labor market, whether located in depressed areas, made recently redundant, long-term unemployed, or young unemployed.[159] These priorities required reorienting the Service away from employers' interests to those of job seekers: rather than searching for applicants for vacancies, this approach implied considering how the skills of individual applicants could be improved as the economy's needs changed.[160] This agenda implied a redefinition of ES's role and breaking the Service's entrenched relationship with employers. In 1962, Louis Levine was appointed director of the Employment Service. He defined the Service's role as successfully implementing this national manpower service at the local level: "Each local office must serve as the local community manpower center and, beyond that, must also function in a strongly linked nationwide network of offices operating to meet national manpower purposes and goals."[161]

From being originally intended to retrain those already in work, the MDTA program quickly shifted its emphasis to those on benefits. Amendments to the 1962 act enacted in 1963, 1965, and 1966 formalized this new emphasis by "broadening the trainee base, liberalizing training allowances and increasing the scope of the program."[162] The 1965 amendment formalized the emphasis upon the long-term unemployed, disadvantaged youth, and the older long-term unemployed who had been made redundant. The period of work experience, a prerequisite to qualifying under the MDTA, was shortened to a year in 1966.

A major component of MDTA's remit was to develop on-the-job training programs for the unemployed and underemployed.[163] Initial on-the-job training grants were subsequently supplemented with grants for education and pre-job entry programs to cater to those unemployed persons whose skill levels were particularly vestigial. State employment offices provided candidates for on-the-job training schemes. Participants received wages equal to those normally paid to entry-level workers. From the mid-1960s onwards, on-the-job training and pre-entry programs were augmented by business-led initiatives to assist the inner-city hard-core unemployed. In Detroit, Chrysler provided a pre-entry class for 125 potential workers, of whom 50 moved into jobs. Such schemes emphasized MDTA training programs' dependence on employers. This subordination was familiar to ES offices.

Reorienting the ES toward the disadvantaged necessitated a novel role for this federal agency. This role was at variance with its practice since the Wagner-Peyser Act of 1933 (with the brief interregnum of the Second World War) and with the political institutions of the United States which advantaged state governance over federal control. In the case of the employment service, state control, particularly after 1946, was considerable and jealously protected: "Many state directors, especially those who were unemployment insurance-oriented, felt they were being overburdened without additional staff."[164] The new orientation was prompted by the formation by Secretary Wirtz of the Human Resources Development program within the Department of Labor in order to coordinate those programs focused on the long-term unemployed concentrated in ghettoes and slums: "In August 1966, with a strong push from the Manpower Administration, HRD was adopted as a major thrust requiring a large portion of USES resources and personnel"; however, state responses were often disappointing as even the official record acknowledges:

> Federal leadership in manpower services . . . has not always resulted in their success at the community level. The Federal-State Employment Service is an affiliation of 54 jurisdictions. These jurisdictions vary widely in orientation and effectiveness. They work within broad guidelines established by the Federal Government, but interpret these within the framework of local and regional laws and traditions.

The implications of this assessment for the USES as a whole were not encouraging:

> the tendency on the part of some State agencies to move at their own pace, and ignore Federal leadership to whatever extent possible, has been costly to the system as a whole. The most serious result has been a doubt in the minds of some Congressional leaders that the public Employment Service was the proper vehicle for administering the numerous new manpower programs created during the 1960's—the Work Incentive Program for welfare recipients, for instance.[165]

Apprenticeship Information Centers were established at Employment Service offices to broaden the base of referrals to apprenticeship and training programs. ES offices developed an early warning system responding to large lay-offs; new systems to test applicant aptitude for positions and training programs; counseling and extramural services to reach those applicants unlikely to visit ES offices; and the recruitment of staff, all to link with the long-term unemployed. Special programs were also developed for the young, both high school dropouts and graduates unable to find work.

As MDTA's remit was expanded, the USES's linchpin location in federal training remained.[166] The MDTA was amended throughout the 1960s to broaden its scope. Table 4.3 lists MDTA with other legislation enacted during the 1960s as part of the federal manpower policy. A considerable number of programs were initiated under the federal manpower policy drive, which was increasingly focused on the disadvantaged rather than the alleged skills crisis which stimulated, in part, the whole undertaking.[167]

These initiatives expanded the role of local employment service offices beyond their traditional administration of unemployment compensation and modest placement efforts. Local ES offices were, in effect, required to assess the training and educational needs of applicants, organize training courses and counseling programs, and liaise with local employers to agree on on-the-job training arrangements. By 1970, the Manpower Administration held a buoyant view of its accomplishments and of the reorganization undertaken between 1968 and 1970 to devolve greater control to local offices:

> Local employment offices recruited more than two million trainees, enrollees, and workers in the nine major programs of the Manpower Administration. Disadvantaged, hard-core unemployed and underemployed have been trained in classrooms in a wide variety of occupations; on-the-job with employers, including projects developed with the assistance of the National Alliance of Businessmen; with city, county and State governments in work experience programs for adults and youths; through the Work Incentive (WIN) program, for adults on welfare; in Public Service Careers to qualify for government jobs; and residential manpower services for youths through the Job Corps.[168]

The Bureau of Apprenticeship and Training (BAT[169]) was drawn into the service of manpower and civil rights policy as the number of apprenticeships rose steadily during the 1960s, from 85,000 in 1966 to 215,000 in 1967, the largest postwar number since 1949.

Discrimination was a problem exercising the minds of all those concerned with apprenticeship programs. The problem exposed the divisions within organized labor, especially between craft unions in the AFL-CIO and civil rights activists such as the NAACP. In 1960, the NAACP prepared an eighty-page report, "Negro Wage Earners and Apprenticeships," which documented the discrimination encountered by blacks seeking to join apprenticeships and the pitiful numbers who were successful. The report observed that "given a continuation of present rates of advance, it will take Negroes 138 years, or until the Year 2094 to secure equal participation in skilled craft training and employment."[170] Of 7,464,120 males working in skilled craft occupations in 1950, a mere 270,420 or 3.5 percent were black workers.[171] In the same year, blacks constituted 1.6 percent of a total 111,750 apprentices.[172]

The bureau's state apprenticeship councils were required under legislation signed in 1964 to ensure nondiscrimination in accepting applicants for apprenticeships. Apprenticeship Information Centers, located in USES offices, assumed responsibility for implementing this new policy and for increasing the number of apprentices.[173] Organized labor supported these initiatives. National Joint Pattern Apprenticeship Standards and Policy Statements were agreed for thirty-five industries. Trades unions controlling entry into craft-based careers, notably in the construction industry, had a poor record in advancing minority opportunities: "BAT has been reluctant to pressure the unions into non-discrimination, and in January, 1971, the Solicitor of the Labor Department expressed the fear that BAT registration of numerous discriminatory apprenticeship programs may be in direct violation of the Constitution."[174] The ES administered the Apprenticeship and Journeymen Outreach Programs[175] through its Office of National Contracts. These programs were designed to attract and prepare minority recruits for apprenticeships. Unions were hostile to them because of their location in inner-city areas with large minority populations. Despite their location, however, fewer than one-fifth of AIC recruits to apprenticeship programs were non-white. This record reflected a general malaise:

> The reactions of the state officials contacted in this survey gave the impression that the ES, with a few exceptions, has virtually given up on the important job of placing minority applicants in apprenticeship programs. Some states, like Florida, still keep no information on placement rates. A Louisiana community leader reported that even when minorities are successfully placed, they get "the traditional black jobs—all muscle and no brain." The Massachusetts ES, in reviewing the prospects of its Boston AIC, wrote: "It is planned to continue this effort despite its disappointing results . . . It is estimated that unless conditions change, at least 50 individuals will enter apprenticeship through this center."[176]

To tackle discrimination in apprenticeships, the Department of Labor established in February 1963 an Advisory Committee on Equal Opportunity in Apprenticeship and Training. It held meetings throughout 1963 and 1964, formulating guidelines for nondiscrimination, particularly for State Apprenticeship Councils.[177] The ES's designated responsibility for increasing minority participation in apprenticeships was not discharged: "One BAT official said that, of all the minorities who enrolled as apprentices in the past few years, more came into the programs on their own than through the Employment Service's AIC's and Outreach programs combined."[178] The role of the AFL-CIO in administering apprenticeships limited the capacity of the Labor Department to achieve reforms. To win labor support it was compelled to locate on-the-job training schemes in BAT offices, whose role was guaranteed by congressional control, where the House chair of appropriations until 1967 was John Fogarty, a staunch defender of the existing ES.[179]

Violations of nondiscriminatory regulations were monitored by the Office of Equality of Opportunity. It formulated compliance agreements with State Employment Services. Violations were documented and sent to the solicitor in the Department of Labor who had power to recommend ending federal funds (which has never occurred) on grounds of noncompliance. Lengthy actions against Ohio and Texas employment services were inconclusive.

After 1968 the Manpower Administration required that each ES return a plan to the federal government before receiving its annual appropriation. However, this strategy did not overcome local ES offices' reluctance to plan:

> Most state plans read alike, reflecting the current DOL rhetoric, but are often contradicted by actual performances. They are so diffuse in content that it is impossible to discern the specific action the state intends to take . . . Most revealing of the plans' significance is the fact that no steps are taken to determine whether a state ES actually did what it said it was going to do in its plan; this reduces the planning exercise to busy work.[180]

Lack of systematic federal evaluation of state proposals echoed a major criticism of the 1958 Thomas study of the USES. The DOL also funded new positions in each governor's office with responsibility for statewide coordination of manpower and employment services. These officials were unable to impose priorities upon local offices whose incumbents maintained existing practices and were financially independent.

The Secretary of Labor also made the USES the implementing agency for WIN. In general it was identified as the principal agency implementing manpower policy programs, including those for the disadvantaged. WIN was the first manpower program for which ES assumed primary responsibility, but the ES failed to fill all of the positions available under WIN with AFDC recipients. Senator Russell Long strongly criticized the ES's role:

> The accomplishments of the Department of Labor in administering the WIN program are dismal. Of the 250,000 welfare recipients found appropriate and referred to the work incentive program during its first twelve months, less than 60% were enrolled in the program, and out of the 145,000 who were enrolled, one-third subsequently dropped out. Only 13,000 welfare cases have been closed following participation in the work incentive program during its first 21 months, while during the same period, 641,000 families were added to the welfare rolls—a ratio of 50 to 1 on the unfavorable side.[181]

On balance, ES officials appeared woefully ill-equipped—in both the sense of lacking skills and lacking the will—adequately to meet the needs of enrollees referred under the WIN program. They failed to implement the not inconsiderable support services available under WIN—such as health care follow-ups, granting of transportation allowances or child-care facilities (though how these were to be funded was unclear from the enabling legislation). And where more committed or interested administrators would have approached WIN's aims as a challenge and an opportunity to enhance the possibilities for the disadvantaged, the average ES official responded, at best, indifferently and, at worst, intemperately. The most fundamental failure, however, was a paradoxical one: the ES's seeming incapacity to place any of the enrollees in WIN programs in jobs. Since WIN was intended to shift nonparticipants with no work experience into the labor market this failing was not trivial. Poor coordination between state welfare and labor departments was an additional source of WIN's poor record, such a problem being a perennial one in the federal system and particularly in work-welfare administration.

The administration of the 1971 amendments to the Food Stamp Act encountered similar difficulties to those of the WIN program. Again, welfare recipients—this time all able-bodied adults in families eligible for assistance—were to be registered at ES offices and to accept appropriate employment, if offered, as a condition of receiving benefits, an early version of workfare. Without ES efforts to improve the employability levels of such recipients, they were sent to whatever jobs were open. However, food stamps are administered by the Department of Agriculture: it failed to provide additional funding for manpower training measures.

The Politics of Training

The attempt to reform the British and American labor exchange networks and to integrate them into national labor market policies, to administer training programs, floundered in both cases. In both the shift from macro- to micro-Keynesianism was distorted by a need to focus on the least skilled and most disadvantaged *unemployed* citizens. Training for the *employed* and those about to enter the workforce was untouched. In Britain, apprenticeships declined because of a crisis in manufacturing while the United States's modest apprenticeship program remained modest. The explanation for this stems fundamentally from the institutional and policy legacies within which the initiatives were embroiled and which were themselves an outcome of political conflicts and choices.

Both British and American training programs began as programs to enhance each country's training framework and workforce's skills, formulated within a micro-Keynesian approach. The transition in training programs for the employed and unemployed in category A (those normally in work) to programs for those in categories B (victims of seasonal or structural unemployment) and C (welfare recipients and/or persons with no work experience) was partly accomplished in both polities because of the weak political and electoral support for the former strategy. These initiatives were also established within a programmatic context whose institutions and values were hostile to such initiatives. In both countries such micro-Keynesianism appears anomalous historically. The institutional concentration on applying work-tests through labor exchanges, the fostering of private sector and voluntarist approaches to training policy and the weak political support from employers and unions for comprehensive training are all manifest during this period.

Training programs for the unemployed reflected in part the ideas of labor economists during the 1960s about appropriate national labor market policies and arguments about pending skills shortages.[182] While these ideas were powerful, mobilized through think tanks, interest groups, and to a lesser extent political parties, they lacked firm political and electoral support, and therefore also defenders. Efforts to implement them confronted the not inconsiderable limitations of British and American work-welfare programs.

The British state is highly centralized, and its legislature is dominated by the executive drawn from it. Its capacity to mold institutions to its own ends, to create new organizations, to modify or destroy old ones, is lightly fettered. Thus the government was able in 1971 speedily to separate placement and benefit activities within the employment service, in a way unthinkable in the United States, where federal authorities were forced to cooperate with states and where building a consensus in Congress is complex. In 1973 it created the Manpower Services Commission (MSC) to provide a national tripartite forum for training policy. In principle, both acts should have fashioned an effective training policy meeting the needs of unemployed persons in categories A and B. In practice, another feature of the British state—policymakers' vulnerability to attempted short-term solutions—diverted these institutions to rising unemployment. What political values informed that response varied with each administration, but since the late 1970s liberal ones, propagated by Conservatives, have prevailed. The opportunity for MSC officials to devise and advance active labor market policy measures of the sort they envisaged—comparable to those of Britain's continental rivals—was limited. The Conservatives, after 1979, were disinclined to broaden the MSC's role in this latter direction but were prepared ruthlessly to exploit its administrative and political anti-unemployment role. Jobcentres, consequently, never enjoyed the opportunity to test the advantages of focusing on placement exclusively.

The trades union movement saw the MSC as a mechanism with which to advance its interests and to influence government policy, but the commission's tripartitism did not create the conditions necessary to erode the traditional voluntarist approach to training policy. Training was conceived principally in apprenticeship terms. When the MSC was forced into a role of serving the long-term and young unemployed, the union movement continued to try to influence its programs but its right to do so was steadily eroded. By the late 1980s, TUC suspicion that the commission's programs were surrogates for punitive work-oriented schemes led to the complete withdrawal of its support.

Officials within the MSC were undoubtedly ambitious to develop a position as a labor market institution rivaling those entrenched in social democratic regimes (which they adopted explicitly as their models) but were unable to accomplish this emulation. The funding they received—while increased after 1975—and the programs they began were all marshalled to serve the political purpose of reducing unemployment by absorbing and removing claimants from the register. This role provided the MSC with a rationale and the political opportunity to survive under a Conservative administration, hostile to tripartitism and labor market intervention, until 1988 (when it was transformed in quick succession into the Training Commission and then Training Agency). By that date, it had been progressively weakened and the influence of the TUC on MSC decisions steadily reduced.

The separation of benefit and placement work did not constitute the expected stimulus to an improved placement record. Part of the reason for this failure was the post-1975 unemployment crisis to which the employment service was quickly directed. In their brief existence, Jobcentres achieved a positive presence in the labor market and succeeded partially in throwing off the image bred by the interwar labor exchange practices. The electoral and political forces empowering the Conservatives from 1979 were too powerful to sustain a commitment to distributing unemployment and social security benefits without policing them more rigorously.

More fundamentally, the policy initiatives undertaken to reform and broaden the British training regime lacked a sufficiently strong electoral or institutional foundation. The MSC institutionalized and barely deflected the agreeable voluntarist approach to training, practiced by employers and unions, centered on apprenticeships. Interest in those excluded by such an approach was slight—in part because of their small number between 1945 and 1975.

As unemployment rose inexorably from the mid-1970s, the trades union movement found itself increasingly unable to reverse the neglect of training or to achieve increased funding for it. High unemployment from 1980 devastated the manufacturing sector of British industry, the unions' principal source of membership,[183] while legislation from 1979 was enacted to weaken the unions and this weakening enabled the Conservative Government to accomplish the shift to the comprehensive work-welfare program, analyzed in chapter 5.

In the United States, the decisions to separate placement and compensation work and to end segregation took far longer to implement than comparable changes in Britain because of the decentralized federal system and the capacity of local employment offices to defend existing routines. Few sanctions were available to the federal government and those few available—principally withholding federal funds—were used sparingly. The National Urban Coalition's severely critical report of the USES unearthed paltry evidence of any modification in the Service's labor market role:

> Unfortunately, the state employment service agencies have not been transformed into comprehensive manpower centers. They are not meeting the national needs. Neither Congress nor the Department of Labor has taken the key steps recommended by the Shultz Task Force to bring the system under federal control. The agencies remain uneven in quality and generally unresponsive to national direction. Some changes have occurred but they have primarily affected the intermediate services performed by the agencies—counseling, testing, referral to other agencies, and computerized job listings. The two basic functions—reaching clients in need of service and placing them in jobs—remain weak.[184]

Absent from this diagnosis is an understanding of the deep administrative bias toward serving employers and administering unemployment benefits. This bias derives from the decision to integrate these activities in 1938 and the USES's historical role of applying work-tests. Critics of the USES's flaccid performance failed to acknowledge this historical context. Former Manpower Administrator Stanley Ruttenberg understood this better:

> There are those who are responsible for the administration of the program in many of the states who feel that it isn't their job to deal with welfare recipients, or to deal with the long-term unemployed, or to deal with the minority, or those individuals who have been less fortunate in receiving education and training . . . If you wanted the employment service to deal with these kinds of individuals, it was necessary to get the employment service to reorient its thinking and reestablish its priorities, stop doing certain of the older things which it always did and begin some of the newer things to adjust itself to the assistance to the hard core.[185]

The National Urban Coalition's damning study had been prepared with the full cooperation of the USES and Bureau of Employment Security in Washington.[186] Despite this cooperation, federal officials were bruised by the final report.[187] Assistant Secretary of Labor Malcolm Lovell, Jr., who met regularly with Sarah Carey of the Lawyers' Committee while the study was being prepared, issued a plaintive response:

> It is difficult to see how a manpower organization, such as the State Employment Service—which has found almost 6 million jobs for minority persons in the past three years—could be viewed with the contempt expressed in a report issued today by the Urban Coalition and the Lawyers' Committee for Civil Rights Under Law. . . . The Employment Service is an institution in transition, moving from a strictly labor exchange operation in 1962 to the more comprehensive manpower agency it is today. . . . Quite frankly, the emphasis of the Employment Service on placing the disadvantaged in jobs has met with disfavor on the part of some employers.[188]

An internal paper later in the year alluded to the "obligatory" need for "speakers from all walks of life and at all stations to demonstrate their membership in the cognoscenti by damning the Employment Service principally for 'not adequately' serving minorities and the disadvantaged. These condemnations typically are not founded in any objective review of the facts or at least not of all the facts . . . "[189] The USES's staunch lobby group, the ICESA, was incensed by the report. It urged the preparation of a detailed response, and the orchestration of a pro-USES "national public relations campaign publicizing the accomplishments and purposes of the state agencies in employer service."[190] In an internal summary of the report (with Manpower Administration comments attached) the Labor Department challenged many of the Urban Coalition's claims. In response to the ES's alleged inability to assist the disadvantaged, the Department noted that "in FY 1970, those applicants who met the poverty and other criteria of disadvantaged were 16.5 percent of all ES applicants, but they received 51.6 percent of the counseling interviews, and 20.9 percent of the nonagricultural placements."[191] Efforts by Sarah Carey to arrange regular meetings between representatives of minority and disadvantaged groups and USES officials were rebuffed.[192]

Since the MDTA program was thought to be demand-driven—that is, training should be designed for known job vacancies—it made sense administratively to charge the employment security offices and Department of Labor, who were responsible for compiling labor market trends data, with its administration. Such an approach seemed ideal for the state employment agencies which, as noted elsewhere, identified themselves as

serving employers' needs. Employers also saw ES offices as the principal medium through which their cooperation in MDTA training programs
should occur. This strategy increased the likelihood of the "creaming off"
of those job seekers least difficult to place since the U.S. Employment
Service wanted to supply employable applicants for employers, their constituency. The implementation of training through the employment service was superimposed upon that system's pre-existing structures and
administrative routines which were biased toward serving employers and
assisting those seeking employment with the fewest fetters to obtaining
work. It limited the programs' capacity to serve the needs of those who
had found it hardest to enter the labor market. These included growing
numbers of black Americans now resident in the Northeast and Midwest
having left the South after 1945. Manpower specialists and economists
within the Department of Labor drafting MDTA understandably looked
to existing institutional and organizational arrangements as implementing agencies. This approach explained the USES's prominent role since,
together with the vocational education system, it offered a national network of delivery agencies theoretically effectively integrated into local
labor markets and skilled in assessing applicants for training courses and
in placing job seekers. Unfortunately, such a picture neglected the internal routines which had produced a pitiful placement record, the discriminatory treatment of black job seekers, and a lack of interest in those
applicants in need of basic skills.

These problems were reflected in the attitudes and behavior of ES staff.
The administrative bias toward compensation work unsurprisingly fostered a parallel bias among employees in the state offices. By the 1970s,
this was exacerbated by the small number of minority staff members.
Appointments were political in two senses. First, ES office appointments
were under the jurisdiction not of federal but state civil service laws,
which varied significantly and in some states were distributed by patronage. The low salaries furthermore discouraged innovative or creative
approaches to work. Second, because some state administrators are political appointments made by governors, the career civil servants, because
of accumulated knowledge and experience, tend to have a greater influence in the ES's routine decision-making and administration. The 1971
National Urban Coalition quoted a former Secretary of Labor and Industry
in Pennsylvania to demonstrate how embedded these patterns were throughout the states and in Washington:

> Of the 4,401 BES [Bureau of Employment Security] employees, 1,800
> or 40% are over 50. Ninety-six are over 65; by contrast, only 765 BES
> employees, or 17% are under 30. Within the BES, there's a red team
> (GOP) and a blue team (Democrat). When there's a change of admin-

istration in Washington, the reds supplant the blues as kingpins in the BES, or vice versa. But each protects the other so that few get hurt and nothing ever changes very much.[193]

Altering the behavior of ES staff had, thus, proved extraordinarily difficult. Finally, the ES lacked an obvious constituency. The disadvantaged job seekers whose needs it disproportionately served were weakly placed politically while the Service had become marginal to skilled and professional workers for whom it was increasingly supplemented by private employment agencies.[194] The advisory committees created under the terms of the Wagner-Peyser Act were innocuous and ineffective, and their only significant constituency was employers.

Work-welfare programs which set out positively to integrate welfare benefits with training programs, such as WIN and food stamps, require a local-level agency administratively capable of both providing the training requisite for labor market entry and for placing trainees when they are ready to assume paid employment. Regrettably, the ES lacked the ability to satisfy these requirements despite its apparently ideally located national network of local offices. Its officers were inappropriately trained, ill-disposed toward assuming additional responsibilities, and thought it unlikely that they would be dismissed for inaction. Finally, the ES's overwhelming focus was on private sector placements where the positions open to recently trained disadvantaged workers remained dead-end or short-term. By the early 1970s, several observers believed that amelioration of labor market opportunities for welfare recipients depended on public-sector job creation schemes. This strategy led logically to the Comprehensive Employment and Training Act's (CETA) public service employment program.

The ES's record did not improve. In 1977 the General Accounting Office (GAO) prepared a critical study of the USES for Congress. It rehearsed familiar failings. The report's authors argued that the USES succeeded in serving only a small part of the labor market—concentrated on the low end of the pay scale since most job seekers used private employment agencies: "We believe ES needs to upgrade the types of jobs that it can offer its applicants and seek a wider range of jobs to better meet the needs of a larger number of its applicants."[195] The GAO urged the Secretary of Labor to establish improved performance indicators since the existing measures overstated ES success rates: "Improvements are needed in data accuracy to ensure that (1) management decisions are based on reliable data and (2) funds are allocated to the States on an equitable basis."[196] The GAO recommended adopting more efficient information systems to match job seekers with openings, though the analysts were skeptical about the importance of computerization in this process:

Using computerized job matching does not guarantee that all possible referrals will be made. We selected 24 jobs which the Salt Lake City office had not filled. Each job had been open for at least 5 days. With the help of office personnel, we used the computer to match available applicants to the jobs. Twenty-nine qualified applicants were available for 9 of the 24 job openings. The Salt Lake City office had referred only one person to one of the nine jobs.[197]

The GAO report was critical also of USES's work in the administration of work-tests. Most states make registration by claimants with the ES a condition of receiving benefits. The ES offices' placement rate was strikingly low:

In fiscal year 1975, ES found jobs for only 8.5 percent of the total claimants registered. The relatively low success rate is evidenced by the fact that they comprised 35 percent of the total number of applicants, yet accounted for only 18 percent of the persons placed in jobs. In addition, only about 1 percent of the registered claimants lost benefits for failure to comply with the work test.[198]

In many cases, the pay for listed openings was so low that the positions could not serve as work-tests. The ES often had difficulty in determining whether a claimant had bothered to appear for a particular job interview.

These recommendations were made known to the Department of Labor, which agreed to pursue most of them, but took umbrage at parts of the report. It agreed yet again that the ES's role needed to be defined lucidly and claimed that the state agencies' labor market placement record was better than the GAO's calculation:

ES internal studies suggest that the overall ES penetration rate over the past decade has been approximately 15 percent. . . . On the other hand, most ES applicants are *unemployed* workers at the time of registering for ES services—95 percent are in this category. If we look only at jobs filled by unemployed workers, rather than all job openings filled, ES placements appear to represent an average of about 38 percent of all new hires of jobless workers in the decade from 1965-75.[199]

The Interstate Conference of Employment State Agencies (ICESA) acted as a lobby group in behalf of ES employees. This powerful pressure group provided the USES with vital political support. It was determined to ensure that the state employment agencies surrendered no power or financial independence while continuing to satisfy employers' needs. As a lobby group, it was remarkably well-placed to influence policy: it was housed in the Department of Labor in Washington, its members paid at federal civil service rates, and its operations financed from the payroll tax trust fund. The ICESA has been treated as a representative of outside views despite its location within the Department of Labor and the receipt of public funding. In the National Urban Coalition's judgment, the organization was little more than a protector of the, often reactionary, interests of state employment agencies:

> The main policy goal of the ICESA has been to retain as much power as possible in the hands of the states, without diluting the flow of federal manpower funds. It has been a staunch supporter of the universal service concept, resisting federal efforts to direct ES resources primarily towards the disadvantaged. In addition, it has directly and indirectly insisted that the ES must meet the needs of employers at least as much as it tries to help job seekers . . . [which has placed] . . . the Conference in direct opposition to many of the DOL and OEO efforts to meet the nation's massive problems of unemployment and underemployment; it explains, in part, why much of the fine-sounding rhetoric of the Manpower Administration has not penetrated far outside of Washington.[200]

The ICESA was instrumental in the postwar efforts to ensure that the USES was returned to the states' control and the federal role minimized, and its members had forged close links with members of Congress on the crucial committees. Instead of acting as a federally funded agency intended to ensure good communication between the Department of Labor and the state ES offices, the ICESA was wholly biased toward the latter. It was a permanently based organization within the DOL capable of capriciously subverting DOL reforms such as those associated with manpower policy. Evidence of the ICESA's influence is provided by its success in ensuring that a bill to increase the power of the Department of Labor over the Employment Service, based on Task Force proposals, failed in 1966.[201] Within the Congress, the only serious opponents of the MDTA initiative were Republican conservatives and some Southerners, the same groups who defended ardently existing USES institutional practices and its placement record. Yet it is remarkable how little resistance there was to this training program, since it constituted such a substantial expansion in the federal government's role. Both the Democrats and Republicans supported new training proposals from the end of the 1950s and voting for the MDTA was high among members of both parties.

The speed with which Secretary Goldberg and President Kennedy responded to growing unemployment early in the 1960s suggests how any proposal focused on this major problem was likely to garner wide cross-party support from elected politicians. By the same token, the fragility and instability of support for such proposals, once politicians perceive them as less important to voters, is also revealed.[202]

Although employers were cited regularly by the USES as their crucial constituency—in the sense that they provided the key commodity, jobs, which the employment service needed—many employers hired directly rather than notifying positions to local employment service offices. A report prepared by an employers' committee established by the Department of Labor in 1972 listed several reasons for employers low use of local offices: the Service's poor reputation and a lack of qualified job seekers among them.[203] Employers sought better personnel service in ES offices and preparation for a wider range of positions than many offices catered to. Assistant Secretary Malcolm Lovell attempted to implement these reforms by improving ES communications with employers, ES personnel standards, and by giving increased emphasis on skilled applicants.

The history of training in the United States became entangled with two perceptions, both detrimental to an active federal role. First, the MDTA initiatives had become transformed by the late 1970s into the Comprehensive Employment and Training Act (CETA), a public-service job creation program widely criticized for favoring those able to find jobs themselves. Mirroring British experience, the pressure of high unemployment during the 1970s required federal action which emphasized short-term job creation rather than longer-term training programs.[204] Employer organizations adamantly opposed training schemes and found ready support among conservative Republicans, electorally well placed after 1980. Second, both MDTA and CETA were accused of "creaming off" the most easily employed or trained clients, neglecting the needs of the hardest to train or place.[205] Training programs were dictated by employers' needs and by community-based schemes vitiated by internecine conflicts between competing agencies, including the Employment Service.

These last criticisms dovetailed with the growing consensus that federal government programs were intrinsically inefficient. This assessment was routinely applied by the end of the 1970s, despite flimsy empirical evidence, and damaged the Democrats after the Carter presidency while benefiting the Reagan Republicans. Symbolically, the term "welfare dependency" was commonly used by them to encapsulate all that was apparently most malign about federal programs. It was not coincidental that the public increasingly thought dependents to be predominantly black.

These developments were anticipated in the 1971 National Urban Coalition study:

> The work requirement is conceptually sound; many of the individuals now trapped on welfare are anxious to assume a productive role in the

society. However, without substantial job creation measures, it will not
work. Further, it is unrealistic to expect the achievement of that goal
via the ES as it is presently constituted. The performance of the ES
under WIN makes it clear that enlarging its role under FAP and the Food
Stamp program—where it would be dealing with similar clients—would
be a great disservice to those who expect substantial economies by moving large numbers of people off the welfare rolls into productive jobs.
More importantly, it could have tragic consequences for the welfare
recipients themselves. ES administration of the work requirement cannot lead to meaningful employment or lasting independence from welfare. It is more likely to mean interrupted, poorly delivered services with
a job previously characterized as "unfillable" at the end of the road. This
could transform the work requirement provision into an uneconomical
measure, creating a cheap pool of forced labor, but not rehabilitating
the economically deprived.[206]

This statement is a prescient account of how work-welfare programs developed in the United States after 1980. It informed the report's recommendation that "the manpower services in connection with the work
requirement provisions of the proposed welfare reform should not be
assigned to the Employment Service."[207] Unfortunately, when the Family
Support Act of 1988 mandated work-welfare throughout the fifty states,
it directed that its JOBS program be administered by state welfare departments in coordination with labor departments and, specifically, ES offices.
The National Urban Coalition study recommended dividing the ES's work
into two branches, one concerned with data collection and labor market
information work, the other with the sort of work necessary to foster
employability skills among job seekers. The new service should, it argued,
be federalized.

The USES's record as a placement agency remained problematic. Its
role was newly defined in Title VI of the Job Training Partnership Act
1982[208] amended in 1988. USES was from 1969 part of the Employment
and Training Administration (ETA) within the Department of Labor, overseeing 25,000 state employment security agency employees and 1,800
local offices. State employment security agencies' placement record of
nonagricultural positions continued to fall in the 1970s to 4 percent in
1987, while the ratio of placement arrangements to new hires fell to 7
percent.[209] Experts were still exercised by the confusion of aims assigned
to the Employment Service. These tasks included: providing special services to groups such as the disadvantaged or veterans; collecting labor
market information; and the traditional work checks on unemployment
insurance claimants.

During the 1970s and 1980s, two significant administrative reforms
affected the USES and three efforts were made to improve its perfor-

mance in placement. The first reform was under President Nixon, whose Secretary of Labor George Schultz changed the funding formula to the states to reward placement performance. The Service's record did not improve greatly. The penetration rate has failed to rise above 7 percent, which can be contrasted with 25 to 30 percent in Britain. The second reform was undertaken by President Reagan who, consistent with his New Federalism program, devolved the USES even more to the states. The USES was made into a special-purpose block grant, federal regulations were revised,[210] weakening the earlier funding changes based on placement performance. At present, one-third of the appropriation is based on each state's relative share of unemployment and the remaining two-thirds on each state's share of population, amendments which abrogated the emphasis on placement. Federal oversight of the state employment agency offices has been reduced: federally specified requirements for labor market trends were reduced and decisions about the priorities of each state's ES were devolved to governors (on the assumption that they would know best their states' needs). The block-grant system eroded the Secretary of Labor's capacity to monitor the system, with his/her powers limited to disapproving an individual state's ES plan.

Efforts to improve the USES's performance have taken three forms. First, Reagan's Secretary of Labor Bill Brock attempted to expand the ES's work in contributing to the U.S. workforce's skills level. He tried to encourage the governors to reform their employment service offices, holding public hearings throughout the United States to elicit proposals for, and reactions to, reform of the ES, and invited formal statements through a notice in the *Federal Register*. Predictably, the public hearings became forums through which those opposed to change could articulate their views, and such opposition could be mobilized on a statewide basis as indeed occurred. A letter-writing campaign was also orchestrated by state-based opponents of the reform and the final legislative proposals were speedily emasculated in Congress.

A second effort was made by Brock's successor, Mrs. McLaughlin, who channeled her reform efforts into administrative initiatives rather than seeking to enact legislation through Congress. The new secretary promulgated "innovative exchange seminars" through which states could learn about others' successes.[211] Some of the best states—Pennsylvania and New York were often cited—had succeeded in combining ES placement and training functions.

Finally, President Bush's first Secretary of Labor, Elizabeth Dole, assumed her office with an ill-hidden antagonism toward the USES's record, which she blamed in part upon ineffectual gubernatorial control. She observed: "I know few areas of government that have shifted missions more frequently than ES, but I am convinced that right now the

American people are not getting enough of a return on the almost $800 million in employer taxes invested in ES each year."[212] She attempted congressional reform and wrote to 200 people throughout the country eliciting suggestions.[213] A response to this approach was instinctively orchestrated by ES supporters who sang the Service's praises. The response from employers mobilized through the Employers' (National) Job Service Committee,[214] however, was almost universally critical and endorsed change. Dole's tenure at the Department of Labor was too short to effect legislative reform, but she prodded states toward formally integrating placement and training services.

Conclusion

The formulation of national manpower planning required the American and British governments to reform their respective labor exchange systems. These constituted the most obvious institutional framework with which to implement the new initiatives. The initiatives were a crucial episode in the history of each country's work-welfare since they signaled an attempt to break with extant programs and approaches. To make this change, work-oriented programs had to be superseded by training-oriented ones. In each case, the attempt to create institutional foundations for successful training systems failed. Schemes that were enacted to deal with those suffering short-term unemployment were transformed into measures primarily for citizens with little or no labor market experience. The initiatives to effect this transformation were imposed upon a set of administrative arrangements which, as the last chapter demonstrated, institutionalized distinctions between types of job seekers and concentrated on assessing willingness to work.

The failure of these reform initiatives, however, arose not only from the strength of existing institutional routines in work-welfare programs but also from the tenuous nature of the political coalition promoting reform. This thesis holds for both Britain and the United States, though the political coalitions differed in each country.

The 1945 Labour government was defeated in 1951 and succeeded by thirteen years of Conservative administrations and high employment. The Tories lacked any motive to reform the apprenticeship-based training framework which allowed a minimal state role.[215] Government Training Centers were run down in the 1950s.[216] Labour's electoral majority in the periods of both 1964 to 1966 and 1974 to 1979 was weak, and both administrations were engaged in constant economic management driven by short-term crises in sterling's value and balance of payments—as was the 1966 to 1970 one which found itself forced to devalue. Labour inherited a voluntarist state approach to training, modified only marginally in the last months of the Conservatives' administration when the Industrial

Training Act was passed. The 1964 initiative failed to disturb significantly prevailing attitudes toward, and institutional arrangements (dominated by apprenticeships) for, training: those seeking jobs and training outside of this framework remained frustrated and marginalized. Neither the main employer (FBI until 1965, then the CBI) nor union (TUC) organizations was especially keen on such initiatives, the latter wanting to maximize job control and wage increases through a highly devolved system, the former resistant to increased government activity in the labor market. The Labour Party's close relationship with the union movement included respecting separate areas of responsibility, such as training.[217] This made initiatives on training by the party rather difficult. It was only with the establishment of the Manpower Services Commission (MSC) in 1973 that the displacement of existing approaches was possible. This, however, failed to occur as the MSC was appropriated by the government to tackle mounting unemployment after the 1973–74 oil crisis. From 1979 on, government policy toward training was based on expediency and short-term political calculation dictated by the problem of unemployment. Policy was molded to create a training program consistent with the Conservatives' New Right neo-liberalism, which entailed integrating it with social security schemes and minimizing program costs. This process was more mechanical and deliberate after 1987, but the rationale predated the Tories' third electoral success. The trades unions which supported the establishment of the MSC in 1973 were principally concerned with industrial relations legislation. Unfortunately, as the unemployment crises of 1974–75 and post-1980 increased the prominence of the commission, so the political power of organized labor declined. Employers' associations, like unionists, were content with the industrial training board regime and any fears that held about the MSC's formulation of comprehensive training programs were quickly allayed after 1975.

In the United States, the electoral coalition underpinning efforts to broaden work-welfare remained essentially the New Deal coalition. The Great Society and War on Poverty programs proved to be this coalition's final gasps. One significant element of the coalition had changed by the 1960s: the civil rights movement, demanding desegregation and equality of opportunity, signaled a fundamental political realignment in American politics. President Johnson was sufficiently adroit to contain this pressure, but conflicts between black Americans' organizations such as the NAACP and sections of organized labor over discrimination in apprenticeships demonstrated the electoral coalition's fragility. Within Congress, the power of Southern Democrats and conservative Republicans was significant throughout the 1960s, and in work-welfare, these members continued to support the ICESA's defense of the USES despite exposure of the latter's failings. This support provided the political underpinning sustaining the extant institutional arrangements of United States' work-welfare. Business associations welcomed the drive to increase skills, as did labor, but rapidly withdrew support as the program focused principally on unemployed persons most marginal to the labor market. The shift to micro-Keynesian policy began with the Manpower Development and Training Act of 1962,[218] the United States government's first major policy with implications for training policy. Federal training was subsumed under the Johnson administration's Great Society initiative and harnessed to address the needs of the profoundly disadvantaged job seekers, including many such persons who had no experience of participation in the labor market (categories B and C)[219] and who lived in a society which judged such nonperformers harshly morally and provided them with little assistance. As Margaret Weir notes, "by the end of the late 1960s, labor market policies had become politically identified as income maintenance policies not much different from welfare . . . The poverty policies of the 1960s incorporated two decisions about the proper focus of labor market policies: such policies should be remedial measures targeted on the lowest end of the labor market, and they should aim to alter the supply of labor by modifying workers' characteristics rather than seeking to change the demand for labor."[220] This led eventually to the work-welfare schemes associated with the JOBS program of the Family Support Act of 1988 (analyzed in chapter 5),[221] through the Comprehensive Employment and Training Act (CETA) of 1973 and the Job Training Partnership Act (JTPA) of 1982. Each of these assigned a central role to the employment service.

In both Britain and the United States, economic policy was separated from labor market policy. Welfare policy was influenced profoundly by the distinction between contributory and noncontributory programs. This distinction was institutionalized through each polity's public employment system. In the United States, the potential effect of the Employment Act of 1946 was significantly diluted during its passage through Congress. It moved from a full-blooded Keynesian commitment to full employment to a more anodyne responsibility for pursuing employment programs. In Margaret Weir's judgment, this diminution of the act's purposes masked a "quite distinct vision of the goals and conducts of economic policy. At the heart of the new conception was a much weaker public role than that envisioned by the New Deal's social Keynesians. . . . Keynesianism was refashioned in ways that severed economic goals from social welfare provision and sharply curbed the authoritative role of the federal executive."[222] According to Gary Mucciaroni, the weakening of the 1946 legislation arose from "deep-seated antistatist beliefs, which take it for granted that the private sector is naturally superior to the public."[223] This severance of work-welfare (and labor market) from economic policy was

a crucial break. It precluded the integration of policy achieved in countries which established Keynesian employment welfare states. The severance of work-welfare from employment policy in federal programs did
not, however, preclude policy overlap. In the United States, labor market policy remained both underdeveloped and tarnished by the institutional limitations of the 1935 Social Security Act's distinction between
contributory and noncontributory programs and the restriction of
Employment Act macroeconomic policy instead of detailed and fully funded labor market programs. When, during the 1960s, more ambitious labor
market policies were attempted, they were distorted by the pressures of
poverty and welfare. The priority of alleviating poverty subsumed that of
establishing an effective training policy, a process reinforced by the inadequacies and obstructionism of the Employment Service. These problems
were exacerbated by the vertical division of powers of federalism and the
difficulty of constructing a political coalition sufficiently robust and coherent to ensure that labor market policy had a remit wider than simply the
poor and unemployed. The federal programs of the 1960s were also subject to major racial distortions: they maintained the tradition of the 1935
act, which excluded from contributory programs those occupations disproportionately held by black Americans. This forged the link between
race and welfare programs that became a commonplace in American political discourse. In Mucciaroni's words, the "policy choices made in the
period from 1945 to 1965 imposed a set of constraints on the federal government's response to unemployment."[224] The power of these constraints
in the 1980s is demonstrated in the next chapter.

In Britain, although the 1944 White Paper produced a governmental
commitment to full employment, this was pursued only through macroeconomic measures. Training was neglected and left to the (limited) initiatives of employers and trades unionists: it was not linked to Keynesian
macroeconomic measures. As in the United States, this propensity was
reinforced by a distinction between contributory and noncontributory welfare programs and by the employment exchanges' concentration on benefits.

In both Britain and the United States, the absence (or weakness in
Britain's case) of left-wing political parties or other social groups advocating labor market policies is an important factor. For instance, in his
comparative study of the United States and West Germany, Janoski
acknowledges the importance of institutional legacies but combines this
with consideration of the role of social groups and political parties in
seeking labor market initiatives. In West Germany, leftist political party
support for these programs was strong, a source of support only ever
weakly articulated in the United States or Britain. Janoski concludes that
"although both social demands and state formation are prominent factors

in explaining active labor market policy in each country, the German case more clearly emphasizes the positive force of social demands, while the American case emphasizes the negative impact of state formation."[225] Janoski contrasts the success of the West German Ministry of Labor in promoting Keynesian employment policies with the weakness of the U.S. Department of Labor. Neither did German policymakers have to contend with a Congress often hostile to an expanded federal role, a hostility especially strong in the Southern states. I have explained above how the British Manpower Services Commission confronted significant difficulties in persuading government ministers to implement European-style labor market programs. These difficulties were never overcome, lost initially in the post-1975 priority of tackling unemployment (which ended also the Labour Party's belated concern about training) and subsequently in the Tories' hostility to government intervention in the labor market. This hostility did not prevent intervention, but it did influence the character of that intervention in a negative way. Trades unionists only weakly advocated labor market initiative in both countries.

The failure of these labor market reforms sets the context for modern work-welfare programs. It is not difficult to see how the collapse of these attempts to build social democratic training programs and the policy responses to unemployment, especially in Britain, facilitated a transition to the harsher work-welfare of the 1980s, the subject of chapter 5. Failure did not signal the death of the labor exchange systems in either Britain or the United States. In Britain, the Conservatives's harsher work-welfare of the 1980s was based, in part, upon reforms to the training and placement system of the 1960s and 1970s. In the United States, the passage of the Job Training Partnership Act (JTPA) in 1982 led to amendments to the 1933 Wagner-Peyser Act regulating the USES.[226]

The Conservatives reverted to the familiar integration of placement and benefit activities, with predictable consequences for the former activity. This is a major reversal of policy since the separation of placement and benefit activities was effectively accomplished. Jobcentres were opened in prominent high street locations in new purpose-built premises. Their mission to place and not to administer benefits was unequivocally institutionalized. Circumstances proved unfavorable to this change and political support for the new system insufficient: high unemployment, an MSC unable to pursue its labor market policy ambitions, declining numbers of union members, and a government influenced by New Right ideas of work-welfare combined to force Jobcentres into an all too familiar role combining placement and benefit responsibilities. A different administration—controlled by Labour—would not have done this; nor, however, would it have been able financially or politically to support the MSC sufficiently to establish an extensive training policy regime.

The programmatic dominance of apprenticeships in post-1945 training policy (and the failure to broaden them into nonindustrial sectors) has resulted in the failure satisfactorily to develop skills' and qualifications' systems for un- or semi-skilled workers and job seekers and for older workers made redundant or possessing outdated skills. Post-1960s training programs in Britain and the United States have been harnessed to the needs of the chronically *unemployed*—a group which, in many cases, includes individuals with no work experience and for whom training often assumes elementary forms.[227] This second characteristic has also ensured that funding is unstable and vulnerable to reduction whenever it is politically expedient.

Breaking the "Spider's Web of Dependency": The Pyrrhic Triumph of Modern Work-Welfare

S peaking in Parliament during the passage of the Social Security Bill of 1989, the then-Minister for Social Security, Nicholas Scott provided a succinct characterization of modern work-welfare programs in Britain and the United States. He argued that the "state . . . has the task of advising and guiding people towards available job opportunities. But surely the unemployed person has a *duty,* as his part of *the contract,* not to sit passively waiting for a job to turn up but *to take active steps to seek work.*"[1] The programs analyzed in this chapter have, at their core, the assumptions that work-welfare beneficiaries have an insufficiently developed sense of their duty to the rest of society.

Unemployment has paralleled the development of capitalist society. The salient problem—the concentration of masses of unemployed unskilled and semiskilled workers—of the late nineteenth century and interwar years which prompted the foundation of labor exchanges in Britain and the United States has become a differently defined, but not a substantially different problem. Large numbers of unemployed persons, in many cases bereft of skills, continue to present needs. If organized collectively, or in combination with those workers in employment, their political strength would be considerable. In the United States, it was principally "welfare dependency" and its links with unemployment which concentrated the minds of legislators and policymakers during the 1980s. In Britain the national problem during the 1980s was unemployment with welfare issues of secondary, though growing, importance.

In this chapter I analyze the evolution, under the impetus of New Right ideas, of work-welfare programs in the United States and Britain since the late 1970s. These schemes constitute a reversion to the basic principles of liberal work-welfare identified in chapter 1. They emphasize excluding the undeserving, stressing with equal vigor the duties and the rights of citizenship and the linkage of the receipt of benefits with work or training activities. They signal the demise of efforts to broaden work-welfare, efforts which, certainly in Britain, and to a lesser extent in America, were the basis for work-welfare programs embarked upon during the 1960s, albeit hesitantly and incompletely. In the United States, participants in these schemes were increasingly identified as welfare recipients, often black and often mothers, unattached to a traditional family structure and devoid of labor market experience—my category C. The new programs demonstrate the resilience of the core institutional and ideological elements of British and American work-welfare policies. Although the training and work elements of modern work-welfare programs are represented as contributions to developing the skills of these two countries' workforces, I contend that for the most part any such effect is marginal and not the measures' principal aim. Their implementation had implications for the labor exchange networks in both countries since the integration of training/work requirements with the receipt of benefit required some formal administrative connections. In Britain, benefits and placement work have been reintegrated (abrogating the brief experiment with separation) and the new offices administer work-tests. In the United States, state employment agencies assess applicants for counseling and training programs.

The legislation on which I focus are Title II of the Family Support Act of 1988 in the United States and, in Britain, the December 1988 Employment and Training Programme (ET) combined with complementary amendments to the social security law (Social Security Acts of 1988 and 1989) and employment law (Employment Act 1989).

Central to an explanation of the adoption of these programs is the political and electoral weakness of the groups, marginal to the labor force, governed by British and American work-welfare programs.[2] They equate with the unemployed categories B and C specified in chapter 1 (the long-term unemployed with little work experience and welfare recipients with no work experience). Conversely, political parties and politicians promoting neoliberal schemes enjoyed an expanding electoral base from the late 1970s onwards in both countries. Neoliberal politicians adopted critiques of welfare programs which stressed the deficiencies of individual recipients and dismissed explanations based on social structural (such as the American racial and class system) or economic (such as Britain's diminishing manufacturing employment base) factors. In the United States, an important source of ideas for work-welfare came from state programs established after 1981. These schemes ranged from training-oriented to work-oriented ones. When federal legislation was enacted in 1988, it was the latter influence which prevailed. One important reason for this outcome is the fragmentation of power in the federal system which forces legislators to compromise to succeed: avoiding a presidential veto in 1988 necessitated the inclusion of a punitive work-oriented provision.

In Britain, the centralized state enabled the Conservatives more easily to manipulate institutions such as the Manpower Services Commission (MSC) and Jobcentre network to their own ends. Even here, however, politicians were forced to proceed toward the integration of benefits and work gradually because of some resistance within the MSC and of trade union hostility to mandatory work-welfare. That the Tories could not act as quickly as they wished is illustrated by the difference between MSC and Department of Employment training proposals in the early 1980s when the latter, mirroring the Government, urged a speedy shift to a program in which the allowance paid to those on training schemes would be lower than those paid to young people participating in the Youth Opportunities Program.[3] Following electoral success in 1983 and 1987, the Conservatives were far more strongly placed to impose their own ends on work-welfare and to undermine the MSC, eventually abolishing it. Electoral success and legislation also diluted the capacity of the TUC to oppose the abolition of any lingering impediments to establishing work-welfare.[4]

The chapter begins with a specification of the new programs and their conception of liberal citizenship. I then explain how these measures were designed to enshrine market-based values and identify the administrative framework for their implementation. I explain how political opposition to these programs was ignored.

Work-Welfare and the Duties of Citizenship

The formulation and enactment of work-welfare programs in Britain and the United States under the Thatcher and Reagan administrations respectively are triumphs for New Right ideas.[5] In both cases, these programs represent a reversion to liberal principles and an abandoning of social democratic pretensions. In Britain, they confirm the weakening of labor interests as an influence on policy decisions, and in both countries they demonstrate the evident electoral and political weakness of unemployed groups in categories B and C, even when growing unemployment expands the size of each group. Such outcomes derive, in part, from the success of New Right advocates in influencing politicians making policy and the electoral success of right-wing parties. In the United States, the ideas for reform came from the "demonstration" work-welfare programs implemented by the states, publicized through congressional committee hearings and policy evaluation studies. These ideas were reconciled with the less liberal views promoted by the White House, to the latter's favor. In Britain the Thatcher administration drew on the proposals advanced by New Right pressure groups and also imitated American programs. The extent of this imitation is suggested by the presence of Cay Stratton, former assistant secretary of economic affairs for employment and training in Massachusetts, in the Department of Employment in London. Stratton designed the British ET program, which integrates the receipt of benefits and training.

Both the conservative critique of British welfare programs and the neoliberal workfare alternative were promoted by New Right interest groups, such as the Social Affairs Unit established in 1981, and in the publications of the Institute of Economic Affairs.[6] By lobbying the prime minister's Downing Street Policy Unit, New Right interest groups were able to promote their radical proposals for work-welfare, particularly a weakening of the benefit entitlement system. Their influence continued after Mrs. Thatcher's loss of power in November 1990. The Conservatives were eager to hear these proposals both because of their ideological appeal and because of their need of ideas for legislation. Expanding public finances also made politicians enthusiastic about ideas for cutting welfare commitments.

The Conservatives sought to reverse the distinction, drawn in the 1944 White Paper,[7] between being unemployed and on a training course and to stress the individual over collectives, such as trades unions, in the labor market. This aim attained its most detailed expression in the Employment Training (ET) Programme launched by the Department of Employment in 1988. It combined existing training programs of the Manpower Services Commission (MSC) and targeted the long-term unemployed, both young adults (over twenty-five years of age), many of whom had never worked, and redundant middle-aged workers. Participants were to attend twelve-month training courses upon completion of which they were to enter work. ET advantaged employers and limited unions in the formulation and administration of the British training regime. Both these maneuvers were the product of almost ten years of Conservative intervention in the labor market, including trade union legislation.[8] They were not outcomes accomplished automatically.

ET was fostered by changes in the social security rules in Acts passed in 1985, 1986, 1988, and 1989, themselves complemented by changes in the Employment Act of 1989.[9] The amendments retain the basic distinction between contributory based benefits[10] (paid for fifty-two weeks and requiring an additional thirteen weeks to requalify) and means-tested noncontributory income support (previously called supplementary benefits[11]) consolidated in the postwar Labour administration.[12] Under income support, claimants receive a basic rate of benefit to meet regular weekly needs with premiums added for families, single parents, pensioners, the long-term sick, and those with disabilities.[13] This change complements those measures requiring participation in the Youth Training (YT) program and disqualifying from unemployment benefits for six months those persons leaving a job voluntarily. The benefit system aims to distinguish between deserving and undeserving applicants, a notoriously difficult exercise. From April 1996 onwards, further changes become operative. First, citizens receiving benefits will enter a contract under which they agree to a personal work plan as a condition of the payment. Second, a new "job-seeker's allowance" will combine the extant unemployment benefit and income-support payments, administering it on a contributory basis for six months; after six months, payment will be means-tested.

The receipt of these benefits is more strictly policed.[14] Claimants for unemployment benefits must provide proof of involuntary unemployment, demonstrate availability for work, must not refuse to take a suitable job opening, and must not have lost their job through misconduct. Since 1986, those unemployed for more than six months are called to Restart interviews at Jobcentres, at which they must demonstrate their availability for work.[15] From autumn of 1990 onwards, Restart courses became compulsory for claimants who have either been unemployed for two years or rejected offers of help at their Restart interview.[16] The Social Security Act of 1989 requires unemployed persons to provide evidence at their Restart interviews that they are "seeking employment actively," a return to the "genuinely seeking work" policy of the 1920s, by producing evidence such as letters or records of telephone calls.[17] The most draconian clause in the Social Security Bill, which became the Social Security Act of 1989, was abandoned by the government during the bill's passage through Parliament. This clause proposed denying unemployed people their benefits if they turned down a job of less than twenty-four hours a week. In November 1991, the government also dropped a proposed rule disqualifying people from claiming unemployment benefit if they declined a job of only sixteen hours a week.

The Social Security Act of 1985 empowered the Employment Secretary to designate training programs "approved training schemes." Under the act, trainees who refuse a reasonable offer of a place on an approved scheme can have their entitlement to social security benefits reduced for six months. Despite the government's denials, the linkage of training and benefits has moved in a work-welfare direction. During the Committee Stage of the 1987 Social Security Bill, then Under Secretary of State for Health and Social Security Michael Portillo argued:

> I entirely rebut the . . . repeated allegation about compulsion. It is true that we are withdrawing income support from 16 and 17-year-olds who have left school, are not in work and have not taken up a YTS place, but the choices for young people are still there. They can stay at school. They can go to college. They can, if they are lucky, take a job. Or they can take the YTS place that is on offer to them. I persist in saying, therefore, that there is no compulsion. We are talking about the guaranteed option of a place on a YTS and the response of the Government and the taxpayer to that new situation.[18]

For young people, the Social Security Act of 1988 makes participation

in Youth Training Schemes virtually compulsory since refusal to participate or leaving a scheme without good cause can result in the loss of
benefits. Norman Fowler, employment secretary at the time, ended the
entitlement to supplementary benefits for 16- to 18-year-olds who have
been guaranteed a YTS place. Part II of the Employment Act of 1988 dis-
qualifies from receipt of benefits persons withdrawing from training
schemes without good cause. The new "job-seeker's allowance," in place
after April 1996, will also tighten assessment of benefit entitlement.
Recipients of payments will agree to a "job-seeker's agreement," in
exchange for accepting benefits, in which they will be required to outline the measures they plan to take to find work—a quasi-contractual
commitment.

To test for "availability for work" among those receiving benefits,
placement and benefit work have been reintegrated. The job counseling
work of Jobcentres can be directly combined, as occurred historically,
with the policing function of Unemployment Benefit Offices.[19] To this
end, a framework, based on the Social Security Act of 1989, which introduced new rules for claimants, including the actively seeking work clause,
was issued to Employment Service offices advising them on the processing of applications by claimants for benefit. This "New Framework
for Advising Claimants" (see table 5.1) is based on a set of compulsory
interviews linked with Restart Courses. They begin with a claimant's first
application for assistance. "Back to work" plans are a series of steps
agreed between the claimant and his/her interviewer (the New Claimant
Adviser) setting out how the former will look for employment. Failure to
find employment produces the follow-up interviews after thirteen weeks,
and then after twenty-six, fifty-two, and seventy-eight weeks of unem-

Table 5.1 The Employment Service and Advising Claimants

Interview	Projected Numbers	Requirements for Claimants
New Claim	4.00m	Interview; back to work plan
13 Weeks	1.85m	10–15% interviewed; back to work plan
26 Weeks (Restart 1)	0.90m	Main interview; back to work plan
Follow Up Caseload		Re-interview; Update back to work plan
52 Weeks (Restart 2)	0.40m	Main interview; back to work plan
78 Weeks (Restart 3)	0.20m	Main interview; back to work plan
104 Weeks (Restart 4)	0.10m	Intensive help: back to work plan; Restart course; target caseload

Source: "New Framework for Advising Claimants," Employment Service Framework for
Customer Management, Guidance, Claimant Services Branch, Employment Service, NF/90/11,
Annex 1, 1990. See also "The New Framework," *Working Brief* (February 1991).

ployment. After 104 weeks unemployment—the fourth Restart interview—the claimant can be required to attend a one-week Restart Course. Failure to attend this course without good cause results in up to 40 percent of the claimants' assistance being reduced. Intensive help is also made available at this stage to find employment.

At the first meeting, after thirteen weeks of unemployment, the claimant advisers check the return-to-work plans. They identify between 10 and 15 percent of the claimants for interviews. In the summer of 1991, this process was extended to two-thirds of all claimants. Instead of taking the act of signing on for benefit as evidence of availability for work, there is now a system of Active Signing. Under this arrangement, clerks check to see whether claimants have fulfilled the steps agreed in their back-to-work plan and inform claimant advisors accordingly. The advisors then decide whether an additional interview is required. At these interviews, applicants are made aware of Job Seminars (a variant of the Job Club approach) and Job Referral service (to assist claimants in applying directly for work), which may be of use since claimants are not eligible for training programs until they have been unemployed for twenty-six weeks. The record of Restart interviews has been mixed: "The experience of compulsory Restart interviews has shown that the interview program has had little success in placing people into jobs and that a significant minority of claimants have experienced 'creeping compulsion' to participate in schemes or otherwise leave the unemployment register."[20] "Creeping compulsion" is an understandable corollary of high unemployment when governments are eager to control unemployment numbers (those entering training schemes are removed from the unemployment register; and, in addition, over twenty amendments to the measurement of unemployment have been introduced since 1979). However, this strategy becomes more and more problematic if the labor market is contracting. In the summer of 1992, the Employment Service ended the distinction between New Client Advisers and Claimant Advisers responsible for carrying out advisory and Restart interviews.

The Family Support Act was signed into law on 13 October 1988 by President Reagan.[21] Title II of the Family Support Act, the "Jobs Opportunities and Basic Skills Training Program," established in federal law a mandatory reform such that each of the fifty states are required to apply work-welfare programs to welfare recipients.[22] Under the JOBS program, states are required to provide work or training activities, one of which must be undertaken by welfare beneficiaries as a condition of their receiving assistance. The work-welfare principle has been placed firmly at the center of American welfare.

At the conference stage of the bill's enactment, Reagan's representative was adamant that failure to make work and/or training a mandatory component of the legislation would result in a veto.[23] It included the provisions sought by the White House. The act amended Title IV of the Social Security Act of 1935 by introducing a condition for the receipt of benefits. It now requires participation in a work program for all parents. This compulsory clause and the participation rates were included over the objections of the state governors and Congress and at the behest of the White House. The act provides support services for children and parents while the latter are participating in the works program, that is, transition costs, and also strengthens the enforcement of child support payment orders.

After October 1990, each state was required to design and implement a JOBS program which included five services: (1) educational activities to provide high school graduation literacy equivalent and English as a second language[24]; (2) job skills training; (3) job readiness programs; (4) job development and placement services; and (5) child-care and transportation support services. Participants also received medicaid—health insurance—during their first year in work, an advantage over those hundreds of thousands of low-income workers with no health insurance coverage. For the work requirement component, states are compelled to offer two of the following four options: (1) job-search assistance; (2) on-the-job training; (3) work supplementation—under which scheme a recipient's benefits are used by the welfare department to subsidize their employment rather than provided directly to the recipients; or (4) the Community Work Experience Program—CWEP—the scheme originally earning the appellation workfare, and generally consisting of menial community work undertaken by the welfare recipient.[25] The first of these programs—job-search assistance—can consist of little more than a room with newspapers and telephones available to recipients. All four employment tasks are undertaken by state welfare departments in coordination with labor departments and USES state employment agency offices. JOBS is also supposed to be coordinated with the federal government's principal training program, the Job Training and Partnership Act (JTPA).

The new American and British work-welfare programs revive and restore aspects of late nineteenth-century and early twentieth-century programs. Each ascribes a traditional role to some sort of labor exchange mechanism. This reversion is more pronounced in Britain. Labor exchanges administer work-tests, provide assistance in finding work, coordinate places on training programs, and monitor labor market needs. The new programs have a liberal conception of social citizenship, an outcome linked to perceptions of the problem addressed and to the political weakness of those groups governed under them.

The principal advocates of work-welfare reform exploited the language of social obligation and duties in support of their aims. In the House of Lords debate on the Social Security Bill of 1988, Lord Boyd-Carpenter emphasized the work-welfare linkage:

> Nothing could be worse than to give them [young people] encouragement to remain without training, living on public benefits—a pointless existence without any of the ambitions or incentives which they will obtain under the Youth Training Scheme.[26]

The then-Minister for Social Security Nicholas Scott provided the most extensive statement of the language of contract and duties.

> The principle at the heart of the clause is that the State rightly accepts a duty to provide benefits for the unemployed under an insurance scheme; if their unemployment is longer than the insurance period, to provide income support for those without other means; and to provide advice, guidance and encouragement for the unemployed. While it accepts the responsibility, as far as it is compatible with broader economic aims, to create an environment of enterprise and job creation, the State is entitled in return to expect individuals to take the trouble actively to seek work. This is not . . . some monstrous imposition on the unemployed. It is a genuine effort to provide a path from the misery of unemployment towards self-respect and the ability of individuals to provide for themselves and their families.[27]

The same language featured in statements from Senator Patrick Moynihan and the National Governors' Association (NGA) in the United States as the Family Support Act was drafted and enacted. Writing of their reforms, the NGA reported:

> The principal responsibility of government in the welfare contract is to provide education, job training and/or job placement services to all employable recipients . . . The *major obligation of the individual* in the public assistance contracts we propose is to prepare for and seek, accept, and retain a job.[28]

These statements imply that rather than stressing the rights of claimants these reforms underline the obligations and duties of such benefit seekers.

In the United States, the new program has been linked frequently with the problem of the underclass.[29] The Family Support Act was a response both to the regularly invoked perception that welfare dependency, as measured by AFDC rolls, had grown and to the U.S. workforce's poor skills. This response was powerfully mediated by the neoliberal politics of the

1980s and 1990s which focused on the failings of the individual, the alleged generosity of state programs, and rejected structural explanations for welfare dependence.[30] Most of the states[31] defined welfare reform as a problem of overcoming dependency, especially among women recipients, though others stressed the shortages of appropriate skills among workers.[32] Many studies emphasized the particular difficulties for women recipients of welfare to achieve the conditions necessary to facilitate entering the labor market.[33] A report to the governor of Alabama concluded that "the very programs that were designed to assist the poor can sometimes encourage long-term dependency," a popular view politically.[34] The problem of welfare was constructed as one of young unmarried women with children receiving benefits under the AFDC program, originally designed for widows. By the 1970s and 1980s, the work ethic in the United States had been sufficiently transformed so that young women were no longer exempt from labor market participation simply for being mothers.[35] The introduction to Wisconsin's Work Experience and Job Training Program declared that "welfare reform . . . represents a shift in emphasis from reliance on welfare payments to an emphasis on employment programs and opportunities . . . The purpose is to reduce dependency on welfare by removing barriers to greater independence."[36]

According to scholars such as Lawrence Mead, welfare programs have eroded the incentives prerequisite to entering the labor force,[37] and Charles Murray's work focuses on the incentives created by federal welfare programs.[38] In this perspective, amelioration of poverty therefore does not require changes to the social and economic order but to the attitudes of work-welfare dependents. This premise requires altering personal attributes. Mead argues that it is a lack of work effort, rather than low wages, which explains the poor's indigence: "Underclass poverty stems less from the absence of opportunity than from the inability or reluctance to take advantage of opportunity. The plight of the underclass suggests that the competence of many of the poor—their capacity to look after and take care of themselves—can no longer be taken for granted as it could in the past."[39] Mead proposed mandatory work and/or training requirements to foster attitudes and organizational skills among welfare beneficiaries apposite to gainful employment. There is no consensus about this view. Politically, Mead and Murray's view is the more attractive during a period of fiscal austerity and inflated rhetoric about the failings of individual welfare recipients, and many Democrats share this interpretation. The latter contributes to the perception that welfare dependency is a peculiarly African-American problem. Analytically, poverty is not necessarily best approached via racial categories, as Orlanda Patterson and Chris Winship recently warned:

> The problem of the black working poor is simple, and it is identical to that of the growing white poor: they do not earn enough and their low wages are declining as a result of structural economic changes and the heartless policies of the 80's that substantially widened income inequality. . . . By further identifying the black poor with the underclass, we reinforce the myth that poverty is a moral problem that only the poor themselves can solve.[40]

There is some evidence from opinion polls that hostility toward noncontributory means-tested welfare programs is greatest among white Americans, irrespective of class, and that a contributing factor to that opposition is the perception that it is disproportionately consumed by black Americans.[41] Low wage levels ensure that working may not be the most cost-effective strategy for welfare recipients, despite a fall in real terms of the median AFDC benefit between 1970 and 1991 of 42 percent.[42]

Reform and the Liberal Tradition

Modifications to, and discussions about, work-welfare programs have been structured by a cardinal dichotomy between contributory insurance based programs and noncontributory schemes. This dichotomy derives from the founding welfare legislation in each country (1935 in the United States and 1945–51 in Britain), as I outline in this section. Consistent with the origins of public welfare programs, contemporary American and British work-welfare programs have been labor-market driven. It is assumed that all citizens should earn their income either directly through labor market participation or indirectly from membership of a wage-earning household. This second characteristic demonstrates how modern work-welfare programs have reified the gender-biased domestic division of labor prevalent and unchallenged until the late 1960s.[43]

Public opinion in each country has supported these systems. In the United States, support for noncontributory programs was weaker than for contributory pension, health and unemployment schemes. The image of the "able-bodied beneficiary" dominated critiques of welfare programs. In Britain, widespread support for the education, health, disability, and old-age dimensions of the welfare state have always been tempered by an easily aroused fear of the malingerer preferring benefits to work.[44]

Within the framework constituted by work-welfare programs, prevailing public sentiments, and the alleged crisis of the 1980s, the neoliberal Reagan and Thatcher administrations undertook systematic reform. Their respective aims coincided. Both sought to consolidate the link between receiving benefits and discharging a work or training activity and to privilege New Right schemes. New Right arguments restated many of the claims and assumptions which informed, and were institutionalized in, the construction of work-welfare in the early twentieth century.

The post–Second World War Labour administration led by Clement Attlee was committed to implementing a comprehensive welfare system which would expand measures introduced before the war. The basis for these reforms was William Beveridge's report, published in 1942.[45] In 1945, a family allowance scheme was introduced together with national insurance for those injured at work. In 1946, national insurance for the sick, unemployed, widows, orphans and retired, and for maternity were all amended and the National Health Service founded. A national assistance scheme was established in 1948. Together these measures expanded prewar programs to create a universal welfare state in which the distinction between benefits claimed as right and those administered as discretion was weakened but not abrogated. Beveridge himself stressed building a set of programs in which those who had contributed to their provision should receive benefits without any means-testing or stigma, though with some means-tested benefits for those individuals who, through disability or the obligation to care for others, were unable fully to participate in the labor-market-based contributory scheme. Neither family nor insurance benefits was ever set at a rate sufficiently high to erode poverty as Beveridge had envisaged.

A buoyant economy and high employment preserved governments from the political problems posed by unemployment and certainly contrasted with the interwar decades. The insurance system to assist unemployed persons was administered through the social security laws enacted in the late 1940s. At the time of their enactment, it was assumed that unemployment was characteristically short-term (despite the experience of parts of the United Kingdom in the 1930s). Unemployed persons who had contributed to the national insurance system while in work received unemployment benefits (UBs), a taxable benefit available for fifty-two weeks. Those lacking sufficient national insurance payments to receive UB applied for means-tested supplementary benefits (SB). This became the most important source of benefits for unemployed persons by the early 1980s, as unemployment grew significantly. Thus, according to the Central Statistical Office in 1985, 62 percent of the unemployed received SB benefits only, while 18 percent received UB and 8 percent received both.[46] Benefit rates are kept below wage levels to avoid any disincentive effect. Government training programs for young and long-term unemployed persons have also kept their payment levels linked to wages and close to benefit levels. The distinction between contributory, non-means-tested insurance and noncontributory means-tested assistance was advocated by Beveridge in his 1942 report, and this separation remains a defining feature of the British welfare state, consistent with neoliberalism. High employment until the 1970s fortuitously rendered the second category marginal.

Once demand for supplementary benefits grew, starting from the mid-1970s and accelerating after 1981, Conservative party politicians influenced by neoliberal arguments about welfare disincentives and unsympathetic to government intervention readily accepted the notion of "welfare scroungers." The Tories' rejection of classes in favor of individuals in social analysis provided a logical underpinning to a minimalist, safety-net welfare state system in which the beneficiaries' status is unappealing. The dichotomy between contributory and noncontributory benefits provided the appropriate institutional framework. Neoliberal pressure groups, including the Adam Smith Institute and the Institute of Economic Affairs, propagated such arguments during the 1980s, and one strong intellectual statement can be found in the work of Friedrich Hayek.[47]

In a speech in September 1987, the then-Secretary of State for Social Services John Moore (and considered a possible party leader by some commentators before his departure from the Cabinet) set out the Conservative approach to the welfare state. Moore emphasized Britain's lengthy tradition of "caring, stretching back four centuries and more." He denied any exclusive Labour Party claim to the welfare system: "One of the most damaging aspects of the myth that the welfare state was created whole by Labour after 1945, is that it was also created perfect: the ultimate, total, flawless Welfare State."[48] Imitating his American ideological counterparts, Moore emphasized what he argued to be the ineluctable tendency of the state benefit system to induce dependency: the postwar welfare state "too often had the effect of increasing people's dependence on the state and its attendant bureaucrats, and reducing the power and control they might have hoped to gain over their own lives." The Conservatives proclaimed an alternative view:

> We have a different vision of what it means to "protect and promote economic and social welfare" in this country. We believe that dependence in the long run decreases human happiness and reduces human freedom. We believe the well being of individuals is best protected and promoted when they are helped to be independent, to use their talents to take care of themselves and their families, and to achieve things on their own . . . Of course we believe real distress must be alleviated and help given to those who cannot help themselves. But . . . welfare measures, if they are to *really* promote economic and social welfare, must be aimed ultimately at encouraging independence, not dependence.[49]

This language is similar to that used by conservative critics of welfare programs in the United States.[50] It resonates also with earlier Conservative party positions.[51] Moore wished to change the climate of opinion, to reject dependence on government assistance: "The job . . . has been to change this depressing climate of dependence and revitalize the belief which has been such a powerful force throughout British history: that individuals *can* take action to change their lives." He identified the social security reforms operative from 1988 as part of this agenda:

> The Act . . . takes a step towards increasing independence by reducing the disincentives to work that the poverty and unemployment "traps" set up, and by increasing the help available to working families on low incomes . . . The indiscriminate handing out of benefits not only spreads limited resources too thinly, it can also undermine the will to self-help, and build up pools of resentment among the taxpayers who are footing the bill, often from incomes barely larger than the money benefit recipients receive. By targeting our welfare resources we will be able to provide more real help where need is greatest.[52]

This last reference is a traditional identification of the burden upon taxpayers created by undeserving and idle benefit claimants. Politically, it is not difficult to explain Moore's emphasis in terms of the Conservative party's electoral support and the marginality of those governed by work-welfare. Similar views were promoted by the New Right policy think tanks which influenced the Conservatives from the mid-1970s onwards and borrowed from the United States. The work-welfare program (ET) discussed earlier is the logical extension of these principles. Historically and institutionally, it is consistent with them.

Moore's sentiments have not evaporated with either his or Mrs. Thatcher's departure from government. Throughout 1993 and 1994, the Conservatives reiterated these themes, targeting invalid benefits, universal schemes, and benefits to unmarried mothers as wasteful. This position was prompted powerfully by the extraordinarily high public-sector borrowing requirement which developed in 1992 and 1993. The newly appointed Welsh (John Redwood) and Employment (David Hunt) Secretaries were at the forefront of this ideological onslaught on the welfare state. In the Conservative party the radical right-wing "No Turning Back" group has advocated dramatic reductions in the welfare state,[53] proposals which are well-timed given the pressures to cut social spending.[54]

The modern American welfare state originates with the Social Security Act of 1935, passed at the height of the New Deal.[55] The act was drafted from proposals prepared by the Committee on Economic Security, which was established by President Roosevelt to formulate a strategy to avoid the catastrophe of another Great Depression. It was the loss of earnings suffered by households through either unemployment of the main wage-earner or his/her dependents which was identified by the committee as the crucial problem confronting citizens. "When earnings cease, dependency is not far off for a large percentage of our people." This prognosis suggested a particular remedy: "The one almost all embracing measure of security is an assured income. A program of economic security . . . must provide safeguards against all of the hazards leading to destitution and dependency."[56] The 1935 act was neither as radical nor as comprehensive as the committee had hoped. Its proposals were doctored. A distinction was made between insurance-type programs derived from citizens' contributions and means-tested noncontributory ones whose distribution imputed the status of mendicant to recipients. Within the first type fell the social security pension scheme, disability allowances, medicare, and a federal-state unemployment insurance program. The principal program within the second was Aid to Dependent Children subsequently modified to Aid to Families with Dependent Children (AFDC). In William Leuchtenburg's judgment, the 1935 act "reversed historic assumptions about the nature of social responsibility, and it established the proposition that the individual has clear-cut social rights."[57] But these "clear-cut social rights" were unproblematic for the insurance type of programs only.[58]

For the second type of programs, the act of 1935 empowered the states to enact their own welfare measures and administrative arrangements. The states are able to set their own eligibility criteria and to set the rates of benefits as they chose. The United States welfare state is a federal-state one and the absence of universal federal standards creates great diversity among the states. Discretionary state powers facilitated the development of a racial dimension in the American work-welfare regime. Black Americans were marginalized by the 1935 act, as they were by other New Deal legislation.[59] The pension and unemployment insurance parts of this act—the key contributory schemes—were designed to exclude a majority of black Americans. This was accomplished by excluding those occupations, in which these latter dominated, from the taxes levied for social insurance. These occupations were principally agricultural laboring and domestic service. Within the noncontributory means-tested components, the division of responsibilities between Washington and state capitals, and the power devolved to states to set and vary rates of benefits, created a flagrant mechanism for discriminating programs (as indeed occurred and as was intended).

In the 1960s, the Johnson administration made major amendments to the U.S. welfare state. The President's War on Poverty initiative produced the Economic Opportunity Act. In 1961 the ADC program was modified to allow children to be included when their deprivation was due to the unemployment of a parent. The decision to include this group was given to the states. Over half of the states took up the option. Most of the new schemes expanded the noncontributory means-tested programs and included enlarged health coverage, childcare, and education schemes such as Headstart. These programs were subject to trenchant criticisms from the mid-1970s onwards as the New Right and neoconservatives mustered their critiques of government programs generally and of federal welfare programs in particular. A consensus rapidly developed in the United States that federal and state welfare programs were not only unsuccessful in achieving their purported aim—alleviating poverty—but fostered a dependence among recipients. The empirical evidence for such claims remains deeply problematic, but the force of the criticisms did not abate.[60] Such claims became far more significant after 1981 with Ronald Reagan's assumption of the presidency. His conservative credentials (and success in achieving a Republican majority in the Senate) made him receptive to arguments for welfare reform. He also had experience with such reforms in California.

Reagan's experience as governor of California influenced his administration's reforms. As governor, Reagan had been in regular contact with the Department of Labor during the Nixon presidency and had met Assistant Secretary of Labor Malcolm Lovell, Jr., in July 1971.[61] Reagan sought to establish a rigorous workfare scheme in his state rather than a training program compatible with the Work Incentive Program (WIN) which the Labor Department was pursuing. He proposed establishing a statewide workfare scheme "based upon the fundamental premise that all employable individuals who are on welfare should be required to work in order to retain their entitlement. Refusal to work would be good cause for removal from the welfare roll."[62] These proposals were different from the schemes advocated by the federal Departments of Labor and of Health, Education and Welfare. In the judgment of the Department of Labor, "although the proposal contains considerable rhetoric about employability development, training and personal growth, the design is deficient in addressing these areas. There are no assurances that work sites will in any way relate to a plan for development of the individual."[63] They met with Reagan and his advisers to reach agreement on a compromise program which would include a significant training component. The meeting was not a success:

> The Governor and his staff were cordial and receptive, but it is clear that they do not fully accept—or perhaps do not fully grasp—the fundamentals of our workfare program (reliance on economic incentives as well as stiff penalties) or agree with *our principle that a person should always be better off working than not working.* Despite repeated discussions with California staff, additional effort seems in order.[64]

Detailed and tortuous negotiations followed between Washington and Californian officials to iron out an acceptable scheme.[65] What is significant about this exchange is how much more strict the Reagan gubernatorial team's work-welfare proposals were compared with those of a conservative Republican administration led by Richard Nixon.[66] Nixon's plans included a public service employment scheme under which participants' welfare benefits were supplemented by the Department of Labor in order to reach the prevailing wage level in the public sector. Eventually agreement was reached with California[67] and this state, together with Illinois and New York, was empowered to conduct work-welfare programs on a demonstration basis. In each case, the state employment service office was assigned administrative responsibility. Clients were required to report every two weeks to their local ES office.[68]

Reagan as President emphasized "dependence" in his pronouncements about the U.S. welfare system prior to the 1988 reform.[69] In his 1986 State of the Union address he said:

> In the welfare culture, the breakdown of the family, the most basic support system, has reached crisis proportions . . . As Franklin Roosevelt warned 51 years ago standing before this chamber. He said welfare is "a narcotic, a subtle destroyer of the human spirit." And we must now escape the spider's web of dependency.[70]

Two weeks after his State of the Union address, the president reiterated the theme of welfare reform in his weekly radio talk; on this occasion he stressed welfare dependency:

> The welfare tragedy has gone on too long. It is time to reshape our welfare system so that it can be judged by how many Americans it makes independent of welfare . . . In 1964 the famous war on poverty was declared and a funny thing happened. Poverty, as measured by dependency, stopped shrinking and then actually began to grow worse. I guess you could say poverty won the war.[71]

In the same talk, Reagan touched upon the traditional neoliberal concern with welfare disincentives. In states where welfare benefits were the highest, "public assistance for a single mother can amount to much more than the usable income of a minimum wage job. In other words, it can pay for her to quit work."[72] Reagan's speech popularized a consensus about welfare and fostered a focus on the work-welfare linkage. Contrary to the 1960s, when this connection was drawn in terms of training—disadvantaged welfare recipients should acquire skills to work—the analysis was now framed in terms of work: welfare recipients should work as a condition of receiving assistance.

The basic antipathy to noncontributory means-tested benefit systems characteristic of neoliberal attitudes was inflamed by such analyses. Because social security benefits are universal and contributory, they have been immensely more popular politically (garnering widespread support within the Congress for obvious political reasons).[73]

The Politics of Reform

In this section I explain how the political weakness of groups and citizens governed in work-welfare regimes facilitated the enactment of neoliberal programs. In the ensuing section, I explain how the institutional framework for the programs' administration complements their neoliberal thrust.

The British government's policy aims clashed with those of trades unions and the MSC. Each opponent was defeated. Technically, trades unionists represent only those who belong to their organizations. In practice, they represent one of the most powerful voices for those unemployed, even if this voice is often muted. Since 1979, the trades unions have been steadily weakened and excluded from government policy, a strategy accomplished with restrictive industrial relations legislation and mass unemployment in the years from 1981 to 1983 and from 1989 to 1992. The administration of ET has been devolved locally to employer-dominated organizations, from which unions are excluded. In place of national direction, the government devolved responsibility for training program delivery to eighty-two Training and Enterprise Councils (TECs) and thirteen Local Enterprise Councils (LECs) in Scotland (modeled on American private industry councils[74]), thereby limiting government influence on the details of training programs and ending tripartitism (in practice the TECs and Department of Employment negotiate about the Department's regulations). These outcomes reflect both the shifting fortunes of employers and unions and the Conservatives' aims in the labor market. The 1992 abolition of NEDC symbolized the virtually complete exclusion of union representation from economic policy.[75]

At their 1988 annual conference, by which date the MSC had been refashioned to a weaker Training Commission, the TUC voted to oppose participation in ET despite the efforts of their leaders and the Training Commission to win cooperation.[76] The largest union, the Transport and General Workers' Union (TGWU), decided as early as March 1988 to oppose the government's new training schemes, as did the Scottish TUC, the General and Municipal Workers' Union (GMWU), the local authority unions—the National and Local Government Officers' Association (NALGO) and the National Union of Public Employees (NUPE)—and voluntary associations. Their views were expressed at meetings of the tripartite MSC. MSC staff shared unionists' view that ET should be voluntary, but lacked the power to enforce this position. The MSC's final report for the February 1988 White Paper concluded that the new program "must be voluntary."[77]

The "workfare" element (in my terms, work-oriented stress) of ET was decisive to the TUC's opposition. The TUC sought a program in which participation was voluntary and believed that ET would emulate American workfare schemes and therefore refused to endorse it.[78] Unionists feared that unemployed persons would be forced to participate in training or lose their benefits,[79] a development the Employment Secretary denied in a letter to the TUC in March 1988.[80] The voluntary participation criterion reflected the TUC's dismay about the requirement from 1988 that young people participate in a training course as a condition of receiving unemployment benefits. In September, the unionist Ron Todd accused the ET program of lacking choice and of "putting unemployed people into low-skilled, low paid placements."[81] Union and voluntary organizations' hostility to ET's predecessors, particularly the Job Training Scheme, limited their implementation.[82] In a pamphlet issued after the decision to boycott ET, the TUC argued that the scheme did not offer adequate adult training. It identified particular weaknesses: "the training is underfunded; the trainees do not receive a proper allowance; there is insufficient provision for trade union monitoring of the scheme; and there are inadequate guarantees against compulsion onto the scheme and job substitution."[83]

The MSC was marginalized in the formulation of policy. In the early 1980s, its officers opposed compulsory training schemes for young people and still had ambitions to create social democratic style programs.[84] The Conservatives' electoral success in 1983 and again in 1987 undermined the commission's position. Internal MSC opposition to compulsory participation in training schemes, particularly the YTS, presented both the need and pretext to modify this organization to render it an effective institutional resource for the Conservatives's work-welfare ambitions.

The marginalization of the MSC facilitated the integration of training programs with benefits. ET has been linked with the distribution of social security benefits, and it enables the government to dovetail training programs with social security benefits to create a work-welfare program not dissimilar to American compulsory workfare programs. The reintegration of Jobcentre placement work (including Restart interviews) with unemployment benefit offices, effected by returning the former to the Department of Employment in 1988, enables them to perform a traditional work-test role. Growing unemployment will again ensure that training programs are pitched as much to work-welfare tests as job creation.

The decision to reintegrate the placement and benefit activities, despite the earlier problems associated with their linkage, symbolized powerfully the political weakness of the training commission. The motive was again concern about the abuse of receipt of unemployment benefits, a priority of the Conservatives' New Right agenda in the 1980s. Reintegration was also claimed to be necessary for the new training initiatives.[85] Jobcentres have subsequently assumed historic policing functions. In the judgment of the Unemployment Unit:

> The direct integration of this service with claimant signing days and benefit eligibility further blurs the distinction between counselling and benefit policing . . . Job Referral staff will be required to take "Refusing Suitable Employment" action against claimants who they believe do not have good reasons for turning down a job, and if they think the claimant is not actively seeking work they will be sent back for a job seeking interview with a Claimant Adviser.[86]

By December 1991, only 1 in 110 claimants succeeded in acquiring employment after a mandatory Restart interview, an outcome plainly related to the deteriorating labor market.[87]

Title II, the JOBS program, was pivotal to the passage of the Family Support Act. Its content and scope determined White House support for the final legislation. It transforms the perception of welfare benefits and integrates them unequivocally to the labor market. Whether this innovation is advocated as a way of realizing "work opportunities," as liberal writers and reformers argue, or excoriated as an unnecessarily punitive workfare system, as critics charge, it constituted a formulation of the welfare "contract" consistent with free-market principles.

The political weakness of American work-welfare recipients was exposed by the way in which state welfare reforms were adapted for the federal program. Despite the governors' emphasis on voluntary participation, the Reagan White House insisted on a mandatory scheme.

The Omnibus Budget Reconciliation Act of 1981 (OBRA) enabled states to replace WIN programs with "demonstration" work-welfare reforms for AFDC recipients. This option had been taken by thirty states by the time the Family Support Act was enacted.[88] Most commonly, so-called "demo" measures were community work experience programs (CWEP), frequently termed workfare. They "required adult AFDC recipients to perform some sort of community work, such as park beautification or as a teacher aide, in exchange for the AFDC benefit. The individual does not become a paid employee but, instead, works off the AFDC benefit. The number of hours a person works may not exceed their AFDC grant divided by the applicable minimum wage."[89]

Some of the state demonstration projects took program participants on a voluntary self-selection basis. Other schemes compulsorily directed AFDC recipients into them. In Massachusetts, Governor Michael Dukakis made ET voluntary because of the unpopularity of the scheme initiated by his predecessor Republican Governor King (1978–82). The main failure of the King program arose in sanctioning nonparticipants. Almost all such sanctions granted were subsequently overruled on appeal, and the Massachusetts Department of Public Welfare was obliged retrospectively to pay checks to recipients unfairly sanctioned.[90] In contrast, California's GAIN program was compulsory. GAIN required all fifty-eight counties to provide a range of services (such as basic education and job-search assistance) to those welfare recipients satisfying particular criteria. Recipients used these services until they left the welfare rolls. Participants were assessed in initial interviews testing their basic education abilities. On the basis of this test, the participants were directed toward either basic education courses, career assessment, or job-search activities. Because mandatory schemes were by definition required to provide places for all comers, they were less selective about program content than voluntary ones. Thus in California, under GAIN, rather than all participants being channeled to either education or career assessment, those with sufficient skills had to undertake job-searches before pursuing other routes.[91]

These state programs did not go uncriticized. A 1987 study by the U.S. General Accounting Office of the post-OBRA WIN demonstration work-incentive programs criticized the diversity between states and the frequently poor coordination between administrative agencies at the local level. The latter criticism referred especially to the welfare and employment security agencies, a perennial problem plaguing work-welfare programs. The report concluded: "The current programs are a patchwork of administrative responsibilities and funding, put together on an ad hoc basis. They lack overall direction or goals. Administration of the various work program authorities, including the regular WIN Program, is split between AFDC and state employment agencies and at the federal level, between HHS and Labor."[92] The study also concluded that a small number of adult AFDC recipients were participating in work-welfare schemes, that most of the programs aimed to shift recipients into employment and not to enhance skills, and that most achieved only modest effect.[93] An earlier study by the GAO (1984) of sixteen community work experience programs criticized their utility and cost-effectiveness: "the evidence on the effectiveness of CWEP is inconclusive. It may or may not be producing AFDC budget savings."[94] Unsurprisingly, states operating CWEP schemes were more sanguine.[95]

Other critics of the shift to workfare type programs were more trenchant than the GAO. The National Urban League maintained that, contrary to popular perceptions, those who are "able-bodied" but unemployed, are unemployed not because they prefer "leisure" but because they often lack the education and experience necessary for long term employment . . . As a rationale for workfare, deterrence would only be valid where there existed a suitable alternative to public assistance. Without adequate educational opportunities, training, availability of jobs and other advantages, that alternative simply does not exist for most recipients of public assistance.[96]

The American Federation of State, County and Municipal Employees (AFSCME) also opposed workfare. They feared that permanent employees would be displaced: "Especially where a sizeable program exists for a sustained period, you will get a substitution effect in which unpaid workfare participants displace regular employees . . . [which] . . . encourages the creation of a subclass of employee."[97]

Work-welfare reform was supported strongly by the state governors. Mobilized by the National Governors' Association, they lobbied for reform both to reduce the program's cost and to enhance the skill levels of their workforces—"training-oriented" programs. The governors' proposals were formulated by an executive committee of the NGA chaired by Bill Clinton, at the time governor of Arkansas, and issued in February 1987. Subtitled a "Job-Oriented Welfare Reform," the proposals stressed creating work opportunities:

> Public assistance programs must . . . provide incentives and opportunities for individuals to get the training they need and to seek jobs. It is our aim to create a system where it is always better to work than be on public assistance . . . The Governors recommend that all employable welfare recipients must participate in an education, job training, or placement program and accept a suitable job when it is offered.

The governors conceived of the welfare problem as exclusion from the labor market. In their view, work-welfare programs should be skill-enhancing schemes supplementing or imparting those qualifications necessary for employment. The NGA believed it was reasonable to expect government to provide the support services—familiar from the 1960s as transportation subsidy, healthcare benefits and childcare facilities—which enabled welfare recipients to participate in training or job search schemes: "Parents cannot be expected to give up welfare if the loss of Medicaid jeopardizes access to health care for their families."[98] The governors wanted a major federal role in the formulation of a jobs-oriented work-welfare strategy.[99]

In the White House, President Reagan advocated a harsher regime. Reluctantly he accepted and endorsed the NGA proposals after his own impeccably workfare measures were obviously going to fail in Congress.

Reagan did succeed, however, as a condition of not vetoing the bill, in imposing the mandatory element in the jobs program included in the Family Support Act (passed in October 1988). Reagan shared with the governors a preference for work schemes but wanted these to be compulsory. He succeeded in this ambition but failed to exclude the provision of transition or support services from public funds.

In the Senate, Senator Daniel Patrick Moynihan organized hearings on welfare.[100] The importance of including work programs in any reform package was quickly aired, though critics feared such schemes would be punitive workfare measures rather than meaningful job opportunities. Congressional hearings provided an opportunity for the results of evaluation studies of state-level work-welfare programs to be publicized.[101] Many of these studies were undertaken by the Manpower Demonstration Research Corporation, which received contracts to evaluate schemes in eight states[102]: Arkansas, California (San Diego), Illinois (Chicago), Maine, Maryland (Baltimore), New Jersey, Virginia, and West Virginia.[103] The MDRC's positive though modest findings that work-welfare schemes could reduce AFDC rolls[104] garnered congressional support for reform.[105] In its own evaluation of MOST, Michigan's Department of Social Services reported a positive effect on welfare dependency for participants, though not a statistically significant one, and a statistically significant effect on a participant's ability to find and retain employment.[106] Ohio contracted evaluations of its "work programs." These schemes were distinguished from other states' programs by their compulsory character—all welfare recipients not exempted were required to participate—and by their use of community work experience programs (that is, workfare) as the primary work-task required of participants. Ohio had a tradition of imposing such work requirements upon recipients of General Relief benefits before extending them under OBRA to AFDC recipients. A 1985 evaluation was ebullient about the state's programs:

> The demonstration counties have achieved marginally greater welfare reductions than the non-WP counties. These incremental reductions appear to have resulted from work programs initiatives. In general, the demonstration counties have achieved success in: putting welfare recipients into jobs or job-related activities; providing valuable community services through the Community Work Experience Program component ("workfare"); and reducing welfare caseloads.[107]

A U.S. General Accounting Office evaluation of the OBRA demonstration programs in Michigan, Massachusetts, Oregon, and Texas also appeared in 1988. Its conclusions were cautious and anodyne.[108] However, the positive evaluation of these state work-welfare programs was an important resource for advocates of federal welfare reform in 1987 and 1988. During congressional hearings, the sanguine assessments of the programs' success in reducing welfare rolls and placing participants in employment were cited authoritatively.

Administering Work-Welfare

The administration of modern work-welfare programs is designed institutionally to advantage labor market forces and to complement the interests of employers. In Britain, giving primacy to industrialists and employers is an ironic strategy since, historically, the failure of this sector to provide adequate training forced government intervention in the first place. In the United States, the Reagan administration was content to expand the private-sector-based administrative apparatus responsible for federal training. In both countries, there is a blurring between industrial training and training for the unemployed, with the former increasingly harnessed (and thereby distorted) to the latter. This blurring arises from both the political need to address mass unemployment and the lukewarm commitment of the Republicans and Tories to training.

The Confederation of British Industry's (CBI) attitude toward training underwent a transformation during the 1980s. From being largely uninterested, the Confederation was, by the end of the decade, advocating a comprehensive national training program.[109] Employers' support for training culminated in the CBI 1988 publication *Towards a Skills Revolution,* which marked a break with industry's postwar indifference toward training.[110] The CBI advocated ending employment of persons under eighteen years of age unless the job included a systematic training component and creating a unified system of vocational and academic targets for the 16- to 18-year-old group.

The CBI supported the ET program. Training and Enterprise Councils (TECs), the primary agency for delivering government training programs,[111] institutionalized the preferential position granted employers. Each TEC has a contract (for approximately £20 million) with the government to spend on training programs for the unemployed (and some employed persons) as it judges most appropriate to local labor and skills circumstances.[112] TECs have an average of fifty members, composed principally of business representatives, in many cases chief executives. Each TEC is chaired by a senior business person who has signed a contract with the Employment Secretary to deliver training programs in his or her local area. They communicate directly with the Secretary of State for Employment.[113] A questionnaire survey by the *Financial Times* to 1,220 TEC members, of whom 506 replied, found that 88 percent had served over a year. A majority wanted better coordination of training and education programs by Whitehall.[114]

The government stressed participation by chief executives on TEC boards for two reasons. First, American experience with PICs revealed that without senior business leaders these organizations would be less successful in winning business community support. Second, emphasizing chief executives is another element in the antitripartite strategy of TECs. Trade union and local authority participation in TECs or LECs is by invitation.[115] Although employers have been advantaged under ET, they have been unwilling simply to administer Department of Employment plans.[116] TECs have won some independence from the Department of Employment.

TECs have had difficulty pursuing the aims underlining their creation: fostering an improved system of training for people in employment in British industry. They lack the power to impose training requirements on firms. They have no equivalent to the old industrywide levy system enjoyed by ITBs and the MSC. And they have been forced to direct their energies to the needs of Britain's burgeoning unemployed. A majority of members are also unhappy with the role assigned to TECs in combating unemployment: "Sixty three per cent rate economic development as their priority, including job creation. Only 17 per cent say training the unemployed is their top priority."[117]

Institutionally, the tradition of a centralized state has been challenged by the network of decentralized TECs, yet the government has been reluctant to devolve power to these local bodies.[118] Training programs have been imposed on this decentralized system. TECs follow the Thatcherite pattern of weak devolved authorities, unelected and dominated by Whitehall.[119] They serve essentially negative functions: destroying trade union influence, for example. They can be compared with most of the post-1979 quangos or even school-governing bodies. Politically and economically, TECs have been compelled to deal with unemployed persons' needs and not with the training requirements of those in employment, as was envisaged when the organizations were founded.[120] This priority fueled an angry memorandum[121] from the GIO body (which represents TEC executives) to the Employment Secretary—declaring that "the TEC movement is on a knife-edge"—in April 1992: "Unless there is a major reform of relationships without delay, the thousand businessmen [on TEC boards] will simply walk away. There will be no mass protest, but the effectiveness will drain away into the sand of inertia."[122] TECs have defined themselves as principally concerned with industrial training and economic development but have been compelled to focus on the unemployed, a replay of the MSC's experience.[123] Both the MSC and TECs were launched as organizations focused on the country's training needs and both have been exploited by governments anxious about unemployment. Civil servant disquiet is apparent too. Sir Geoffrey Holland, then-Permanent Secretary at Employment, expressed concern about the quality of TEC board members and judged the whole system "fragile."[124]

Concurrently with the introduction of ET, the Conservatives reintegrated placement and benefit work to facilitate the implementation of their work-welfare program. The process began in 1982. A study undertaken by Sir Derek Rayner for the government concluded that the employment service should complement and not compete with other media for job placements in the labor market.[125] The Rayner study recommended removing and privatizing the branch of the service dealing with professional and executive recruitment, thereby reducing the number of Jobcentres and shifting their location away from high streets to cheaper out-of-the-way premises. A common criticism of the Jobcentre service in the years after Rayner's report was its inadequate work for the long-term unemployed. By succeeding in broadening their service to help the non-long-term unemployed and nonmanual job seekers, the service was accused of providing less for that very group most associated with the dole image. Such concerns rapidly focused on the abuse of benefits which, it was claimed, was no longer effectively policed. This provided the pretext for reintegration.[126]

Jobcentres' priorities are integrally linked with those of the government's programs to combat unemployment among the long-term unemployed and the young and to administer Restart interviews.[127] In their 1987 manifesto, the Conservatives promised to "take steps to provide a comprehensive service to the unemployed."[128] In the same year, the government informed the MSC that the commission would no longer be responsible for the Jobcentre network and its placement work. Jobcentres together with the Enterprise Allowance Scheme and Restart interviews were transferred under direct Department of Employment control. The Employment Service became jointly responsible for Jobcentres and benefit offices. In 1989, the government decided to reorganize the service into an executive agency.[129] By March 1992, close to 670 integrated Jobcentre and benefit offices had been created by the Employment Service (when this initiative began there were 2,000 Jobcentres and unemployment benefit offices). A breakdown of the first 500 of these integrated sites revealed that 39 percent were located at old unemployment benefit offices and 21 percent at previous Jobcentres.[130] The most serious implication is the return to a previous style of organization considered to be flawed: the integration of placement and benefit systems. This criticism was rejected by the government, who anticipated a more "effective service. Unemployed people would be able to visit one place, as at least a starting point, for a range of services including the advertisement of job vacancies, jobclubs, jobshare, employment training, enterprise allowances and employment rehabilitation."[131] According to newspaper and other reports, these proposals were a considerably watered-down version of the Secretary of State for Employment's original plans. These included complete integration of the two services and the transfer of offices to cheap backstreet locations.[132] A report in the *Guardian* claimed that the "Employment Secretary, Mr Norman Fowler, drew back from a program of mass integration in the face of widespread criticism that this reflected a lowering of the Government's commitment to solving unemployment after it had dipped below two million."[133] The persistence of high long-term unemployment and a fourth consecutive electoral victory has increased the attraction of such an option, however.[134]

The administration of the Family Support Act advantaged the private sector and weakened opponents in two ways.[135] First, it was linked directly to the Job Training Partnership Act (JTPA)—a federal program and a private-sector-based scheme. Second, the participation rates which it required states to satisfy to maintain their funding ineluctably forced administrators to push participants into work-oriented schemes and to neglect long-term training needs. Both features were compounded by the federal system.

State JOBS programs are implemented in coordination with the existing JTPA framework. JTPA is based in the private sector and administered by private industry councils (PICs), a deliberate shift away from the public-sector location of the Comprehensive Employment and Training Act (CETA). CETA grew significantly during the Carter administration to address unemployment.

JTPA provides federal funding for employment and training programs and is distributed across states by an unemployment-based formula. Title II-A provides the bulk of funds for both economically disadvantaged adults and youth; funds under Title II-B are for summer youth programs; Title III funds are for the reemployment of dislocated workers; and Title IV funds cover native Americans and migrant workers. Although JTPA's enactment coincided with severe unemployment, and while meeting the needs of the unemployed was its primary focus, the subsequent decline of unemployment fostered an increasing link between JTPA services and the work-welfare programs initiated by state and local welfare departments under the 1981 OBRA demonstration scheme. The linkage was well developed in Massachusetts, for instance.[136] It is this linkage which is supposed to be forged in all states to cope with the implications of the FSA JOBS program.[137] There is considerable variation in the relations between the placement service offices (based in the Department of Labor in each state) and the welfare departments, with suspicion and poor communications not uncommon.

Administratively, the JTPA program required each governor to establish a State Job Training Coordinating Council with responsibility for coordinating training programs under the scheme.[138] States were divided into service delivery areas for each of which a private industry council (PIC) was appointed by local officials and approved by the governor. Each local PIC devises an annual plan for providing disadvantaged adults and youth with training services and employment placement services. This plan must be approved each year by the governor. The states consider JTPA a valuable instrument in improving the skills of their workforces.[139] Governor of New Jersey Thomas Kean established a Task Force on Employment Policy, which reported in 1987 and whose authors drew an unambiguous linkage between economic needs and work-welfare programs:

> The success of New Jersey's economy in the years ahead will depend upon its ability to develop the higher quality labor force essential to efficiently produce the high quality goods and services the marketplace will demand from us. To realize this ability, a number of things must happen. The skills of working people will have to be enhanced. The disadvantaged will have to be brought more fully into the economic mainstream. The coordination and performance of education and training programs will have to be improved.[140]

A study conducted by the National Alliance of Business concluded that JTPA was a success in most states. Their survey in 1985 found that "almost three-quarters of the PIC chairs whose firms have hired JTPA graduates believe that they make equally as good or better employees than those from other sources."[141] A 1989 U.S. General Accounting Office study, based on a national survey, was less sanguine. It found that the JTPA program was serving the needs of the less job-ready and the more job-ready in roughly similar proportions; within both groups, however, high school dropouts were underserved and there was relatively little skill enhancement with program participants entering jobs for which their previous skills were appropriate. A survey by the United States Conference of Mayors of the impact of the JTPA program on the job needs of thirty-one large cities praised the scheme at a general level but criticized its provision of services for the most disadvantaged, the constituents of JOBS: "Officials surveyed warn that too many unemployed are left behind because JTPA fails to provide enough money to more than scratch the surface when targeting the disadvantaged unemployed and underemployed." Furthermore, the funding provided for assisting welfare recipient participants was insufficient: "In Louisville, local data indicate that $7 an hour is needed in order for welfare recipients to become independent. To earn $7 an hour, long term training programs are necessary. Short term programs, such as those provided by JTPA, are ill-equipped to do this. There is simply not enough money in JTPA to meet these needs."[142] The JTPA's own national advisory committee issued a report in March 1989 which was generally positive but highlighted also the inadequate funding if the United States intended to develop a comprehensive national training system.[143] The committee made several recommendations, including developing a more direct focus upon disadvantaged persons with serious skill inadequacies, designing training programs for individual needs, setting out clear measures such as wage rates and permanency of employment, and expanding the public-private network underpinning JTPA.[144]

The Family Support Act JOBS component has implications for the U.S. Employment Service network in addition to JTPA. The job search and placement element of JOBS involves the local employment security offices. The success of this linkage varies by state with some, for example, Massachusetts, impressive, others far less so. In New Jersey, Kean's committee on employment policy recommended a much fuller integration of ES activities with the training framework provided by JTPA to create a new system of training and placement:

> The State should adopt an all-purpose employment and training program title . . . under which all participating agencies would operate . . . [W]e believe a common identification is essential to avoid fragmentation of what ought to be a unified system in the minds of not only the client and prospective employer but also of service deliverers. Each agency would retain its structural independence but all participating agencies would provide basic intake and referral services for all other participating agencies. In this way, the client would be served without being confused by a variety of agency names and titles which are of importance only to administration of the system.[145]

The ES, private industry councils, and service delivery areas were to be integrated into a "Jobs New Jersey," and decisions about the allocation of employment service resources would be undertaken jointly by this organization. This arrangement was accepted and implemented in 1989.

While such a system of agency integration may seem unremarkable, it is in fact an exceptional achievement within the United States federal system where agency autonomy at all levels is tenaciously defended. Formally, the state employment services are supposed to be closely linked with state JTPA offices, but their closeness varies considerably. In many states, the employment service and department of labor have representatives on private industry councils but little further effective coordination. One study of innovative activities performed by the U.S. Employment Service throughout the United States identified coordination with JTPA programs as one of four such innovations.[146] It is remarkable that such a link was considered novel.

The Family Support Act set monthly participation rates for the states' JOBS programs for fiscal years 1990 to 1995, that is, percentages at which participants should be guaranteed to be included in the program. This clause was also a point of controversy between the Congress and the White House during enactment, the latter insisting upon its inclusion. The rates were fixed at: 7 percent in FY 1990 and FY 1991, 11 percent in FY 1992, 15 percent in FY 1994, and 20 percent in FY 1995. If states fail to meet these rates, they suffer a cut in the federal grant received by up to 50 percent. The first version of the federal regulations[147] for the Family Support Act provided a narrow reading of these participation rates in that, to satisfy them, state administrators would have to force participants to engage in unproductive activities; limit the states' ability to give volunteers first consideration; and limit childcare provision. If administrators tried to place participants in permanent, well-paid jobs, they would be unlikely to satisfy their participation requirements. These regulations were widely criticized as too stringent by congressional supporters of FSA, including Moynihan and interest groups. Speaking before a congressional hearing convened by Senator Moynihan in May 1989, Delaware's Republican Governor Michael Castle concluded that "the proposed rules will actually force significant changes in current programs—often the very programs that served as the models for the law itself."[148] In other words, those state programs initiated after 1981 which paved the way for the FSA would themselves be subverted by strict federal regulations.

Implementing the JOBS program in California meant far greater numbers of compulsorily directed participants.[149] An analysis of the program's implementation throughout the state reported, rather blandly, that "available data show that GAIN registrants continue to obtain jobs in an increasingly large number with a steadily progressing hourly wage. Lawmakers recognized that GAIN was a long-term commitment in an area where 'quick-fixes' have not been successful."[150] Using a simple measure of participation in GAIN—"entering a job search, education, or training activity"—a MDRC study of four counties found that there was considerable variation between the counties, reflecting in large part the different types of registrants (for instance, whether participants were fluent in English) and different philosophies.[151] Those counties with conservative philosophies prioritized job searches before enrolling registrants in education.

As anticipated by critics, satisfying the participation rate requirements of the JOBS program has been difficult. There are two participation rate requirements—one for AFDC recipients and one for AFDC-UP recipients. Each state must achieve participation rates for the JOBS Program of 7 percent in FY 90 and reach 20 percent by FY 95. The criteria for meeting these rates are extremely complex, as the American Public Welfare Association appreciated:

> It will be difficult for states to predict in advance how many people they must serve in order to reach the participation rate target each year. They will have to monitor and track a running average *each* month of how many hours *each* participant in JOBS is scheduled in an approved activity. This presumes, of course, that a state has the automation capability to track each individual in this manner. States without the necessary automation will find this process to be extremely cumbersome, particularly as the size of their program increases to meet the rising participation rate requirements for AFDC and AFDC-UP recipients.[152]

Conclusion

The British and American work-welfare programs analyzed in this chapter demonstrate the political power of advocates of liberal market-oriented policies. A number of factors illustrate this judgment.

First, although both sets of programs include a mandatory training component, neither scheme succeeds in addressing fundamental training needs. The framework within which they have been conceptualized and administered is contradictory. Training programs have to serve first and foremost as anti-unemployment or anti-welfare dependency instruments and not as significant training measures. This problem is most explicit in Britain where work-welfare reforms have been associated confusingly with the crisis in training, discussed in chapter 4. This association has resulted in the imposition of reforms for training, such as the ET program, on a framework, based in the old MSC schemes, designed to combat unemployment. Training programs are thus fundamentally flawed by their location in a framework for unemployment and not employment. It is ironic that the construction of neoliberal work-welfare programs necessitates extensive state intervention both to police more rigorously benefit claims and to address the inadequacies of market-based training schemes.

Second, both British and American work-welfare programs conserve and perpetuate defining characteristics of extant liberal institutional arrangements. Both assume a distinction between deserving and undeserving recipients of public assistance or unemployment benefits and a dichotomy between contributory and noncontributory programs. Rather than offering an opportunity to dissolve such selective and stigmatizing distinctions, these programs compound them. The dubious training component makes it unlikely that participants will acquire the qualifications necessary for a transition to contributory programs and hence earn social rights of citizenship. Self-sufficiency is intended to be accomplished through job placement, but it is quite possible for welfare recipients to be placed in low-paying, unattractive jobs and still to discharge their obligation. Such an outcome was predicted by critics of the regulations issued to accompany the JOBS program in the United States.

Third, these schemes reveal the weak electoral and political power of program participants. The success of New Right ideas in influencing politicians formulating these programs demonstrates their political power and the weakness of those governed by them. Policymakers had to decide whether the new work-welfare programs should be compulsory or voluntary. Both the Reagan and Thatcher administrations advocated compulsory schemes: that is, all those receiving welfare benefits in the United States should be required either to undertake work or to participate in a training scheme; and all those unemployed in Britain have to demonstrate evidence of searching for employment and to participate in a training program. This drive to compulsion was against the advice of the interest and policy-making groups in each country. In the United States, the state governors—whose policies and initiative for welfare reform shaped national policy—maintained that work-welfare programs, to be most effective, should be voluntary. The most successful state training program—Massachusetts's ET—was voluntary and its organizers believed this a necessary condition of success.[153] Indeed, Massachusetts experimented with a mandatory program in the early 1980s under Dukakis's predecessor Governor King and its resounding failure shaped subsequent policy. In Britain, the MSC was a firm believer in voluntary training programs. The commission believed that their programs should attain a standard and success rate which would make them sufficiently attractive so as not to require compulsory participation. Unions and the Labour Party also opposed compulsion.

The combination of these second and third points creates the potential for a transition to a harsher workfare regime, and recent discussions echo this potential. The Conservatives argue that their work-welfare program does not equate with workfare. A review in August 1992 of government spending on anti-unemployment programs was undertaken to sharpen the linkage between receipt of benefits and return to employment.[154] Again workfare has been rejected but measures to tighten the connection between benefits and refusing places are imminent.[155] That claimants can lose 40 percent of their benefits if after two years of unemployment they refuse to attend a Restart counseling course provides a foundation for such a policy choice. Gillian Shephard, the Employment Secretary (1992–93), reportedly considered a merger of ET and Employment Action to create community work projects, such as clearing derelict sites, on a large scale to absorb, and impose work activities upon, the large number of unemployed.[156] The appeal of such schemes for the government can only grow as disorder and riotous behavior increases in rundown inner-city areas and on council estates. Despite losing his seat in Parliament in 1992, the former Treasury Minister Francis Maude's enthusiasm for work-welfare was undaunted. In a radio interview he argued: "I think it is not good for people who are unemployed simply to pay them not to work. I think people generally are happier when they have something to do. . . . I think the principle of Workfare is an excellent one and is a Christian approach to providing help to people."[157] Support for such schemes is not restricted to the Tories. The lobby group, Full Employment UK, has advocated compulsory workfare schemes for some time, though they see this approach as benign. The organization urged the government "to launch a major new temporary work program in the inner-cities, to provide constructive activities for Britain's growing underclass. . . . we need an obligatory work program, offering the '12 month plus' unemployed community work for three days a week in return for their 'community benefit'—which would replace income support."[158] The Labour MP Frank Field has also expressed support for approaching the "idea of 'workfare' positively" and chastises the government for failing to offer such a program: "I believe many unemployed people would prefer a system which, while requiring them to be available for work (as at present), offers a place on a temporary work scheme or a training place."[159]

The tenacity of unemployment has placed an enormous strain upon this package of government work-welfare programs (the rise in December 1992 represented the thirty-first consecutive month's rise and the number of long-term unemployed is especially serious; the number has fallen since 1993). While some observers believe this problem reflects in itself the historic failure of training policy in Britain, it is improbable that significant improvements to training will occur during a major recession. What are called training programs in Britain are more accurately characterized as anti-unemployment measures. Fiscally, the government's principal target is to control public spending—greatly increased by the combination of reduced revenue and expanded expenditures caused by unemployment—and the work-welfare system, carefully constructed during the last six years, provides a powerful mechanism with which to identify and exclude the alleged undeserving from the receipt of public assistance. The unprecedented numbers of homeless in London personify this strategy and its outcomes.

The Conservatives introduced Employment Action (as a temporary measure in October 1991[160]) to counter the new rise in unemployment. Employment Action (EA) is designed to provide work experience on projects near to home for 37,500 people in its first year and 60,000 a year thereafter. EA is targeted toward those living in inner cities who have been out of work for at least six months. Participants are paid their benefit and an additional £10; they are provided with minimal skills training since the emphasis of the scheme is to get participants into a work-experience program. EA has generated conflict with the TECs about administration. TECs want to emphasize training for employed persons whereas the government's priority is to provide training programs capable of absorbing the unemployed. TECs have also encountered difficulties in their relationship with local Chambers of Commerce who represent smaller firms. TECs and chambers may be performing similar roles; the latter assisted in implementing YTS.[161] By the end of August, Labour was accusing the government of failing to provide a promised 10,000 places on the program.[162]

In principle, all unemployed young persons are guaranteed a place on a Youth Training (YT) scheme, though demand exceeds available places.[163] A survey by the Labour Party concluded that the reductions in TECs' budgets would result in 60,000 fewer YT places.[164] Vouchers may be introduced for the YT program in the next year or two; some TECs have been granted permission to introduce pilot studies of vouchers under the "Gateway to Learning" initiative. Young school-leavers—aged 16 or 17— have been especially hard hit by government tightening and reduction of benefits since September 1988; they are no longer allowed unemployment benefits, and receiving income support has been restricted.[165] By April 1992, of 103,000 unemployed 16- and 17-year-olds, one study calculated 80,000 had no income at all and no access to employment or training program or right to state benefits.[166] As noted earlier, after April 1996 the benefit regime in Britain will be tightened further. The "job-seeker's allowance" will replace the existing unemployment benefit and recipients, in exchange for the payment, will enter into an agreement outlining how they will search for gainful employment. This latter arrangement is termed the "job-seeker's agreement."

In the United States, Democratic President Bill Clinton proposes to tighten federal welfare programs, also by introducing a more punitive element. His likely proposals will expand federal spending on education, training, and childcare for welfare recipients, but will require those who have received benefits for over two years to enter a work program in exchange for payment. This contractual obligation will expand the work component of the federal JOBS program and introduces an unambiguously workfare character. The work program will run for one year, and re-enrollment would continue as long as the recipient searches actively for work. Those beneficiaries declining a job or failing to search with sufficient diligence would have their benefits stopped. This movement to a harsher regime is consistent with the position of Southern governors, among whom Bill Clinton was a leading member while in his gubernatorial office in Little Rock, Arkansas. Whether Congress will embrace this new workfare emphasis has yet to be determined.

In both Britain and the United States, recent discussion of work-welfare has assumed a gendered character.[167] The JOBS program established under the Family Support Act affects principally women in households, though some male heads-of-households are also covered. In Britain, the incidence of women brought into work-welfare is not so high but is nonetheless a significant number. The concept of "welfare dependency" privileged in American reforms and British aspirations has particular ramifications for households composed of mothers and dependent children. Abramovitz and Piven chastise the consequences of this focus for the United States:

> The welfare rolls stabilized in the early 1970s at about 3.6 million families and began to grow only with the 1989 recession. Even now, Aid to Families with Dependent Children accounts for only 1 percent of the Federal budget, or about $22 billion a year. And rather than supporting families so generously as to encourage "dependency," the grants are painfully low, averaging $370 a month in 1992. No state brings families up to the poverty line, even when food stamps are included.[168]

They continue by noting that it is economic circumstances rather than individual failure which explains the difficulty citizens encounter in finding employment: "If there were good job training, adequate child care and decent wages at the end of the road, many women would eagerly leave welfare. But such programs would cost upward of $50 billion, so that is not what Government is doing. Instead, the harassment of welfare mothers in the name of reform continues."[169] Comparable rhetoric began to dominate Conservative politicians' statements about welfare in Britain after the 1992 election. Lone parents have been singled out for criticism by the Secretary of State for Social Security supported by right-wing think tanks. At their 1993 annual conference, the Secretaries of State for both the Home Office and Social Security attacked state benefits to single-parent families and endorsed American schemes which penalized mothers on welfare who had additional children.[170]

Fourth, the fiscal context of British and American work-welfare programs not only means that comprehensive training programs are highly unlikely but that even the modest training measures now included may be downgraded. In the United States, this problem manifests itself in the choice of options used by states in the JOBS program: lack of resources compels state policymakers to limit the training component to the most inexpensive options.[171] Many state governments are under enormous fiscal pressure as federal funds decline in real terms and local tax revenues are eroded through recession. Thus, despite the riots in Los Angeles and California's large welfare recipient population, Governor Pete Wilson has had to propose sharp cuts in state spending. Close to forty states have opted for a strategy of tightening eligibility criteria and reducing benefits available under state work-welfare programs.[172] Other states and some British politicians have combined moral arguments about welfare dependency with support for schemes which reduce benefits to welfare parents and mothers having additional children. Arguments about family responsibility are mobilized to underpin such schemes as Wisconsin's "learnfare," which reduces benefits to mothers whose children are truant from school; Maryland's "healthfare," which reduces benefits when children fail to receive immunizations; and New Jersey's "wedfare" increases the benefits to welfare mothers who marry while the state's "family cap" has the opposite effect. This last scheme was cited enthusiastically by the Home Office secretary to the Tory conference in October 1993.

CHAPTER SIX

Conclusion: The Politics of Institutions

What I hope this book has demonstrated is the tenacity of the origins of British and American work-welfare once they were established. This viscidity has survived attempts to broaden the types of programs implemented or to modify understandings about the conditions of participants. It has, however, accommodated reforms consistent with the political principles and interests embedded in these programs. I have argued that, within the conflux of political forces (including strong craft and decentralized trades unions and organizationally weak labor movements), electorally powerful right-wing political parties, government structures, and the interplay of these factors (manifest, for instance, in the advantaging of Southern Democrats' interests in Congress), work-welfare assumed a liberal form. Furthermore, from their establishment, the programs acquired administrative solidarity, strengthened by later policy. The attempts of Labour and Democratic party politicians to reform this liberal heritage largely failed because of the difficulty of building and sustaining electoral and political support for such measures. Conversely, Conservative and Republican party politicians enjoyed sufficient electoral and political power to reinforce aspects of this liberal heritage.

In this chapter, I review my theoretical argument through a consideration of the failure of radical reform in the 1960s and 1970s and the success of conservative programs in the 1980s. I assess the implications of this analysis for historical institutionalism and conclude by emphasizing the importance of the problems intended to be addressed by work-welfare for British and American society.

As explained in chapter 1, in Britain and the United States the institutional arrangements through which work-welfare programs were administered significantly shaped their character and, by creating distinct policy legacies, influenced the limitations and possibilities for reform. This claim required an analysis of the origins of work-welfare programs, particularly of the political interests affected by them. I argued in chapter 2 that the establishment of public employment exchanges required policymakers to accommodate divergent and opposing interests in Britain (those of employers and trades unionists) and to define a new role for the American state in the federal polity (an activism resisted by Southern Democrats, fearful of the effect upon race relations, and by conservative Republicans). Winning agreement from these divergent interests, or at least withstanding their opposition, produced a propensity to design policy satisfying the lowest common denominator (for example, combining the establishment of labor exchanges and unemployment benefit with a work-test mechanism). Thus, in 1909 the president of the Board of Trade, Winston Churchill, assured trades unionists that labor exchanges would not be used to supply strike breakers while placating employers' fears that exchanges would become a "sort of permanent club for the unemployed." Honoring both assurances ineluctably limited labor exchanges' role in the labor market. In 1964, British unionists and employers were allowed to maintain their existing apprenticeship schemes under the newly created industrial training boards. In the United States, ending discrimination in the state employment services and in apprenticeship programs faced comparable strictures. These examples illustrate the pressures constraining the scope of reform.

These original arrangements were maintained, after establishment, not only through administration but also by the preferences of organized interests and political coalitions. As I explained in chapter 3, the most powerful organized groups' interest in work-welfare declined. This not only allowed the status quo to persist but hindered amendment.[1] In the United States, the lobbying activities of the ICESA and the support of powerful committee chairmen in Congress gave work-welfare institutional arrangements political support. Administratively, in both Britain and the United States, public employment exchange officials were irresistibly pushed into a greater concern with applying work-tests of varying types than with placing applicants in jobs. These routines proved so stalwart and deadening that they precluded administrators from widening the remit of their institution to enrich the opportunities of those seeking assistance, especially supplicants lacking any labor market experience or requisite skills. Exchange officials proved uncooperative to new initiatives intended to widen work-welfare. The administration of unemployment benefit by British labor exchange officials in the interwar years gave this institution a devastating legacy. I have not advanced administrative inadequacy as a sole explanation for the disappointing record of job placement agencies; rather, administrative weaknesses reflected political choices and interests.

The institutional bias within work-welfare toward serving the most marginal not only trammeled reform initiatives in the 1960s and 1970s but was reinforced by the programs enacted. For instance, in both countries training schemes were established to ameliorate national skill standards. Although these schemes were intended to serve the needs of job seekers throughout the labor market, the absence of support from business associations or trades unionists, and the powerful presence of an institutional structure targeted on the most disadvantaged, resulted in a further concentration on this group. The Manpower Services Commission, established in Britain in 1973 to improve training, was compelled to target youth and long-term unemployment rather than to formulate a national training program. Training programs have been anti-unemployment programs, conceived of in short-term, low-skill terms, politically motivated and separated from the concerns of those workers in employment. In Britain, such programs have been expanded recently to force down unemployment figures.[2] In the United States, when policymakers in the 1960s attempted to shift Keynesian policy from macroeconomic management to labor-market training programs, they lacked electoral support or an appropriate administrative framework.[3]

The Reform of Work-welfare: Coalitions and Institutional Legacies

Two significant efforts to reform the British and American work-welfare programs have been undertaken. First, during the 1960s and 1970s attempts were made in both Britain and the United States to effect social democratic reform of each polity's work-welfare programs.[4] Each initiative failed. Second, the 1980s were dominated by the revival of right-wing and employer-biased political reforms, and work-welfare was not immune to this trend. British and American policymakers succeeded in tightening the rules governing participation in work-welfare schemes and in linking participation directly with the receipt of benefits or as substitutes for benefits. Several reasons explain the *success* of right-wing policies in the 1980s and the *failure* of the earlier more radical initiatives.

The electoral coalition which is a prerequisite for the initiation and consolidation of social democratic programs did not develop. Historically and comparatively, it has been rare in either Britain or the United States for governments unequivocally committed to social democratic policies to hold office or to hold it with a majority of sufficient magnitude to ensure successful enactment of proposals. In Britain, the natural party of social democracy—Labour—found itself in a sufficiently powerful position to implement such programs on few occasions, notably 1945 (but was then excluded from office for thirteen years after 1951) and in the second half of the 1960s.[5] Labour, for historical and party political reasons, was more concerned with macroeconomic policy, including measures such as nationalization, than with the work-welfare dimension of social citizenship. The more common pattern in Britain has been for Conservative administrations or Labour governments with precarious majorities. Between 1945 and 1992, Labour held power for seventeen years (including the Lib-Lab pact period), the Conservatives for twenty-nine years; during the interwar years, the Conservatives held power for seventeen years. More recently, the Labour Party has suffered a long-term decline in its working-class support.[6] That decline has steepened since 1979. In two of the postwar periods when Labour held power (1945–51 and 1964–70), the party did introduce important work-welfare measures but within the contributory-noncontributory framework. The party neglected training during both periods. In its third period in office (1974–79), Labour expanded training programs through the Manpower Services Commission, but these were responses to unemployment rather than comprehensive schemes, a pattern followed by their successors in the 1980s.

In the United States, as I explained in chapter 1, the construction of the New Deal coalition did succeed in building alliances between diverse groups of voters but these were precarious. They unraveled during the 1960s, as civil rights dominated national politics. The New Deal coalition rested upon a subservient position for black Americans, and once this role was demolished, expectations about work-welfare also changed. The contributory-noncontributory framework and divisions between participants in work-welfare programs and other voters ensured that these programs possessed little capacity to transform attitudes or to win broader support.[7] In the United States before the 1960s, two political systems existed side-by-side: a democratic system in the Northeast, West, and Midwest and an oligarchic one in the South. In the second, black residents were both systematically disenfranchised and subordinated to a repressive agricultural system in which upper-class and many poor whites acquiesced, and to which most Northerners turned a blind eye. Far from building solidarity, an essential feature of New Deal policy was to ensure that dormant hostility between its electoral components was not disturbed. The brief period during which liberal work-welfare appeared to be dissolving in favor of quasi-social democratic measures—the post-1964 War on Poverty era when Johnson made poverty pivotal—quickly failed as the fragile balance of electoral interests underpinning Democratic presidential support was vitiated by conflicts between different parts of the coalition and by the impending Vietnam crisis.[8] Within Congress, Southern control of key committees shaped policy decisions. Choices made during the New Deal determined the dichotomy between contributory and noncontributory programs. For instance, the Roosevelt administration and members of the Congress resolved that a condition of implementing a federal unemployment benefit system was an institutional capacity to test willingness to work, a condition advanced by the President's Committee on Economic Security.[9] This role was devolved to the employment service. As opponents of devolution anticipated, implementing work tests administratively overshadowed the employment service's placement work and reinforced the relief-status public perception of the service. The division of powers between executive and legislature encouraged compromise in public policy, making radical initiatives very difficult.

The weakness of left-wing parties and the difficulty of constructing electoral coalitions to support social democratic reforms contrasts with the capacity of right-wing parties and politicians to win power in the 1980s. In Britain, the electoral weakness of Labour has provided opportunities from which the Conservative party has benefitted. Although the Tories made little effort to modify the programs implemented by the 1945–51 Labour administration before the 1970s, since 1979 they have made decisive changes to work-welfare. Exploiting four consecutive electoral successes, the Conservatives have integrated unemployment and social security rules, abolished the tripartite training commission (MSC), and introduced employer-dominated training councils.

In the United States, the differences between the Democratic and Republican parties' approach to work-welfare have declined since the 1970s. Both have focused on the need to reform welfare by reducing the numbers claiming benefits and imposing work or training requirements upon beneficiaries as a condition of assistance. The overlap reached its fullest expression in the Family Support Act of 1988 when the Reagan White House combined with the Democratic Congress, supported principally by New York Senator Daniel Patrick Moynihan, to agree on the legislation. While Democrats wanted a greater emphasis upon training in work-welfare, the Republicans emphasized mandatory workfare. By threatening to exercise a veto, the Reagan administration ensured that this component was included in the act. There are differences between the two parties in emphases and in their view of compulsion. A Democratic reform would have had less emphasis upon work and compulsion,[10] demonstrating the importance of Republican control of the presidency in 1988.

Efforts to build active labor market policies received little support from either trades unions or employers. In both countries, trades unions have been internally divided, dominated by craft rather than industrial organization and highly decentralized. Alliances between unionists and nonunionists have been unusual. In the United States, hostility rather than cooperation has characterized relations between white unionized workers and black Americans. In Britain, trades unions have suffered an exceptional onslaught in terms both of membership decline and restrictive legislation since the 1970s. At times of mass unemployment, such as the 1930s in both countries or 1981 through 1983 and 1991 through 1993 in Britain, when the potential to forge a widely based political coalition of the unemployed and marginalized has been greatest, the ability of labor to effect policy has been weakest. The role of unions and employers in British and American training programs illustrates how these groups accepted arrangements which excluded the unemployed in categories B and C (the long-term unemployed with little work experience and welfare recipients with no work experience), limited the scope of work-welfare programs and protected contributory-based schemes. In training, this pattern has resulted in a system dominated by apprenticeships,[11] the underdevelopment of vocational educational programs, and a limited approach to training for unemployed persons and benefit recipients. The response of the AFL-CIO to Nixon's family assistance plan (FAP), a negative income tax scheme, is indicative of organized labor's approach. In a memorandum discussing welfare reform, AFL-CIO staffer Bert Seidman noted that Nixon's scheme "violates principles the labor movement has long espoused, including opposition to wage subsidies and minimum reliance on means-tested programs."[12] Nixon's program would have extended a basic minimum-income support to all families, something the AFL-CIO opposed. Organized labor feared any likely increase in cheap labor stimulated by the removal of work disincentives. As Quadagno writes of the same proposal, the AFL-CIO did not support a universal welfare state: "Unionists had little concern for the nonunionized black and female low-wage service industry workers for they did not compete in the same labor market, and they took action to ensure that gender and racial barriers to class fragmentation remained."[13] Since few women worked in industries organized by craft unions, their interests were excluded from those of highly skilled wage-earners. The AFL-CIO lobbied for civil rights and workers' rights after 1945, but such activity has limited benefit for those outside of the workforce and affected by work-welfare. Organized labor has been glad to support selective noncontributory programs allocated on a means-tested basis for nonunion members but has been disinclined to mobilize its political strength to build universal public welfare programs.[14]

In Britain, union density has been high compared with many other industrial countries but still only covers about 50 percent of its potential.[15] Whereas American unions have been limited by their concentration on organizing in manufacturing workplaces, British trades unions have been hampered by strong local organizations determined to maintain job control at the plant level. In this ambition they were successful. Collective bargaining was decentralized, a strategy most appropriate to periods of economic prosperity such as the postwar decades rather than to recessions, as witness the progressive weakening of the unions since 1981. British unions have had the enormous advantage, compared with American ones, of being wedded to a historically effective political party. The Labour Party indeed began as an offshoot of the trades unions movement.[16] The relationship between trades unions and the Labour Party was, until recently, productive, providing the electoral and financial base

for achieving important social democratic initiatives such as those associated with the 1945–51 government, but not powerful enough to with-
stand the conservative political challenge of the 1980s and 1990s.[17]

Trades unionists' acceptance of the divisions between workers, whether
based on skills or race, has hampered efforts to ameliorate work-welfare
programs. Among workers formally organized, unions based in decentralized craft traditions have been most influential. British unionists have
placed a higher value on local job and training control than on national
initiatives. Consequently, the national union organization was often in
conflict rather than harmony with Labour governments. The union movement did not provide the support requisite for the Labour Party to ensure
its electoral renewal and, hence, the conditions to transcend liberal work-
welfare. For instance, although the industrial training boards were established by the Conservatives in 1964, they functioned first during the
Wilson Labour administration of 1964 to 1970. As many observers subsequently noted, the boards simply consolidated extant training practices,
particularly in apprenticeships, rather than becoming an opportunity to
expand training into new areas and to broaden the apprenticeship system.
Both trades unions and employers colluded in this process, the former
dominated by craft unions who considered local job control and high
wages for their members a greater priority than a successful national training scheme.

Important groups of workers affected by work-welfare programs have
been excluded from organized labor, whether intentionally (for example,
black workers in the United States) or unintentionally as a consequence
of union organization (for example, arising from the influence of craft
unions). This tendency was more pronounced in the United States than
in Britain because it assumed a racial dimension, but even in Britain the
skilled-unskilled dichotomy has been divisive.[18] It was also accepted and
reinforced in government policy. A 1948 Conservative party document
analyzed apprenticeships in terms of this dichotomy:

> A more difficult, but not less important task in the field of education
> and training in industry, is the provision of appropriate means of devel-
> opment for those who are destined to accept in the future the more menial
> tasks and for which no formal apprenticeships are required. Good instruc-
> tional method on the job, together with educational and training activ-
> ities away from the job, can help these people to appreciate the significance
> of their work. These schemes, in providing an opportunity for develop-
> ment and an understanding of purpose, have an important function to
> fulfil in contrast to the more formal apprenticeship schemes available
> to other employees.[19]

The way in which workers were organized in trades unions, and the control exercised by those unions over training and apprenticeship programs, was as powerful a factor in work-welfare as any employer-worker distinctions. During the Second World War, when black American workers had an opportunity to work in industry in substantial numbers, especially in defense-related plants, this opportunity occurred only after employers had exhausted sources of white and female workers and after President Roosevelt issued an executive order requiring equality of employment. Federal attempts to establish equal civil rights for black American workers included reforming industries controlled by craft unions, who ardently resisted such modifications.[20]

Organized employers have rarely advocated extensive training policies. They have protected their own interests, conceived of as being outside of state labor market policy. This position proved increasingly problematic in the 1980s as skill shortages affected production. In the United States, both the U.S. National Association of Manufacturing and the U.S. Chamber of Commerce have urged greater investment in education[21] and proposals to broaden apprenticeships have appeared in the 1990s.[22] The U.S. National Alliance of Business has also advocated skills improvement.[23] In Britain, the CBI issued a pamphlet in July 1989 urging a "skills revolution" as they too accepted the long-term implications of underfunding education and training.[24] Business associations faced crises in the levels of skills which their own indifference to earlier programs had helped foster. These problems derive from the voluntarist approach to training in both countries, an approach condoned by the state.[25] Voluntarism has meant that training remains minimal and consistent with the interests of employers (minimizing costs) and trades unions (protecting their members' interests whether they be highly paid apprenticeships or excluding part-time workers). A group established in the 1960s—the U.S. National Alliance of Business[26]—has been sympathetic to the plight of the most disadvantaged and has participated in schemes to improve their labor market prospects. In Britain, the Association of British Chambers of Commerce, a group representing smaller businesses and employers has been brought into training policy in the 1980s and 1990s. Unaffected by early labor organization and largely excluded from the postwar voluntarist training policy regimes, these organizations have been placed at the center of the Conservatives's measures since 1988 displaying union representation. They lack the legitimacy and organizational infrastructure of their continental counterparts, though these may of course develop.[27] They must also compete with TECs.

The structure of the U.S. state has helped conservative, and hindered radical, reform. The threat of a presidential veto ensured the inclusion of conservative measures in policy in 1988. Before the 1960s, congressional committee structures reinforced the dominance of Southern Democrats.

Because committee assignment rested upon seniority and because the Democratic party was overwhelmingly dominant in the Southern states, the capacity of conservative white Democrats to ensure that work-welfare programs did not disturb landlord-tenant or black-white power relations was high. For example, the 1933 Wagner-Peyser Act establishing the public employment service was created as a federal-state program giving considerable power and autonomy to state administrators. This arrangement ensured that eligibility rules advantaged white, and disadvantaged black, job seekers. On those rare occasions when Democrats failed to control the House or Senate, a coalition of conservative Republicans and Southern Democrats ensured that Congress still remained a bulwark against reforms disruptive of Southern power relations. Filibustering was a powerful tool in the service of white dominance in the South.

In Britain, the centralized state offered a much more powerful resource for legislating policy. However, the preference of both employers and unionists to retain autonomy and to minimize their costs constituted a barrier to implementing training programs; the articulation of interests by these two groups also influenced significantly the way in which labor exchanges were organized. By the same token, government policies—such as those in the 1980s—effecting retrenchment rather than expansion could rely upon a powerful executive for enactment.

Right-wing political parties have been ably assisted by pressure groups and policy networks promoting conservative policy proposals. Both the Conservative and Republican parties, but especially the former, have been closely associated with the revival of a liberalism characterized as the "new right," and both have striven to restore liberal tenets in work-welfare programs. The modern version of social citizenship,[28] promulgated by New Right pressure groups and conservatives, is to match any rights to assistance a citizen holds with a corollary set of duties which must be satisfied as a condition of the former.[29] Not only did the Conservative and Republican parties achieve sufficient electoral strength to leave their imprint upon work-welfare programs in the 1980s, but they served also as conduits for liberal ideas and proposals. In Britain, the Conservatives promoted free-market remedies promulgated by so-called New Right interest groups. These groups advocated radical reforms to restore and strengthen the liberal character of work-welfare. In the United States, liberal proposals were also favored by the Republicans and by advisers to President Reagan, although their influence on legislation was somewhat diluted by Republican weakness in Congress. The Congress had alternative proposals for reform, notably those formulated by the National Governors' Association. However, the dominant actor was the Republican president, Ronald Reagan, who threatened to use his presidential veto if a mandatory work requirement was not included in the Family Support Act.

History, Institutions, and Politics

There is undoubtedly some validity in the claim that institutional arrangements influence policy outcomes and shape, in part, subsequent policies.[30] More puzzling from my analysis, and inadequately explained in this historical institutionalist perspective, is the commonality of policy outcomes in Britain and the United States despite the fundamental differences in formal state structures. In this respect, these theorists seem to neglect unduly the political origin of programs and the political conflicts and interests reflected in institutional arrangements—which also differ across the two cases. These factors can best be understood through detailed historical analysis of the programs' origins and development. Institutionalist theories need to be much more informed by historical analysis than is often the case. Such an approach is required both better to understand the functioning of programs and to understand how they embody solutions to political conflicts which either limit or enhance subsequent modification. It is not just institutional arrangements that are tenacious, but the political interests and choices reflected in them may remain influential upon future policies. I have argued that the failure of the reform initiatives in the 1960s and 1970s and the success of reform in the 1980s reflects not only the compatibility (or incompatibility) of the respective schemes with extant institutions' expressions of political interests but also efficacious political coalition formation. The compromises and interests influencing institutional arrangements do not necessarily evaporate or dissipate over time. Institutionalists are in danger of neglecting the politics and history of institutions.[31]

Institutional and policy legacies set the framework within which politicians and political parties undertake reform. They define ideas and transform them into proposals suitable for enactment, from Churchill and Roosevelt to Thatcher and Reagan. Furthermore, they have, on occasion, the electoral mandate and authority to effect reforms. The strength of the mandate matters for the scope of reform: Roosevelt in 1933, Labour in 1945, and the Conservatives in 1987 were all well-placed to pursue reforms. The sources of ideas for parties are also important. For instance, the Conservatives, from 1975 to 1992, were well connected with New Right radical think tanks whose members formulated and propagated a range of ideas and proposals useful for politicians seeking both solutions to enduring problems and radical schemes. President Reagan enjoyed comparable support in the United States, and the state demonstration programs provided a further source of proposals. President Clinton is well supplied with proposals. It is commonplace that the Labour Party has lacked innovative proposals since the 1970s despite establishing its own think tank.[32] Other sources of ideas include government commissions or reformers who win the ear of politicians. Of the former type, notable historical instances are the proposals and ideas emanating from the Royal Commission on the Poor Laws in the first decade of this century through Roosevelt's Committee on Economic Security in 1935 to Beveridge's report in 1942. Prominent individuals have included Beveridge, Commons, and their contemporaries. I have tried to demonstrate, in earlier chapters, the extent to which these proposals were consistent with liberal and market tenets. Thus, Beveridge and Commons were determined to harness government powers to organize the labor market but not in any way to supplant or replace it. The principle of the public employment exchange was driven by a desire to increase the efficiency of the labor market. These reformers undoubtedly wished to address the poverty and waste their societies faced but did not advocate any substantial collectivist solutions. Not surprisingly, both Britain and the United States opted for insurance-based welfare programs, and in each case legislators were mindful of the relationship between state support and disincentives. Thus, politicians and political parties play a more important role in policy formulation than some scholars acknowledge.[33] The importance of institutions, and the activities of bureaucrats, rest upon prior political conflicts and the mobilization of (or failure to mobilize) interests.

British and American work-welfare programs have been consistently designed to accommodate, rather than to perturb, conflicting interests. They have been underfunded and have had to depend on inadequate administrative frameworks. Work-welfare programs have also been constructed around categories of inclusion and exclusion rather than designed to transcend such divisions. This practice has reinforced the inadequacies of the programs implemented, inadequacies best understood by examination of their historical origins. Governments fear the effects of unemployment and attempt to control them. In one version of this priority, the president of the Board of Trade, Winston Churchill, observed to employers in 1909 that "there is no reason at all why people should wander about in a loafing and idle manner; if they are not earning their living they ought to be put under some control."[34] Other approaches are more benign, assume that "idleness" is not universally voluntary, and attempt to assist the unemployed in obtaining work. The preceding chapters have examined this range of responses.

Citizens actively seeking work arrive at this destination from different paths, in some cases from welfare status, in others from previous experience of jobs no longer existing. However experienced, unemployment is the most fundamental social and political problem confronting Britain and the United States, a challenge to politicians and parties of all ideologies. For whatever reason—technological change, demographic changes affecting labor market participation, higher productivity, decline of labor-intensive industries—the numbers of permanently unemployed have grown and most efforts to reduce them have failed. This intractability brings with it a host of mostly unwanted social and political consequences for Britain and the United States. Unemployment is not an exclusive cause of social malaise, but its persistence and salience indisputably contributes to this condition. Work-welfare programs in Britain and the United States—workfare schemes, training programs for the unemployed, and job placement assistance—are the principal government response to this pervasive problem. For the most part, the schemes included under these rubrics have been inadequate to their tasks. Without a more serious commitment to developing apprenticeship-style vocational skills (skills transferable across jobs) for the unemployed and most marginal members of the British and American workforces, thereby facilitating the erosion of the division between the employed and the unemployed, the pernicious effects of unemployment will remain. Furthermore, the divisions (whether on criteria of work, skills, race, or gender) between those citizens fully included in society and those rendered marginal will increase within these two polities, whose respective political cultures attach a distinctive value to working as a source of self-respect.

Comparative Tables on Work-Welfare

Table 1 Changing Status of the United States Employment Service after 1940

Year	Legislation or Modification
1942	State employment security agencies federalized and USES transferred to War Manpower Commission from the Department of Labor.
1943	State employment security agency administrators begin lobbying Congress for agreement to return agencies to state control at the end of the war.
1945	Truman issues executive order transferring USES back to the Department of Labor.
1948	Congress uses appropriation bill to transfer USES from Department of Labor to the Federal Security Agency under the Social Security Board.
1949	Congress reorganizes federal agencies and shifts both the USES and the unemployment insurance agency to the Department of Labor.
1962	Manpower Development and Training Act passed and to be administered through a new Office of Manpower Automation and Training (OMAT).
1963	OMAT replaced by new Manpower Administration except for research and development.
1964	Economic Opportunity Act passed, creating community action agencies with tasks similar to those of the USES-state employment security agencies.
1967	Changes within Manpower Administration and USES confirmed within the Bureau of Employment Security.
1973	Comprehensive Employment and Training Act (CETA) passed, creating local primary-sponsor agencies free to use or ignore USES system.
1975	Manpower Administration renamed Employment and Training Administration (ETA).
1982	Wagner-Peyser Act amended for the first time under Title V of the Job Training Partnership Act of that year.
1988	Omnibus Trade and Competitiveness Act passed, replacing Title V of the JTPA and placing USES authority under Title VI.

Table 2 Selected List of State Demonstration Work-Welfare Programs[1]

State	Program
Arkansas	Arkansas Work Program (Project SUCCESS)
California	Greater Avenues for Independence (GAIN)
Connecticut[2]	JOB CONNECTION
Georgia	Positive Employment and Community Help (PEACH)
Indiana	Indiana Manpower Placement and Comprehensive Training (IMPACT) program
Kansas	Replaces WIN with CWEP in 1982
Maine[3]	Welfare Employment, Education & Training Program (WEET)
Massachusetts	Employment Training Choices (ET)
Michigan[4]	Michigan Opportunity and Skills Training (MOST)
Nebraska	Job Support Program
New Jersey[5]	Realizing Economic Achievement (REACH)
Ohio[6]	Fair Work Program
Oklahoma	Employment and Training Program (E and T)
Oregon[7]	JOBS program
Tennessee[8]	Victory Network
Virginia	Employment Services Program (ESP)
Wisconsin	Work Experience and Job Training program (WEJT)/Building Employment Skills Today (BEST)

Notes:

1. For a comparison of pre- and post-1981 state programs, see Emmett Carson et. al., *AFDC, Food Stamps, and Work: History, Rules and Research* (Washington, DC: Congressional Research Service 87-599 EPW, 17 July 1987).

2. See report to the General Assembly on the Job Connection, Connecticut's Work Incentive (WIN) Demonstration Project (Hartford, CT: Connecticut Department of Income Maintenance, 1 January 1987).

3. See Maine Department of Human Services, Division of Welfare Employment, *WEET: The Welfare Employment, Education and Training Program: Its Creation, Operation and Future Direction* (Augusta, ME: Department of Human Services, January 1987): "The WEET program goal is to assist participants to move toward maximum economic and personal self-sufficiency by helping them prepare for, obtain and maintain employment" (p. 13). See also The Statewide Work Group on Adult Welfare Recipients, *A Path of Self Sufficiency for Maine's Welfare Recipients,* Interim Report (Augusta, ME: Department of Welfare Employment, September 1985).

4. Established in 1984. For details, see Office of Planning Budget and Evaluation, Planning and Evaluation Division, *Michigan Opportunity and Skill Training (MOST) Evaluation: Interim Report* (January 1989) and *Interim Evaluation of the Michigan Opportunities Skills Training Program* (March 1989), both produced by the Michigan Department of Social Services.

5. See New Jersey Department of Human Services, *REACH: County Plan Guidelines* (Trenton, NJ: NJDHS, December 1987). This document provides a detailed account of how each of the twenty-one counties were to prepare their REACH programs in accordance with state requirements. The document declares that REACH "is New Jersey's program to replace welfare with work, dependence with self-sufficiency, and less than fully productive lives with opportunity" (p. 2).

6. Ohio Department of Human Services, *Ohio Fair Work Program* (Columbus, OH: Department of Human Services, December 1987).

7. See State of Oregon Plan for Operating the Work Incentive Demonstration Program, submitted by Governor Victor Atiyeh 1 January 1982 (Salem, OR: Department of Human Resources, 1982).

8. Tennessee Department of Human Services, *Victory Network Program: Interim Findings,* prepared by Kay S. Marshall and Ronald Randolph January 1987 (Memphis, TN: TDHS, 1987).

Table 3 Apprenticeships in the United States

Year	In training on January 1	New Registrations	Completions	Cancellations	In training on December 31
1941	18,300	14,177	1,289	5,051	26,137
1942	26,127	20,701	2,011	4,683	40,144
1943	40,144	11,661	1,715	6,975	43,115
1944	43,115	7,775	2,122	8,197	40,571
1945	40,571	23,040	1,568	5,078	56,965
1946	56,695	84,730	2,042	8,436	131,217
1947	131,217	94,238	7,311	25,190	192,954
1948	192,954	85,918	13,375	35,117	230,380
1949	230,380	66,745	25,045	41,257	230,823
1950	230,823	60,186	38,533	49,747	202,729
1951	202,729	63,991	38,754	56,845	171,011
1952	172,477	62,842	33,098	43,689	158,532
1953	158,532	73,620	28,561	43,333	160,528
1954	160,258	58,939	27,383	33,139	158,675
1955	158,675	67,265	24,795	26,423	174,722
1956	174,722	74,062	27,231	33,416	188,137
1957	189,684	59,638	30,356	33,275	185,691
1958	185,691	49,569	30,647	26,918	177,695
1959	177,695	66,230	37,375	40,545	166,005
1960	172,161	54,100	31,727	33,406	161,128
1961	161,128	49,482	28,547	26,414	155,649
1962	155,649	55,590	25,918	26,434	158,887
1963	158,887	57,204	26,029	26,744	163,318
1964	163,318	59,960	25,744	27,001	170,533
1965	170,533	68,507	24,917	30,168	183,955
1966	183,955	85,031	26,511	34,964	207,511
1967	207,511	97,896	37,299	47,957	220,151
1968	207,517	111,012	37,287	43,246	237,996
1969	237,996	123,163	39,646	47,561	273,952
1970	269,626	106,779	45,102	53,610	279,693
1971	278,451	78,535	42,071	43,104	274,024
1972	247,840	103,527	53,059	56,750	264,122
1973	243,956	133,258	43,580	49,860	283,774
1974	280,965	112,830	46,454	56,292	291,049
1975	284,562	83,018	45,765	55,338	266,477
1976	265,647	88,418	49,447	49,650	254,968
1977	253,993	107,897	54,347	44,957	262,586
1978	263,660	131,139	50,464	54,111	290,224
1979	289,168	136,786	43,454	58,634	323,866

**Table 4 Registered Apprentices in Workloads of the Federal Bureau of
Apprenticeship Training (BAT) and State Apprenticeship (SAC) Councils**

Year	BAT/SAC End-of-Period Apprentices	Percentage of minorities	Percentage of females
1980	320,073	17.1	4.8
1981	315,887	18.4	5.7
1982	286,698	18.7	6.0
1983	253,187	20.2	6.6
1984	232,583	18.9	6.7
1985	222,591	19.9	6.4
1986	224,778	19.8	6.4
1987	243,261	20.1	6.4
1988	253,134	20.9	6.9
1989	263,023	21.6	7.2
1990	283,352	22.5	7.1

Table 5 Manpower Services Commission Staffing

Date (mo/yr)	Employment division	Training division	Special programs	Skillcentre agency	Total
10/78	15,394	9,101	813.5		25,720
10/79	14,960	8,649	1,156		26,172
10/80	13,667	8,309	1,923		24,622
10/81	12,925	7,933	2,055		24,251
10/82	12,684	7,596	2,634		24,184
4/83	11,753	5,156		4,733	22,688
4/84	11,179	5,299		4,310	21,929
4/85	10,726	5,069		3,805	20,803
4/86	11,310	5,539		2,943	21,075
4/87	13,332	6,248		2,958	23,953
3/88	*	8,143.5		2,936	12,164

Source: Adapted from various *MSC Annual Reports* and the *Training Commission Annual Report* for 1987/88.

*In 1988, the MSC was renamed the Training Commission and its former employment service was transferred to the Department of Employment.

Table 6 Manpower Services Commission budget (£ million)

Year	Total MSC	Total Employment* & Enterprise Group	Total Vocational** Education & Training
1978/79	641.3		
1979/80	727.1		
1980/81	869.3		
1981/82	1,111.4		
1982/83	1,343.2		
1983/84	1,897.3	677.6	1,181.4
1984/85	2,110.1	929.9	1,133.5
1985/86	2,386.7	293.6	1,212.3
1986/87	3,102.2	420.4	1,448.5
1987/88	3,232.0	227.6	1,774.8

Source: *Manpower Services Commission Annual Reports* for 1978–1988.

*Includes Jobcentres, Restart, enterprise allowance scheme; the content of this category changes almost every year, limiting comparability.

**Includes YTS, new JTS, Job Training Program, and technical and vocational education initiative; the content of this category changes almost every year, limiting comparability.

Table 7 Key Work-Welfare Legislation in the United States

Date	Legislation
1933	Wagner-Peyser Act passed, creating United States Employment Service.
1935	Social Security Act passed.
1946	Employment Act passed.
1950	Social Security Act Amendments broadened coverage to children and the elderly.
1953	Department of Health, Education and Welfare created.
1957	Civil Rights Act set up Commission on Civil Rights.
1962	Social Security Act Amendments extended services for families with dependent children. Community Work and Training Program provided eduction for AFDC male recipients.
1962	Manpower Demonstration and Training Act, first major federal training legislation.
1964	Civil Rights Act. Food Stamps Act. Economic Opportunity Act, Title V, established Work Experience and Training Program as option for states.
1965	Older Americans Act established Administration on Ageing. Medicare and Medicaid. Elementary and Secondary School Act provides federal assistance for schools in poor neighborhoods.
1967	Work Incentive Program (WIN) provides employment skills to recipients of AFDC benefits.
1973	Comprehensive Employment and Training Act (CETA), federal employment creation program.

Table 7 Key Work-Welfare Legislation in the United States *(cont.)*

Date	Legislation
1975	Social Security Act Amendments provide services through block grants to states.
1978	CETA amended to create public service employment (PSE) program.
1981	Omnibus Budget Reconciliation Act and Social Service Block Grant Act reduced federal grants to states and allowed demonstration WIN/work-welfare programs.
1982	Job Training Partnership Act, replaced CETA.
1983	Food Stamp Employment and Training Program.
1988	Family Support Act.

Source: Various sources, including Robert S. Magill, "United States of America," in John Dixon and Robert P. Scheurell, eds., *Social Welfare in Developed Market Countries* (London: Routledge, 1989); and Desmond King "Citizenship as Obligation in the United States: Title II of the Family Support Act of 1988," in U. Vogel and M. Moran, eds., *The Frontiers of Citizenship* (London: Macmillan, 1991).

Table 8 Key Work-Welfare Legislation and Measures in Britain

Date	Legislation
1601	43d Elizabeth, Chapter 2 Poor Law
1662	Amendment to 1601 Act: Law of Settlement; right to return a person to former residence if justices anticipated he would require assistance at a future date.
1782	Gilbert Act, ended practice of contracting out care for the poor and established right to erect poorhouses.
1834	Poor Law reform: Poor Law Amendment Act introducing principle of less eligibility and requirement to be confined in workhouse.
1905	Unemployed Workmen's Act.
1909	Labour Exchanges Act.
1911	National Unemployment Insurance.
1920	Unemployment Insurance Act, increased the number of insured workers from 4 to 11.4 million.
1921	Unemployment Insurance Act; widened numbers of those eligible for unemployment benefits. "Genuinely seeking work" clause established for testing applicants for unemployment benefits; abolished in March 1930.
1930	Unemployment Act.
1942	Beveridge Plan: Social Insurance and Allied Services. The report emphasized universality for unemployment insurance whereby all working citizens would contribute and be entitled to receive benefits; contributions and benefits would be set at flat rates equal for all citizens; and the benefits paid out should provide for subsistence but not provide anything beyond that. Recommended an unlimited period of benefit receipt if the recipient attended a work or training center; not enacted.
1944	White Paper on Employment Policy.
1945	Family Allowance scheme established.
1946	National Insurance Act. Enacted main element of the Beveridge Plan with Labour agreeing to the contributory basis to insurance with payments by both employees and employers. Assistance Board (subsequently renamed National Assistance Board) to set benefit levels.

Table 8 Key Work-Welfare Legislation and Measures in Britain *(cont.)*

Date	Legislation
1948	National Assistance Act, provided assistance to the destitute with no income or savings.
1966	Government introduces earnings-related unemployment insurance benefits and contributions, first significant modification to the 1946 program.
1971	"People and Jobs" policy statement recommends separation of placement work (Jobcentres) from distribution of benefits (unemployment benefit offices). First Jobcentre opened in 1973, with 550 in place by 1979.
1982	Abolition of compulsory registration for employment at Jobcentres.
1985	Social Security Act, empowered the Employment Secretary to designate training programs "approved training schemes": trainees refusing a place without good cause on such a scheme could lose their benefits.
1986	Social Security Act, began reforms of the benefit system operative from April 1988. Renamed "supplementary benefits" for those with insufficient income to live on "income support"; provides a basic weekly rate (£33.40 for those over 25 years of age) with premiums for particular needs. "Family credit" replaced "income support" for low-income working families with children. New housing benefit. All these benefits means-tested. Social Fund established to replace one-off single payments system, which is cash-limited. Money lent, not given, to claimants.
1986	New requirement that everyone on the unemployment register for more than six months is called to a Restart interview to determine their availability for work and to give advice about training programs. Failure to attend can result in loss of benefits. Pushes the Employment Service back to its traditional role of serving the unemployed. Imposition of a six-month disqualification from unemployment benefit on people leaving a job voluntarily.
1988	Social Security Act, mandated participation for young people in a YTS scheme with refusal resulting in loss of benefits.
1988	Employment Act, Part II, disqualified unemployed persons from receiving unemployment benefits if they withdraw from a training scheme "without good cause."
1988	Jobcentres and unemployment benefit offices reintegrated into a single Employment Service, which has been increasingly privatized. UBOs police benefits and test applicants availability for work; Jobcentres conduct Restart interviews and place recipients of training schemes.
1989	Social Security Act, requires unemployed persons to demonstrate that they are "seeking employment actively" as a condition of receiving unemployment benefits. Evidence includes letters and records of telephone calls. Initial proposal that unemployed people would be threatened with loss of benefits if they turned down jobs of less than twenty-four hours a week was dropped during parliamentary passage.
1989	February: easing of new social security rules that had prevented many 16- and 17-year-olds from receiving state benefits when they left home and/or were not participating in a YTS scheme.
1990	July: training courses made compulsory for those unemployed for two or more years and who reject assistance at their Restart interviews.
1996	New "Job-Seeker's Allowance" to replace unemployment benefit. Recipients to enter "Job-Seeker's Agreement" in exchange for the payment.

NOTES

Introduction

1. Stalin declared that socialism of the Soviet variety transformed labor "from a shameful and heavy burden into a matter of honour, matter of fame, matter of valour and heroism." Quoted in P. T. Kilburn, "A Labor Day Message No One Asked to Hear," in the *New York Times,* 5 September 1993, E:1.

2. For this term, see T. H. Marshall, *Class, Citizenship and Social Development* (New York: Doubleday, 1964), and discussions in Desmond S. King and J. Waldron, "Citizenship, Social Citizenship and the Defence of Welfare Provision," *British Journal of Political Science* 18 (1988): 415–43; R. Lister, "Women, Economic Dependency and Citizenship," *Journal of Social Policy* 19 (1990): 445–67; and M. Roche, *Rethinking Citizenship* (Oxford: Polity, 1992).

3. House of Commons-7182/1893, "Report on Agencies and Methods for Dealing with the Unemployed," *Parliamentary Papers, 1893–94,* vol. LXXXII, p. 11, my emphasis.

4. Karl Polanyi, *The Great Transformation* (Boston: Beacon, 1944), p. 135.

5. Despite forcing most citizens, especially the poorest, to earn a living through labor market participation, the market economy seldom provided a sufficient number of openings for this precept to be realized. For some analysts of capitalism the maintenance of reserve labor (that is, unemployed and available for work) is a crucial aspect of productivity and seen as such by employers. See M. Kalecki, "Political Aspects of Full Employment," *Political Quarterly* 14 (1943): 322–31.

6. *Parliamentary Debates,* House of Commons, 5th series (1909–), vol. 5, (19 May) col. 503.

7. Throughout this book I use the terms "liberal" and "liberalism" in a British-European sense and not in the common American usage.

8. I use the terms "public employment exchange," "public employment system," "employment service," and "labor exchange" interchangeably.

9. See C. Forman, *Industrial Town: Self-Portrait of St Helens in the 1920s* (London: Cameron and Taylor in association with David Charles, 1978), p. 69.

10. A. P. Jephcott, *Rising Twenty* (London: Macmillan, 1953), p. 120.

11. House Committee on Education and Labor, Select Subcommittee on Labor, *The Role and Mission of the Federal-State Employment Service in the American Economy,* House of Representatives 88th Cong., 2d sess., December 1964, p. 31.

12. Public Record Office (PRO) LAB2/210/33/LE716/1909. Copy of evidence taken before the Royal Commission on Labour, August 1892, p. 11.

13. B. Bjornaraa, "A Historical Sketch of Public Employment," *Employment Service News* 2, no. 2 (February–March 1935).

14. This enthusiasm seems endless. In October 1993, the Tory party's endorsement of the New Jersey work-welfare scheme which penalized mothers who had additional children while receiving public benefits was a crowd-winner at its annual conference.

15. See C. C. Ragin, *The Comparative Method* (Berkeley: University of California Press, 1987), with whose characterization of case-oriented research I would broadly agree: "The goals of case-oriented investigation often are both historically interpretive and causally analytic. Interpretive work . . . attempts to account for significant historical outcomes or sets of comparable outcomes or processes by piecing evidence together in a manner sensitive to historical chronology and offering limited historical generalizations which are sensitive to context. Thus, comparativists who use case-oriented strategies often want to understand or interpret specific cases because of their intrinsic value. [The causal-analytic] goal is to produce limited generalizations concerning the causes of theoretically defined categories of empirical phenomena (such as the emergence of class-based political parties) common to a set of cases" (p. 35).

Chapter One

1. House of Commons-7182/1893, "Report on Agencies and Methods for Dealing with the Unemployed," *Parliamentary Papers 1893–94*, vol. LXXXII, p. 407. For the best study of such policies in Britain, see José Harris's seminal study, *Unemployment and Politics* (Oxford: Clarendon Press, 1972), especially chap. 3.

2. See, among a vast literature, Karl de Schweinitz, *England's Road to Social Security* (Philadelphia: University of Pennsylvania, 1943); William R. Brock, *Welfare, Democracy and the New Deal* (New York and Cambridge: Cambridge University Press, 1988); and Michael B. Katz, *In the Shadow of the Poorhouse* (New York: Basic Books, 1986). The principal characteristics of the Elizabethan Poor Law of 1601—including the principle of local responsibility, outdoor relief for the deserving poor, and the later workhouse regime—were adopted by the American states both during and after the colonial period.

3. For recent reviews, see A. S. Orloff, *The Politics of Pensions* (Madison, WI: University of Wisconsin Press, 1993), chap. 2, and T. Skocpol, *Protecting Soldiers and Mothers* (Cambridge, MA: Harvard University Press, 1992), Introduction.

4. "Labor movement" and "power resources" are terms used interchangeably. In the analysis of the welfare state neo-Marxists have been influential with the labor mobilization and power resources views. See, among others, G. Esping-Andersen, *Politics Against Markets* (Princeton, NJ: Princeton University Press, 1985); W. Korpi, *The Democratic Class Struggle* (London: Routledge, Kegan and Paul, 1983); J. Stephens, *The Transition from Capitalism to Socialism* (London: Macmillan, 1979). For different variants, particularly a discussion of the role of agrarian interests, see P. Baldwin, *The Politics of Social Solidarity* (New York and Cambridge: Cambridge University Press, 1990), chap. 1.

5. Classically, in Sweden the solidaristic wages policy was designed to win the support of as large a part of the electorate of the Social Democratic Party as possible. Furthermore, Swedish governments, controlled by the Social Democrats, have spent more on training programs than on unemployment benefits, thereby

keeping unemployment to low levels comparatively. The standard account is G. Esping-Andersen, *Politics Against Markets* (Princeton, NJ: Princeton University Press, 1985), whose study examines a much greater range of policies than considered in this book.

6. See Stephens, *The Transition from Capitalism to Socialism;* see also the power resources model in Walter Korpi, "Power, Politics, and State Autonomy in the Development of Social Citizenship: Social Rights during Sickness in Eighteen OECD Countries since 1930," *American Sociological Review* 54 (1989): 309–28. On the limits of the social democratic strategy in Sweden, see J. Pontusson, *The Limits of Social Democracy* (Ithaca, NY: Cornell University Press, 1992).

7. As Stephens recognizes. On more general problems with this thesis, see P. Swenson, "Bringing Capital Back In, or Social Democracy Reconsidered: Employer Power, Cross-Class Alliances and Centralization of Industrial Relations in Denmark and Sweden," *World Politics* 43 (1991): 513–44.

8. Esping-Andersen offers the following definition of a social democratic model: "The principles of universalism and decommodification of social rights were extended to the new middle classes . . . [T]he social democrats pursued a welfare state that would promote an equality of the highest standards, not an equality of minimal needs as was pursued elsewhere." This is contrasted with a liberal model in which "means-tested assistance, modest universal transfers, or modest social-insurance plans predominate. Benefits cater mainly to a clientele of low-income, usually working-class, state dependents. In this model, the progress of social reform has been severely circumscribed by traditional, liberal work-ethic norms" (G. Esping-Andersen, *The Three Worlds of Welfare Capitalism* [Oxford: Polity Press, 1990], pp. 27, 26). See also C. Pierson, *Beyond the Welfare State?* (Oxford: Polity Press, 1991), and Baldwin, *The Politics of Social Solidarity.*

9. As Piore and Sabel write, "Craftsmen monopolize the skills in their trade, and the craft is perpetuated by transmission of these skills from one generation to another on the job, through apprenticeship. Limitation of the number of apprentices and of what is taught to outsiders is the craft community's best long-term defense against scarcity of work. Indirectly, through the market, this limitation upon entry into the trade also facilitates the craft's control of wages" (M. Piore and C. Sabel, *The Second Industrial Divide* [New York: Basic 1984], p. 116).

10. See Library of Congress, National Association for the Advancement of Colored People (NAACP) Papers III-A, Box A180, Folder: Labor, Apprenticeship Training. NAACP, "Negro Wage Earners and Apprenticeships" (Washington, DC: NAACP, 1960), p. 80.

11. See W. Galenson, *The CIO Challenge to the AFL: A History of the American Labor Movement, 1935–41* (Cambridge, MA: Harvard University Press, 1960).

12. See Paul Bagguley, "Protest, Acquiescence and the Unemployed: A Comparative Analysis of the 1930s and 1980s," *British Journal of Sociology* 43 (1992); or F. F. Piven and R. Cloward, *Poor People's Movements: Why They Succeed, How They Fail* (New York: Vintage, 1979).

13. It is not self-evident that those at the margins of the labor market in countries such as Sweden or Germany have been any more powerful than their counterparts in Britain and the USA. Rather, they have been linked to powerful labor movements. One example of the latter sort of phenomenon is provided by Ruggie's

comparative study of the state's policies for working women in Britain and Sweden, in which the author argues that the latter's more favorable policy reflects not a greater openness to women but the extent to which Swedish trades unions have embraced class solidarity. See M. Ruggie, *The State and Working Women* (Princeton, NJ: Princeton University Press, 1984).

14. C-7182/1893, "Report on Agencies and Methods for Dealing with the Unemployed," *Parliamentary Papers, 1893–94,* vol. LXXXII, p. 17. For a detailed account of how these union rules operated in different trades, including engineering, shipbuilding, metal, building, printing, textiles, clothing, furnishing, mining, baking and waterside labor, see pp. 20–90.

15. On the difficulties of defining unemployment in the nineteenth century, see Harris, *Unemployment and Politics,* chap. 1, and Gareth Stedman Jones, *Outcast London* (Oxford: Oxford University Press, 1971), chaps. 2 and 3. It would not be possible to extend the work of these historians—both in interpreting contemporary analyses of unemployment and in constructing their own accounts— in this study; furthermore, my principal interest lies with the work-welfare regimes constructed around the categories and not with the details of their definition or numbers.

16. From his study of London's labor market, Stedman Jones summarizes the generality of this condition in the second half of the nineteenth century: "Very few workers could expect a working life of stable employment . . . and occupations which appeared relatively immune to the hazards of seasonality, cyclical depression, or technological development—brewery or railway employment for instance—were eagerly sought after despite indifferent wage rates" (G. Stedman Jones, *Outcast London,* p. 53).

17. He continued: "Any workman who becomes repeatedly unemployed through lack of skill or knowledge may be tested at a suitable place for the purpose, and if in any case it appears that his defects could be removed by a course of technical instruction, and that the burden on the Unemployment fund would thereby be diminished, arrangements may be made for his attendance accordingly." In W. H. Beveridge, Paper on "State Unemployment Insurance in the U.K.," delivered to the Unemployment Conference at Ghent, September 1913, para 59. Public Record Office (PRO) LAB2, Box 1482, Folder: LE 10237/8/1913.

A similar view was held by the authors of the Minority Report of the Royal Commissioners on the Poor Law (drafted by Beatrice and Sidney Webb), who criticized the "lack of any systematic provision for training in new means of livelihood, whether in industry or in land settlement, of men displaced by new processes, machinery or other industrial changes." In Cd.4499/1909, "Minority Report of the Royal Commission on the Poor Laws and Relief of Distress," *Parliamentary Papers, 1909,* vol. 37, p. 1180.

18. For details, see D. S. King and H. Ward, "Working for Benefits: Rational Choice and the Rise of Work-Welfare Programmes," *Political Studies* 40 (1992): 479–95.

19. See D. R. Roediger, *The Wages of Whiteness* (London: Verso, 1991).

20. Among many studies, see Robert Moffitt, "Incentive Effects of the U.S. Welfare System: A Review," *Journal of Economic Literature* 30 (1992): 1–61; and Patrick Minford and Paul Ashton, "The Poverty Trap and the Laffer Curve— What Can the GHS Tell Us?" *Oxford Economic Papers* 43 (1991): 245–79.

21. As Himmelfarb records: "Outdoor relief in general, and the allowance system in particular, were held responsible for a vicious cycle of evils: an increase of poor rates, a decrease in wages (which were supplemented out of the rates), a decline of the yeomanry (who had to pay the rates but did not profit by the wage subsidy since they did not employ laborers), a rise in agricultural unemployment (the displaced yeomen swelling the ranks of the agricultural laborers), a fall in productivity (pauper labor being less efficient than independent labor), higher food prices (resulting from the decline of productivity), an increase of population (relief encouraging the poor to marry earlier and to have more children), still lower wages (resulting from this increase of population), and so on." In Gertrude Himmelfarb, *The Idea of Poverty* (London: Faber, 1984), pp. 154–55; see also K. Polanyi, *The Great Transformation* (Boston: Beacon, 1944), chap. 7.

22. See S. Steinmo, K. Thelen, and F. Longstreth, eds., *Structuring Politics: Historical Institutionalism in Comparative Analysis* (Cambridge and New York: Cambridge University Press, 1992). See also P. A. Hall, *Governing the Economy* (New York: Oxford University Press, 1986), a book which stimulated this approach among comparativists, and the influential article by J. March and J. Olsen, "The New Institutionalism: Organizational Factors in Political Life," *American Political Science Review* 78 (1984): 734–49. For the state-centric approach, see the important collection, *Bringing the State Back In,* edited by P. Evans, D. Rueschmeyer, and T. Skocpol (New York and Cambridge: Cambridge University Press, 1984), especially the Introduction, "Bringing the State Back In," by Skocpol.

23. See R. McKibbin, "The 'Social Psychology' of Unemployment in Interwar Britain," in R. McKibbin, *The Ideologies of Class* (Oxford: Clarendon Press, 1990).

24. Trades Union Congress, Report of Annual Conference 1911, "Trade Unionists and the Labor Exchange," (London: TUC), pp. 19–20.

25. G. Stedman Jones, *Outcast London,* p. 338.

26. Friendly Societies did not, of course, undertake any organization of the disadvantaged or most marginal members of the labor market, but assisted those in work before state programs were enacted.

27. C-7182/1893, "Report on Agencies and Methods for Dealing with the Unemployed," *Parliamentary Papers, 1893–94,* vol. LXXXII, p. 91.

28. See Himmelfarb, *The Idea of Poverty,* chap. 6. The 1834 New Poor Law is the crucial institutional development which established the principle of less eligibility to deter laborers and their families from seeking assistance or poor relief.

29. C-7182/1893, "Report on Agencies and Methods for Dealing with the Unemployed," *Parliamentary Papers, 1893–94,* vol. LXXXII, p. 144.

30. See the useful recent analysis in V. C. Hattam, *Labor Visions and State Power* (Princeton, NJ: Princeton University Press, 1993), and in Ira Katznelson, *City Trenches* (New York: Pantheon, 1981). For a comparative analysis, see G. Marks "Variations in Union Political Activity in the United States, Britain and Germany from the Nineteenth Century," *Comparative Politics* 22 (1989): 83–104.

31. This thesis is forcefully developed by Katznelson in *City Trenches*; see also D. Rueschemeyer, E. H. Stephens, and J. Stephens, *Capitalist Development and Democracy* (Oxford: Polity, 1992), and R. H. Tawney, *The American Labor Movement and Other Essays* (Brighton: Harvester, 1979).

32. For an analysis of the evolution of the AFL's business unionism strategy,

see A. Joseph, "The Solidarity of Skilled Workers: Creating a Logic of Particularism," *Journal of Historical Sociology* 6 (1993): 288–310. Joseph emphasizes the rational nature of the AFL's concentration upon craft workers within the particular environment of U.S. capital and labor.

33. P. S. Foner, *Organized Labor and the Black Worker, 1619–1981* (New York: International Publishers, 1981).

34. See C. Phelan, *William Green* (Albany, NY: State University of New York Press, 1989), pp. 75, 27.

35. See ibid., generally.

36. At the founding of national employment exchanges (in 1933) union membership was small. Membership declined throughout the 1920s and was under three million in 1933. As a percentage of the labor force, union membership in 1930 was 6.8 percent, falling to 5.2 percent in 1933. It began to grow from the late 1930s, stabilizing at circa 23–25 percent during the 1940s. For data, see M. Goldfield, *The Decline of Organized Labor in the United States* (Chicago: University of Chicago Press, 1987), p. 10.

37. See J. Brenner and M. Ramas, "Rethinking Women's Oppression," *New Left Review* 144 (1984).

38. Ibid., pp. 44–45.

39. E. Meehan, *Women's Rights at Work* (London: Macmillan, 1985).

40. See, among others, J. Lewis, "Gender and the Development of Welfare Regimes," *Journal of European Social Policy* 3 (1992): 159–73; A. S. Orloff, "Gender and the Social Rights of Citizenship: The Comparative Analysis of Gender Relations and Welfare States," *American Sociological Review* 58 (1993): 303–28; and L. A. Tilly and J. W. Scott, *Women, Work and Family* (New York and London: Routledge, 1978). See also T. Skocpol and G. Ritter, "Gender and the Origins of Modern Social Policy in Britain and the United States," *Studies in American Political Development* 5 (1991): 36–93.

41. See Roediger, *The Wages of Whiteness*, and Foner, *Organized Labor and the Black Worker 1619–1981*.

42. See also National Archives and Record Administration (NARA) Record Group (RG) 183 USES, Oxley Papers, Box 1, Folder: "Building Trades, Discrimination Against Negro Workers, Chicago," especially the letter from Harold Gould, Chicago Urban League, to Oxley, 26 January 1935, pp. 1–3.

43. See hearings held by the President's Committee on Fair Employment Practice (FEPC) in Records of the Committee on Fair Employment Practice, Record Group 228, National Archives and Record Administration. See also NARA RG 228, Records of the Committee on Fair Employment Practice, Official Files of George M. Johnson, Box 76: H. R. Northrup, "An Analysis of the Discriminations Against Negroes in the Boiler Makers Union," pp. 1–18, n.d.; and RG 228, Records of the Committee on FEP, Legal Division, Box 338: "Summary of Hearings on Complaints of Negro Steamfitters against the Steamfitters' Protective Association Local 597 held in Chicago Ill April 4 1942 before the President's Committee on Fair Employment Practice with Findings and Directions," pp. 1–5. On page 2, the report noted of Local 597 that "although there is no written rule against the admission of non-white persons to its membership, through practice, rules, customs, traditions, or other devices, colored persons, otherwise known as Negroes, have

been for many years last part, and are now, denied membership in said union, solely on account of their race or color; that said Local 597 also refuses to grant permits to colored Steamfitters to enable them to obtain work on defense projects solely on account of the race or color of said steamfitters." The FEPC encountered numerous cases of discrimination among AFL-affiliated trades unions as the archival records amply demonstrate.

44. Library of Congress, NAACP III-A, Box A180, Folder: Labor, Apprenticeship Training. NAACP, *Negro Wage Earners and Apprenticeship* (Washington, DC: NAACP, 1960), p. 19.

45. See P. Burstein, *Discrimination, Jobs and Politics: The Struggle for Equal Employment Opportunity in the United States since the New Deal* (Chicago: University of Chicago Press, 1985); H. Northrup and R. L. Rown, eds., *The Negro and Employment Opportunity: Problems and Practices* (Ann Arbor, MI: Bureau of Industrial Relations, 1965); F. R. Marshall and V. Briggs, *The Negro and Apprenticeships* (Baltimore, MD: Johns Hopkins University Press, 1967), and B. Wolkinson, *Blacks, Unions and the EEOC: A Study of Administrative Failure* (Lexington, MA: Lexington Books, 1973).

46. However, on a visit to Washington and New York in 1934, Keynes was surprised and aghast at business's, especially financial, hostility toward and loathing of Roosevelt's programs: Robert Skidelsky, *John Maynard Keynes: The Economist as Saviour, 1920–1937* (London: Macmillan, 1992), pp. 504, 506.

47. The U.S. Chamber of Commerce, more closely tied with small businesses, has been less hostile to government intervention and certainly supported it during the Great Depression.

48. See R. M. Collins, *The Business Response to Keynes, 1929–1964* (New York: Columbia University Press, 1981), and I. Katznelson and B. Pietrykowski, "Rebuilding the American State: Evidence from the 1940s," *Studies in American Political Development* 5 (1991): 301–39.

49. For opinion data to support this view, see Benjamin Page and Robert Y. Shapiro, *The Rational Public* (Chicago: University of Chicago Press, 1992), chap. 4, though on differences between black voters and white voters, see Lee Sigelman and Susan Welch, *Black Americans' Views of Racial Inequality* (New York and Cambridge: Cambridge University Press, 1991).

50. E. D. Berkowitz and K. McQuaid, *Creating the Welfare State* (Lawrence, KS: University Press of Kansas, 1992).

51. *Parliamentary Debates,* House of Commons, 4th series, vol. 190, 15 June 1908, col. 564.

52. The commitment to this division was maintained by the Tories during the 1950s: see discussion in Conservative Research Department, 2/30/17: Minutes of National Insurance Policy Subcommittee, 1953. In Conservative Party Archives, Bodleian Library, Oxford.

53. Kristi Andersen, *The Creation of a Democratic Majority, 1928–1936* (Chicago: University of Chicago Press, 1979); James L. Sundquist, *Dynamics of the Party System* (Washington, DC: Brookings, 1983); and D. Rueschemeyer, E. H. Stephens, and J. Stephens, *Capitalist Development and Democracy* (Oxford: Polity, 1992).

54. In the nineteenth century, fragility came from the integration of new Catholic

ethnic immigrants into politics. In the 1830s and 1840s, "nativist" parties (most famously the Know Nothing party) representing Protestantism and nativism developed seeking to lengthen the period of required residency before naturalization to twenty-one years; despite some striking electoral successes, this movement failed to modify the United States's immigration and naturalization rules. In part, the local politicians' need to win the votes of immigrants of whatever ethnic origin undercut this populist drive. This pattern helps explain the early establishment of pensions in the United States, since these would be enjoyed principally by citizens holding a sufficiently long residence to have served in the United States armed forces.

55. L. Hartz, *The Liberal Tradition in the United States* (New York: Harcourt, Brace and World, 1955); J. Gray, *Liberalism* (London: Routledge, 1991); R. Bellamy, *Liberalism and Modern Society* (Oxford: Polity, 1992). See also B. Bailyn, *The Ideological Origins of the American Revolution* (Cambridge, MA: Harvard University Press, 1967), and G. Wood, *The Creation of the American Republic, 1776–1787* (New York: Norton, 1969).

56. See H. Heclo, "General Welfare and Two American Political Traditions," *Political Science Quarterly* 101 (1986): 179–96; R. Goodin, "Self-Reliance versus the Welfare State," *Journal of Social Policy* 14 (1985): 25–47; C. Murray, *Losing Ground* (New York: Basic Books 1984); L. Mead, *Beyond Entitlement* (New York: Free Press, 1985); N. Barry, *Welfare* (Milton Keynes: Open University Press, 1990); G. Gilder, *Wealth and Poverty* (New York: Basic Books, 1981); and the debate between Raymond Plant and Norman Barry, *Citizenship and Rights in Thatcher's Britain: Two Views* (London: Institute of Economic Affairs, 1990).

For an illuminating discussion of how the conception of American liberalism should be enlarged, see R. M. Smith, "Beyond Tocqueville, Myrdal, and Hartz: The Multiple Traditions in America," *American Political Science Review* 87: 549–66.

57. Michael Freeden, *The New Liberalism* (Oxford: Clarendon Press, 1978), p. 40.

58. Michael Freeden, *Liberalism Divided* (Oxford: Oxford University Press, 1986), p. 371.

59. Jimmy Carter Presidential Library, Domestic Policy Staff—Eizenstat, Box 317, Folder: Welfare Reform [CFR,O/A 732][1]. Letter from Senator Moynihan to Carter, 8 February 1979, p. 2.

60. J. Quadagno, "From Old-Age Assistance to Supplemental Security Income: The Political Economy of Relief in the South, 1935–1972," in M. Weir, A. S. Orloff, and T. Skocpol, eds., *The Politics of Social Policy in the USA* (Princeton, NJ: Princeton University Press, 1988), p. 236.

61. For instance, the Social Service Act of 1982 enacted in Sweden requires "eighteen- and nineteen-year olds who were not in training or apprenticeship positions . . . to work in municipal jobs in exchange for their allowance." Quoted in H. Heclo and H. Madsen, *Policy and Politics in Sweden* (Philadelphia: Temple University Press, 1987), p. 171. The authors observe that "because none of the opposition parties wanted to argue that it was better to pay young persons for not working, the new law commanded near unanimous consent" (p. 171).

62. For comparative analyses of this phenomenon, see D. S. King and B. Rothstein, "Institutional Choices and Labor Market Policy: A British-Swedish Comparison," *Comparative Political Studies* 26 (1993): 147–77, and "Government Legitimacy and the Labor Market: A Comparative Analysis of Employment Exchanges," *Public Administration* 72 (1994): 289–306.

63. See G. Esping-Andersen, *Politics Against Markets*; D. S. King and B. Rothstein, "Institutional Choices and Labor Market Policy: A British-Swedish Comparison"; and S. Olsson, "Sweden," in J. Dixon and R. Scheurell, eds., *Social Welfare in Developed Market Countries* (London: Routledge, 1989).

64. For an early statement, see A. Shonfield, *Modern Capitalism* (Oxford: Oxford University Press, 1965), chap. 4, and more recently, M. Albert, *Capitalism Against Capitalism* (London: Whurr Publishers, 1993). Albert contrasts an Anglo-American version of capitalism with a Rhine-Japanese one. The latter makes training a priority pursued by the state, individuals, business associations and unions, the former leaves it to market processes with predictable consequences: see pp. 12–13, 114, 117.

65. For an outstanding analysis, see D. Finegold and D. Soskice, "The Failure of Training in Britain: Analysis and Prescription," *Oxford Review of Economic Policy* 4 (1988) 21–51. See also D. Finegold, "Institutional Incentives and Skill Creation: Preconditions for a High-Skill Equilibrium," in Paul Ryan, ed., *International Comparisons of Vocational Education and Training for Intermediate Skills* (London: Falmer Press, 1991).

66. D. Finegold and D. Soskice, "Britain's Failure to Train," *Oxford Review of Economic Policy* 4 (1988): 21–51, p. 22. The formidable difficulties confronting the Clinton administration's reformers are analyzed in D. Finegold, "Making Apprenticeships Work," *Rand Issue Paper* (March 1993): 1–6.

Chapter Two

1. *Parliamentary Debates,* House of Commons, 5th series, 19 May 1909, vol. 5, col. 503.

2. On the systems operative in each country before these pieces of national legislation see: for the United States, NARA, RG 47 (Records of the Social Security Administration), Committee on Economic Security, Special Staff Reports, Box 22, Folder: Gladys L. Palmer, "The History and Functioning of the United States Employment Service"; B. Bjornaraa, "A Historical Sketch of Public Employment," *Employment Service News* 2, no. 2 (February–March 1935); M. D. Meyer, "Public Employment Bureaus," *American Labor Legislation Review* 18 (1928); R. Kellogg, *The United States Employment Service* (Chicago: University of Chicago Press, 1933); and U. Sautter, *Three Cheers for the Unemployed* (New York and Cambridge: Cambridge University Press, 1991), chap. 2. For Britain, see Lord Beveridge, "The Birth of Labor Exchanges," *Minlabour,* January 1960, "Employment Exchanges" Box, Department of Employment Library, London; the correspondence between Mrs. A. Spencer Buck, the Ministry of Labour and the Board of Trade, PRO LAB2, Box 211, Folder: LAB2/211/LE20734A; and House of Commons-7182/1893, "Report on Agencies and Methods for Dealing with the Unemployed," *Parliamentary Papers, 1893–94,* vol. LXXXII.

3. Cd 4499/1909, *Report of the Royal Commission on the Poor Laws and Relief of Distress*. In *Parliamentary Papers*, 1909, vol. 2, p. 267.

4. See Roy Jenkins, *Mr Balfour's Poodle* (London: Heinemann, 1954)—Arthur Balfour led the Conservative party in the Commons. For the period more generally, see Michael Bentley, *The Climax of Liberal Politics* (London: Edward Arnold, 1987).

5. As Beveridge observed, "The two parties of the Commission, while differing in so much else, agreed in their advocacy of a national system of Labour Exchanges as the basis of any effective dealing with unemployment." W. H. Beveridge, "Labour Exchanges in the U.K.," to Conference Internationale du Chomage, Paris, 18–21 September 1910, p. 1. PRO LAB2/1482/LE10237.

6. *Parliamentary Debates*, House of Commons, 6th series (1909), vol. 6, 16 June, col. 1005. Painter based his remarks from observations on a trip to Berlin: "In Berlin we saw the experiment in actual working, and we saw amongst the unskilled men, 500 or 600 of them, all classified in regard to groups of trades and the time they had been out of employment. As we saw the messages coming over the telephone, the letters being opened from employers asking for men, and men and women going out in response to those indications, we were encouraged to give a cordial support to the Bill."

7. *Parliamentary Debates*, House of Commons, 5th series, 20 May 1909, vol. 5, col. 381.

8. *Parliamentary Debates*, House of Commons, 6th series, 16 June 1909, vol. 6, col. 997. Other critics opposed exchanges as too weak a response to the unemployment problem. Exchanges did not create jobs, a view embraced by Sir Frederick Banbury: "The only way, so far as I know, to secure employment is to find people who are willing to employ workmen to do certain work, and I do not believe that the provision of Labour Exchanges will in any way advance this." Churchill skirted this issue by emphasizing the placement role of the proposed exchanges: "The principle which the management of the Labour Exchanges will bear in mind always will be the desire to find men for jobs and jobs for men. That is the main object" (cols. 995, 1036).

9. Cd 4499/1909, *Report of the Royal Commission on the Poor Laws and Relief of Distress*. *Parliamentary Papers*, 1909, vol. 2, p. 398.

10. Metropolitan Employment Exchanges were established in: Battersea, Bermondsey, Bethnal Green, Camberwell, Chelsea, Deptford, Finsbury and Holborn, Fulham, Greenwich, Hackney and Stoke Newington, Hammersmith, Hampstead, Islington, Kensington, Lambeth, Lewisham, Paddington, Poplar, St. Pancras, St. Marylebone, Shoreditch, Southwark, Stepney, Wandsworth, and Woolwich.

11. W. H. Beveridge, *Unemployment* (London: Longmans, Green and Co,. 1908), p. 199.

12. Michael Freeden, *The New Liberalism* (Oxford: Oxford University Press, 1978); and Michael Bentley, *The Liberal Mind* (New York and Cambridge: Cambridge University Press, 1977).

13. Cd 4499/1909, *Report of the Royal Commission on the Poor Laws and Relief of Distress*. *Parliamentary Papers*, 1909, vol. 37, p. 400.

14. Confidential minutes of the 1st conference between the Parliamentary Committee of the TUC and Winston Churchill, president of the Board of Trade,

17 June 1909, p. 17. PRO LAB2, Box 211. The statement was made by TUC delegate Cooper.

15. Ibid., p. 18. PRO LAB2 Box 211.

16. W. H. Beveridge, Paper read at the International Conference on Unemployment at Ghent, September 1913. Draft 6/13, p. 6. PRO LAB2, Box 1482, Folder: LE 10237/8/1913.

17. Cd 4499/1909, *Report of the Royal Commission on the Poor Laws and Relief of Distress. Parliamentary Papers,* 1909, vol. 37, p. 401.

18. *Parliamentary Debates,* House of Commons, 5th series, 19 May 1909, vol. 5, col. 503.

19. Ibid.

20. W. H. Beveridge, Paper read at the International Conference on Unemployment at Ghent, September 1913. Draft 6/13, p. 26. PRO LAB2, Box 1482.

21. *Parliamentary Debates,* House of Commons, 5th series, 19 May 1909, vol. 5, col. 510.

22. *Parliamentary Debates,* House of Commons, 6th series, 16 June 1909, vol. 6, col. 1044.

23. W. H. Beveridge, *Memorandum on the Future of Labour Exchanges,* submitted to the Local Government Board about July 1907. British Library of Political and Economic Science, Beveridge Papers: Unemployment (Coll. B), vol. XIV.

24. Beveridge, *Unemployment,* p. 215.

25. Ibid.

26. These were:

1. LEs have always failed in this country and will fail again;
2. LEs will never secure the voluntary support of employers;
3. LEs will interfere with the employer's choice and control of his staff;
4. LEs will be of no use for skilled men, since these are already dealt with by trade union registration; nor for the unskilled men, since employers can always get as many of these they want at their own gates;
5. LEs will not make fresh employment; they will only re-distribute it, giving to A the job that would otherwise have gone to B;
6. LEs will not put an end to unemployment. They must be accompanied by provision for the unemployed—by maintenance and insurance;
7. LEs will make labor more casual than before;
8. LEs will lower the rate of wages;
9. LEs will injure trade unionism by giving to nonunionists facilities in finding work which are now confined to trade unionists;
10. Workmen will object to being sent away from home to jobs at great distances; and
11. LEs by registering unemployed will give a handle to Socialist agitators to force through "the right to work."

From W. H. Beveridge, "Labour Exchanges," General Memorandum, Confidential, 1909, pp. 9–12. Beveridge Papers: Unemployment (Coll. B), vol. XIV.

27. *Parliamentary Debates,* House of Commons, 5th series, 19 May 1909, vol. 5, col. 500.

28. Ibid., col. 501.

29. Ibid.

30. Ibid., col. 502.

31. Labour Exchanges Act, 1909 [9 EDW. 7. c. 7.].

32. Labour Exchanges Act, 1909, section 1 (2), p. 2.

33. This decision referred to the exchanges operated by the local government board and the Metropolitan Employment Exchanges operated by the Central (Unemployed) Body of the Unemployment Workmen Act of 1905. It was the Treasury who had to agree to these new arrangements. See PRO LAB2/211/LE345/09.

34. Labour Exchanges Act, 1909, 2 (2).

35. Labour Exchanges Act, 1909, 2 (5).

36. *Parliamentary Debates,* House of Commons, 5th series, 19 May 1909, vol. 5, col. 507.

37. Ibid., col. 510.

38. *Parliamentary Debates,* House of Commons, 6th series, 16 June 1909, vol. 6, cols. 1045–49.

39. See *Parliamentary Debates,* House of Lords, 1909, vol. 2, 3 August, cols. 877–78.

40. *Parliamentary Debates,* House of Commons, 5th series, 19 May 1909, vol. 5, col. 504. Churchill outlined the proposals: "We should propose, the House assent to the Bill, to divide the whole country into about ten divisions, each with a Divisional Clearing House, and presided over by a divisional chief, and all coordinated with a National Clearing House in London. Distributed amongst those ten divisions will be between 30 and 40 first-class Labour Exchanges in towns of 100,000 or upwards and about 45 second-class Labour Exchanges in towns of between 50 and 100 thousand, and 150 minor offices and sub-offices, third-class Labour Exchanges with waiting rooms will be established in the smaller centres. The control of this system will be exercised by the Board of Trade."

41. PRO File LAB 2/211/9 E20734A, see Annex A to its March 1909 report. The committee was established at the suggestion of Beveridge; its brief was to "consider and report to me [President] as to the organisation and finances of a system of Labour Exchanges" (p. 21). It was to consider salaries, recruitment, office costs, and the territorial distribution of offices.

42. "Labour Exchanges Committee Report" (Confidential), 27 March 1909, p. 9. PRO Folder LAB 2/211/9 E 20734A.

43. Ibid., p. 13.

44. Letter from Metropolitan Employment Exchanges, South Central District Branch, from District Manager to President of the Board of Trade, 5 August 1909. PRO Folder LAB2/428/LE780/1909.

45. Reply from Board of Trade to Metropolitan Employment Exchanges, South Central District Branch, 9 August 1909 (signed by George J. Stanley). PRO File LAB2/428/LE780/1909.

46. United Kingdom. *Labour Bureaux.* Copy of the report made to the Local Government Board by Arthur Lowry, 1906, p. 18. In Beveridge Papers: Unemployment (Coll. B), vol. XIV.

47. Committee on Women in Industry, National League of Women Voters, *A*

Federal-State Employment Service (Washington, DC: National League of Women Voters, March 1932), p. 9.

48. On Keeler's "mandate-crisis reform hypothesis," Roosevelt had the strongest score from eight cases: J. T. S. Keeler, "Opening the Window for Reform: Mandates, Crises and Extraordinary Policy-Making," *Comparative Political Studies* 25 (1993): 433–86.

49. In the press release from Senator Wagner's office accompanying the introduction of the bill it was described as, "except for a few slight modifications, the same as the employment exchange bill which . . . was pocket vetoed by the President." Georgetown University Library, Papers of Robert F. Wagner, Speech Files, Box 102, Folder 22, p. 1.

50. *Congressional Record,* House Proceedings and Debates of the 73d Cong., 1st sess., 77, pt. 5:4777.

51. Franklin D. Roosevelt Presidential Library (FDRL hereafter), Papers of Frances Perkins, Box 1, Folder: Frances Perkins, Drafts of Articles, "The United States Employment Service," in *Conference Board Service Letter,* 30 July 1933, p. 49.

52. The system in place before 1933 was also called the USES, creating some confusion about terminology.

53. *Congressional Record,* House Proceedings and Debates of the 66th Cong., 1st sess., 58, pt. 1:490. This bill was the basis for subsequent efforts by Wagner to enact legislation authorizing a nationwide employment system. It was introduced by Senator William Kenyon (R-Iowa) and Representative John Nolan (R-California). It was opposed by Democrats on grounds of cost.

54. Wagner relied on other strategically placed members of the Congress for support in passing his legislation, including Hiram Johnson (R-California), chairman of the key Senate Commerce Committee, and Representatives Fiorello LaGuardia (R-New York) and Emanuel Celler (D-New York), both from congressional districts in New York City.

55. It was accompanied by two other bills from Wagner to fund public works programs (S. 3059) and to expand the Department of Labor's statistical information work (S. 3061).

56. *Congressional Record,* Senate Proceedings and Debates of the 71st Cong., 2d sess., 72, pt. 7:6822. The bill was passed by the Senate on 12 May and by the House on 26 June.

57. Papers of Robert F. Wagner, Georgetown University Library. Legislative Files, Box 188, Folder 406: Analysis and Memos. Memorandum, n.d., p. 3.

58. See Margaret Weir, *Politics and Jobs* (Princeton, NJ: Princeton University Press, 1992) on the difficulties of expanding the federal government's role in employment policy.

59. Papers of Robert F. Wagner, Legislative Files, Box 188, Folder 406: Analysis and Memos of S. 3060: Employment Exchanges (Analysis), p. 3. A similar strategy had been adopted in Britain in the 1909 Labour Exchanges Act.

60. Proposals for a national employment service in 1919 were opposed by the Texan Democratic Representative Thomas Blanton while conservative Republicans (Rep. George Graham of Pennsylvania and Senator Hiram Bingham of Connecticut)

opposed the 1930–31 initiatives: see *Congressional Record,* 1919: 2 February, H.R. 4653; 1930: April 28, S. 7796-7807; and 23 February 1931 H.R. 5745.

61. Senator Jones, *Congressional Record,* Senate Proceedings and Debates of the 71st Cong., 2d sess., 72, pt. 7:7804.

62. Ibid., 8:8741.

63. S. Rept. 63, 73d Cong., 1st sess., p. 4.

64. Ibid.

65. *Congressional Record,* Senate Proceedings and Debates of the 73d Cong., 1st sess., 77, pt. 5:4467.

66. Hearings before the House Committee on Labor, 73d Cong., 1st sess., on "H. R. 4559: A Bill to Provide for the Establishment of a National Employment System," 17 and 18 May 1933, p. 2. House of Representatives

67. Ibid., p. 3.

68. Ibid., p. 13.

69. RG 172, Box 59, Folder: Employment—General: January–May 1937. By May 1937, forty-eight states had affiliated according to USES Director Frank Persons in a talk to the International Association of Public Employment Services on 5 May 1937. He observed that "not so many years ago, in a discussion of this nature, one might have been called upon to defend public ES as a legitimate function of government. That time has passed."

70. RG 47, Box 22, Folder: Palmer "History and Functioning of the USES," p. 17. Palmer notes that the "function of the federal office under this arrangement is to develop and maintain minimum standards of operation, promote uniformity in procedures and record-keeping, maintain interstate clearance of labor, and thus integrate the local and state services into a nation-wide employment system."

71. The Federal Advisory Council nominated an Executive Committee. The first council was chaired by Robert Maynard Hutchins and consisted of: Frederic A. Delano (treasurer), Henry S.Dennison, William Green, Henry I. Harriman, Louis Johnson, Miss Rose Schneiderman, Robert F. Wagner, and Arthur H. Young; USES Director Frank Persons was secretary.

72. Frances Perkins Oral History, Columbia University Oral History Collection, Part 3, Book 4, 1953, p. 275.

73. FDRL Official File 15h, Labor Department, Box 8, Folder: U.S.E.S. 1933–37.

74. Frances Perkins Oral History, Columbia University Oral History Collection, Part 3, Book 4, 1953, p. 275.

75. FDRL Papers of Harry Hopkins, Box 25, Folder: CWA Conference—Minutes, 15 November 1933, p. 8.

76. FDRL Papers of Harry Hopkins, Box 25, Folder: CWA Conference—Minutes, 15 November 1933, p. 9.

77. Papers of Harry Hopkins, Box 50, Folder: Reemployment Reports. Address by Persons to the National Reemployment Service conference on 15 July 1933, p. 13.

78. RG 47, Box 22, Folder: Palmer "History and Functioning of the USES," p. 25.

79. RG 174, Box 58, Folder: Employment—General: March-July 1933. In a letter to the governor of Virginia, Perkins observed that "the reemployment of

millions of unemployed, which is the object of the President's Industrial Recovery and Public Works Program, will require an adequate and efficient system of public employment offices on a national scale" (20 July 1933).

80. FDRL Papers of Harry L. Hopkins, Box 25, Folder: WP Administrators' conference on 16 June 1935, p. 48.

81. FDRL Papers of Frances Perkins, Box 1, Folder: Perkins—Drafts for Speeches. "Public Employment Offices: Their Present Possibilities and Limitation," Address by Persons at the Second Metropolitan Conference on Employment and Guidance Procedure of the Welfare Council, New York, 26 October 1934, p. 2.

82. In 1938, thirty states required state advisory councils, six made them optional and twelve had no provision; fourteen states required local advisory councils, seventeen were optional, and seventeen had no provision. Raymond C. Atkinson, Louise C. Odencrantz, and Ben Deming, *Public Employment Service in the United States* (Chicago: Committee on Public Administration of the Social Science Research Council, 1940), p. 145.

83. Ibid.

84. Ibid., chap. 9.

85. Trades Union Congress, Report of Conference, 1904 (London: TUC Library), p. 7.

86. Keir Hardie, *The Unemployed Bill* (London: Independent Labour Party, 1905), pp. 7–8. London Trades Union Congress Library.

87. John Barton Seymour, *The British Employment Exchange* (London: P. S. King & Sons, 1928), p. 10.

88. Joint Board's letter of 9 October 1906, pp. 1–2. Beveridge Papers: Unemployment (Coll. B), vol. XIV. Letter 9 October 1906 to Local Government Board from W. C. Steadman, M.P., A. Henderson, M.P., and I. H. Mitchell, London City Council. There is no record of to whom the letter was sent, but since the Distress Committees were the responsibility of the Local Government Board this body is the logical addressee. In a memorandum to the board in 1907, Beveridge urged the administration of labor exchanges by the Board of Trade. See "Memorandum about the Future of Labour Exchanges" (Submitted to the Local Government Board July 1907). Both in Beveridge Papers: Unemployment (Coll. B), vol. XIV.

The content of the letter is the same as that reported to a meeting of the Trades Unions Subcommittee of the Employment Exchange Committee of the Central (Unemployed) Body of London, 14 February 1907: Beveridge Papers: Unemployment (Coll. B), vol. XIV.

89. Joint Board's letter of 9 October 1906, p. 2. Beveridge Papers: Unemployment (Coll. B), vol. XIV.

90. Ibid.

91. Trades Union Congress, Report of Annual Meeting, 1909, p. 150.

92. Ibid.

93. Ibid.

94. Ibid.

95. Ibid., p. 160. The relationship of labor exchanges and blackleg work featured in earlier TUC conferences. In 1907 the conference heard a report from a delegation to the Central Unemployed Body (London) which pressed the case that

unemployed men should not be sent to places in which an industrial dispute was in progress. The delegation reported that the CUB was sympathetic to the TUC case and to their request that local committees advising exchanges should be composed of local employers and trades unionists. See "Report of Deputation to Central Unemployed Body re. Labour Exchanges," Trades Union Congress, Report of Annual Conference, 1907, p. 120.

96. Labour Exchanges Bill, 1909. 1st conference with the Parliamentary Committee of the TUC and Churchill, President Board of Trade, Confidential, 17 June 1909, p. 3. PRO LAB2, Box 211.

97. Ibid.

98. Ibid., p. 4.

99. Confidential minutes of the conference between the Federation of Engineering and Ship-Building Trades and the Board of Trade, 18 June 1909, p. 12. PRO LAB2, Box 211.

100. Mosses alluded critically to the proposal that union vacancy books should be placed in the exchanges since these included information which, in addition to registering vacancies, constituted a "fund of information which is the exclusive property of our own members . . . and which certainly we will resent very strongly being placed through the labour exchanges at the disposal of men who have no right to [them]" (Ibid., p. 13).

101. Ibid., pp. 17–18.

102. Ibid., pp. 24–25.

103. Ibid., pp. 25–26.

104. Ibid., p. 27.

105. Ibid., p. 33. Several European governments established labor colonies to remove vagrants, tramps, and ex-prisoners—the least employable—from the countryside and cities in the nineteenth century. Labor colonies existed in Germany, Holland, Belgium, France, Austria and Switzerland, though they were most important in the first two countries. Writing in 1893, James Mavor concluded that such colonies were advantageous as institutions to "suppress begging, to clear the tramps from the highways, and the beggars from the streets, to hide them out of sight, to keep them out of mischief, and to compel them to work." But for the "workman who has been accustomed to regular employment, and who is suddenly thrown out, or, indeed for the intermittently employed low-grade workmen, the labour colony is a very questionable resort." House of Commons-7182/1893, "Report on Agencies and Methods for Dealing with the Unemployed," *Parliamentary Papers, 1893–94,* vol. LXXXII, part IV, pp. 335, 338.

106. Confidential minutes of Conference between the Federation of Engineering and Ship-Building Trades and Board of Trade, 18 June 1909, p. 34. PRO LAB2, Box 211.

107. W. M. Mosses wrote Churchill that "if the interests of the Federated Trades are safeguarded as you indicated would be the case at our Conference than every assistance possible will be rendered by the Federation to make your proposed Labour Exchanges what we believe you are desirous they should be—a real help to workless men and women in the direction that assistance can best be given and accepted by self-respecting workpeople." Letter from W. M. Mosses to

Churchill, 19 June 1909, PRO LAB2, Box 211, LE 178291. The tone of Mosses's letter conveys an indifference toward workless men and women.

108. Confidential minutes of the Board of Trade Conference with the Engineering Employers' Association and the Ship-Building Employers' Federation, 18 August 1909, p. 3. PRO LAB2, Box 211.

109. Ibid., p. 4.

110. Ibid., p. 5.

111. Ibid.

112. Ibid., pp. 5–6.

113. Ibid., p. 7.

114. Ibid., p. 8.

115. Ibid., p. 9.

116. Ibid., p. 10, my emphasis.

117. Ibid.

118. Labour Exchanges Bill, 1909. 1st conference between Parliamentary Committee of the TUC and Winston Churchill, president of the Board of Trade. Confidential, 17 June 1909, Davis, p. 7. PRO LAB2, Box 211. Bowerman cited German practice where it was the trades unions who acted on behalf of labor, an example disputed by Beveridge who claimed that in Germany "there is not any one universal method" (p. 8).

119. Ibid., p. 10.

120. Ibid., p. 11.

121. Ibid., p. 14.

122. Ibid.

123. Ibid., pp. 52, 53.

124. "To the President of the Board of Trade," 1 March 1910, in Trades Union Congress, *Annual Report,* 1910, p. 35. Churchill had been replaced by Sydney Buxton as president of the Board of Trade.

125. Ibid., p. 39. An early advisory committee established for the London labor exchanges had a membership divided equally between representatives of employers and workmen. See *The Board of Trade Journal,* 4 August 1910, p. 219.

126. Confidential minutes of the 2d Conference between the Parliamentary Committee of the TUC and Board of Trade, 8 July 1909, p. 28. PRO LAB2, Box 211.

127. Ibid.

128. He continued: "Whenever you come to a question which raises an issue between capital and labor, then you will have a sub-committee of perhaps three or four on each side, and they would be absolutely three or four trade unionists and three or four employers, as it might be—which is quits—with an independent chairman" (ibid., p. 32).

129. Ibid.

130. Confidential minutes of the conference between the Federation of Engineering and Ship-Building Trades and the Board of Trade, 18 June 1909, p. 6. PRO LAB2, Box 211.

131. Ibid., p. 5.

132. Ibid., p. 8.

133. Ibid.

134. Ibid., p. 9.

135. Ibid., p. 22.

136. 8th, 9th, 10th annual reports of the Egham Free Registry for the Unemployed, 1892–94. In Beveridge Papers: Unemployment (Coll. B), vol. XIV.

137. W. H. Beveridge, *Memorandum on Relationship of Employment Exchanges to Trade Unions.* 17 December 1906, Confidential, p. 1. Beveridge Papers: Unemployment (Coll. B), vol. XVI.

138. Ibid.

139. "Employment Exchanges cannot consistently with the principle of impartiality, refuse to register and notify vacancies either (1) On the ground that they are inconsistent with the conditions as to wages, hours, etc., laid down on behalf of one party (employer or employed) alone. or (2) On the ground that they are inconsistent with conditions as to wages, hours, etc, which are merely 'customary' or vaguely 'recognised'" (ibid., p. 4).

140. Churchill was equivocal however when negotiating with the employers' federation—see J. Harris, *Unemployment and Politics* (Oxford: Clarendon Press, 1972), pp. 278 passim, and J. Harris, *Lord Beveridge: A Biography* (Oxford: Clarendon Press, 1977), chap. 7.

141. *Parliamentary Debates,* House of Commons, 6th series, 16 June 1909, vol. 6, col. 1037.

142. Confidential minutes of the 1st conference between the Parliamentary Committee of the TUC and Winston Churchill, president of the Board of Trade, 17 June 1909, p. 24. PRO LAB2, Box 211.

143. Ibid., p. 18.

144. Ibid., p. 27.

145. Ibid., p. 31.

146. Ibid., p. 32.

147. Ibid., p. 33.

148. Ibid., p. 35.

149. Confidential minutes of the 2d conference between the Parliamentary Committee of the TUC and the Board of Trade, 8 July 1909, p. 4. PRO LAB2, Box 211.

150. Confidential minutes of Board of Trade Conference with the Engineering Employers' Association and the Ship-Building Employers' Federation, 18 August 1909, p. 26. PRO LAB2, Box 211.

151. Ibid., p. 19.

152. Ibid., p. 20.

153. Ibid., p. 24.

154. Confidential minutes of the 1st conference between the Parliamentary Committee of the TUC and Winston Churchill, president of the Board of Trade, 17 June 1909, p. 33. PRO LAB2, Box 211.

155. Ibid., pp. 33–34.

156. Ibid., p. 36.

157. Ibid., p. 37.

158. "I personally am all for the standard rate, and for everything that arrives at it" (ibid., p. 42).

159. Ibid.
160. Ibid.
161. Ibid., p. 45.
162. Ibid., p. 48. The Post Office was Churchill's favorite analogy.
163. Ibid., p. 49.
164. Ibid., p. 49.
165. Ibid., pp. 51–52.
166. Ibid., p. 52.
167. Confidential minutes of the 2d conference between the Parliamentary Committee of the TUC and Churchill, 8 July 1909, p. 4. PRO LAB2, Box 211. Churchill responded with bewilderment to this claim: "Do you mean to say a work man goes to an employer and works there for a whole week, and does not know till the end of the week what he is going to get paid?" (p. 5).
168. Ibid., p. 6. Shackleton cited the practice of the Public Labour Exchange in Berlin in support of this proposal.
169. Ibid., p. 12.
170. Ibid., p. 13.
171. Ibid., p. 16.
172. Ibid., p. 17.
173. Ibid., p. 18.
174. Ibid., p. 25.
175. Ibid., pp. 22, 24.
176. Ibid., p. 24.
177. Confidential minutes of Board of Trade Conference with the Engineering Employers' Association and the Ship-Building Employers' Federation, 18 August 1909, p. 17. PRO LAB2, Box 211.
178. Lord Beveridge, "The Birth of Labour Exchanges," *Minlabour,* January 1960, p. 2. Employment Exchanges Box, Department of Employment Library, London.
179. Trades Union Congress, *Report of Annual Meeting,* 1910, p. 160.
180. Ibid., p. 161.
181. Ibid., pp. 161–62. The unionists were: W. Friend (Bookbinders), J. V. Stevens (Tinplate and Sheet Metal Workers), T. Warner (Bleachers and Dyers), L. Russell (London Cab Drivers), B. Tillett (London Dockers), B. Cooper (Cigar Makers), and A. Gould (Amalgamated Carpenters and Joiners).
182. Ibid., p. 163.
183. Ibid., p. 164.
184. Ibid., p. 164–65. The circular continued: "Such families must, of course, be clean, healthy, respectable, and have good eyesight. The wages offered are the standard rates—that is, 8s and 9s per week when learning, and afterwards rising, according to the ability of the worker to 12s 6d and 14s per week. There is also a chance for smart girls to be raised in the department to a still higher rate of wage. The rents of the cottages vary. The villages are healthy, and the conditions of labour in the mills are good. The present employees are of high standard physically. I should be glad therefore if your Board would consider the possibility of co-operating with the Yorkshire Division Labour Exchanges in this matter and shall be pleased to hear from you at your earliest convenience."

185. Ibid., p. 165.

186. "To the President of the Board of Trade," 1 March 1910, Trades Union Council, *Annual Report,* 1910, p. 40.

187. "That this Conference is prepared to support Labour Exchanges provided these are conducted on the lines proposed to the President of the Board of Trade by the representatives of the Trades Union Council" (Trades Union Council, *Report of Annual Conference,* 1911, p. 19).

188. Trades Union Congress, *Report of Annual Conference,* 1911, "Trade Unionists and the Labor Exchange," pp. 19–20.

189. M. Olson, *The Logic of Collective Action* (Cambridge, MA: Harvard University Press, 1965), chap. 1.

190. See "Cabinet: Unemployment (Secret) 4 August 1920" CP-1714. Joint Memorandum of the Minister of Health (Addison) and the Minister of Labor (McNamara). PRO Folder LAB2/502/ED 27444/1919. The memo noted (p. 1): "1. It is therefore obvious that if unemployment even approximating to that of 1905 to 1908 were encountered the country would be face to face with a situation the difficulty of which it is impossible to exaggerate unless the Government were prepared in advance with far-reaching measures." And also, "2. There are indications at the present moment that we are on the eve of serious and even alarming unemployment."

191. C.O. Circular 151/1918, Confidential, T. W. Phillips, Acting Assistant Director, 20 February 1918, to all Divisional Officers and Managers. PRO Folder LAB2/295/ED 17163/1918.

192. One observer, Thomas Janoski, disputes this view of the AFL's support. He argues that AFL support for a national labor exchange system began only in November 1932. Janoski gives David Robertson's dissertation as a source for the claim that "from 1917 to 1932, the AFL was lukewarm with its voluntaristic anti-policy stand." It is difficult to reconcile Janoski's assessment with the evidence offered in the primary source, the *American Federationist.* I suspect his analysis refers more generally to the AFL's attitude toward government policy. See Thomas Janoski, *The Political Economy of Unemployment* (Berkeley: University of California Press, 1990), p. 50; and David Robertson, "Politics and Labor Markets," Ph.D. diss., Indiana University, 1981. Robertson kindly made his dissertation available to me, and his original analysis is contrary to Janoski's reading: "the American Federation of Labor, after 1916, put its weight behind the Nolan and Wagner bills" (pp. 109–10).

193. *American Federationist* 37, no. 2 (February 1930): 148.

194. *American Federationist* 37, no. 10 (October 1930): 1196. The November issue carried an editorial reiterating the need for a national employment service and condemning the United States's comparative slowness in establishing one, noting that "our government provided such a service for war-time emergencies when the supply of labor was small and employers were harassed by the difficulties in finding workers. Now when the emergency of unemployment throws the burden of finding employment on workers, the need for such a service is equally inescapable" (*American Federationist* 37, no. 11 (November 1930): 1334.

195. Proceedings of the AFL Conference, 1930. *Report of the Proceedings of the AFL 50th Annual Convention* (Washington, DC: Department of Labor Library), p. 59.

196. "A nationwide system of employment, the state to establish local services and the federal government to provide the channels for policy information and experience is essential to any plan for assuring continuous employment for workers." See *Report of the Proceedings of the AFL 50th Annual Convention*, p. 61.

197. Article in *American Federationist* 40, no. 3 (March 1933): 265.

198. *Report of Proceedings of the AFL 51st Annual Convention*, p. 80.

199. Ibid., p. 83.

200. See V. C. Hattam, *Labor Visions and State Power* (Princeton, NJ: Princeton University Press, 1993) and the discussion in C. Phelan, *William Green* (Albany, NY: State University of New York Press, 1989), chaps. 2, 3.

201. This bill was almost identical to one enacted in 1933.

202. Papers of Robert F. Wagner, Legislative Files, Box 188, Folder: 417a: S.R. 2687. Press release of talk by Secretary Doak on NBC, 10 May 1932, "The Federal Employment Service," pp. 1–2.

203. Ibid., p. 4.

204. *Public Papers of the Presidents of the United States: Herbert Hoover*, 1 January–31 December 1931 (Washington, DC: Government Printing Office, 1976), p. 132.

205. Ibid., p. 134. A similar concern was expressed by Doak: "In the midst of our emergency we are to be compelled to abandon this vital help to labor and the new system, founded upon an old plan of State subsidies, could not be substituted for many months and even years" (p. 135).

206. George H. Trafton, "The Wagner Bill and the Hoover Veto," *American Labor Legislation Review* 21, no. 1 (March 1931): 85.

207. Quoted in Trafton, "The Wagner Bill," pp. 85–86.

208. *American Federationist* 38, no. 4 (April 1931): 407–8.

209. Sumner H. Slichter, "Misleading Attack on Wagner Bill," *American Labor Legislation Review* 21 (1931): 192. He continued thus: "In view of the fact that this has been pointed out by dozens of employment experts during the last several weeks, it is difficult to understand why Secretary Doak should attempt to mislead the public by repeating the statement."

210. Papers of Robert F. Wagner, Speech Files, Box 102, Folder 19: CBS Radio Address, 25 April 1931: "Veto of Employment Service Bill," pp. 3–5. On page 2, Wagner noted that "were I to permit this imputation to go unchallenged I would be unfair to the hundreds of men and women identified with the labor movement who steadfastly exerted all their energies to bring about the enactment of the legislation." On Hillman, see S. Fraser, *Labor Will Rule: Sidney Hillman* (New York: Basic Books, 1992).

211. Papers of Robert F. Wagner, Speech Files, Box 102, Folder 19: CBS Radio address, 25 April 1931: "Veto of Employment Service Bill," pp. 7–8.

212. See Green to Hoover, 24 November 1930, Reel 7, frame 382, William Green Collection, Ohio Historical Society; cf C. Phelan, *William Green* (Albany, NY: State University of New York Press, 1989), p. 187.

213. That the 1933 act devolved so much power to the states suggests how significant a constraint this factor was.

214. William J. Barber, *From New Era to New Deal* (Cambridge and New York: Cambridge University Press, 1985), pp. 190–92.

215. For NAM's early opposition, see S. Harrison et al., *Public Employment*

Offices: Their Purpose, Structure and Methods (New York: Russell Sage Foundation, 1924); see also David Brian Robertson, "Politics and Labor Markets," Ph.D. diss., Indiana University, 1981, chap. 4.

216. M. Kalecki writes: "In the great depression of the thirties, big business opposed consistently experiments for increasing employment by Government spending in all countries . . . This was to be clearly seen in the USA (opposition to the New Deal)" ("Political Aspects of Full Employment," *Political Quarterly* 14 [1944]:324).

217. F. F. Piven and R. Cloward, *Regulating the Poor* (New York: Vintage 1971), p. 82. See also R. M. Collins, *The Business Response to Keynes, 1929–1964* (New York: Columbia University Press, 1981).

218. See Edward Berkowitz and Kim McQuaid, *Creating the Welfare State,* rev. ed. (New York: Praeger, 1992; originally published in 1980), p. 100.

219. See William E. Leuchtenburg, *Franklin D. Roosevelt and the New Deal* (New York; Harper and Row, 1963), who writes: "In the early years of the depression, the nation was united by a common experience. People felt genuine compassion for the victims of hard times. By Roosevelt's second term, as it seemed that the country might never wholly recover, the burden of the unemployed had become too exhausting a moral and economic weight to carry. Those who held jobs . . . could hardly but feel that the depression had been a Judgment which divided the saved from the unsaved" (pp. 273–74).

220. However, according to one study in 1938, the use of the ES offices for distributing unemployment compensation benefits was not inevitable: "In this country, the Social Security Act contemplates, *though it does not specifically require,* the payment of unemployment benefits through public employment offices. In practice all states have provided for the participation of the employment service in the administration of unemployment compensation upon the beginning of benefit payments." In Raymond C. Atkinson, Louise C. Odencrantz, and Ben Deming, *Public Employment Service in the United States* (Chicago: Committee on Public Administration of the Social Science Research Council, 1940), p. 38, my emphasis.

221. RG 174, Box 55, Resolution No. 1 Under the Agreement of 30 March 1937 Between the Secretary of Labor and the Social Security Board, p. 2.

222. Ibid., p. 4.

223. Evidence about the extent and depth of the conflict over reorganization comes indirectly from the Oral History of the Unemployment Insurance project undertaken by the Department of Labor. A number of interviewees who joined the Social Security Board in the late 1930s or early 1940s refer to the legacy of this conflict. For example, see the interviews with Ralph Altman (21 and 27 January 1981) and with Philip Booth (9 April 1981) in the Oral History, Department of Labor. One interviewee, Edward L. Keenan, stressed the "differences of opinion . . . between the Social Security Board and the U.S. Department of Labor about the relationship of unemployment insurance and the employment service program" in the late 1930s (interview, 4 February 1981, p. 5).

224. Since 1937, previously second Assistant Secretary of Labor. For his account of the controversy, see Arthur J. Altmeyer, *The Formative Years of Social Security* (Madison, WI: University of Wisconsin Press, 1966), especially chap. 2.

225. RG 174, Box 56, Summary of Proceedings, Meeting of the Federal Advisory Council of the USES, 10 February 1934, p. 28.

226. RG 174 (General Records of the Department of Labor), Box 100, Folder: "Unemployment Compensation 1938–1939." Address by Altmeyer to Interstate Conference of Unemployment Compensation Agencies, 20 October 1938, pp. 6, 10.

227. RG 174, Box 93, talk by Altmeyer to the 25th annual convention of the International Association of Public Employment Services, titled, "Coordination of Employment Service and Unemployment Compensation Administration," 6 May 1937, pp. 2, 3, 5.

228. Persons's public statements, however, were less critical of the proposed merger. See "State Employment Services Prepared for New Responsibilities," *American Labor Legislation Review* 27 (1937): 161–62, and "The Role of the United States Employment Service," *Employment Service News*, no. 4 (1937): 3–4.

229. RG 174, Box 57, Folder: Agreement between Secretary of Labor and Social Security Board. Memo from Persons to Perkins, 9 April 1937, p. 3.

230. Ibid., pp. 4–5.

231. Ibid., p. 6.

232. The one exception was Wisconsin where there was an industrial commission with overall authority for work-welfare with staff members responsible respectively for administering the Employment Service and the unemployment compensation function; this dualism maintained a distinction between the two functions throughout the state to the lowest administrative unit.

233. RG 174, Box 56. See contribution by Altmeyer to "Social Security and the Employment Service: Their Cooperative Relationships and Respective Administrative Responsibilities," 10 February 1934, pp. 29–30, for a description of the alternative arrangements.

234. RG 174, Box 60, Folder: Employment—General: January–July 1939. Memo from Persons to Perkins, 10 January 1939, p. 3.

235. See memo from Mary La Dame, an assistant to Persons, to Perkins, 9 April 1937, who had originally intended to oppose the merger because of the "reports of conflicts produced by the present set up . . . [and] my own conviction that the development of intelligent policies and practices can provide the necessary safeguards for the placement function" (p. 1). In RG 174, Box 57, Folder: Agreement between Secretary of Labor and Social Security Board.

236. 76th Cong., 1st sess., S. Rept. 2, Part 1: "Unemployment and Relief," p. 3. The report was prepared pursuant to S. Res. 36 in the 75th Congress.

237. RG 174, Box 60, Folder: Employment—General: January–July 1939. Letter from Altmeyer to Perkins, 21 March 1939. In a subsequent letter on 18 April 1939, Altmeyer again urged public clarification upon Perkins: "In my conference with you on March 31 I urged that you clarify the situation and reconcile conflicting views at this time so that there would be no later embarrassment in undertaking to set up a single bureau as recommended in the study of the SSRC 'Public Employment Service in the U.S.' which you stated to me was acceptable to you although you were not prepared to spell out the exact arrangements within the bureau."

238. RG 174, Box 55, Folder: Transcripts of the Record of the Meeting of the Federal Advisory Council of the USES, 7–8 June 1937, p. 37.

239. Ibid., p. 44.

240. Ibid., pp. 45, 46.

241. For details, see Richard Polenberg, *Reorganizing Roosevelt's Government: The Controversy over Executive Reorganization, 1936–1939* (Cambridge, MA: Harvard University Press, 1966).

242. Papers of Harold Smith, Box 1, Folder: Daily Memoranda April–June 1939, April 27 (FDRL).

243. Ibid.

244. Ibid., 6 May 1939.

245. Ibid.

246. FDRL Official File 15, Labor Department, Box 2, Folder: Department of Labor—1939. Memorandum from Dimock to Perkins, 16 January 1939, p. 1.

247. Ibid.

248. Ibid.

249. Ibid., p. 2.

250. Ibid.

251. FDRL Official File 15h, Labor Department, Box 8, Folder: USES 1938–45. Letter from Green to FDR, 11 May 1939, p. 1.

252. FDRL Official File 15h, Labor Department, Box 8, Folder: USES 1938–1945. Letter and memorandum from Senator James Mead to FDR, 21 June 1940, pp. 1–2.

253. Papers of Harold Smith, Box 1, Folder: Daily Memoranda, July–September 1939, 19 July 1939 (FDRL).

254. FDRL Official File 15h, Labor Department, Box 8, File: U.S.E.S. (1933–37). Emil Hurja, Assistant to the Chairman of the Democratic National Committee, forwarded on 27 January 1936 to FDR's assistant Marvin (Mac) McIntyre from Senator Lewis B. Schwellenbach about difficulties in the ES in his state of Washington. The incident also suggests that Persons was not the easiest official with whom to deal. Persons approached Schwellenbach in January of 1935 requesting the latter's assistance regarding the Reemployment Service: "What Persons wanted was a man who had the friendship of the labor groups in the State and upon whom I could rely to take over the task of 'fronting' for the Administration and attempting to alleviate some of the difficulties which were arising. This place was to be handled by a nonsalaried State Director . . . The chief cause of difficulty has been the attitude of the Assistant State Director, Major Hutton . . . I was notified by the Executive Council of the State Federation of Labor that unless Mr. Hutton was removed that organization would oppose the President in the election next year . . . I have consistently attempted to protect Mr. Persons and the Administration and I have been personally subjected to very bitter criticism within the State for this attitude . . . Mr. Persons' attitude is certainly the most ungrateful, after all we have done to try to assist him during the past year. Of course, Mr. Persons has no knowledge about conditions within the State and no conception of the problem."

255. Ruth M. Kellogg, *The United States Employment Service* (Chicago:

University of Chicago Press, 1933), p. 96. Kellogg details a series of political charges against the old ES including appointments, open partisan bias, and peculiar administrative practices. In partial response to the controversy provoked by Hoover's veto, Secretary of Labor Doak attempted to reorganize the existing service in 1931 after the veto. He first introduced a substitute bill to the House, which was overwhelmingly rejected and which, according to Senator Wagner, "did not involve a single improvement over the existing deplorable conditions except to change the title and raise the salary of the Director in Charge of the present decrepit employment service." (Papers of Robert F. Wagner, Speech Files, Box 102, Folder 19: CBS Radio Address, 25 April 1931: "Veto of Employment Service Bill," p. 21.)

Doak conducted an internal reorganization of the service, establishing a new set of federal ES offices in competition with the existing service. The reform was criticized widely for the quality of appointees: the 1931 September meeting of the International Association of Public Employment Services adopted a resolution declaring that "the now existing so-called reorganised Federal Employment Service is wrong in principle, has failed and cannot succeed in developing an efficient worthwhile public employment service." Quoted in "State Employment Service Officials Condemn Doak Reorganization," *American Labor Legislation Review* 21 (September 1931): 393.

256. Kellogg, *The United States Employment Service,* pp. 103–4.

257. RG 172, Box 93. A cutting from the *Washington Post* dated 21 February 1939 reports Persons's resignation and his move to the CCC: "Persons' resignation was concerned with the controversy as to whether the employment service, a bureau of the Labor Department, should be merged with the Unemployment Compensation Bureau of the Social Security Board . . . Unconfirmed reports were that Miss Perkins had forced Persons' resignation. It was stated that his continuance as head of the Employment Service had become an embarrassment to her, since he had opposed the proposed merger."

258. FDRL Official File 15h, Labor Department, Box 8, File: U.S.E.S. 1938–45. Letter from Fechner to Roosevelt, 20 January 1939. He added: "I do not need to tell you how readily I would comply with any request that you might make but I thought you should know the situation as I see it. One of the things that has given me great satisfaction in this work has been the fact that I have operated the Civilian Conservation Corps on an efficient and economical basis. I have been constantly importuned by Senators, Congressmen and others to place both men and women on my payroll. I have consistently refused to do so on the basis that their services were not needed" (pp. 1–2).

259. FDRL Official File 15h, Labor Department, Box 8, File: U.S.E.S. 1938–45. Memorandum for Mr. Early in the White House, recording Fechner's phone call with "K" on 16 February 1939. In place of the letter of dismissal Roosevelt sent one on 16 February 1939 accepting Persons's resignation. The same file contains a copy of the dismissal letter dated 15 February 1939 and signed conditionally by the President, who wrote: "Since our recent conversation I have given further consideration to the adjustments which must be made to coordinate the work of the United States Employment Service in connection with the operation of other

agencies in the State and Federal Governments and have concluded that some changes in personnel are necessary. I therefore am constrained to request your resignation as Director of the USES."

260. M. Goldfield, *The Decline of Organized Labor in the United States* (Chicago: University of Chicago Press, 1987), p. 10.

261. The AFL supported legislation to improve the conditions of employment for particularly weak groups such as women or child workers, but it refrained from advocating laws which compromised its voluntarist approach. See R. L. Horowitz, *Political Ideologies of Organized Law* (New Brunswick, NJ: Transaction Books, 1978), chap. 1.

262. And, of course, the opponents of integration, notably Persons, predicted unwanted results.

263. W. H. Beveridge, *Unemployment,* part 2, p. 295.

264. RG 174, Box 56, Summary of Proceedings, Meeting of the Federal Advisory Council of the USES, 10 February 1934, p. 27. He stated: "Under any unemployment compensation act that will probably be passed in this country, compensation will be provided only for *involuntary* unemployment, so that under each act there will be the necessity of establishing that the man or woman is involuntarily unemployed through what has been called in other countries a 'work test' . . . In Great Britain you will recall that the expression in the act used to be 'genuinely seeking employment.' In Great Britain at the present time the situation is reversed so that the burden of proof is placed upon the administrative authority to establish that the person is unwilling to accept suitable employment which is actually offered him. That, probably, is the sort of test that will be put in the American Unemployment Compensation Acts" (p. 27).

265. Ibid., p. 28.

266. RG 174, Box 60, Folder: Employment—General: January–June 1938. *Employment Service News* 5, no. 3 (March 1938): 13.

Chapter Three

1. Minutes of meeting of the Federal Advisory Council, USES, 9 January 1936, pp. 31, 32, my emphasis; in fact, as explained in the last chapter, Altmeyer became an advocate of integration. In Subject Files of James Mitchell, Box 290, Folder: ES-2 Public Employment Service 1959, National Archives and Record Administration (NARA) Record Group (RG) 174.

2. These numbers are from B. Showler, *Onto a Comprehensive Employment Service* (London: Fabian Research Series 309, 1973), p. 5.

3. Ibid., p. 4.

4. Department of Employment and Productivity, *Future of the Employment Service, Consultative Document* (London: Department of Employment and Productivity, 1970), p. 7.

5. Ibid.

6. Dwight D. Eisenhower Library (hereafter cited as DDE), Library Papers of James P. Mitchell, Box 60, Folder: 1955—Bureau of Employment Security—Personnel. Address by Goodwin to International Association of Public Employment Services (IAPES) Convention, 1955, p. 5.

7. Ibid., p. 8.

8. DDE Library Papers of James P. Mitchell, Box 78, Folder: 1955—Administration—Rocco Siciliano, Speech by Siciliano: "Employment Security Actions—Performance and Promise," 7 June 1955.

9. DDE Library Papers of James P. Mitchell, Box 69, Folder: 1958 DOL Report. "A Review of the Major Aspects of the Public Employment Service 1947–57," by Robert L. Thomas, 1958, p. 1. See also, Thomas Janoski, *The Political Economy of Unemployment* (Berkeley: University of California Press, 1990), pp. 92–103.

10. DDE Library Papers of James P. Mitchell, Box 69, Folder: 1958—DOL Report. "A Review of Major Aspects of the Public Employment Service, 1947–1957," by Robert Thomas, 1958, p. 1.

11. Ibid., p. 2.

12. Ibid.

13. Ibid., p. 3.

14. DDE Library Papers of James P. Mitchell, Box 69, Folder: 1958—DOL Report. Memorandum from Charles Stewart to DOL Under Secretary, 6 August 1958, p. 2.

15. DDE Library Papers of James P. Mitchell, Box 78, Folder: 1955—Administration—Rocco Siciliano. Speech by Siciliano, 7 June 1955, p. 3.

16. Ibid.

17. DDE Library Papers of James P. Mitchell, Box 69, Folder: 1958—DOL Report, "A Review of Major Aspects of the Public Employment Service, 1947–1957," by Robert Thomas, 1958, p. 10.

18. Ibid., p. 11.

19. Ibid., p. 12.

20. Ibid., p. 13.

21. Ibid.

22. U.S. General Accounting Office, *Uneconomical Practices in the Administration of Employment Service and Unemployment Compensation Programs,* Report to the Congress, May 1963 (Washington, DC: U.S. General Accounting Office, 1963).

23. *The Role and Mission of the Federal-State Employment Service in the American Economy,* Subcommittee on Labor, Committee on Education and Labor, House of Representatives, 88th Cong., 2d sess., December 1964 (Washington, DC: Government Printing Office, 1965), p. 35.

24. *A Report of the Secretary of Labor from the Employment Service Task Force,* U.S. Employment Service Task Force, 1965, p. 13.

25. Memorandum from Goodwin to Goldberg, 4 December 1962, p. 1, in M. Cass Papers, Box 17, Folder: ES-2-1, Administration of State Programs (November–December). NARA RG 174.

26. "Employment Service Placement Activities," *Research and Education,* Bulletin No. 82 (Washington, DC: Employment Security), 15 December 1970, p. 1.

27. National Urban Coalition and the Lawyers' Committee for Civil Rights Under Law, *Falling Down on the Job* (Washington, DC: National Urban Coalition and the Lawyers' Committee for Civil Rights, June 1971), p. 37.

28. U.S. General Accounting Office, *Employment Service: More Jobseekers Should Be Referred to Private Employment Agencies* (Washington, DC: General Accounting Office, March 1986).

Since some scholars blamed the continued operation of private employment agencies in Britain and the United States as part of the reason for the inadequacies of the public systems, this recommendation was ironic. Some American scholars cite the outlawing of private employment agencies in other advanced industrial countries, except notably Britain, as an important element supporting publicly funded arrangements. The claim is that the absence of private competitors enabled the public system to expand and to centralize placement work. The most valid aspect of this argument is the failure of British and especially American public labor exchange systems to extend their services beyond the most disadvantaged and least-skilled workers. In their early decades, both systems failed to attract job seekers in the professional and executive occupations; subsequent strategies to serve these groups had some success in Britain, though far less in the United States. The significance of these patterns is that they reinforced the propensity of British and American exchanges to serve those holding the weakest position in the labor market.

29. Harry S. Truman Library (HST Library) Papers of Robert C. Goodwin, Box 1, Folder: Papers Relating to the War Manpower Commission, 1943–45. Circular from McNutt to all employees of the WMC, 11 August 1945. The phrase is that of WMC Chairman Paul McNutt.

30. HST Library Papers of Robert Goodwin, Box 1, Folder: *A Short History of the WMC* (USES, DOL: Technical Services Division, June 1948), p. 13.

31. Ibid., p. 77.

32. Ibid., p. 14.

33. Ibid., p. 76.

34. L. D. A. Baron, "United Kingdom," in *The Public Employment Services and Management* (Paris: OECD, 1965), p. 65.

35. NARA RG 174, Secretary's Office, General Subject Files, Box 139, Folder: Federal Advisory Council 1942. Summary of Meeting, Washington, DC, 29 and 30 October 1942, p. 4.

36. Ibid., p. 2.

37. HST Library Papers of Robert Goodwin, Box 1, Folder: *A Short History of the WMC* (USES, DOL: Technical Services Division, June 1948), p. 15.

38. HST Library Papers of John W. Gibson, Box 8, Folder: Reorganization— Department of Labor, Memorandum from J. Donald Kingsley to Robert Goodwin, "The Future Status and Program of the Employment Service," 26 June 1945, p. 2.

39. These anticipated circumstances dictated the following roles for the postwar service: labor market information service; technical personnel services for small- and medium-sized businesses; employment counseling; and selective placement service for minority groups and workers with physical handicaps. These proposals were mirrored within the War Manpower Commission, which anticipated a substantial reorganization of manpower activities after the war to centralize policy-making and increase efficiency. HST Library Papers of John W. Gibson, Box 9, Folder: Confidential. Proposed Report of the Director of War

Mobilization and Reconversion on Consolidation of Executive Agencies in the Manpower Field, 9 August 1945, p. 6.

40. 1944 White Paper on Employment Policy, pp. 19, 27.

41. As for most legislation on employment or training in Britain, the focus of debate during its passage through Parliament was the proposed legislation's implications for industrial disputes. See Standing Committee A, "Employment and Training Bill," 4–11th May 1948, *Hansard Parliamentary Debates,* House of Commons Official Report, Standing Committees 1947–48, vol. III.

42. International Labour Organization, *National Employment Services: Great Britain* (Geneva: ILO, 1952), p. 3.

43. Ministry of Labour, "Changing Role for the Employment Service," *Ministry of Labour Gazette,* June 1966, pp. 285.

44. Ibid.

45. HST Library Oral History of Robert C. Goodwin, 13 October 1977, p. 16.

46. HST Library Papers of John Gibson, Box 8, Folder: Reorganization— Department of Labor, Memo (personal and confidential) from Edward Cushman to Gibson, "The Future of the Public Employment Service," 7 September 1945, p. 3.

47. HST Library Papers of John W. Gibson, Box 8, Folder: Reorganization— Department of Labor, Memo from J. Donald Kingsley to Robert Goodwin, "The Future Status and Program of the Employment Service," 26 June 1945, p. 1. Emphasis in original.

48. HST Library Papers of John W. Gibson, Box 9, Folder: Speeches and background material. Confidential. Proposed Report of the Director of War Mobilization and Reconversion on Consolidation of Executive Agencies in the Manpower Field, 9 August 1945, pp. 9–10.

49. Ibid., p. 10.

50. HST Library Papers of Robert Goodwin, Box 1, Folder: Papers relating to the War Manpower Commission, 1943–45. Memo from McNutt to all WMC employees, "Post-War Program of the United States Employment Service," 11 August 1945.

51. HST Library Papers of Robert Goodwin, Box 1, Folder: Papers relating to the War Manpower Commission, 1943–45. USES "Post-War Program of the USES," 11 August 1945, p. 1.

52. Ibid., p. 2.

53. Ibid., p. 10.

54. Among the counselor's responsibilities were: "1. Assist the person to discover, analyze, and evaluate his vocational assets; 2. provide current information on job requirements and employment opportunities; 3. assist in formulating a vocational plan and in putting it into effect; 4. put the person in touch with community facilities, including training through which he may better equip himself for employment in his chosen field" (HST Library Papers of Robert Goodwin, Box 1, Folder: Papers relating to the War Manpower Commission, 1943-45, USES "Post-War Program of the USES," 11 August 1945, p. 7).

55. Ibid., p. 16.

56. It was noted that the "Federal-State system of employment services has an important part to play in reducing unemployment . . . [and should] . . . be

strengthened so that it can better fulfil these purposes." In the DDE Library Papers of Arthur Burns, Box 117, Folder: Economic Report of 1955—Chapter 3 Part IV—Public Works (1). Memo from Albert Rees to Neil Jacoby, 20 December 1954, "The Employment Service," p. 1. The same piece observes that, "of course, an employment service cannot create jobs."

57. HST Library Papers of John W. Gibson, Box 8, Folder: Reorganization—Department of Labor, Memorandum from J. Donald Kingsley to Robert Goodwin, "The Future Status and Role of the Employment Service," 26 June 1945, p. 3.

58. *A Report to the Secretary of Labor from the Employment Service Task Force,* U.S. Employment Service Task Force, 1965, p. 1.

59. T. S. Chegwidden and G. Myrddin-Evans, *The Employment Exchange System in Great Britain* (London: Macmillan, 1934), p. 3.

60. Rodney Lowe, *Adjusting to Democracy* (Oxford: Clarendon Press, 1986).

61. Cmd.1054/1920, *Report of the Committee of Enquiry into the Work of Employment Exchanges,* p. 10. In Reports from Commissioners, Inspectors, and Others, vol. XIX, 10 February to 23 December 1920 (London: HMSO). Chaired by G. Barnes, M.P., with thirteen members representing industry, unions, and exchange administrators.

62. A similar distinction was drawn in the United States in the *Social Security Act of 1935.*

63. This clause was originally formulated as "genuinely seeking whole-time employment but unable to obtain such employment" in the 1921 legislation but was modified in the *Unemployment Insurance (No. 2) Act of 1924.*

64. Alan Deacon, *In Search of the Scrounger,* Occasional Papers on Social Administration, No. 60 (London: G. Bell & Sons, 1976), p. 9.

65. Figures cited in Rodney Lowe, *Adjusting to Democracy* (Oxford: Clarendon Press, 1986), p. 146.

66. Chegwidden and Myrddin-Evans, *The Employment Exchange System of Great Britain,* p. 75.

67. Cmd.1054/1920, *Report of the Committee of Enquiry into the Work of the Employment Exchanges.* In Reports from Commissioners, Inspectors, and Others, vol. XIX, 10 February to 23 December 1920 (London: HMSO). Chaired by G. Barnes, M.P., with thirteen members representing industry, unions, and exchange administrators.

68. John Barton Seymour, *The British Employment Exchange* (London: P. S. King & Son, 1928), p. 62. Seymour advocated compelling employers to notify vacancies to the exchanges since this requirement would increase the exchanges' pool of applicants and ensure that they were informed about vacancies. Such a proposal would not create undue hardship or injustice, Seymour ventured, since "the workpeople have compulsory registration of unemployment now; employers could justly be asked to do what employees are required to do." Seymour anticipated little employer resistance and recorded comparable regulations in other countries, including Germany and Switzerland.

69. B. Showler, *The Public Employment Service* (London: Longman, 1976), pp. 22–23.

70. Cmd.4185/1932, *Royal Commission on Unemployment Insurance,* 1931–32. Final Report paras. 594–96. These staff held unestablished positions.

71. See, for example, *Labour and the Unemployment Crisis,* Parliamentary Committee of the TUC and the National Executive of the Labour Party (London, 1921); *Workless: A Social Tragedy,* TUC (London, 1933); and Joint Meetings of the Committee of the TUC General Council and the Representative Group of Employers, *Unemployment,* working draft, 1928, TUC Library.

72. TUC, *Royal Commission and the T.U.C.* (London: TUC, 1932). The TUC was far more critical of the commission's work on Unemployment Insurance; see TUC, *Fair Play for the Unemployed: The Trade Union Case against the Royal Commission's Report,* published in 1931 before the commissioners completed their work.

73. Deacon, *In Search of the Scrounger,* p. 88.

74. Ross McKibbin, "The 'Social Psychology' of Unemployment in Inter-war Britain," in Ross McKibbin, *The Ideologies of Class* (Oxford: Clarendon Press, 1990), p. 246.

75. Ibid.

76. Ibid., p. 249.

77. Lowe, *Adjusting to Democracy,* pp. 134, 146.

78. McKibbin, "The 'Social Psychology' of Unemployment," p. 252.

79. Lowe, *Adjusting to Democracy,* chap. 5.

80. ILO, *National Employment Services: Great Britain,* p. 134.

81. Ibid., p. 135.

82. The expansion of national assistance and of pensions was a constant worry for the Conservatives in the 1950s, and several papers were drafted about the problem by the Conservative Research Department. For example, see François Lafitte, "Some Reflections on Social Security," July 1951, p. 10. Covering note to Mr. Lafitte's memo: "We believe that great economies could be effected by concentrating public expenditures upon persons who are in need of assistance instead of dissipating the assistance indiscriminately over goods supplied" (p. 2). In CRD2/30/5: *Insurance and Assistance Subcttee 1951.* See also CRD2/30/8: *Insurance Subcommittee Briefs 1952–53* and CRD2/30/4: *National Assistance 1948–50: Sir Geoffrey Hutchinson's* [chairman of the National Assistance Board] *Talk to Insurance Sub-Cttee.,* 24 March 1954. Personal and Confidential. All in Conservative Party Archives, Bodleian Library, Oxford.

83. ILO, *National Employment Services: Great Britain,* p. 136.

84. Baron, "United Kingdom," p. 75.

85. Ibid.

86. Goodwin notes that Canada separated two functions but concludes that "they're putting them back together again." HST Library Oral History of Robert C. Goodwin, 1977, p. 13. Statutorily, claimants for UI were required to register at ES offices and demonstrate that they were searching for work; this latter clause was not rigorously enforced. It is important to note that it is unemployment insurance and not welfare benefits (AFDC) which the ES offices dispensed.

87. Proposed Report of the Director of War Mobilization and Reconversion on Consolidation of Executive Agencies in the Manpower Field. HST Library Papers of John W. Gibson, Box 9, Folder: Labor Speeches and background material. Confidential. 9 August 1945, p. 10.

88. Ibid., pp. 10–11.

89. *A Report to the Secretary of Labor from the Employment Service Task Force,* U.S. Employment Service Task Force, 1965, pp. 12–13.

90. A private organization: for details see, B. L. Jones, "The Role of Keynesians in Wartime Policy and Postwar Planning, 1940–46,"American Economic Review 62 (1972): 125–33.

91. HST Library Official File 1392, Folder: 552—Misc. (January 1946), "A National Employment Service," National Planning Association, 17 December 1945, pp. 2, 3.

92. Ibid., p. 3.

93. HST Library Papers of Robert Goodwin, Box 1, Folder: Papers relating to the War Manpower Commission, 1943–45. USES "Post-War Program of the USES," 11 August 1945, p. 15, my emphasis.

94. HST Library Papers of Robert Goodwin, Box 1, Folder: *A Short History of the WMC* (USES, DOL: Technical Services Division, June 1948), p. 14.

95. Ibid.

96. Ibid., p. 15.

97. For one account, see CRD2/30/4: *National Assistance 1948–50: Sir Geoffrey Hutchinson's* [chairman of the National Assistance Board] *Talk to Insurance Sub-Cttee.,* 24 March 1954. Personal and Confidential. In Conservative Party Archives, Bodleian Library, Oxford.

98. ILO, *National Employment Services: Great Britain,* p. 29.

99. CRD2/30/4: *National Assistance 1948–50: Sir Geoffrey Hutchinson's* [chairman of the National Assistance Board] *Talk to Insurance Sub-Cttee.,* 24 March 1954, Personal and Confidential, p. 1. In Conservative Party Archives, Bodleian Library, Oxford.

100. See the brief discussion on the "social bases of the Employment Service" in Showler, *The Public Employment Service,* pp. 9–15.

101. The nine aims identified as appropriate for a national employment service included: notifying job vacancies and retraining opportunities between districts; providing a "comprehensive placing service and information about available openings, supplemented by employment advice and vocational guidance in depth in cases of need"; labor market research; special guidance, placing retraining "operations in the context of big redundancies"; assisting regional policy; linking employers with specialist advisory services of the Department of Employment and Productivity (DEP); and collecting statistics about employment. See Department of Employment and Productivity, *Future of the Employment Service, Consultative Document,* 1970, p. 4.

102. Ibid., p. 6.

103. Ibid.

104. See, for example, the paper on "Employment Policy," 27 October 1948, 14 pp. With memorandum from C. J. M. Alport to Mr. Clarke Con, Political Centre, 23 November 1948. "The 'Employment Policy' White Paper [i.e., 1944] was presented to Parliament by Lord Woolton when he was Minister of Reconstruction in the Coalition Govt. It is a most admirable document and has never had sufficient attention" (p. 9). In CRD2/9/7 *Employment 1946–48,* in Conservative Party Archives, Bodleian Library, Oxford.

105. DDE Library Papers of James P. Mitchell, Box 69, Folder: 1958—DOL

Report, "A Review of Major Aspects of the Public Employment Service, 1947–1957," by Robert Thomas, 1958, p. 21.

106. Ibid., p. 22.
107. Ibid., p. 23.
108. Ibid., p. 24.
109. Ibid., p. 25.
110. Ibid., p. 35.
111. Ibid., p. 25.
112. Ibid., p. 26.
113. Ibid., p. 27.
114. Ibid., p. 30.
115. Ibid.
116. Ibid., p. 31.
117. Ibid., p. 32.
118. Ibid., p. 33.
119. Ibid., p. 34.
120. Ibid., p. 36.
121. Ibid., p. 38.
122. Ibid., p. 4.
123. Ibid., p. 7.
124. Ibid., p. 15.
125. Ibid.
126. Ibid., p. 18.
127. See the account in DDE Library Papers of James P. Mitchell, Box 78, Folder: 1955—Administration, Rocco Siciliano, Speech by Siciliano, 7 June 1955, p. 4.
128. DDE Library Papers of James P. Mitchell, Box 69, Folder: 1958—DOL Report, "A Review of Major Aspects of the Public Employment Service, 1947–1957," by Robert Thomas, 1958, p. 18.
129. Ibid., p. 19.
130. Ibid., p. 20.
131. Ibid., p. 21.
132. Ibid., p. 40.
133. Ibid.
134. Ibid. p. 41.
135. Cmnd.6527/1944, *White Paper on Employment Policy,* in *Parliamentary Papers, 1943–44,* vol. VIII.
136. Ibid., p. 27.
137. ILO, *National Employment Services: Great Britain,* p. 130.
138. Ibid., p. 2.
139. W. H. Beveridge, *Full Employment in a Free Society* (London: Allen & Unwin, 1944; 2d ed., 1960).
140. ILO, *National Employment Services: Great Britain,* p. 30.
141. Ibid.
142. See S. Blank, *Government and Industry in Britain: The Federation of British Industry in Politics, 1945–65* (Lexington: Heath, 1973), and W. Grant and D. Marsh, *The CBI* (London: Hodder and Stoughton, 1977).

143. This association, like the Committee for Economic Development, was a private organization acting as a forum for policy discussions between representatives of business, unions, and economists. They were founded during the Second World War. Both organizations proved strong supporters of Keynesian economics. See H. Stein, *The Fiscal Revolution in America* (Chicago: University of Chicago Press, 1969), and B. L. Jones "The Role of Keynesians in Wartime Policy and Postwar Planning 1940–46," *American Economic Review* 62 (1972): 125–33.

144. DDE Library Office of Special Assistant to President for Personnel Management, Box 27, Folder: Labor (2). Talk by Edison Bowers, "The Employment Security Elephant," March 1958.

145. In 1942, when the USES was federalized and placed under the WMC, the state governors and Interstate Conference of State Employment Security Administrators attempted to "insure that the USES would be returned to state control after the war. In order to accomplish this the Interstate Conference was successful in having provisions attached to the Appropriation Bills which limited the salary scales of the transferred USES personnel in state and local offices to those paid in other State Agencies of Government." HST Library Papers of Robert Goodwin, Box 1, *A Short History of the WMC*, 1948, p. 33.

146. HST Library Official File, Box 1392, Folder: 552 (January 1946). Includes an example of this form. The same folder includes numerous letters urging Truman to keep the USES under federal control.

147. See RG 174 Office of the Secretary, Subject Files, Box 14, Folder: ES 1945, Memorandum from Robert Goodwin USES Director to Second Assistant Secretary Labor Department Edward Moran, "Proposed Strategy for Dealing with the Legislative Situation as it Affects the USES," 3 October 1945; and Letter from Secretary of Labor L. Schwellenbach to Harold Smith, Director, Bureau of the Budget, 20 December 1945.

148. *Public Papers of the Presidents of the U.S.: Harry S. Truman* (Washington, DC: Government Printing Office, 1961), pp. 579–80; and see "Control of Employment Services," *Congressional Digest* 25 (April 1946): 97–128.

149. *Public Papers of the Presidents of the U.S.: Harry S. Truman* (Washington, DC: Government Printing Office 1961), pp. 580–81.

150. For a discussion of this organization, see "Statement on Interstate Conference," July 1955, DDE Library Papers of James P. Mitchell, Box 77, Folder: 1955—Administrative—John Gilhooley.

151. Janoski maintains that the ICESA "even opposed raising state workers' salaries for doing the same work as more highly paid federal workers during World War II; it was also accused of lobbying against appropriation bills for the employment service in 1947" (Janoski, *The Political Economy of Unemployment*, p. 77); he cites Arthur Butler, "The Public Employment Service in the U.S.," Ph.D. diss., University of Wisconsin, Madison (1951), as the source of this claim.

152. DDE Library Office of the Special Assistant to President for Personnel Management, Box 27, Folder: Labor (2), Bowers, "The Employment Security Elephant," 27 March 1958, p. 4.

153. On labor's view, see the letter from AFL President William Green to Secretary of Labor Schwellenbach dated 27 September 1945 opposing returning

the ES to the states, in NARA RG 174, Labor Office of the Secretary, Subject Files of the Secretary, Box 3, Folder: AFL 1945.

154. HST Library Papers of John W. Gibson, Box 9, Folder: Labor—Speeches and background material. Confidential. Proposed Report of the Director of War Mobilization and Reconversion on Consolidation of Executive Agencies in the Manpower Field, 9 August 1945.

155. HST Library Oral History of Robert C. Goodwin, 1977, p. 10.

156. Ibid., p. 9.

157. "The Question of Federal or State Control of the Employment Services," *Congressional Digest* 25 (April 1946).

158. I. Katznelson and B. Pietrykowski, "Rebuilding the American State: Evidence from the 1940s," *Studies in American Political Development* (1991) 5:301–39, p. 332.

159. Figures from the Federal Security Agency, *Annual Report,* 1949 (Washington, DC: Government Printing Office) and cited in Katznelson and Pietrykowski, "Rebuilding the American State: Evidence from the 1940s," p. 333.

160. HST Library Papers of John W. Gibson, Box 8, Folder: Reorganization— Department of Labor, Memo from J. Donald Kingsley to Robert Goodwin, "The Future Status and Program of the Employment Service," 26 June 1945, p. 1.

161. HST Library Official File 1392, Folder: 552-Misc. (January 1946). "A National Employment Service," National Planning Association, 17 December 1945, p. 2.

162. Ibid.

163. See D. W. Brady, *Critical Elections and Congressional Policy Making* (Stanford, CA: Stanford University Press, 1988).

164. HST Library. Oral History of Robert C. Goodwin, 13 October 1977, p. 7. In his request to Congress to continue the wartime Fair Employment Practice Committee, Truman also requested increased funds for the federal Employment Service: D. R. McCoy and R. T. Ruetten, *Quest and Response* (Lawrence, KS: University Press of Kansas, 1973), pp. 25–26.

165. The state affiliation of the chairmen of these committees in the two decades before the *Civil Rights Act* was passed are instructive. In the Senate, Finance was chaired by Eugene D. Millikin (R-Colorado, 1947–49), Walter F. George (D-Georgia, 1949–53), Millikin (1953–55), and Harry F. Byrd (D-Virginia, 1955–65); Labor and Public Welfare was chaired by Robert A. Taft (R-Ohio 1947–49), Elbert D. Thomas (D-Utah, 1949–51), James E. Murray (D-Montana, 1951–53), H. Alexander Smith (R-New Jersey, 1953–55), and Lister Hill (D-Alabama, 1955–65). With the exception of Smith, these committees were controlled either by conservative Republicans or Southern Democrats. In the House, the Ways and Means chairmen were: Harold Knutson (R-Minnesota, 1947–49), Robert L. Doughton (D-North Carolina, 1949–53), Daniel A. Reed (R-New York, 1953–55), Jere Cooper (D-Tennessee, 1955–57), and Wilbur D. Mills (D-Arkansas, 1958–65).

166. In 1945, Dirksen succeeded in attaching an amendment to the Rescission Bill (H.R. 4407) in the House Appropriations Committee requiring the Service to be defederalized within thirty days of enactment. The bill was vetoed by Truman.

167. H.R. 6793, PL—79-549.

168. Figures cited in Katznelson and Pietrykowski, "Rebuilding the American State: Evidence from the 1940s," p. 335.

169. *The Role and Mission of the Federal-State Employment Service in the American Economy,* Subcommittee on Labor, Committee on Education and Labor, House of Representatives, 88th Cong., 2d sess., December 1964 (Washington, DC: Government Printing Office, 1965), pp. 49 my emphasis, 52.

170. *A Report to the Secretary of Labor from the Employment Service Task Force,* U.S. Employment Service Task Force, 1965, p. 38.

171. Cited in letter from Secretary Schwellenbach to AFL President William Green, 5 December 1950, NARA RG 174, Office of the Secretary, Subject Files of Tobin, Box 32, Folder: 1950 AFL, p. 2.

172. Ibid.

173. NAACP Group II, Box B 95, Folder: Labor: State Employment Services, 1947–49. Memorandum prepared for President Marshall, 20 June 1949, p. 1. The memo added: "Job orders received at the central—white—employment service in which no specification of white or colored is made receive first attention from the white office with the result that white workers have a prior opportunity for the job . . . [T]he existence of a segregated office initiates the suggestion that an employer express a preference by calling one or the other of the agencies" (p. 2).

174. NAACP Group II, Box A 653, Folder: USES 1940–42, General. From a memorandum of a conference between Ewan Clague, Head of the USES, and Walter White of the NAACP, 17 December 1940, p. 1.

175. NAACP Group II, Box B 95, Folder: Labor: State Employment Services, 1947–49. Letter from Clarence Mitchell, NAACP Labor Secretary, to Robert Carter, Assistant Special Counsel at the NAACP, commenting on a letter from J. Donald Kingsley, Acting Administrator of the Federal Security Agency, 27 April 1949, p. 1.

176. NAACP Group II, Box A 653, Folder: USES 1940–42, General. Letter from Byron Mitchell to Addison Cutler, 17 April 1940, p. 1.

177. For details, see Desmond King, "'The Longest Road to Equality': The Politics of Institutional Desegregation under Truman," *Journal of Historical Sociology* 6 (1993): 119–63.

178. NAACP Group II, Box A 653, Folder: USES Discrimination, 1944–47. Statement from NAACP to Secretary of Labor Lewis Schwellenbach on the return of the USES to the states, 11 September 1946; and memo on meeting with Department of Labor on Transfer of USES to the states, 17 September 1947, p. 4. The NAACP was one of ten organizations meeting with the Labor Secretary.

179. NAACP Group II, Box A 653, Folder: USES Clarence Mitchell, 1946–47.

180. NAACP Group II, Box A 653, Folder: USES Discrimination, 1944–47. National Citizens' Political Action Committee, "Retention of Employment Service as National Agenda Essential to Fair Employment in Reconversion Period," 10 November 1945, p. 3.

181. NAACP Group II, Box A 653, Folder: USES Discrimination, 1944–47. NAACP press release, 25 April 1947, p. 1.

182. NARA RG 174, Office of the Secretary, Subject Files, Box 14, Folder: ES 1946, Memorandum from Philip Hannah and Goodwin to the Secretary, 26

August 1946, "Meeting with AFL Representatives re Segregation in District Employment Office," p. 1.

183. NARA RG 174, Office of the Secretary, Subject Files, Box 14, Folder: ES 1945. See letter from Henry Beitscher, president of the Washington Industrial Union Council to Secretary of Labor Lewis Schwellenbach, 22 August 1946: "As you undoubtedly know, the Washington CIO, with the cooperation of other community organizations, has been conducting a vigorous campaign along these lines. The purpose of our meeting with you would be to correct the systematic distortion of the facts in the situation on the part of some USES officials, as well as to propose specific steps for the elimination of segregation in the local office."

184. NARA RG 174, Office of the Secretary, Subject Files, Box 14, Folder: ES 1945, Memorandum from Goodwin to Second Assistant Secretary Edward Moran Department of Labor, 4 October 1945, "Need for Legislation to Transfer the USES to the States," p. 1.

185. See NARA RG 174, Office of the Secretary, Subject Files, Box 14, Folder: ES 1946 Memorandum from USES Deputy Director E. L. Keenan to Secretary of Labor, 30 August 1946, "Program for the Transfer of USES Employees to State Service," p. 10.

186. DDE Library, James Mitchell Papers, Box 55, Folder: 1953—Reorganization of DOL—Suggestions. American Federation of Labor, "Reorganization of the U.S. Department of Labor," n.d., p. 2. See also NARA RG 174, Office of the Secretary, Subject Files, Schwellenbach, 1945–48, Box 3, Folder: AFL 1945, "Labor's Demand for a Fair and Just Administrative Procedure," submitted to the president by John Frey, president of the Metal Trades Department of the AFL, p. 8.

187. DDE Library, James P. Mitchell Papers, Box 55, Folder: 1953— Reorganization of the DOL—Suggestions, "Post-War Planning Committee Draft for the Reorganization and Development of the U.S. DOL," n.d., p. 1.

188. Ibid., p. 6.

189. Ibid., p. 7.

190. HST Library, Papers of Gerhard Colm, Box 1, Folder: Full Employment— Misc. Memorandum from Atkinson to Colm, "Significance of a Full Employment Program for Location of USES," 13 July 1945, p. 4.

191. HST Library, Papers of Gerhard Colm, Box 1, Folder: Full Employment— Misc. Memorandum from Clark to Colm, "U.S. Employment Service and the Full Employment Program," 26 July 1945, pp. 1–2.

192. Ibid., p. 5.

193. Ibid., p. 6.

194. NARA RG 174, Office of the Secretary, Subject Files, Box 14, Folder: ES 1946 Memorandum from Goodwin to the Secretary, 28 October 1946, "Unresolved Differences Between the USES and the Bureau of Employment Security, Federal Security Agency, with Respect to the Organization of the Employment Service in the States," p. 2.

195. HST Library, Papers of John W. Gibson, Box 8, Folder: Reorganization— Department of Labor. Memo from J. Donald Kingsley to Robert Goodwin, 26 June 1945, p. 1.

196. S. Barkin, "The Evolving New Public Employment Service," in OECD,

The Public Employment Services and Management (Paris: OECD, 1965), p. 11.

When Oscar Ewing, the American postwar Federal Security Administrator, visited European countries to study their unemployment and welfare systems, he was given or acquired in Sweden, Karl Hojer's, *Social Welfare in Sweden.* Hojer proclaimed that "Swedes have decided that, basically, it is neither logical nor really humanitarian to help people only after they are already ensnarled in misfortune. The primary goal should be to attack the *causes* of the misfortunes, to root out and eliminate these causes so far as possible." This objective was embodied in Swedish labor market policy—"the Swedish worker wants, first, to be sure of a job; financial aid when he is out of work is a secondary concern"—which required integrating labor and social welfare legislation. According to Hojer, this task was relatively easy in Sweden. It was facilitated by the country's labor exchange system: "An effective labor-exchange service is considered an important weapon in Sweden's social-welfare arsenal." Hojer stresses the dominance of the exchange system's placement work over the unemployment insurance system and the pivotal role of union representatives in exchange administration. See HST Library, Papers of Oscar R. Ewing, Box 34, Folder: Sweden—Public Welfare, 1945. Statement of Oscar R. Ewing, U.S. Federal Security Administrator, Stockholm, 19 December 1949, pp. 23, 30, 32.

197. *The Role and Mission of the Federal-State Employment Service in the American Economy,* Subcommittee on Labor, Committee on Education and Labor, House of Representatives, 88th Cong., 2d sess., December 1964 (Washington, DC: Government Printing Office, 1965), p. 68.

198. As McKibbin noted, the exchanges were "grim and shabby" places, consistently underfunded, which "remained not a credit to them [the Ministry of Labor] for another forty years" ("The 'Social Psychology' of Unemployment," p. 246).

199. Department of Employment and Productivity, *Future of the Employment Service: Consultative Document,* 1970, and *Manpower Policy in the United Kingdom* (Paris: OECD, 1970). See also "Manpower policies in Britain," *Employment and Productivity Gazette,* August 1969, pp. 720–24.

200. Department of Employment and Productivity, *Future of the Employment Service: Consultative Document,* 1970, pp. 1–2.

201. Ibid., p. 2.

202. Ibid.

203. Ibid., p. 3.

204. Ibid., p. 5.

205. Ibid., pp. 10, 11.

206. Ibid., p. 11. That the 1970 report made this recommendation is evidence of the failure of a previous step in this direction issued in 1965 by the Ministry of Labour. The National Plan of that year included the injunction that the employment service was to "swing" from being an unemployment benefit institution to "an economic agency which is predominantly about employment." Obviously this imperative had not been achieved, despite its restatement of one of the earliest aims of a national employment service. See Ministry of Labour, "Changing Role for the Employment Service," *Ministry of Labour Gazette,* June 1966, p. 285.

207. Department of Employment and Productivity, *Future of the Employment Service: Consultative Document,* 1970, p. 12.

208. Ibid., p. 20.

209. See Brian Showler, *Onto a Comprehensive Employment Service,* and *The Public Employment Service.*

210. Showler, *Onto a Comprehensive Employment Service,* pp. 2–3.

211. Ibid., p. 11.

212. DDE Library, Papers of James P. Mitchell, Box 69, Folder: 1958—DOL Report, "A Review of Major Aspects of the Public Employment Service," 1958, p. 43.

213. Ibid., p. 45.

214. DDE Library, Papers of James P. Mitchell, Box 134, Folder: 1958—Federal Advisory Council—Employment Security January–June 1958 (2). Progress Report of Committee on Employment Service, Metropolitan Area Offices, November 1957.

215. Ibid., p. 6.

216. DDE Library, Papers of James P. Mitchell, Box 135, Folder: 1959—Federal Advisory Council on Employment Security (April–November). Staff working paper by Federal Advisory Council, "Role of the Employment Service," 16 October 1959, p. 1.

217. Ibid., p. 2.

218. Ibid.

219. DDE Library, Official File 851, Folder: 156-1 (1) Unemployment Insurance. Memo from Mitchell to the President, 7 April 1954.

220. DDE Library, Papers of James P. Mitchell, Box 135, Folder: 1959—Federal Advisory Council on Employment Security (April–November). Staff working paper, "Role of the Employment Service," 16 October 1959, p. 9.

221. *The Role and Mission of the Federal-State Employment Service in the American Economy,* Subcommittee on Labor, Committee on Education and Labor, House of Representatives, 88th Cong., 2d sess., December 1964 (Washington, DC: Government Printing Office, 1965), p. 37.

222. DDE Library, Whitman File: Cabinet Series, Box 15, Folder: Cabinet Meeting, 26 February 1960. "Manpower—Challenge of the 1960s," February 1960.

223. DDE Library, Papers of James P. Mitchell, Box 62, Folder: 1960—Bureau of Employment Security—Summary Plan (1). Minutes of ES Conference of University Consultants, June 1960.

224. Ibid., p. 2.

225. Ibid., p. 7.

226. Ibid., p. 9. Similar points emerged from the discussions of working group "A."

227. *A Report to the Secretary of Labor from the Employment Service Task Force,* U.S. Employment Service Task Force, 1965, p. 4.

228. Ibid., p. 14.

229. For a discussion, see P. Milgrom and J. Roberts, *Economics, Organization and Management* (Englewood Cliffs, NJ: Prentice-Hall, 1992), chap. 7.

230. HST Library Oral History of Robert Goodwin, 1977, pp. 29–30.

Chapter Four

1. The term is borrowed from Andrew Shonfield, *Modern Capitalism* (Oxford: Oxford University Press, 1965).

2. Ibid., pp. 64–65.

3. See Memorandum to the President from Secretary of Labor Willard Wirtz, 23 December 1966, "A Report on Employment and Unemployment in Urban Slums and Ghettoes," NARA RG 174, Office of the Secretary.

4. Solomon Barkin, "Introduction: The Evolving New Public Employment Agencies," in OECD, *The Public Employment Services and Management* (Paris: OECD, 1965), pp. 11, 12. For a British application, see Brian Showler, *The Public Employment Service* (London: Longman, 1976), chap. 1.

5. For discussions, see the essays in Peter Hall, ed., *The Political Power of Economic Ideas: Keynesianism Across Nations* (Princeton, NJ: Princeton University Press, 1989), especially chap. 3 by M. Weir, "Ideas and Politics: The Acceptance of Keynesianism in Britain and the United States."

6. Shonfield, *Modern Capitalism,* p. 65. This was partially achieved by the creation of the tripartite National Economic Development Council (NEDO) in 1962 by the Macmillan government to provide a forum for cooperation between government, industry, and unions; the idea was copied from French indicative planning models.

7. For discussions, see Peter Hall, *Governing the Economy* (Oxford: Polity Press, 1986).

8. HMSO, *Employment Policy* (London: HMSO Cmnd 6527 1944). See also Jim Tomlinson, *Employment Policy: The Crucial Years, 1939–1955* (Oxford: Clarendon Press, 1987).

9. See paper on "Employment Policy," 27 October 1948, pp. 14 and 9, in Folder: Conservative Research Department (CRD) 2/9/7: Employment 1946–48, Conservative Party Archives, Bodleian Library, Oxford; and C. A. R. Crosland, *The Future of Socialism* (London: Cape, 1956).

10. HMSO, *Employment Policy* (London: HMSO Cmnd 6527 1944), p. 26.

11. Ibid., p. 27.

12. See Desmond King and Bo Rothstein, "Government Legitimacy and the Labor Market: A Comparative Analysis of Employment Exchanges," *Public Administration* 72 (1994): 289–306.

13. Published in 1974 as "There's Work to Be Done: Unemployment and Manpower Policies" (London: HMSO, 1974).

14. Hall, *Governing the Economy,* p. 77; see also S. Blank, *Government and Industry in Britain: The Federation of British Industry, 1945–65* (Lexington: Heath, 1973) and W. Grant and D. Marsh, *The CBI* (London: Hodder and Stoughton, 1977).

15. See Herbert Stein, *The Fiscal Revolution in America* (Chicago: University of Chicago Press, 1969); Margaret Weir's chapters, "Ideas and Politics: The Acceptance of Keynesianism in Britain and the United States," in Peter Hall, ed., *The Political Power of Economic Ideas* (Princeton, NJ: Princeton University Press, 1989) and "The Federal Government and Unemployment: The Frustration of Policy Innovation from the New Deal to the Great Society," in M. Weir et al., eds., *The Politics of Social Policy in the United States* (Princeton, NJ: Princeton University Press, 1988), and *Politics and Jobs* (Princeton, NJ: Princeton University Press, 1992). The much more radical Full Employment Bill, requiring the federal government to pursue policies guaranteeing full employment was defeated in Congress

in 1945. For this transformation, see Stephen Kemp Bailey, *Congress Makes a Law* (New York: Vintage Books, 1950), and for business opposition influencing this dilution, see Robert M. Collins, *The Business Response to Keynes, 1929–1964* (New York: Columbia University Press, 1981).

16. Proposals from the National Resources Planning Board (an agency in the Executive Office of the President) envisaged a full employment Keynesian program after 1945. See National Resources Planning Board (NRPB), "Full Employment Now and Tomorrow: An Approach to Post-War Planning," 1941, in FDRL Official File 1092, Box 4.

17. President Roosevelt's 1944 state of the union address to Congress presenting his "Economic Bill of Rights" presaged this development.

18. HST Library, Official File, Box 1104, Folder: 407 (1945) Letter of 3 June 1945 from Vinson to Wagner.

19. HST Library, President's Secretary's Files: General File, Box 121, Folder: Full Employment. Letter from Truman to McCormack, 29 October 1945.

20. HST Library Oral History of Robert C. Goodwin, 1977, p. 16.

21. Ibid., pp. 47–48.

22. See HST Library Oral History of Leon H. Keyserling, 1971, p. 41. Training issues touched policymakers only fleetingly before the Second World War period. Some of the policies formulated to respond to the Great Depression included training components. Both the measures adopted and the accompanying discussions were modest. See the correspondence between Grace Abbott, the distinguished University of Chicago social scientist, and the USES Director Persons. Letter from Grace Abbott to Frank Persons, 8 November 1937, National Archives, RG 174: General Records of the Department of Labor, Office of the Secretary, Box 60, File: Employment—General August through December 1937. Memo by Persons, 20 January 1938, p. 2. See also National Archives, RG 174: General Records of the Department of Labor, Office of the Secretary, Box 60, File: Employment—General: January–July 1939.

At the end of World War II, President Truman established a Training and Retraining Administration (TRA) under General Groves Erskine to develop training programs. See HST Library, Official File, Box 86, Folder: OF 15-1 Retraining and Reemployment Administration, letter from Secretary Schwellenbach to Truman nominating Erskine, 7 February 1946.

The administration established 1,500 community centers throughout the country. Despite a broad brief, the TRA principally assisted in the return of veterans to their former peacetime positions, as evidenced by the quote, "To supervise and coordinate all government programs at the national level as they relate to retraining, reemployment, vocational education and vocational rehabilitation," from a speech by Groves Erskine, 5 December 1945, p. 6. HST Library, Papers of Groves B. Erskine, Box 1, Folder: Whole Blood Broadcast NBC.

23. HST Library, Papers of Leon H. Keyserling, Box 7, Folder: Manpower—Memoranda and Reports, re. 1947–1951. Memo from Davis to Keyserling, 3 March 1947, pp. 2–3.

24. Writing in 1947, Nourse outlined a very modest role for the Council of Economic Advisers (CEA), distant from the activist Keynesianism associated with a social democratic full-employment model. The CEA was deemed responsible

for synthesizing a "large and complicated body of data and interpretation so that
it focuses effectively upon the issues which are at a given time most significant
for future welfare . . . Under this interpretation . . . our agency should always
remain a small assembly plant, using subassemblies, parts and materials drawn
from all corners of the field" (E. G. Nourse, "The *Employment Act of 1946* and
a System of National Bookkeeping," *American Economic Review* 37:23). See also
N. P. Bowles, "'Playing the Old Record': The Presidency and the Politics of Fiscal
Disorder," in R. Maidment and J. Thurber, eds., *The Politics of Relative Decline*
(Oxford: Polity Press, forthcoming).

25. For an account, see Ira Katznelson and Bruce Pietrykowski, "Rebuilding
the American State: Evidence from the 1940s," *Studies in American Political
Development* (1991) 5: 301–39.

26. They included William Haber, John Dunlop, Clark Kerr, and particularly
Eli Ginzberg. See also Weir, *Politics and Jobs.*

27. See G. Mucciaroni, *The Political Failure of Employment Policy, 1945–1990*
(Pittsburgh, PA: University of Pittsburgh Press, 1990), pp. 264–65.

28. See *Report of the Special Committee on Unemployment Problems,* U.S.
Congress Senate Report no. 1206, 86th Cong., 2d sess., March 1960. Bills to
expand training programs introduced after the report failed to be enacted.

29. "Report of Consultants on Future Policy and Program of the Federal-State
Employment Service," by Dale Yoder, Charles A. Myers, Carroll L. Shartle, and
Leonard P. Adams, 14 December 1959, p. 2, in Subject Files of James Mitchell,
Box 290, Folder: ES-2 Public Employment Service 1959, NARA RG 174.

30. Ibid., p. 3.

31. Department of Employment, *People and Jobs: A Modern Employment
Service* (London: HMSO, 1971), p. 4.

32. Ibid., p. 6.

33. Ibid., p. 8.

34. Ibid., p. 9.

35. Department of Employment, *Into Action: Plan for a Modern Employment
Service* (London: HMSO, December 1972).

36. Department of Employment, *Action Plan* (London: HMSO 1972), p. 6.

37. "How Well Are the Jobcentres Working?" *Department of Employment
Gazette,* July 1978, p. 791.

38. Ibid., pp. 791–92.

39. Department of Employment, *People and Jobs: A Modern Employment
Service* (London: HMSO, December 1971), p. 12.

40. The report owed much to the *Future of the Employment Service Consultative
Document* published by the Department of Employment and Productivity in May
1970 and discussed at length in chapter 3.

41. Department of Employment, *People and Jobs: A Modern Employment
Service* (London: HMSO, 1971), p. 12.

42. Ibid.

43. Ibid., p. 10.

44. Ibid., p. 12.

45. Ibid.

46. For details, see Desmond King, "Training Policy and the Conservatives,

1979–1992: From a Tripartite to a Neoliberal Regime," *Political Studies* 41 (1993): 214–35; Patrick Ainley and Mark Corney, *Training for the Future* (London: Cassell, 1990); and Kenton Worcester, chap. 2 of "From Tripartitism to the Enterprise Culture," Ph.D. diss., Columbia University, Department of Political Science, 1990.

47. Manpower Services Commission/Employment Services Agency, *The Employment Service: Plans and Programs* (London: ESA, October 1974).

48. Ibid., p. 1.

49. Ibid.

50. "How Well Are the Jobcentres Working?" *Department of Employment Gazette,* July 1978, p. 791.

51. See Manpower Services Commission/Employment Services Agency, *The Employment Service: Plans and Programs* (London: MSC, October 1974), which defined its central aim as assisting people to choose and to train for appropriate jobs and for employers to acquire suitable applicants speedily. See also Department of Employment, *People and Jobs: a Modern Employment Service* and *Into Action: Plan for a Modern Employment Service.*

52. "How Well Are the Jobcentres Working?" *Department of Employment Gazette,* July 1978, p. 793, and see also Manpower Services Commission, *Jobcentres—An Evaluation* (London: MSC Employment Service Division, May 1978).

53. "How Well Are the Jobcentres Working?" *Department of Employment Gazette,* July 1978, p. 793.

54. Dan Finn and Steve Preston, "A Better Employment Service," *Unemployment Bulletin* 30 (Summer 1989): 8.

55. Ibid., pp. 8–9.

56. LBJ Library, Administrative History, Department of Labor, Box 1, vol. II—Programs of the Department of Labor: Chap. I, "Manpower Development Assistance," p. 172.

57. General letter from the AFL-CIO dated 21 November 1947, p. 2, in Papers of Lewis B. Schellenbach, Box 31, Folder: Employment Service—General, NARA RG 174.

58. Between 1960 and 1967, the Unemployment Trust Funds were completely divorced from the annual budgetary agreements, resulting in considerable incomes for the state employment agencies. See Thomas Janoski, *The Political Economy of Unemployment* (Berkeley: University of California Press, 1990), p. 97.

59. House Report No. 228, 81st Cong., 1st sess., 8 March 1949; see also Senate Report No. 265, 81st Cong., 1st sess., 14 April 1949, Conference Report No. 892, 81st Cong., 1st sess., 23 June 1949, House Report No. 228, 84th Cong., 1st sess., 18 March 1955, Senate Report No. 410, 84th Cong., 1st sess., 2 June 1955, House Report No. 1845, 84th Cong., 2d sess., 2 March 1956, and Senate Report No. 2093, 84th Cong., 2d sess., 1 June 1956. The issue of ICESA appropriations is discussed in a memorandum to Secretary Wirtz dated 5 July 1963, in M. Cass Papers, Box 54, Folder: 1963—ICESA, NARA RG 174.

60. For accounts, see Mucciaroni, *The Political Failure of Employment Policy, 1945–82,* pp. 136–37; Weir, *Politics and Jobs,* pp. 80–83; and Weir, "The Federal Government and Unemployment: The Frustration of Policy Innovation from the

New Deal to the Great Society," in M. Weir et al., eds., *The Politics of Social Policy in the United States.*

61. Califano succeeded Bill Moyers as chief presidential adviser on domestic affairs to President Johnson. He was appointed secretary of Health, Education and Welfare by Carter in 1979. Schultze served as director of the Bureau of the Budget under Johnson and chairman of the CEA under Carter. Both were committed to broadening federal work-welfare programs.

62. LBJ Library, WHCF Confidential File, Box 30, Folder: 160-6 U.S. Employment Service, memo to Charles Schultze, 17 August 1967, pp. 1, 2. The memo also endorsed the 1965 Employment Service Task Force. In 1986, the U.S. General Accounting Office recommended that ES refer more clients to private employment agencies: see *Employment Service: More Jobseekers Should Be Referred to Private Employment Agencies* (Washington, DC: General Accounting Office, March 1986).

63. See E. S. Redford and M. Blissett, *Organizing the Executive Branch: The Johnson Presidency* (Chicago: University of Chicago Press, 1981), and J. Grossman, *The Department of Labor* (New York: Praeger, 1973).

64. Summary of Recommendations of the Employment Service Task Force, in M. Cass Papers, Box 201, Folder: Employment Service Task Force, NARA RG 174.

65. *A Report to the Secretary of Labor from the Employment Service Task Force,* U.S. Employment Service Task Force, 1965, p. 10. This task force was chaired by George Schultz, dean of the Graduate Business School at the University of Chicago.

66. In 1947, the USES had decided against issuing a nondiscrimination statement because "such a policy is already a matter of government-wide policy expressed in executive orders." See memorandum to Secretary Schellenbach from R. M. Barnett, USES, 13 February 1947, in Papers of Lewis B. Schellenbach, Box 31, Folder: Employment Service—General, NARA RG 174.

67. Memorandum from Goodwin to Secretary of Labor Lewis Schellenbach, 20 September 1948, p. 1 [my emphasis], in Papers of Lewis B. Schellenbach, Box 31, Folder: Employment Service—General, NARA RG 174.

68. Confidential draft memo prepared for Mitchell by John W. Leslie, "Draft of a Position on Civil Rights," 5 June 1959, p. 3. DDE Library, Papers of James P. Mitchell, Box 68, Folder: 1959 DOL Misc.

69. DDE Library, Whitman File: Cabinet Series, Box 15, Cabinet Meeting, 18 December 1959, p. 4.

70. NAACP Papers, Box A-146, Folder: Government—National: DOL, 1960–65. Memo from Bureau of Employment Security to All State Employment Security Agencies, 12 March 1964: "Implementation of Policy and Procedure With Respect to Serving Minority Groups."

71. LBJ Library, memo for the President from Willard Wirtz, 20 January 1964, WHCF FG Box 237, Folder 160-6 U.S. Employment Service, p. 1.

72. Ibid., p. 2.

73. Under Secretary of Labor's Order No. 9-68, 22 May 1968.

74. LBJ Library, Box 1, Administrative History Department of Labor, Folder: Vol. II, Chap. 1, Manpower Development Assistance, pp. 339, 340.

75. For a useful discussion, see U.S. Congress Office of Technology Assessment, *Worker Training: Competing in the New International Economy* (Washington, DC: Government Printing Office, September 1990).

76. In 1967, the percentage of blacks in the employment service offices by type of job was: Employment-Security Agencies: 9.4 percent; managerial-supervisory: 3.5 percent; professional-technical: 7.3 percent; clerical-office: 12.1 percent; and custodial-service: 56.0. In the LBJ Library, Box 1, Administrative History Department of Labor, Folder: Vol., II, Chap. 1, Manpower Development Assistance, p. 343.

77. One strategy to address discrimination and segregation in ES offices was known as the "Philadelphia Plan," formulated during the Johnson years by Secretary Wirtz, but it was activated only after 1969 by the new Secretary George Shultz. The plan centered upon a set of proposals to eradicate discrimination in the building industry and to impose requirements to hire certain numbers of minorities on federally funded building projects.

For AFL-CIO hostility to this plan, see material in George Meany Memorial Archives, Legislative Reference Files, Box 6, Folder 2.

78. National Urban Coalition and the Lawyers' Committee for Civil Rights Under Law, *Falling Down on the Job* (Washington, DC: National Urban Coalition and the Lawyers' Committee for Civil Rights Under Law, June 1971), p. 64.

79. Ibid.

80. Training policy receives hardly any mention in P. Hall's excellent analysis of Britain in *Governing the Economy.* For an outstanding overview, see D. Finegold, "The Low-Skill Equilibrium: An Institutional Analysis of Britain's Education and Training Failure," D.Phil. thesis, Oxford University, 1992, chap. 5.

81. Shonfield, *Modern Capitalism,* p. 117.

82. See, among others, John Sheldrake and Sarah Vickerstaff, *The History of Industrial Training in Britain* (Aldershot: Avebury, 1987); David Finegold and David Soskice, "The Failure of Training in Britain: Analysis and Prescription," *Oxford Review of Economic Policy* 4, no. 3 (1988): 21–51; and P. J. C. Perry, *The Evolution of British Manpower Policy* (London: Eyre and Spottiswoode, 1976).

83. Cmd.6527/1944, *White Paper on Employment Policy,* in *Parliamentary Papers, 1943–44,* vol. VIII.

84. On trades unions, see L. Ulman, "Collective Bargaining and Industrial Efficiency," in R. E. Caves et al., *Britain's Economic Prospects* (London: Allen and Unwin, 1968); and J. Zeitlin, "The Emergence of Shop Steward Organization and Job Control in the British Car Industry: A Review Essay," *History Workshop Journal* 10 (1980): 119–37. On the origin and persistence of the apprenticeship system, see B. Elbaum, "The Persistence of Apprenticeship in Britain and Its Decline in the United States," in H. Gospell, ed., *Industrial Training and Technological Innovation* (London: Routledge, 1991).

85. CRD2/7/27: Training for Industry (draft pamphlet) 1947, pp. 4, 6, 7. See also the Conservative party document in 1948, "Opportunity, Education and Training in Industry," p. 7, 1 October 1948, in CRD2/7/2: Govt. Education and Training in Industry, 1948, both in the Conservative Party Archives, Bodleian Library, Oxford.

86. See H.M. Inspectorate Department of Education & Science, *Aspects of Vocational Education and Training in the Federal Republic of Germany* (London: HMSO, 1991).

87. Christel Lane, *Management and Labor in Europe* (London: Edward Elgar, 1989), p. 71.

88. For discussions, see Sidney Pollard, *The Development of the British Economy, 1914–1980,* 3d ed. (London: Edward Arnold, 1983); Sidney Pollard, *The Wasting of the British Economy* (London: Croom Helm, 1982); and Shonfield, *Modern Capitalism.*

89. For a general statement, see Shonfield, *Modern Capitalism.*

90. For the influence of business upon the National Economic Development Council's (NEDC) establishment, see Blank, *Industry and Government in Britain: The Federation of British Industries, 1945–65,* chap. 6. Blank reports the deliberations of the FBI's Committee on Economic Programs and Targets whose report in 1961 called for a NEDC type organization.

91. National Economic Development Council, *Conditions Favourable to Faster Growth* (London: HMSO, 1963), p. 7.

92. See the Labour Party, *Labour and the Scientific Revolution* (London: Labour Party National Executive Council, 1963), and H. Wilson, *The New Britain* (Harmondsworth: Penguin Books, 1964).

93. Cmd. 1892/1962 White Paper, Ministry of Labour, "Industrial Training: Government Proposals," *Parliamentary Papers, 1962–63,* vol. 31, p. 3. The government's proposals were contained in the White Paper Cmnd. 1892/1962, "Industrial Training: Government Proposals" (London: HMSO, 1962); see also hearings for the Industrial Training Bill in 1963: *Hansard Parliamentary Debates,* House of Commons Official Report, Standing Committee A, 1963–64, vol. I, 3–12 December 1963. See also D. Finegold, "The Low-Skill Equilibrium," pp. 193–94.

94. In the summer of 1993, the Labour party returned to the principle of a levy on companies in their proposals for training: see *Labour's Economic Approach,* 1993 conference paper (London: Labour Party, 1993).

95. Union members of ITBs sat as representatives of their union and not of the TUC. However, TUC representatives were members of the Central Training Council established by the 1964 act.

96. This view was reported to the 1970 Review of the Central Training Council, chaired by Mr. Frank Cousins: see TUC, "Unions, TUC and Industrial Training" (London: TUC, 1970), p. 2.

97. See A. Sorge and M. Warner, "Manpower Training, Manufacturing Organization and Workplace Relations in Great Britain and West Germany," *British Journal of Industrial Relations* 18 (1980): 321.

98. *Manpower Services Commission Annual Report, 1974–75* (Sheffield: Manpower Services Commission), p. 8.

99. Ibid.

100. See John Corina, "Planning and the British Labour Market: Incomes and Industrial Training," in Jack Hayward and Michael Watson, eds., *Planning, Politics and Public Policy* (New York and Cambridge: Cambridge University Press, 1975), pp. 194–200, who stresses the autonomy achieved by the ITBs.

101. Sheldrake and Vickerstaff, *The History of Industrial Training in Britain,* p. 39.

102. For the act's parliamentary passage, see House of Commons, *Parliamentary Debates,* Official Report, 5th Series, 1972–73, vol. 852, cols. 1133–1242, and *Parliamentary Debates,* Official Report, 5th Series, 1972–73, vol. 857, cols. 495–626.

103. *Parliamentary Debates,* House of Commons Official Report, 5th Series, 1972–73, vol. 852, 13 March 1973, col. 1137.

104. For an account, see "The Manpower Services Commission: The First Five Years," n.a. 1979, ref. 1628, unpublished (Sheffield: MSC Library), p. 55. See also P. Ainley and M. Corney, *Training for the Future* (London: Cassell, 1990).

105. Department of Employment, "Training for the Future: A Plan for Discussion" (London: HMSO, 1972). For a summary of the government's proposals, see pp. 46–48.

106. The TUC had expressed dissatisfaction with the lack of executive powers of the Central Training Council, which was limited to an advisory role. See TUC, *Unions, the TUC and Industrial Training* (London: TUC, 1970), pp. 1–2. See also TUC, *Trade Unions and Training for the Future* (London: TUC, 1972), p. 11 as evidence of the TUC's long advocacy of a national training agency.

107. See Santosh Mukherjee, *Making Labor Markets Work* (London: P.E.P., 1972).

108. The Fulton Committee of Enquiry recommended the creation of small, distinctly defined units hived off from departments within the civil service, of which the MSC was a good example. See Fulton Report, Cmnd 3638, chap. 5, paras. 147 and 150. An OECD report was critical of British manpower policy and again influenced the MSC formation (see *Manpower Policy in the United Kingdom* [Paris: OECD, 1970]).

109. MSC, "Manpower Services Commission: The First Five Years," n.a. 1979 (Sheffield: MSC Library), p. 5.

110. This tripartite pattern was reproduced in Area Manpower Boards.

111. In the Commons, Chichester-Clark reported that the "make-up of the commission—three employers, three trade unions, two local authority representatives and one educational representative—was arrived at after full discussion and consultations, and it seemed to be almost the unanimous view that that was about the right balance." See *Parliamentary Debates,* House of Commons Official Report, 5th series, 1972–73, vol. 857, 23 May 1973, col. 502.

112. Sheldrake and Vickerstaff, *The History of Industrial Training in Britain,* p. 45.

113. For details, see *Manpower Services Commission Annual Report, 1974–75,* p. 17.

114. F. W. S. Craig, *British General Election Manifestoes, 1900–1974* (London: Macmillan, 1975), p. 457. For the Conservatives' 1974 manifesto, see pp. 435–44. In their 1970 manifesto, the Tories promised to "closely examine the work of the ITBs and the operations of the levy/grant system" (p. 332).

115. *Department of Employment Gazette,* April 1975, p. 328.

116. For details, see MSC, "The Manpower Services Commission: The First Five Years," p. 17.

117. Ibid., p. 10.

118. Finegold and Soskice, "The Failure of Training in Britain: Analysis and Prescription," p. 30.

119. MSC, *Training for Skills: A Program for Action* (London: MSC, 1977), p. 20.

120. Department of Employment, White Paper Cmnd.8455/1981, *A New Training Initiative: A Programme for Action* (London: HMSO, December 1981). On union opposition to abolishing the ITBs, see TUC Consultative Conference: Industrial Training, Discussion Paper, 13 March 1981 (London: TUC Library).

121. See, for example, T. Nichols, *The British Worker Question* (London: Routledge and Kegan Paul, 1986). In 1989, a study by the government reported that British employers still adopted a haphazard and short-term approach to training: training reflected short-term necessity and the majority of workers had received no vocational training while in employment. See *Training in Britain: A Study of Funding Activity and Attitudes* (London: HMSO, November 1989), a summary report and five research volumes. Training was skewed toward the already-skilled.

122. The CBI urged education and industry to "work more closely together to ensure a better match between those leaving the education system and the employment opportunities available" (*CBI National Conference Report,* 1979, p. 39). Similar issues were aired at their 1980 meeting: CBI, *National Conference Report,* 1980, pp. 38–47. See also "Joining the Club—National Approaches to Vocational Education and Training," *Department of Employment Gazette,* September 1984, pp. 422–23.

123. The MSC chairmen were as follows: 1974–76, Sir Denis Barnes; 1976–81, Sir Richard O'Brien; 1981–84, Lord Young; 1984–86, Bryan Nicolson; and 1986–88, Sir James Munn.

124. For the Department of Employment's understanding of ET, see "Coming Up to the Start—The Employment Training Program," *Department of Employment Gazette,* August 1988, pp. 444–47.

125. Arthur M. Goldberg, Secretary of Labor, 1961–62; appointed Supreme Court Justice August 1962 and replaced by W. William Wirtz, 1962–69, previously Under Secretary of Labor (1961–62).

126. Memorandum from Arthur Goldberg to the President, 16 February 1961, in the Papers of President Kennedy, President's Official Files, Box 81, File: Labor 1/61–3/61, John F. Kennedy Library (JFKL).

127. See Andrew Martin, *The Politics of Economic Policy in the United States* (London and Beverly Hills: Sage, 1973); Stein, *The Fiscal Revolution in America*; and Weir, "The Federal Government and Unemployment: The Frustration of Policy Innovation from the New Deal to the Great Society," in *The Politics of Social Policy in the United States.*

128. For education and training policy, such as vocational education and vocational rehabilitation programs, in other areas of the United States, see Janoski, *The Political Economy of Unemployment.*

129. Labor Day (29 August 1961) Statement by the President, Papers of President Kennedy, President's Official Files, Box 81, File: Labor 8/61–9/61. (JFKL).

130. "Report of Consultants on Future Policy and Program of the Federal-State Employment Service," by Dale Yoder, Charles A. Myers, Carroll L. Shartle, and Leonard P. Adams, 14 December 1959, in Subject Files of James Mitchell, Box 290, Folder: ES-2 Public Employment Service, 1959, NARA RG 174.

131. Addressing the Federal Advisory Council of the Bureau of Employment Security in 1963, Secretary Wirtz declared that manpower policy was the Department of Labor's principal problem. See the Minutes of Federal Advisory Council Meeting, 5 April 1963, in M. Cass Papers, Box 56, Folder 1963—Council—Federal Advisory Council on Employment Security (January–July) RG 174 NARA.

132. Memorandum from Goldberg to the President, 28 March 1961, p. 1, in Papers of President Kennedy, President's Official Files, Box 81, File: Labor 1/61–3/61. (JFKL).

133. Both groups were represented on the Federal Advisory Council of the Bureau of Employment Security where the development of manpower policy was regularly discussed in the early 1960s.

134. See Nicholas Lemann, *The Promised Land* (New York: Knopf, 1991).

135. Memorandum from Secretary of Labor W. Wirtz to Johnson, 23 December 1966, p. 2. NARA RG 174, Office of the Secretary. The survey was conducted in November 1966.

136. Ibid., p. 23.

137. LBJ Library Oral history of Stanley H. Ruttenberg, Economic Adviser to Secretary of Labor Wirtz, 1963–64, and Manpower Administrator from January 1965, p. 6.

138. For a readable account, see Leman, *The Promised Land*; see also J. T. Patterson, *America's Struggle Against Poverty, 1900–1980* (Cambridge, MA: Harvard University Press, 1981), chaps. 6–12.

139. The National Urban Coalition and the Lawyers' Committee for Civil Rights, *Falling Down on the Job*, p. 8.

140. Ibid., pp. 11–13.

141. Ibid., p. 20.

142. Ibid., p. 22, my emphasis. The most successful work-welfare programs of the 1980s—ET in Massachusetts—made placing participants in permanent jobs paying above the minimum wage a standard practice.

143. More generally, computerization of job openings from the early 1970s gave a better service to job seekers who did not require special assistance, though the number of placements did not rise significantly. See Stanley H. Ruttenberg and Jocelyn Gutchess, *The Federal-State Employment Service: A Critique* (Baltimore, MD: Johns Hopkins University Press, 1970), pp. 62–65.

144. See chapter 5 for a full discussion. For the latter view, see Lawrence Mead, *The New Politics of Poverty* (New York: Basic Books, 1992).

145. LBJ Library, Box 1, Administrative History, Department of Labor, Vol. II: Programs of the Development of Labor; Chap. 1: Manpower Development Assistance, p. 102.

146. Formulated by Southern and conservative Democrat Russell Long, senator from Louisiana and chairman of the Finance Committee. See Desmond King, "Sectionalism and Welfare Policy in the United States: The Failure of President Carter's Initiative, mimeo., Oxford, 1993.

147. LBJ Library, Box 1, Administrative History, Department of Labor, Vol. II: Programs of the Development of Labor; Chap. 1: Manpower Development Assistance, p. 105.

148. Ibid., p. 108.

149. *A Report to the Secretary of Labor from the Employment Service Task Force,* U.S. Employment Service Task Force, 1965, p. 4.

150. Memorandum from Robert Goodwin to Secretary of Labor Wirtz on the annual meeting of the ICESA 1963, 18 October 1963, in M. Cass Papers, Box 54, Folder: 1963-Conference-ISCEA, NARA RG 174.

151. *A Report to the Secretary of Labor from the Employment Service Task Force,* U.S. Employment Service Task Force, 1965, p. 6.

152. Letter to Larry Runder Personnel Consultants, Florida, from Director of Bureau of Employment Security Robert Goodwin, 16 November 1964, in response to a letter directed to President Johnson. LBJ Library, WHCF FG Box 237, Folder: FG 160-6. Many other such letters are included in the presidential files: see, in particular, that from Tyson Lee of Lee's Associates, 5 August 1964, who maintained that "every day in every way we see signs of the USES trying to expand—expand in the wrong direction."

153. Letter to Lee's Associates from Ralph Dungan, Special Assistant to the President, 31 July 1964, pp. 2, 1, LBJ Library, WHCF FG Box 237, Folder: FG 160-6. In his original letter to LBJ, Tyson Lee maintained that the "USES was formed to help the unemployed get a job, but in recent years, in their eagerness to expand, they are now in the placing of white collar workers and executives who are now working" (*sic*), a revealing statement of public perception of the ES. Letter from Lee's Associates to LBJ, 7 July, p. 1, LBJ Library, WHCF FG Box 237, Folder: FG 160-6.

154. *A Report to the Secretary of Labor from the Employment Service Task Force,* U.S. Employment Service Task Force, 1965, p. 23.

155. Ibid., p. 39.

156. The act's focus upon category A unemployment (the temporarily unemployed, normally employed group) is suggested by the preamble: "It is . . . the purpose of this Act to require the Federal government to appraise the manpower requirements and resources of the Nation, and to develop and apply the information and methods needed to deal with the problems of unemployment resulting from automation and technological changes and other types of persistent unemployment" (*Manpower Development and Training Act,* 1962, section 101).

157. This impression is also conveyed by the minutes of the Federal Advisory Council—see, for example, minutes of meeting on 30 July 1963, in M. Cass Papers, Box 56, Folder: 1963 Federal Advisory Council on Employment Security, NARA RG 174.

158. The Department of Labor established an Advisory Committee on Employment Service Research in October 1966 charged with improving the USES's labor-market information base as a corollary to the new roles implied by the task force. It gave itself a year to produce suggestions for this improvement, none of which were dramatic. See "Advisory Committee on Employment Service Research," U.S. Department of Labor, 19 October 1966, p. 8, in M. Cass Papers, Box 201, Folder: Employment Service Task Force, NARA RG 174.

159. Early in his presidency, Kennedy emphasized the importance of the USES and provided it with additional resources.

160. LBJ Library, Box 1, Administrative History, Department of Labor, Vol. II: Programs of the Development of Labor; Chap. 1: Manpower Development Assistance, p. 174.

161. Louis Levine, "An Employment Service Equal to the Times," *Employment Security Review* (June 1963): 11–12.

162. LBJ Library, Box 1, Administrative History, Department of Labor, Vol. II: Programs of the Development of Labor; Chap. 1: Manpower Development Assistance, p. 117.

163. Garth Mangum and John Walsh, *A Decade of Manpower Development and Training* (Salt Lake City, UT: Olympus, 1973), and David Brian Robertson, "Politics and Labor Markets," Ph.D. diss., Indiana University, 1981.

164. LBJ Library, Box 1, Administrative History, Department of Labor, Vol. II: Programs of the Development of Labor; Chap. 1: Manpower Development Assistance, p. 175.

165. Ibid., p. 176.

166. Manpower programs existed before 1964, as the following list indicates: (1) *Wagner-Peyser Act of 1933,* as amended; (2) Titles III, IX, XII and XV of the *Social Security Act of 1935,* as amended; (3) *Federal Unemployment Tax Act*; (4) *Servicemen's Readjustment Act of 1944*; (5) EO 10366, 26 June 1952; (6) *Farm Labor Contractor Registration Act of 1963*; (7) *Immigration and Nationality Act,* as amended; (8) Titles I, II, and III of MDTA 1962, as amended; (9) *Trade Expansion Act of 1962*; (10) EO 11075, 18 January 1963, as amended; (11) *Public Works and Economic Development Act of 1964*; (12) *Public Works Acceleration Act of 1962*; (13) *Automation Products Trade Act of 1965*; (14) *National Apprenticeship Act of 1937*; (15) *D.C. Apprenticeship Act*; (16) *Appalachian Regional Development Act of 1965*; (17) *Economic Opportunity Act of 1964*; (18) *C.R. Act of 1964*; (19) E.O. 11141; (20) E.O. 11000; (21) Vocational Rehabilitation Amendments of 1954; (22) Defence Manpower Policy No. 4; (23) *Vocational Education Act of 1963*; (24) E.O. 10582; (25) E.O. 10651; (26) E.O. 11122; and (27) E.O. 11152, establishing the President's Committee on Manpower.

167. On 18 April 1963, the Department of Labor established the Coordinating Committee on Manpower Research (CCMR) as an extension of the Manpower Administration under MDTA. The CCMR was given responsibility to coordinate administration manpower policies and was composed of representatives from each bureau within the department whose activities impinged upon labor policy. The committee's principal task has been preparation of the annual *Manpower Report of the President.*

168. Memorandum prepared for Lovell's meeting with the Secretary of Labor, 22 December 1970, p. 2, in Papers of Malcolm Lovell, Jr., Folder: Secretary of Labor, Historian's Office, Department of Labor Library, Washington, DC.

169. Created under the Fizgerald (National Apprenticeship) act of 1937, which set standards for federal regulation but not administration of apprenticeships.

170. Library of Congress, NAACP III-A, Box A180, Folder: Labor, Apprenticeship Training. NAACP, *Negro Wage Earners and Apprenticeship* (Washington, DC: NAACP, 1960), pp. 80, 4.

171. Ibid., p. 15.

172. Ibid., p. 20.

173. However, by October 1970, 34 percent of applicants were from minorities, but only 22 percent were accepted as apprentices, statistics which, in Assistant Secretary Lovell's words, "don't strike me as overly impressive." See memorandum from Lovell dated 28 September 1970, in Papers of Malcolm Lovell, Jr., Folder: Apprenticeship Information Centers, Historian's Office, Department of Labor Library, Washington, DC.

174. National Urban Coalition and the Lawyers' Committee for Civil Rights Under the Law, *Falling Down on the Job,* p. 74.

175. For details and evaluations, see Papers of Malcolm Lovell, Jr., Folder: Apprenticeship Outreach Programs, and Folder: Apprenticeship Information Centers, Historian's Office, Department of Labor Library, Washington, DC.

176. National Urban Coalition and the Lawyers' Committee for Civil Rights Under the Law, *Falling Down on the Job,* p. 76.

177. Memorandum by Millard Cass, 12 May 1967, of Advisory Committee's first seventeen meetings, pp. 1–5, in M. Cass Papers, Box 200, Folder: Advisory Committee on Equal Opportunity in Apprenticeships and Training (Minutes and Agenda) RG 173 NARA. The committee was ended in 1971.

178. National Urban Coalition and the Lawyers' Committee for Civil Rights Under the Law, *Falling Down on the Job,* p. 77.

179. See David Robertson, "Politics and Labor Markets," pp. 241–43.

180. See the National Urban Coalition and the Lawyers' Committee for Civil Rights Under the Law, *Falling Down on the Job,* p. 26.

181. Family Assistance Plan Hearings, Senate Finance Committee, U. S. Congress, 91st Cong., 1st sess., 4 August 1970, pp. 763–64.

182. The idea of structural unemployment—joblessness caused by technological development—was especially influential during this decade.

183. To the extent British trades unions remain a significant presence, it is in the public sector.

184. See the National Urban Coalition and the Lawyers' Committee for Civil Rights Under the Law, *Falling Down on the Job,* p. 35.

185. LBJ Library Oral history of Stanley Ruttenberg, 1969, p. 8.

186. See the extensive correspondence between Lovell and Carey in Malcolm Lovell, Jr., Papers, Folder: Employment Service Report by Lawyers' Committee, Historian's Office, Department of Labor Library, Washington, DC.

187. The report received wide coverage in the quality press: see the *New York Times, Washington Post* and *Wall Street Journal,* 22 April 1971.

188. Press release, U.S. Department of Labor, 21 April 1971, p. 1. In Malcolm Lovell, Jr., Papers, Historian's Office, Department of Labor Library, Washington, DC.

189. "Should a Blue Ribbon Task Force Be Established to Review the Employment Service?" 15 June 1971, Papers of Malcolm Lovell, Jr., Folder: Employment Service Task Force, Historian's Office, Department of Labor Library, Washington, DC.

190. For details, see letter from William Heartwell, President of ICESA, to

Lovell, dated 11 June 1971, in Papers of Malcolm Lovell, Jr., Folder: Employment Service Report by Lawyers' Committee, Historian's Office, Department of Labor Library, Washington, DC.

191. "Falling Down on the Job: The USES and the Disadvantaged Report," n.d., p. 1, in Papers of Malcolm Lovell, Jr., Folder: Employment Service Report by Lawyers' Committee, Historian's Office, Department of Labor Library, Washington, DC.

192. See letter from Carey to Lovell, dated 2 February, and Lovell's reply of 17 February 1972, in Papers of Malcolm Lovell, Jr., Folder: Employment Service Report by Lawyers' Committee, Historian's Office, Department of Labor Library, Washington, DC.

193. Quoted in the National Urban Coalition and the Lawyers' Committee for Civil Rights Under the Law, *Falling Down on the Job,* p. 42.

194. See also Weir, *Politics and Jobs.*

195. Comptroller General of the United States, *The Employment Service— Problems and Opportunities for Improvement,* Report to the Congress (Washington, DC: U.S. General Accounting Office, 1977), p. 7.

196. Ibid., p. 14.

197. Ibid., p. 27.

198. Ibid., p. 30.

199. Ibid., Appendix 1, p. 47.

200. See the National Urban Coalition and the Lawyers' Committee for Civil Rights Under the Law, *Falling Down on the Job,* p. 90.

201. See U.S. Congress, Senate, Joint Hearings before the Subcommittee on Employment and Manpower, *Manpower Services Act of 1966* and *Employment Service Act of 1966,* 89th Cong., 2d sess., 1966. The administration's substitute (though weaker) version of the legislation also failed.

202. For one account of this unraveling, see Thomas Edsall and Mary Edsall, *Chain Reaction* (New York: Norton, 1992).

203. Report of the National Employers' Committee for Improvement of the State Employment Service, July 1972, in Papers of Malcolm Lovell, Jr., Folder: Employment Service, Historian's Office, Department of Labor Library, Washington, DC.

204. Other programs included the New Jobs Tax Credit of 1977 and its successor, the Target Jobs Tax Credit in 1979.

205. "Creaming off" the best applicants was a general problem for federal manpower programs: see memorandum to Lovell and paper, "Discussion Paper on the Potential of Creaming in Manpower Programs," 15 August 1972, p. 9, which identified the problem as arising from funding pressures—success in placing trainees was a condition for future funding which encouraged the enrollment of more advantaged applicants. In Papers of Malcolm Lovell, Jr., Historian's Office, Department of Labor Library, Washington, DC.

206. National Urban Coalition and the Lawyers' Committee for Civil Rights Under the Law, *Falling Down on the Job,* pp. 59–60.

207. Ibid., p. 97.

208. Public Law 97–300.

209. See Malcolm S. Cohen and David W. Stevens, *The Role of the Employment Service* (Ann Arbor: Institute of Labor and Industrial Relations, University of Michigan 1989).

210. See *Federal Register* 48, no. 213 (2 November 1983): 60662–68.

211. See *Building a Job Service for the Year 2000: Innovative State Practices,* A Special Report of the Interstate Conference of Employment Security Agencies (Washington, DC: Bendick and Egan Economic Consultants, January 1989), prepared by Marc Bendick for the Employment Training Administration, Department of Labor.

212. See Elizabeth Dole, "A Public Employment Service for the 1990s," *Perspective* 6 (1990): 3–6.

213. USES, *Briefing Paper on the Public Employment Service* (Washington, DC: USES, 21 September 1990), p. 16.

214. Such committees exist in each state funded by the ES to work with the local ES.

215. The Conservatives recognized that they lacked support among skilled trade union members, the main beneficiaries of formal training schemes: see Conservative Party Archives, CRD2/7/6: Trade Unions and Employment Papers, 1950–59, Report of a Subcommittee of the Parliamentary Labour Committee, 20 July 1950, Strictly Confidential, see especially p. 1.

However, the Tories were aware of the need for improvements in national training. A pamphlet on this topic prepared in 1947 provided a good analysis of Britain's training needs:

> Organised training enables a person to gain a specific mental or manipulative skill as quickly and as easily as possible by teaching step by step the right way of doing a particular job. In the absence of systematic training schemes, employees are forced by circumstances to train themselves, because they must learn somehow to do new jobs. Neglect to give proper instruction however may result in the formation of wrong and wasteful habits of work. This is a widespread result. Without going into further detail . . . it is considered obvious that the best use cannot be made of available manpower . . . without a carefully coordinated training organization, with reports at every stage.
>
> At the present time there is a strong demand for training of all kinds, and a considerable multiplication of training facilities for industry and other occupations has recently occurred. Three main reasons for this are suggested:
>
> (a) War-time dislocation of normal procedure of entry into occupations.
>
> (b) War-time manpower shortages which in many cases gave birth to schemes for improving efficiency. These schemes are now being further developed under the pressure of continued manpower shortage.
>
> (c) The search for security. On the one hand, this is seen in the desire of the individual to increase his market value by equipping himself with a particular skill. On the other, it is seen in the vested interest of members of a trade or profession desiring to narrow the road to entry and to raise their own status.

CRD2/7/27: Training for Industry (draft pamphlet), 1947, "Training for Industry," pp. 10, 1, 2. See also CRD2/7/26: Manpower, 1946–50. Conservative Parliamentary Secretariat, 12 March 1948, Secretariat Brief on "Manpower," p. 5. Both in Conservative Party Archives, Bodleian Library, Oxford.

216. See memorandum, "Building Labor Training Schemes," Conservative Research Department, 9 May 1950, CRD2/7/6, Conservative Party Archives, Bodleian Library, Oxford.

217. See L. Minkin, *The Contentious Alliance: Trade Unions and the Labour Party* (Edinburgh: Edinburgh University Press, 1991).

218. See also the *Area Redevelopment Act of 1961,* which funded public works schemes in depressed areas and a limited amount of occupational training. There were vocational education measures in the 1940s and 1950s, but these were not conceived of in terms of a federal active manpower policy as was the MDTA.

219. Persons falling within the third category of unemployed, as identified in chapter 1.

220. Weir, *Politics and Jobs,* pp. 63, 64. G. Mucciaroni reaches a similar conclusion: "The employment component of the poverty program consisted of a grab bag of small, underfunded programs to provide a variety of services, including training and work experience for poor youth . . . [I]nstead of a comprehensive and positive labor market policy, the 1960s saw the creation of remedial training programs for the disadvantaged, programs that were puny in relation to the problem they were intended to address" (*The Political Failure of Employment Policy, 1945–1982,* p. 47).

221. I do not address the proposals which failed to be enacted, of which the most important was the Family Assistance Plan formulated by the Nixon administration in 1969 based on a negative income tax mechanism. See Daniel Patrick Moynihan, *The Politics of a Guaranteed Income: The Nixon Administration and the Family Assistance Plan* (New York: Random House, 1973).

222. Weir, *Politics and Jobs,* p. 53.

223. Mucciaroni, *The Political Failure of Employment Policy, 1945–1982,* p. 43.

224. Ibid., p. 19.

225. Janoski, *The Political Economy of Unemployment,* pp. 260–61.

226. President Clinton's Secretary of Labor Robert Reich has unveiled a "Draft Proposal for a Comprehensive Worker Adjustment Program," which proposes merging existing programs for displaced workers and widening eligibility. It is costed at $1.1 billion and aimed at placing laid-off workers back in permanent employment. Clinton has also proposed a *School-to-Work Opportunities Act,* which provides for modern-state vocational and apprenticeship schemes implemented at the state level with business and labor cooperation. Both initiatives depend on Congress for enactment.

227. This feature has increased under the training component of modern work-welfare programs.

Chapter Five

1. *Hansard Parliamentary Debates,* House of Commons Official Report (26 January 1989), col. 134. My emphasis.

2. See G. Mucciaroni, *The Political Failure of Employment Policy, 1945–1988*

(Pittsburgh, PA: University of Pittsburgh Press, 1990), chap. 8, and K. L. Schlozman and S. Verba, *Injury to Insult: Unemployment, Class and Political Responses* (Cambridge, MA: Harvard University Press, 1979).

3. Contrast MSC, *A New Training Initiative—A Consultative Document* (London: MSC, May 1981), with Department of Employment White Paper, *A New Training Initiative: A Program for Action,* Cmnd. 8455/1981 (London: HMSO, December 1981). For Norman Tebbit's acceptance of the MSC's proposals, see *Hansard Parliamentary Debates,* House of Commons, 1982, vol. 26, ser. 6, cols. 22 et seq.

4. See G. Garrett, "The Politics of Structural Change: Swedish Social Democracy and Thatcherism in Comparative Perspective," *Comparative Political Studies* 25 (1993): 521–47, and J. T. S. Keeler, "Opening the Window for Reform: Mandates, Crises and Extraordinary Policy-Making," *Comparative Political Studies* 25 (1993): 433–86.

5. On the international influence of New Right ideas, see H. Glennerster and J. Midgley, eds., *The Radical Right and the Welfare State* (Hemel Hempstead Hertfordshire: Harvester Wheatsheaf, 1991). For Britain and the United States, see D. S. King, *The New Right* (London: Macmillan, 1987), and K. Hoover and R. Plant, *Conservative Capitalism* (London and New York: Routledge, 1989). See also D. S. King, "The Establishment of Work-welfare Programs in Britain and the USA: Ideas, Institutions and Politics," in S. Steinmo, K. Thelen, and F. Longstreth, eds., *Structuring Politics* (New York and Cambridge: Cambridge University Press, 1992).

6. H. Parker, *The Moral Hazards of Social Benefits* (London: Institute of Economic Affairs, 1982); A. Seldon, *Whither the Welfare State* (London: Institute of Economic Affairs, 1981); Digby Anderson, ed., *The Ignorance of Social Intervention* (London: Croom Helm, 1980); D. Anderson, J. Lait, and D. Marsland, *Breaking the Spell of the Welfare State* (Leeds: Social Affairs Unit, 1981); and R. Segalman and D. Marsland, *Cradle to Grave* (London: Macmillan Press in association with the Social Affairs Unit, 1989).

7. Cmd.6527/1944, *White Paper on Employment Policy,* in *Parliamentary Papers, 1943–44,* vol. VIII, p. 14.

8. F. H. Longstreth, "From Corporatism to Dualism? Thatcherism and the Climacteric of British Trade Unions in the 1980s," *Political Studies* 36 (1988): 413–32.

9. Further changes are suggested by the government's need to limit spending pushed up by falling revenues and increasing unemployment benefits. One proposal aired recently is to reduce UB from twelve to six months.

10. However, the flat-rate unemployment benefit has fallen by two-thirds in real terms since 1979, and it requires claimants to have paid in two years' National Insurance.

11. In 1982, the government abolished the earnings-related supplement.

12. For analyses, see N. Wikeley, "Unemployment Benefit, the State and the Labor Market," *Journal of Law and Society* 16 (1989): 291–309; S. Deakin and F. Wilkinson, "Labor Law, Social Security and Economic Inequality," *Cambridge Journal of Economics* 15 (1991): 125–48; and A. B. Atkinson, "Income Maintenance for the Unemployed in Britain and the Response to High Unemployment," *Ethics* 100 (April 1990): 569–85.

13. In addition, family income supplement was replaced by family credit as a benefit to help low-income working people with children.

14. The 1988 White Paper observed that "it is an obligation on all Governments to take whatever steps are necessary to make sure that the social security system is not abused" (Cm 316/1988 Training for Employment, White Paper [London: HMSO, 1988], p. 33).

15. See Department of Employment Group, "Your Guide to Our Employment Training and Enerprise Programmes," PL856 (9/88) (London: HMSO, 1988), p. 7. See also "Restart: Where You Stand," Unemployment Unit (London: Unemployment Unit, July 1989); "Actively Seeking Work," Unemployment Bulletin (Autumn 1989).

16. "A Compulsory Offer," Unemployment Unit, Working Brief (July 1990), and "No Option Course," Working Brief (January 1991).

17. See Unemployment Unit, Working Brief (May 1989) and (July/August 1989) for discussions.

18. Hansard Parliamentary Debates, House of Commons Official Report, Standing Committee E (1 December 1987), col. 313. See also Desmond S. King and Hugh Ward, "Working for Benefits: Rational Choice and the Rise of Work-Welfare Programmes," Political Studies 40 (1992): 479–95.

19. See the discussion in Dan Finn, "Employment Service," Unemployment Bulletin (Summer 1988): 9.

20. Unemployment Unit, Working Brief (August/September 1991): 5.

21. For an inventory of unsuccessful welfare reform proposals before the 1988 law, see Vee Burke and Carmen D. Solomon, Welfare Reform: Brief Summaries of Selected Major Proposals (Washington, DC: Congressional Research Service 88-223 EPW, 17 March 1988).

22. For an analysis which stresses the incremental, undramatic nature of the FSA, see T. R. Marmor, J. L. Mashaw, and P. Harvey, America's Misunderstood Welfare State (New York: Basic Books, 1990).

23. For details, see Ron Haskins, "Congress Writes a Law: Research and Welfare Reform," and Erica Baum, "When the Witch Doctors Agree: The Family Support Act and Social Science Research," Journal of Policy Analysis and Management 10, no. 4 (1991): 613–30.

24. In California, the state work-welfare program—GAIN—was already implemented before the FSA quickly confronted the problem of educational needs, with administrators discovering illiteracy among 60 percent of participants.

25. Family Support Act of 1988, Public Law 100-485, Title II, section 482.

26. Hansard Parliamentary Debates, House of Lords Official Report (25 January 1989), vol. 492, col. 438.

27. Hansard Parliamentary Debates, House of Commons Official Report (31 January 1989), col. 164.

28. National Governors' Association, Job-Oriented Welfare Reform (Washington, DC: NGA, February 1987), pp. 1–2, my emphasis.

29. For the best discussions of this widely used term, see C. Jencks and P. Peterson, eds., The Urban Underclass (Washington, DC: Brookings, 1991); W. J. Wilson, The Truly Disadvantaged (Chicago: University of Chicago Press, 1987); Isabel Sawhill, "Poverty and the Underclass," in I. Sawhill, ed., Challenge to Leadership (Washington, DC: Urban Institute, 1988); and M. Katz, ed., The

Underclass Debate (Princeton, NJ: Princeton University Press, 1993).

The concept of underclass has been used in Britain also, though less successfully. See Charles Murray et al., *The Emerging British Underclass* (London: Institute of Economic Affairs, May 1990).

30. This view was developed in state demonstration work-welfare enacted after 1981 OBRA.

31. See U.S. General Accounting Office, *Welfare Simplification: Thirty-Two States' Views on Coordinating Services for Low-Income Families* (Washington, DC: General Accounting Office, October 1986); and Demetra Nightingale and Lynn Burbridge, *The Status of Work-Welfare Programs in 1986* (Washington, DC: The Urban Institute, 1987).

32. See, for example, *Jobs for Connecticut Future: Executive Report* (Hartford, CT: Connecticut Department of Income Maintenance, January 1986), which emphasized mismatches in the labor market: "The expansion of the Connecticut workforce lags behind the growth in the numbers of jobs, and workers are not appropriately skilled for the challenge of the future knowledge-based and service-oriented economy" (p. 5).

33. See, for example, Final Report of the Work Opportunities Committee, *Women, Work and Welfare* (Maine: Maine Department of Human Services, September 1981), a national report funded in part by the National Governors' Association coordinated through Maine, and *Opportunities for Self-Sufficiency for Women in Poverty,* 25th Report by the Committee on Government Operations (Washington, DC: U.S. Government Printing Office, 31 December 1985). For a state-specific analysis, see Report of the Governor's Task Force on Self-Sufficiency, *"New Directions": The Colorado Action Plan* (Denver, CO: Colorado Department of Social Services, October 1988), and on Washington, DC, Women's Employment and Training Coalition, *An Urgent Agenda: Women, Employment and Training in the District of Columbia* (Washington, DC: Women's Employment and Training Coalition, 1986).

34. The Governor's Welfare Reform Commission, *Welfare in Alabama and the Need for Change* (Montgomery, AL: Alabama Department of Human Resources, September 1988), p. 1. The commission focused on teenage pregnancy, intergenerational welfare dependence, the cost of state welfare programs, and the rise in the number of single-parent families in Alabama. The commission reported "a growing consensus that welfare recipients who *can* work, *should* work. People who have barriers to work, such as lack of skills or child care, should have help in removing these barriers" (p. 5). See also *The Alabama Welfare Reform Vision: A Report to the Governor* by the Governor's Welfare Reform Commission (Montgomery, AL: Department of Public Welfare, April 1988).

35. On the statistical patterns, see Christopher Jencks, *Rethinking Social Policy* (Cambridge, MA: Harvard University Press, 1992), p. 166 passim, and Mary Jo Bane, "Politics and Policies of the Feminization of Poverty," in M. Weir et al., eds., *The Politics of Social Policy in the United States* (Princeton, NJ: Princeton University Press, 1988). On the political implications of the "marriage of gender politics and the welfare state," see H. Brackman et al., "Wedded to the Welfare State," in J. Jenson et al., eds., *Feminization of the Labour Force* (Oxford: Polity Press, 1988).

36. Department of Health and Social Services, *Year 2 of WEJT* (Madison, WI: Office of Policy & Budget Department of Health & Social Services, March 1989), p. 1. The results were encouraging: "The evaluation found that the WEJT program participants tended to get better jobs, with higher average wages, more hours worked per month, better job retention after six months and more employment-related fringe benefits, including health insurance and sick leave" (p. 4).

37. L. Mead, *The New Politics of Poverty* (New York: Basic Books, 1992); see also Mead's earlier book *Beyond Entitlement* (New York: Free Press, 1985) and the debates around the "new consensus" in *The Public Interest*, no 89 (1987), and M. Novak et al., *The New Consensus on Family and Welfare* (Lanham, MD: American Enterprise Institute, 1987).

38. C. Murray, *Losing Ground* (New York: Basic Books, 1984).

39. Lawrence M. Mead, "The New Politics of the New Poverty," *Public Interest*, no. 103 (1991): 3.

40. Orlanda Patterson and Chris Winship, "White Poor, Black Poor," *New York Times*, 3 May 1992, E:17. See also Lawrence Mishel and Jacqueline Simon, *The State of Working America* (Washington, DC: Economic Policy Institute, 1988).

41. "While support for welfare among the working class is somewhat greater than among the middle class (28 percent favored increased spending compared to 21 percent), blacks are over twice as likely as whites to favor spending increases (44 percent to 20 percent) . . . not only do blacks and whites differ dramatically in their support for welfare, but among whites, it is racial attitudes that most strongly determine welfare support." In Martin Gilens, "Race, Class, and Opposition to Welfare in the United States," APSA paper, 1991, pp. 8–9. See also Benjamin Page and Robert Shapiro, *The Rational Public* (Chicago: University of Chicago Press, 1992), pp. 124–27.

42. Paul Taylor, "In the Belly of the Untamed Beast," *Washington Post National Weekly Edition*, 17–23 February 1992, p. 24.

43. See C. Pateman, "The Patriarchal Welfare State," in A. Gutmann, ed., *Democracy and the Welfare State* (Princeton, NJ: Princeton University Press, 1988), and R. Lister, "Tracing the Contours of Women's Citizenship," *Policy and Politics* 21 (1993): 3–16. See also C. Pierson, *Beyond the Welfare State?* (Cambridge: Polity Press, 1991).

44. See A. B. Atkinson, "Income Maintenance for the Unemployed in Britain and the Response to High Unemployment," *Ethics* 100 (1990): 569–85. The Conservatives continue to contemplate further eroding social security benefits, discussing on 10 August 1992 a reduction from twelve to six months for unemployment benefit.

More generally, see also R. Jowell et al., *British Social Attitudes: The 1986 Report* (Aldershot: Gower, 1986), and subsequent years; for a critique of these and other opinion polls, see R. Harris and A. Seldon, *Welfare Without the State* (London: Institute of Economic Affairs, 1987).

45. William Beveridge, *Social Insurance and Allied Services* (London: HMSO, Cmd. 6404, 1942).

46. Central Statistical Office, *Social Trends 1987* (London: HMSO, 1987).

47. F. A. Hayek, *The Constitution of Liberty* (London: Routledge, Kegan and Paul, 1960), chaps. 17–24. Hayek opposed welfare state policies because he argued

they diminished freedom: "Though they are presented as mere service activities, they really constitute an exercise of the coercive powers of government and rest on its claiming exclusive rights in certain fields" (p. 258). See also N. Barry, *Welfare* (Milton Keynes: Open University Press, 1990).

48. Speech by John Moore to a Conservative Political Centre Conference, 26 September 1987, p. 2. Conservative Party News Service.

49. Ibid., p. 3. The emphasis is in the text.

50. Among academics, Norman Barry's work also draws heavily upon American sources such as C. Murray and L. Mead: see his section in Raymond Plant and Norman Barry, *Citizenship and Rights in Thatcher's Britain: Two Views* (London: Institute of Economic Affairs, 1990).

51. For example, in 1954 the chairman of the National Assistance told a Conservative party committee about the need to exclude abusers from the welfare system:

> There was a need to differentiate between the pensioner applying for assistance and the person of working age. He believed that the pensioner should be encouraged to apply and for this reason favoured changing the name to supplementary pension when given to pensioners. The psychological effect of this change would be considerable.
>
> On the other hand the person of working age who was unemployed or ill for a short while should be discouraged from seeking assistance and a different attitude should be adopted in dealing with these applicants.

In Sir Geoffrey Hutchinson's [chairman of the National Assistance Board] Talk to Insurance Sub-Cttee, 24 March 1954. Personal & Confidential, CRD2/30/4: National Assistance 1948–50, Conservative Party Archives, Bodleian Library, Oxford.

52. Speech by John Moore to a Conservative Political Centre Conference, 26 September 1987, pp. 6, 10. Conservative Party News Service.

53. No Turning Back Group of Conservative MPs, *Who Benefits? Reinventing Social Security* (London: Conservative Political Centre, 1993).

54. See "Lilley Warns on Benefits Spending," *Financial Times,* 21 July 1993.

55. Before this period, several states had established various welfare initiatives; federally, only pensions had been enacted for reasons explained in the previous chapter. For accounts, see Ann Shola Orloff and Theda Skocpol, "Why Not Equal Protection? Explaining the Politics of Public Social Spending in Britain 1900–1911, and the United States 1880s–1920," *American Sociological Review* 49 (1984): 726–50, and Theda Skocpol and John Ikenberry, "The Political Formation of the American Welfare State," *Comparative Social Research* 6 (1983): 87–148. Theda Skocpol has extended this thesis in detail in her book, *Protecting Soldiers and Mothers* (Cambridge, MA: Harvard University Press, 1992), in which she analyzes civil war pensions and programs for women and children enacted in the early decades of the twentieth century: for a discussion of this interpretation, see G. William Domhoff, "The Death of State Autonomy: A Review of Skocpol's *Protecting Soldiers and Mothers,*" *Critical Sociology* 19 (1992): 103–16, and the review by F. F. Piven, *American Political Science Review* 87 (1993): 790–91.

56. Committee on Economic Security, "Report to the President," January 1935,

FDR Official File 1086, Folder: Committee on Economic Security, 1935–40, pp. 7–8, 10. FDR Library. See also the illuminating account by Edwin E. Witte, *The Development of the Social Security Act* (Madison, WI: University of Wisconsin Press, 1963), the committee's executive director.

57. William E. Leuchtenburg, *Franklin D. Roosevelt and the New Deal* (New York: Harper and Row, 1963), pp. 132–33.

58. Skocpol and Ikenberry, "The Political Formation of the American Welfare State," 87–148; and Desmond King, "Citizenship as Obligation in the USA: Title II of the *Family Support Act of 1988,*" in U. Vogel and M. Moran, eds., *The Frontiers of Citizenship* (London: Macmillan, 1991).

59. Black Americans complained extensively about their exclusion from many of the public works programs established in the 1930s.

60. For discussions, see contributions by neoconservatives to *Public Interest* during the 1970s and 1980s, including James Q. Wilson, "The Rediscovery of Character: Private Virtue and Public Policy," *Public Interest* 81 (Fall 1985): 3–16; C. Murry et al., "In Search of the Working Poor," *Public Interest* 89 (1987): 3–19. A book by Michael Novak and colleagues was also influential: *The New Consensus on Family and Welfare* (Lanham, MD: American Enterprise Institute, 1987). For empirical studies, see Sheldon Danziger, Robert Haveman, and Robert Plotnick, "How Income Transfers Affect Work, Savings and the Income Distribution," *Journal of Economic Literature* 19 (1981): 975–1028; Sheldon Danziger and Daniel Weinberg, eds., *Fighting Poverty: What Works and What Doesn't* (Cambridge, MA: Harvard University Press, 1986). For positive assessments, see Danziger and Weinberg, eds., *Fighting Poverty: What Works and What Doesn't;* Robert H. Haveman, *Poverty Policy and Poverty Research* (Madison, WI: University of Wisconsin Press, 1987); and especially John E. Schwartz, *America's Hidden Success* (New York: W. W. Norton, 1988).

61. Memorandum to the Secretary of Labor Hodgson, "Brief Overview of Meeting with Governor Reagan and Staff," 14 July 1971, in Papers of Malcolm Lovell, Jr., Historian's Office, Department of Labor Library, Washington, DC.

62. "California Work Relief Proposal," 28 July 1971, p. 1, in Papers of Malcolm Lovell, Jr., Folder: Welfare Reform/WIN, Historian's Office, Department of Labor Library, Washington, DC.

63. Ibid.

64. Memorandum for the President from Secretary of HEW Richardson, 16 July 1971, my emphasis, in Papers of Malcolm Lovell, Jr., Folder: Welfare Reform/WIN, Historian's Office, Department of Labor Library, Washington, DC.

65. See Memorandum for Richard Nathan from Malcolm Lovell, Jr., "California Work Relief Demonstration," 5 August 1971, and "Emergency Employment Act Apportionment to California," 16 August 1971, in Papers of Malcolm Lovell, Jr., Folder: Welfare Reform/WIN, Historian's Office, Department of Labor Library, Washington, DC.

66. Nixon's proposals were included in his Welfare Reform legislation (H.R. 1), which failed to be enacted.

67. Not until the California scheme had been formally rejected by Washington and resubmitted, however. See Malcolm Lovell, Jr., Memorandum for the Secretary, "The President's Work Relief Demonstration Projects," in Papers of Malcolm

Lovell, Jr., Folder: Welfare Reform/WIN, Historian's Office, Department of Labor Library, Washington, DC.

68. Many of the problems associated with these programs—such as the need for childcare and the increased workload for the USES—faced work-welfare schemes after 1981.

69. See, among others, George Gilder, *Wealth and Poverty* (New York: Basic Books, 1981); N. Glazer, *The Limits of Social Policy* (Cambridge, MA: Harvard University Press, 1988); and Charles Murray, *Losing Ground* (New York: Basic Books, 1984). For discussions, see David T. Ellwood, *Poor Support* (New York: Basic Books, 1988); Christopher Jencks, *Rethinking Social Policy* (Cambridge, MA: Harvard University Press, 1992); and Nicholas Lemann, *The Promised Land* (New York: Knopf, 1991). On the American Right in the 1980s, see G. Peele, *Revival and Reaction* (Oxford: Clarendon Press, 1984), chaps. 1–3.

70. *Public Papers of the Presidents of the United States: Ronald Reagan, Book 1,* January–June 27, 1986 (Washington, DC: Government Printing Office, 1986), p. 1281.

71. Reported in the *New York Times,* 16 February 1986, 1,37:1.

72. Ibid.

73. This dichotomy is explained by Hugh Heclo as a division between welfare as self-sufficiency and welfare as mutual dependence. The first type is

> supremely individualistic, for it has to do with the capacity of an individual to go his own way, to enjoy the fruits of his own labor . . . To paraphrase President Reagan . . . we Americans do not get together to celebrate Dependence Day . . . the second [conception] has to do with a social or group-oriented rationality . . . This is not a question asking us to choose between rational individualism and all other behavior that is somehow irrational. It is . . . asking us to apply rational criterion to the self-in-group rather than to the self-in-isolation as the point of reference.

Perceptions about the legitimate bases of welfare assistance in the United States fall under Heclo's first category, a position which limited American generosity toward the less fortunate in society. See H. Heclo, "General Welfare and Two American Political Traditions," *Political Science Quarterly* 101 (1986): 182, 183.

74. PICs administer the federal *Job Training Partnership Act.*

75. In August 1992, the TUC issued a plaintive call for the government to spend £600 million on training measures to tackle unemployment but such pleas fall on deaf ears. There are also within the Labour Party some pressures to make the achievement of full employment party policy.

76. A year after declining to support ET, the TUC expressed concern about Britain's skill levels comparable to that of the CBI. See "Skills 2000," *TUC Bulletin* (August 1989); see also TUC, *Skills for Success: A TUC Statement on Training* (London: TUC, 1988).

77. Quoted in *Financial Times,* 6 January 1988. However, in an interview in August 1988, Bryan Wolfson, chairman of the Training Agency, expressed the view that workfare could not be ruled out because "you could have a situation where the only way you could do something is by making it compulsory," quoted in the *Independent,* 24 August 1988.

78. That Fowler was aware of and studied American schemes is widely known.

The Employment Secretary visited several United States' schemes, including the trumpeted Massachusetts ET Choices program, which he examined in Boston in February 1988. However, the Massachusetts program was in fact the most liberal of the post-1981 state programs, stressing voluntary participation for its trainees. For details, see King, "Citizenship as Obligation in the United States"; see also "Poor America: Workfare in the 1990s," *Unemployment Bulletin* (Autumn 1990).

79. According to the Unemployment Unit, the scheme was originally to be compulsory: "A confidential policy review prepared for the Employment 'Secretary's Strategy Group' in March 1989 suggests that participation in ET will be made compulsory. The document considers ways to increase the pressure on unemployed people who refuse to participate in ET" (Unemployment Unit, *Working Brief* [November 1989]).

80. See the *Financial Times,* 24 March 1988, for a report of the letter.

81. *Financial Times,* 8 September 1988.

82. The Job Training Scheme was designed to absorb over a 100,000 trainees but in fact achieved a figure of only 30,000, partly because the unions refused to endorse the program.

83. TUC, *TUC Guidance on Employment Training* (London: TUC, December 1988), p. 2. See also TUC, "Adult Training for the Unemployed" (London: TUC Library, 1988), and *TUC Training Bulletin,* no. 17 (Winter 1988/89), which is devoted to responding to the "Employment for the 1990s" White Paper.

84. As Margaret Beckett noted in the House of Commons during consideration of the 1987 social security bill: "As long ago as 1982 the MSC expressed strong reservations about compelling people to go on YTS." *Hansard Parliamentary Debates,* House of Commons Official Report, Standing Committee E, 26 November 1987, col. 239.

85. In August 1992, the government went further, proposing to create a "one-stop" benefit service under which all of the services and benefits available to claimants would be concentrated in one location. See Paula Green, *One Stop, Benefits Agency Service Delivery* (Leeds: Benefits Agency Publishing, 1992).

86. Unemployment Unit, *Working Brief* (August/September 1991): 5. Between January 1991, when the compulsory interview program began, and June 1991, 925 long-term unemployed claimants had had their benefits reduced for failure to attend or to complete Restart courses—*Working Brief* (December 1991): 5.

87. Ibid., p. 4.

88. Congress failed to accede to Reagan's request to make this substitute compulsory.

89. Committee on Ways and Means, U.S. House of Representatives, *Background Material and Data on Programs within the Jurisdiction of the Committee on Ways and Means* (Washington, DC: Government Printing Office, 15 March 1989), p. 523.

90. Tennessee's work-welfare demonstration program, VICTORY, was also voluntary: Tennessee Department of Human Services, *Victory Network Program: Interim Findings,* prepared by Kay S. Marshall and Ronald Randolph (Tennessee: TDHS, January 1987), p. viii.

91. For details about the formulation and content of the work-welfare programs in California, Georgia, and Massachusetts, see King, "Citizenship as Obligation in the United States."

92. U.S. General Accounting Office, *Work and Welfare: Current AFDC Work Programs and Implications for Federal Policy* (Washington, DC: U.S. General Accounting Office, January 1987), prepared for the House of Representatives Committee on Government Operations, Subcommittee on Intergovernmental Relations and Human Resources, p. 120.

93. Ibid., p. 123. The authors were skeptical of the measurements of program success: "To measure success, most programs use placement rates that are not compared to the performance of control groups. Such data can be misleading with regard to a program's true effects and tell little about the quality of jobs found."

94. U.S. General Accounting Office, *CWEP's Implementation Results To Date Raise Questions about the Administration's Proposed Mandatory Workfare Program* (Washington, DC: U.S. General Accounting Office, 2 April 1984), p. 27.

95. See, for example, the report in North Carolina Department of Human Resources, *Community Work Experience Program Annual Report, 1987–1988* (Raleigh, NC: Department of Human Resources, 1 October 1988), p. 1.

96. National Urban League, "Workfare," *Point-Counterpoint* 82, no. 1 (June 1982): 3.

97. AFSCME press release. Testimony of Nanine Meiklejohn before Subcommittee on Public Assistance and Unemployment Compensation, 17 June 1986, p. 5.

98. National Governors' Association, "Job-Oriented Welfare Reform" (Washington, DC: National Governors' Association, February 1987), pp. 2–3.

99. Thus chairman Bill Clinton observes in the introduction to *Making America Work: Productive People, Productive Policies:* "As important as it is to prepare people to succeed in a highly competitive world, education alone will not guarantee them opportunities. They also need sound economic policies to provide good jobs" (National Governors' Association, *Making America Work: Productive People, Productive Policies* [Washington, DC: National Governors' Association, 1987], p. vi).

100. See "Welfare Reform" hearings before the Committee on Finance, U.S. Senate (100th Cong., 1st sess., 14 and 28 October 1987, 4 February 1988); "Welfare: Reform or Replacement," hearing before the Subcommittee on Social Security and Family Policy of the Committee on Finance, U.S. Senate (100th Cong., 1st sess., 23 February 1987); and "Welfare Reform," hearing before the Subcommittee on Public Assistance and Unemployment Compensation of the Committee on Ways and Means, House of Representatives (100th Cong., 1st sess., 28 January, 19 February, 4, 6, 10, 11 and 13 March 1987).

101. For details, see Haskins, "Congress Writes a Law: Research and Welfare Reform," and Baum, "When the Witch Doctors Agree." A similar marshaling of expert advice and policy research is documented by Janoski during the passage of War on Poverty legislation in 1964: Thomas Janoski, *The Political Economy of Unemployment* (Berkeley: University of California Press, 1990), p. 203.

102. For a pre-OBRA MDRC evaluation, see Barbara S. Goldman, *Impacts of the Immediate Job Search Assistance Experiment: Louisville WIN Research Laboratory Project* (New York: MDRC, June 1981), which concluded that providing access immediately to job information, bypassing the eight- to twelve-

week WIN process, "proved effective in increasing the employment and earnings of the experimentals and in reducing the amounts of their AFDC payments" (p. x).

The head of MDRC declared in 1987 that "the results of recent research suggest that introducing a stronger work emphasis into the AFDC program ultimately will not cost but save money—although it will cost money in the short run." In Judith Gueron, *Reforming Welfare With Work* (New York: Ford Foundation Project on Social Welfare and the American Future, 1987), p. 37.

103. For a sample, see Daniel Friedlander et al., *Arkansas: The Demonstration of State Work/Welfare Initiatives* (New York: MDRC, September 1985); John Wallace and David Long, *GAIN: Planning and Early Implementation* (New York: MDRC, April 1987); Janet Quint and Cynthia Guy, *Interim Findings from the Illinois Win Demonstration Program in Cook County* (New York: MDRC, June 1986); Daniel Friedlander et al., *West Virginia: Final Report on the Community Work Experience* (New York: MDRC, 1986); Daniel Friedlander et al., *Maryland: Final Report on the Employment Initiatives Evaluation* (New York: MDRC, 1985); and Barbara Goldman et al., *Final Report on the San Diego Job Search and Work Experience Demonstration* (New York: MDRC, 1986).

104. For instance, in Virginia, MDRC concluded that the state's 1983 created Employment Services Program (ESP) "led to modest employment gains and welfare savings. This was particularly true for the women who came into the program at the time they were applying for welfare . . . For the recipient group—or women already receiving welfare at program entry—immediate improvements in employment and welfare savings were short-lived. The program, in addition, did not reduce the size of the caseload for either group; there was no increase in case closings." In James Riccio et al., *Final Report on the Virginia Employment Services Program* (New York: MDRC, August 1986), p. viii. ESP was implemented by 11 of the state's 124 local welfare agencies.

For Arkansas, the same organization concluded that the "WORK program achieved modest increases in employment and earnings." In Daniel Friedlander et al., *Arkansas: Final Report on the WORK Program in Two Counties* (New York: MDRC, September 1985), p. 12. However, the findings for reducing welfare costs were stronger.

105. MDRC has continued to evaluate work-welfare programs: see, for example, Karin Martinson and James Riccio, *GAIN: Child Care in a Welfare Employment Initiative* (New York: MDRC, May 1989); Stephen Freedman and James Riccio, *GAIN: Participation in Four Counties* (New York: MDRC, May 1991); James Riccio et al., *GAIN: Early Implementation Experiences and Lessons* (New York: MDRC, April 1989); and Gayle Hamilton and Daniel Freidlander, *Final Report on the Saturation Work Initiative Model in San Diego* (New York: MDRC, November 1989).

106. Established in 1984. For details, see Office of Planning Budget and Evaluation, Planning and Evaluation Division, *Michigan Opportunity and Skill Training (MOST) Evaluation: Interim Report* (January 1989) and *Interim Evaluation of the Michigan Opportunities Skills Training Program* (March 1989), both produced by the Michigan Department of Social Services.

107. Potomac Institute for Economic Research, *The Ohio Work Programs:*

Assessing the First Two Years, Final Report (Washington, DC: Potomac Institute for Economic Research, October 1985), p. 5. See also *Impact of the 1984 and 1985 Work Programs: A Brief Glimpse* (Washington, DC: Potomac Institute for Economic Research, March 1988).

108. U.S. General Accounting Office, *Work and Welfare: Analysis of AFDC Employment Programs in Four States* (Washington, DC: General Accounting Office, January 1988), p. 3.

109. In a publication in 1985, the Confederation of British Industry (CBI) observed how many companies were expanding their training program and "taking initiatives to help unemployed people, via government schemes or independently, and sometimes in programs organised and executed jointly by the private sector, voluntary organizations and local authorities." In CBI, *Company Responses to Unemployment* (London: CBI, July 1985), p. 7. However, the CBI's findings conflict with those of a government study which found persistently inadequate training: *Training in Britain: A Study of Funding Activity and Attitudes* (London: HMSO, November 1989), summary report and five research volumes.

110. CBI, *Towards a Skills Revolution* (London: CBI Publications, July 1989). It was prepared by the CBI's vocational education and training task force. In June 1993, the CBI Director-General Howard Davies criticized the United Kingdom's training system for being insufficiently market-oriented (*Financial Times,* 2 June 1993).

111. See Department of Employment, *Training and Enterprise Councils: A Prospectus for the 1990s* (Sheffield: Training, Enterprise and Education Directorate Department of Employment, 1988). For analyses, see Desmond S. King, "The Conservative and Training Policy, 1979–1992: From a Tripartite to a Neoliberal Regime," *Political Studies* 41 (1993): 214–35; and Jon Tonge, "Training and Enterprise Councils: The Privatisation of Britain's Unemployment Problem?" *Capital and Class* 51 (1993): 9–16.

112. Most TECs have connections with local enterprise agencies. A significant number of TEC chairpersons have come from enterprise agencies and many agency directors or board members sit on the new TECs.

113. This direct communication is threatened by the formation of G10, a self-appointed group of representatives drawn from the earlier TECs to represent TEC chief interests.

114. *Financial Times,* 10 May 1993.

115. As one observer noted about ET: "The Government is committed to reducing the power of local authorities and the Unions over a range of local economic and tax-funded activities" (Alan Bartlett, "Training and Enterprise Councils—Will They Succeed?" [London: Association of British Chambers of Commerce, May 1989], pp. 1–2).

116. For the formal framework, see Department of Employment, *TEC Operating Agreement* (Sheffield: Training, Enterprise and Education Directorate, 1992).

117. *Financial Times,* 10 May 1993.

118. See Tonge, "Training and Enterprise Councils: The Privatisation of Britain's Unemployment Problem?"

119. See D. S. King, "Government Beyond Whitehall: Local Government and Urban Politics," in P. Dunleavy, G. Peele, A. Gamble, and I. Holliday, eds., *Developments in British Politics 4* (London: Macmillan, 1993).

120. The major initiative from TECs for training those in work has been the Investors in People program established by the National Training Task Force in 1990 and transferred now to the TECs.

121. Relations between TEC leaders and Whitehall have been tenuous from their foundation: in May 1991 there was a heated meeting between G10 and Sir Geoffrey Holland: see *Working Brief* (July 1991). For the G10 official version, see Executive Summary, *TEC Conference, July 1992* (London: TECs' Secretariat, 1992).

122. Quoted in B. Clement, "Revolution? What Revolution?" *Independent,* 13 July 1992.

123. Disquiet has been growing among TEC members and directors. At the TECs' third annual meeting in 1993, the common theme was to shift away from training and problems of unemployment toward enterprise. See L. Wood, "Good Try, but Could Do Better," *Financial Times,* 14 July 1993.

124. B. Clement, "Revolution? What Revolution?" *Independent* 13 July 1992. Holland became permanent secretary at education in August 1992, but took early retirement in 1994.

125. MSC, *The General Employment Service in Great Britain,* Report of the Employment Service, D. Rayner Scrutiny, 1982.

126. Dan Finn and Steve Preston, "A Better Employment Service," *Unemployment Bulletin* 30 (Summer 1989): 9. See also Dan Finn and David Taylor, *The Future of Jobcentres,* Employment no. 1 (London: Institute for Public Policy Research, 1990).

127. See Department of Employment Group, "Your Guide to Our Employment Training and Enterprise Programs" PL856 (9/88) (London: HMSO, 1988), p. 7. See also Unemployment Unit, "Restart: Where You Stand," (London: Unemployment Unit, July 1989), and "Actively Seeking Work," *Unemployment Bulletin* (Autumn 1989).

Unemployment Unit, "A Compulsory Offer," *Working Brief* (July 1990), and "No Option Course," *Working Brief* (January 1991).

128. Quoted in D. Finn, "Employment Service," *Unemployment Bulletin* (Summer 1988): 9.

129. See Efficiency Unit, *Improving Management in Government: The Next Steps* (London: HMSO, 1988), and House of Commons Treasury and Civil Service Committee Fifth Report, "Developments in the Next Steps Program," 1988–89, 19 July 1989, and Eighth Report, "Civil Service Management Reform: The Next Steps," vol. 1, 25 July 1988.

130. *Working Brief* (June 1992): 5.

131. *Financial Times,* 2 December 1989.

132. *Guardian,* 4 March 1989. A report advocating workfare was prepared for the Department of Employment by John Burton; it was commissioned by Lord Young, Fowler's predecessor, but Young rejected the compulsory option.

133. *Guardian,* 13 September 1989.

134. Labour Party spokesman Michael Meacher argued that the administrative reorganization and integration of activities was part of the government's effort to impose tighter regulations for benefit receipt and to direct more unemployed persons toward compulsory training schemes: "This year will see the most decisive moves yet to reduce the number of people claiming benefit, by forcing them into

any job or training scheme, however inappropriate, or simply ending their entitlement." Quoted in the *Guardian,* 4 March 1989.

135. For examples of detailed accounts of state JOBS programs, see Rhode Island Department of Human Services, *Rhode Island Job Opportunities and Basic Skill Program: Pathways to Independence* (Rhode Island: Department of Human Services, May 1989); Department of Income Maintenance, *Connecticut's State Plan for JOBS under the Family Support Act of 1988* (Hartford, CT: Department of Income Maintenance, 15 May 1989); New Jersey Department of Labor, *Instructions for the Preparation of the JOBS New Jersey PY 89 Plan* (New Jersey: New Jersey Department of Labor, April 1989); New Hampshire Department of Health and Human Services, *Proposed State Plan for a JOBS Program Under the Family Support Act of 1988 for New Hampshire* (Concord, NH: New Hampshire Department of Health and Human Services, 15 June 1989); and Department of Health and Social Services, *Building Employment Skills Today, "BEST": JOBS State Plan* (Madison, WI: Wisconsin Department of Health and Social Services, 15 May 1989).

136. See "My Mom and ET," Department of Public Welfare Massachusetts (1989), Annual Report, 1988, Department of Employment Training, Massachusetts 1988.

137. For example, the South Dakotan Employment Service plan for fiscal year 1989 recorded its commitment to implementing the Title II JOBS program as one of its responsibilities: "The State Agency in conjunction with the South Dakota Department of Social services and other state agencies are involved in the design of the newly enacted Family Support Act . . . the transition from WIN to JOBS will begin during 1989. The South Dakota Department of Labor will be involved in the delivery of the JOBS program." In South Dakota Department of Labor, *Employment Service State Operational Plan Program Year 1989* (Aberdeen, SD: South Dakota Department of Labor, 1989), p. 4.

138. For an overview, see U.S. General Accounting Office, *JTPA: Initial Implementation of Program For Disadvantaged Youth and Adults* (Washington, DC: U.S. General Accounting Office, 4 March 1985), prepared for the United States Senate.

139. States continue to emphasize problems of skills in their workforce requiring education and training: see *Retooling Utah's Work Force,* A Report from the Governor's Utah Workforce 2000 Task Force (Salt Lake City, UT: State Capitol, September 1988); *The Next Steps: The Development of a Fully Productive Work Force in Virginia,* Governor's Job Training Coordinating Council Private Sector Task Force (Richmond, VA: State Capitol, January 1986); and Task Force Report, *Education and Job Training* (Harrisburg, PA: Pennsylvania Economic Development Partnership Office of the Governor, January 1988).

140. Task Force on Employment Policy, Report to the Governor, *New Jersey's Employment Challenge* (New Brunswick, NJ: Task Force on Employment Policy, December 1987), p. i.

141. National Alliance of Business, *Is the Job Training Partnership Working?* (Washington, DC: National Alliance of Business, 1986).

142. U.S. Conference of Mayors, *The Impact of the JTPA on Urban Employment Needs* (Washington, DC: U.S. Conference of Mayors, June 1988), p. 14.

143. JTPA Advisory Committee, *Working Capital: JTPA Investment's for the 90's* (Washington, DC: JTPA Advisory Committee, March 1989), p. 8.

144. A GAO study of JTPA programs for dislocated workers found a high success rate, with 69 percent of participants placed in employment, far higher than rates for other federal employment and training programs. See U.S. General Accounting Office, *Dislocated Workers: Local Programs and Outcomes under the JTPA* (Washington, DC: U.S. General Accounting Office, March 1987); see also *Dislocated Workers: Exemplary Local Projects Under the JTPA* (Washington, DC: U.S. General Accounting Office, April 1987).

145. New Jersey Department of Labor, *Recommendations of the ES/JTPA Coordination Committee* (Trenton, NJ: Department of Labor, 9 September 1988), p. 4.

146. Marc Bendick, Jr., *Building a Job Service for the Year 2000: Innovative State Practices,* A Special Report of the Interstate Conference of Employment Security Agencies (Washington, DC: ICESA, January 1989), p. vi; the study was funded by the Employment Training Administration of the U.S. Department of Labor. Given the discussion of the ICESA in earlier chapters, there is room for caution in interpreting this report: one view might be that this lobby group is ensuring the USES has a continuing function.

147. See *Federal Register* 54, no. 156 (1989): 38–95.

148. Reported in J. Rovner, "Draft Welfare Regulations Draw Fire From States," *Congressional Quarterly Weekly Report* 47, no. 20 (May 1989): 119. See also Mark Greenberg, "JOBS Regs: A First Look at Some Big Problems" (Washington, DC: Center for Law and Social Policy, April 1989).

149. JOBS provisions were implemented in California on 1 July 1989 with the passage of AB 2171.

150. California Department of Social Services, *California GAIN Program: Report* (Sacramento, CA: Department of Social Services, 10 January 1991), p. 31; see also *California GAIN Program: Report,* January 1990.

151. Stephen Freedman and James Riccio, *GAIN: Participation Patterns in Four Counties* (New York: MDRC, May 1991).

152. American Public Welfare Association, *Early State Experiences and Policy Issues in the Implementation of the JOBS Program* (Washington, DC: APWA, 1990), p. 30. See also Jan L. Hagen and Irene Lurie, *Implementing JOBS: Initial State Choices* (Albany, NY: The Nelson A. Rockefeller Institute of Government, March 1992), and Department of Health and Human Services Memo on "JOBS Participation Rate Status Update," 26 June 1992 (Washington, DC: DHHS).

153. This judgment is based on interviews by the author with officials in Massachusetts in 1989.

154. A report that £36.8m was overpaid in unemployment benefit according to a National Audit Office study may fuel such propensities; report in *Financial Times,* 4 June 1992.

The Secretary of State for Employment Gillian Shephard also urged employers to notify Jobcentres about vacancies, airing a historical problem about labor exchanges: should employer modification be compulsory? In 1909, policy was decided against compulsion; in the 1950s, the government also urged notification but because of labor shortage, not excess as in the 1990s.

155. *Sunday Times,* 3 July 1994, and *Financial Times,* 4 July 1994, *Working Brief,* July 1994, citing "Stricter Benefit Regime—Hard to fill Vacancies," Memorandum for ES Benefit Management Branch to ES Regional Director, 11 May 1994.

156. In March 1993, the government announced a Community Action program for the unemployed in their budget. The program is to provide benefit plus £10 for 60,000 people who wish to work part-time.

157. Quoted in the *Guardian,* 12 August 1992.

158. Letter to the *Independent* from Peter Ashby, Full Employment UK, 4 May 1992. Ashby gave his proposals in some detail in *Citizenship, Income and Work,* Parts One and Two (Windsor Castle, Berkshire: St. George's House, Autumn 1988 and February 1989).

159. Letter to the *Independent,* 14 August 1992. Field urges the government to establish a commission to develop a temporary work training program. See also Richard Layard and John Philpott, *Stopping Unemployment* (London: Employment Institute, 1992).

160. The program was subject to cross-party criticism by the House of Commons employment committee in August 1991 for lacking any compulsory training element. See *Training and Enterprise Councils and Vocational Training,* Employment Committee, Fifth Report, vol. 1 (London: HMSO, 1991).

161. For a first reaction, see Bartlett, "Training and Emterprise Councils—Will they Succeed?" In Germany, Chambers of Commerce have a leading role in training policy and hold responsibility for examining and certifying apprentice and trainee programs: see *Aspects of Vocational Education and Training in the Federal Republic of German* (London: HMSO, 1991), chap. 8.

162. See Tony Blair, *Training in Crisis: A Report on the Underfunding of Training and Enterprise Councils* (London: Labour Party, June 1992) and "Labour Renews Attack over Jobs," *Financial Times,* 31 July 1992.

163. "According to the Labour Party, as many as 55,000 cannot find suitable courses and under government rules about 11,000 are refused social security benefit" (*Independent,* 13 July 1992). The government has denied these claims. See also *Working Brief* (October 1991) and (April 1992).

164. D. Summers, "Blair Claims Survey Shows Cuts in Training Provision," *Financial Times,* 12 June 1992.

165. In May 1988, 32,000 16-year-olds received income support; by May 1990, the figure was 4,000; for 17-year-olds the drop was from 69,000 to 17,000 (*Working Brief* [February 1992]: 6).

166. *Working Brief* (April 1992): 4.

167. For the more general context of gender and welfare, see A. S. Orloff's discussion, "Gender and the Social Rights of Citizenship: The Comparative Analysis of Gender Relations and Welfare States," *American Sociological Review* 58 (1993): 303–28.

168. M. Abramovitz and F. F. Piven, "Scapegoating Women on Welfare," *New York Times,* 2 September 1993.

169. Ibid. For a defense of work-welfare, see B. Gotbaum, "When Workfare Is Just Make-Work," *New York Times,* 4 September 1993. On the implementa-

tion of JOBS, see R. P. Nathan, *Turning Promises into Performance* (Washington, DC: Twentieth-Century Fund, 1993).

170. See reports in the *Financial Times,* 6 and 7 October 1993.

171. See the discussion in Kay E. Sherwood and David A. Long, "JOBS Implementation in an Uncertain Environment," *Public Welfare* (Winter 1991): 17–27. See also CBO, *Work and Welfare: The Family Support Act of 1988* (Washington, DC: Congressional Budget Office Staff Working Paper, January 1989).

172. See, *New York Times,* 4 April 1992. A March 1992 study of ten states found that the states were satisfying their enrollment requirements and that the relevant state agencies were cooperating more effectively. However, state administrators were tending to allocate the resources under the program less imaginatively or extensively than intended, favoring limited job search and CWEP schemes over fuller training projects. The report was prepared by Jan L. Hagen and Irene Lurie at the Rockefeller Institute of Government at SUNY and reported in the *New York Times* 30 March 1992.

Chapter Six

1. G. Mucciaroni writes of the United States that "unlike many other areas of domestic policy, the absence of sustained involvement by well-established interest organizations is a distinctive feature of the employment-training subsystem." In *The Political Failure of Employment Policy, 1945–1982* (Pittsburgh, PA: University of Pittsburgh Press, 1990), p. 199.

2. D. S. King, "The Conservatives and Training Policy 1979–1992: From a Tripartite to a Neoliberal Regime," *Political Studies* 41 (1993): 214–35.

3. See Mucciaroni, *The Political Failure of Employment Policy, 1945–1982,* and M. Weir, *Politics and Jobs* (Princeton, NJ: Princeton University Press, 1992).

4. By social democratic, I mean work-welfare programs with most of the following elements: national organization of the labor market through a service such as the employment service; a commitment by the government to funding training programs as the economy encounters difficulties; extensive training programs (providing high-quality vocational skills easily transferable between jobs) for those seeking first-time entry to the labor market and retraining for those made redundant—programs all coordinated with detailed information about labor market trends; effective job-placement services to which employers are required to notify vacancies and unimpeded by private agencies. For an analysis which contrasts the United States model with the social democratic Swedish system, see H. Ginsburg, *Full Employment and Public Policy: The United States and Sweden* (Lexington, MA: Lexington Books, 1983), chap. 6.

5. The Wilson-Callaghan administration (1974–79) rarely achieved the unity necessary for significant reforms, though, of course, they did defend existing social democratic achievements.

6. See discussions in Ivor Crewe, "Labor Force Change, Working Class Decline, and the Labor Vote: Social and Electoral Trends in Postwar Britain," in F. F. Piven, ed., *Labor Parties in Postindustrial Societies* (Oxford: Polity, 1991); and Desmond King and Mark Wickham-Jones, "Social Democracy and Rational

Workers," *British Journal of Political Science* 20 (1990): 387–413.

7. Contrast the success of social security in the United States, a contributory program with wide electoral support.

8. For one account, see Thomas Byrne Edsall and Mary Edsall, *Chain Reaction* (New York: W. W. Norton, 1991).

9. In its submission to the committee, the Technical Board's members believed linking these two activities was crucial given the "willingness to work" eligibility criterion for receipt of benefits: "These offices must function as efficient placement agencies if the 'willingness to work' test of eligibility for benefits in unemployment compensation is to be made effective." See NARA RG 47 (Records of the Social Security Administration), Box 1, Folder: Reports and Minutes of the Committee on Unemployment Insurance, Technical Board on Economic Security, "Report of the Technical Board on the Major Alternative Plans for the Administration of Unemployment Insurance," p. 89.

10. Though the Carter administration's welfare reform proposals also emphasized work. See Desmond King, "Sectionalism and Welfare Policy in the United States: The Failure of President Carter's Initiatives," mimeo, Oxford 1993.

11. See B. Elbaum, "The Persistence of Apprenticeships in Britain and Its Decline in the United States," in H. Gospell, ed., *Industrial Training and Technological Innovation* (London: Routledge, 1991); "Why Apprenticeship Persisted in Britain but Not in the United States," *Journal of Economic History* 49 (1989): 337–49. On the United States, see also Thomas Janoski, *The Political Economy of Unemployment* (Berkeley: University of California Press, 1990).

12. George Meany Memorial Archives, Legislative Reference File, Box 54, File 62, Memorandum from Bert Seidman, "Welfare Reform Alternatives," p. 2.

13. Jill Quadagno, "Race, Class, and Gender in the U.S. Welfare State: Nixon's Failed Family Assistance Plan," *American Sociological Review* 50 (1990): 22.

14. This point has been made well by V. Hattam in *Labor Visions and State Power* (Princeton, NJ: Princeton University Press, 1993). She writes: "The AFL only supported laws targeted at especially vulnerable segments of the population—women, children, government employees . . . In contrast, it consistently opposed regulation of its core constituents—white adult males—for fear of weakening their organizational base" (p. 5).

15. On the failure of Labour to construct a social democratic regime in Britain, see Jonas Pontusson, *Swedish Social Democracy and British Labour: Essays on the Nature and Conditions of Social Democratic Hegemony* (Ithaca, NY: Cornell Studies in International Affairs, Western Societies Program, 1988).

16. For the early organization of the Labour Party and its relationship with the TUC, see Ross McKibbin, *The Evolution of the Labour Party, 1910–1924* (Oxford: Clarendon Press, 1974).

17. The Conservatives were well aware of their lack of support among skilled union-member voters. A committee was established by the Conservative Central Office in 1950 to examine the "question of the factors which have so far prevented the greater part of the skilled workers of this country from supporting the Conservative Party." It was a subcommittee of the Tory's Parliamentary Labour Committee. It concluded that most factors arose from "the loyalty which is given to the Labour Party by large members of Trade Unionists on the basis rather that

it is 'their' Party than because they approve of particular items of its policy. Interlocked with this conception is a profound suspicion of the motives and intentions of our own Party, based partly on an identification of it with the employers, partly on a comprehensible feeling about the past and partly as the result of years of propaganda. The obstacle to be overcome can be summed up as the inculcation of trust and confidence in our Party. The problem is, in fact, the creation of that confidence." In CRD2/7/6: Trade Unions and Employment Paper, 1950–59, 20 July 1950, Strictly Confidential, pp. 4, 1. Conservative Party Archives, Bodleian Library, Oxford.

18. The racial dimension should not be underestimated in Britain, however. In 1954 the chairman of the National Assistance Board raised the issue in an address to a Conservative Party Insurance Subcommittee. He raised nine points, of which the ninth was as follows:

> There was the problem of coloured people coming to this country from the Commonwealth. Again nothing much could be done about this from the assistance angle as these people were British subjects. There was, however, a Government Cttee which was considering possible ways of discouraging these persons from coming to Britain unless they had reasonable means of support.

Sir Geoffrey Hutchinson's [chairman of the National Assistance Board] Talk to Insurance Sub-Cttee. In CRD2/30/4: National Assistance, 1948–50, 24 March 1954, Personal & Confidential, Conservative Party Archives, Bodleian Library, Oxford.

19. In Conservative Research Department papers, CRD2/7/2: (B) Govt. Education and Training in Industry, 1948, 1 October 1948, "Opportunity, Education and Training in Industry," p. 3. Conservative Party Archives, Bodleian Library, Oxford.

20. For instance, the AFL-CIO opposed the so-called Philadelphia Plan devised in 1970 to increase the number of black participants in apprenticeships. See George Meany Memorial Archives, Legislative Reference Files, Box 6, Folder 2, pamphlet by G. Meany, "Labor and the Philadelphia Plan," January 1970.

21. See U.S. Chamber of Commerce, *Business and Education: Partners for the Future* (Washington, DC: U.S. Chamber of Commerce, 1985), prepared by Robert L. Martin; National Alliance of Business, *Employment Policies: Looking to the Year 2000* (Washington, DC: NAB, 1986), and *Shaping Tomorrow's Workforce* (Washington, DC: NAB, 1988); American Society for Training and Development, *Workplace Basics: The Skills Employers Want* (Washington, DC: U.S. Department of Labor Employment and Training Administration, 1988), prepared by A. P. Carnevale, L. J. Gainer, and A. S. Meltzer.

22. These calls are not unrelated to Clinton's election: see S. Berryman, "Apprenticeship as a Paradigm for Learning," in William T. Grant Foundation, *Youth Apprenticeship in America* (Washington, DC: William T. Grant Foundation, 1992).

23. U.S. National Alliance of Business, *Real Jobs for Real People* (Washington, DC: National Alliance of Business, 1992).

24. CBI, *Towards a Skills Revolution* (London: CBI Publications, July 1989).

25. Both governments have been involved in vocational training schemes.

26. Founded by President Johnson in 1968 to administer the Job Opportunities

in the Business Sector program, an element of the Great Society reforms.

27. See H. M. Inspectorate, Department of Education and Science, *Aspects of Vocational Education and Training in the Federal Republic of Germany* (London, HMSO 1991).

28. Social rights include public unemployment insurance, health and education systems. For the development of this concept, see T. H. Marshall, "Citizenship and Social Class," in *Citizenship and Social Development* (New York: Doubleday, 1964); Desmond King and Jeremy Waldron, "Citizenship, Social Citizenship and the Defence of Welfare Provision," *British Journal of Political Science* 18 (1988): 415–43; and for the United States, A. L. Schorr, *Common Decency* (New Haven, CT: Yale University Press, 1986). See also Raymond Plant and Norman Barry, *Citizenship and Rights in Thatcher's Britain: Two Views* (London: Institute of Economic Affairs, 1990), and David Miller, *Market, State and Community* (Oxford: Clarendon Press, 1989), chap. 9. Marshall's arguments were formulated principally in respect of Britain and he evidently believed they were firmly based; this is no longer the case.

29. See, for example, L. M. Mead, *Beyond Entitlement* (New York: Free Press, 1987).

30. See K. Thelen and S. Steinmo, "Historical Institutionalism in Comparative Politics," in S. Steinmo et al., eds., *Structuring Politics: Historical Institutionalism in Comparative Analysis* (New York and Cambridge: Cambridge University Press, 1992); P. A. Hall, *Governing the Economy* (Oxford: Polity, 1986); and S. Steinmo, "Political Institutions and Tax Policy in the United States, Sweden and Britain," *World Politics* 41 (1989): 500–535.

31. This lesson was, of course, emphasized many years ago by E. E. Schattschneider in *The Semi-Sovereign People* (New York: Holt, Rinehart and Winston, 1960), p. 71: "All forms of political organization have a bias in favor of the exploitation of some kinds of conflict and the suppression of others because organization is the mobilization of bias. Some issues are organized into politics while others are organized out."

32. It also established a Commission on Social Justice to review the welfare state. Both it and the Institute of Public Policy Research may bear fruit as a source of ideas for Labour.

33. Perhaps more so than scholars in the state-centric perspective concede— see P. Evans, D. Rueschmeyer, and T. Skocpol, eds., *Bringing the State Back In* (Cambridge and New York: Cambridge University Press, 1986). For instance, H. Heclo, *Modern Social Policies in Britain and Sweden* (New Haven, CT: Yale University Press, 1974), concluded his study of the origin of social policies in Britain and Sweden by observing that "the bureaucracies of Britain and Sweden" have been "consistently important. While parties and interest groups did occasionally play extremely important parts, it was the civil services that provides the most constant analysis and review underlying most courses of government action. Parties and interest groups typically required a dramatic stimulus, such as a spurt in unemployment, to arouse their interest, but administrative attention remained relatively strong throughout these fluctuations" (p. 301).

34. Confidential minutes of Board of Trade Conference with the Engineering Employers' Association and the Ship-Building Employers' Federation, 18 August 1909, p. 8. PRO LAB2 Box 211.

BIBLIOGRAPHY

Primary Sources
Detailed citations to quoted material are provided in the endnotes. Here I list
the major collections and documents consulted.

Britain
Archival Sources
Various papers and collections were consulted in the following libraries, as ref-
erences in the text and endnotes indicate. Here I list the principal papers in
each of the collections.

1. British Library of Political and Economic Sciences
   William Beveridge Papers: Unemployment (Coll. B)
2. Public Record Office
   LAB2
3. Department of Employment Library
   Employment Exchanges Boxes
4. International Heritage Centre, Salvation Army, London
   Records of Land and Industrial Colony, Hadleigh Essex
5. Manpower Services Commission/Training Agency Library, Sheffield
   N.A., 1979, "Manpower Services Commission: The First Five Years"
   Annual reports and various studies
6. Trades Union Congress Library
   TUC files on training, employment exchanges, and unemployment
7. Bodleian Library, Oxford University
   Papers of the Conservative Party, Research Department

Selected Published Primary Sources
Department of Employment and Productivity. 1970. *Future of the Employment
Service: Consultative Document.* London: HMSO.
Department of Employment. 1972. *People and Jobs—A Modern Employment
Service.* London: HMSO.
Department of Employment. 1972a. *Into Action—Plan for a Modern
Employment Service.* London: HMSO.
Department of Employment. 1972. *Training for the Future: A Plan for Discus-
sion.* London: HMSO.
Department of Employment White Paper. 1981 (December). *A New Training
Initiative: A Programme for Action.* London: HMSO, Cmd. 8455.

Department of Employment White Paper. 1988. *Training for Employment.* London: HMSO, Cm 316.

Ministry of Labour Gazette

Department of Labour Gazette

Parliamentary Papers (1893–94). "Report on Agencies and Methods for Dealing with the Unemployed." Vol. LXXXII. London: HMSO, C-7182/1893.

Parliamentary Papers (1920). Report of the Committee of Enquiry into the Work of the Employment Exchanges Reports from Commissioners, Inspectors and Others. Vol. XIX. London: HMSO, Cmd. 1054.

Parliamentary Papers (1943–44). White Paper on Employment Policy. Vol. VIII. London: HMSO, Cmd. 6527.

Parliamentary Papers (1947–48). Employment and Training Bill. Vol. II. London: HMSO.

Parliamentary Papers (1962–63). Industrial Training: Government Proposals. Vol. XXXI. London: HMSO, Cmd. 1892.

Parliamentary Papers (1956). The Economic Implications of Full Employment. Vols. XXVI–XI. London: HMSO, Cmd. 9725.

Parliamentary Papers (1983–84). Training for Jobs. Vol. 58. London: HMSO, Cmnd. 9135.

Poor Law Commissioners (1909). *Royal Commission on the Poor Laws and Relief of Distress.* London: HMSO, cd 4499.

Royal Commission on Unemployment Insurance (1932). *Final Report.* London: HMSO, Cmd 4185.

Parliamentary Debates and Standing Committee reports.

Trades Union Congress, General Council, and the Representative Group of Employers, joint meetings. 1928. *Unemployment,* working draft. London: TUC.

Hardie, Keir. 1905. *The Unemployed Bill.* London: Independent Labour Party.

Trades Union Congress. 1931. *Fair Play for the Unemployed.* London: TUC.

Trades Union Congress. 1932. *The Royal Commission and the TUC.* London: TUC.

Trades Union Congress. 1933. *Workless: A Social Tragedy.* London: TUC.

Trades Union Congress. 1970. *Unions, TUC, and Industrial Training.* London: TUC.

Trades Union Congress. 1972. *Trade Unions and Training for the Future.* London: TUC.

Trades Union Congress. 13 March 1981. *TUC Consultative Conference: Industrial Training, Discussion Paper.* London: TUC.

Trades Union Congress. 1988. *Adult Training for the Unemployed.* London: TUC.

Trades Union Congress. 1988. *Vocational Education and Training.* Background Document for a TUC Consultative Conference on Vocational Education and Training. London: TUC.

Trades Union Congress Training Bulletin. Various issues.

Trades Union Congress-Labour Party Liaison Committee. 1984. *A Plan for Training.* London: TUC.

Parliamentary Committee of the TUC and the National Executive of the Labour Party. 1921. *Labour and the Unemployment Crisis.* London: TUC.

Manpower Services Commission annual reports.

Manpower Services Commission. 1977. *Training for Skills: A Programme for Action.* Sheffield: MSC.

Manpower Services Commission. 1981 (May). *A New Training Initiative—A Consultative Document.* Sheffield: MSC.

Manpower Services Commission. 1987. *The New Job Training Scheme: The Facts.* Sheffield: MSC.

Business in the Community. 1988. *Putting the Enterprise into TECs.* London: Business in the Community.

H.M. Inspectorate Department of Education and Science. 1991. *Aspects of Vocational Education and Training in the Federal Republic of Germany.* London: HMSO.

National Economic Development Council. 1963. *Conditions Favourable to Faster Growth.* London: HMSO.

Confederation of British Industry. *National Conference Report.* Various years.

Confederation of British Industry. 1985. *Company Responses to Unemployment.* London: CBI.

Confederation of British Industry. 1989 (July). *Towards a Skills Revolution.* London: CBI.

Association of British Chambers of Commerce. 1989. *Training and Enterprise Councils—Will they Succeed?* by Alan Bartlett. London: ABCC.

Network Training Group. 1983. *Training and the State: Responses to the Manpower Services Commission.* London: Network Training Group.

Centre for Alternative Industrial and Technological Systems. 1989 (May). *ET in London.* London: CAITS.

Centre for Alternative Industrial and Technological Systems. 1989. *ET: There Are Alternatives.* London: CAITS.

Full Employment UK. 1989 (October/November). *TECs, Training Vouchers and the Long-term Jobless.* London: Full Employment UK.

Society of Civil and Public Servants. 1982. *Back to Work: An Alternative Strategy for the Manpower Services Commission.* London: Society of Civil and Public Servants.

Greater London Council. 1983. *The Future of YTS.* London: Greater London Council.

Greater London Manpower Board, Industry, and Employment Committee. 1983.

Youth Training Scheme. Report by Director of Industry and Employment and Chief Economic Adviser. London: Greater London Council.

Jarvis, Valerie, and Sig Prais. 1988. *Two Nations of Shopkeepers: Training for Retailing in France and Britain.* London: National Institute for Economic and Social Research, Discussion Paper 140.

Unemployment Unit. April 1988. *Training or Workfare? The New Job Training Scheme in London.* London: Unemployment Unit.

Unemployment Unit. *Working Brief.* Various issues. London: Unemployment Unit.

Unemployment Unit. *Unemployment Bulletin.* Various issues. London: Unemployment Unit.

United States
Archival Sources
1. National Archives and Record Administration
   Record Group 25: Office of War Mobilization and Reconversion
   Record Group 47: Records of the Social Security Administration
   Record Group 146: Records of the U.S. Civil Service Commission
   Record Group 174: General Records of the Department of Labor,
       Records of the Secretary of Labor Arthur Goldberg
       Records of the Office of the Deputy Under Secretary, Millard Cass
       Papers of Lewis B. Schellenbach
       Office of the Secretary, 1933–37
       Subject Files of James P. Mitchell
   Record Group 183: Bureau of Employment Security; includes U.S.
       Employment Service (1907–49), Social Security Board (1936–42)
   Record Group 211: War Manpower Commission; includes Bureau of
       Training, Bureau of Manpower Utilization, Bureau of Placement, and
       the Women's Advisory Committee
   Record Group 228: Records of the Committee on Fair
       Employment Practices
   Record Group 244: Retraining and Reemployment Administration

2. Franklin D. Roosevelt Presidential Library
   Presidential Official File
   Papers of Harry Hopkins
   Papers of Frances Perkins
   Papers of Harold Smith
   Papers of John Wanat
3. Library of Congress
   Papers of the National Association for the Advancement of Colored People (NAACP).
4. George Meany Memorial Center, American Federation of Labor-Committee of Industrial Organization (AFL-CIO) Archives
   Legislative Reference Files
   Green Papers: Office of the President AFL, William Green (1909–1952):
       0003/0006/023, Unemployment Insurance, 1930–1934;
       0003/0007/0008, Wagner-Lewis Bill

Frances Perkins Oral History, Columbia University Oral History
    Collections, Part 3
5. Georgetown University Library
    Papers of Robert F. Wagner
6. John F. Kennedy Presidential Library
    Kermit Gordon Papers
    Papers of President Kennedy, President's Office Files;
    Departments and Agencies; Cabinet Meetings; Inter-Cabinet Briefing Book
7. Harry S. Truman Presidential Library
    Papers of Oscar Ewing
    Oral History of Robert C. Goodwin
    Papers of Robert C. Goodwin
    Papers of John Gibson
    Presidential Official File
    Papers of Gerhard Colm
    Papers of Graves B. Erskine
    Papers of Philleo Nash
    Oral History of Leon H. Keyserling
8. Dwight D. Eisenhower Presidential Library
    Office of Special Assistant to President for Personnel Management
    Papers of James P. Mitchell
    Presidential Official File
    Presidential Whitman File
9. U. S. Department of Labor Library, Washington, DC
    Oral History of the Unemployment Insurance project: interviews with
        Philip Booth, Edward L. Keenan and Ralph Altman
    Papers of Malcolm Lovell, Jr.
10. Lyndon B. Johnson Presidential Library
    Stanley Ruttenberg Oral History
    Department of Labor administrative history
11. Jimmy Carter Presidential Library
    White House Central File: Welfare and Labor
    Domestic Policy Council

Selected Published Primary Sources

Congressional Record. 1933. Proceedings and Debates of the 73d Cong., 1st
    sess., 77, pt. 5: 4467–69, 4801–2 (Senate), 4766–83 (House).
Committee on Education and Labor, House of Representatives. 88th Cong., 2d
    sess. Select Committee on Labor. December 1964. "The Role and Mission
    of the Federal-State Employment Service in the American Economy."
    Washington, DC: Government Printing Office.
Committee on Labor, House of Representatives. 73d Cong., 1st sess. Hearings
    on "H. R. 4559," 17 and 18 May 1933.
Public Papers of the Presidents of the United States: Herbert Hoover. 1976.
    Washington, DC: Government Printing Office.
Public Papers of the Presidents of the United States: Harry S. Truman. 1961.
    Washington, DC: Government Printing Office.
Public Papers of the President of the United States: Ronald Reagan. 1986.

Washington, DC: Government Printing Office.

Hudson Institute. 1987. *Workforce 2000.* Indianapolis, IN: Hudson Institute.

Subcommittee of Trade, Productivity and Economic Growth of the Joint Economic Committee "Workfare versus Welfare." 99th Cong., 2d sess., 23 April 1986.

National Governors' Association. February 1987. *Job-Oriented Welfare Reform.* Washington, DC: National Governors' Association.

National Governors' Association. 1987. *Making America Work: Bringing Down the Barriers.* Washington, DC: National Governors' Association.

Council of State Policy and Planning Agencies. 1988. *The Safety Net as Ladder.* By Robert Friedman. Washington, DC: Council of State Policy and Planning Agencies.

National League of Women Voters. 1932. *A Federal-State Employment Service.* Washington, DC: Committee on Women in Industry, National League of Women Voters.

National Coalition on Women, Work, and Welfare Reform. April 1987. *Changing Welfare: An Investment in Women and Children in Poverty.* Washington, DC: Wider Opportunities for Women.

U.S. Chamber of Commerce. 1985. *Business and Education: Partners for the Future.* Washington, DC: U.S. Chamber of Commerce.

National Council on Employment Policy. May 1985. *Policy Statement on the United States Employment Service.* Washington, DC: NCEP.

National Alliance of Business. 1992. *Real Jobs for Real People.* Washington, DC: National Alliance of Business.

U.S. General Accounting Office. 31 October 1989. *Testimony: Statement of William J. Gainer Director of Education and Employment Issues before the Subcommittee on Employment Opportunities House of Representatives.* Washington, DC: Government Printing Office.

Pedro, Peter G., ed. 1973. *Symposium on the Changing Mission of the United States Employment Services.* Washington, DC: U.S. Department of Labor, Employment, and Training Administration.

U.S. Employment Service. 1937. *Filling Nine Million Jobs.* Washington, DC: Government Printing Office.

U.S. Employment Service. September 1990. *Briefing Paper on the Public Employment Service.* Washington, DC: USES.

The Lawyers' Committee for Civil Rights under the Law and the National Urban Coalition. June 1971. *Falling Down on the Job: The United States Employment Service and the Disadvantaged.* Washington, DC: Lawyers' Committee for Civil Rights under the Law and the National Urban Coalition.

Cohen, Malcolm S., and David W. Stevens. 1989. *The Role of the Employment Service.* Ann Arbor, MI: Institute of Labor and Industrial Relations, University of Michigan.

Comptroller General of the United States. May 1963. *Uneconomical Practices in the Administration of Employment Service and Unemployment Compensation Programs.* Report to the Congress. Washington, DC: Comptroller General of the United States.

Comptroller General of the United States. 22 February 1977. *The Employment*

Service—Problems and Opportunities for Improvement. Report to the Congress. Washington, DC: Comptroller General of the United States.

U.S. Employment Service Task Force. 1965. *A Report to the Secretary of Labor from the Employment Service Task Force.* Washington, DC: Department of Labor.

Office of Technology Assessment, Congress of the United States. 1990. *Worker Training: Competing in the New International Economy.* Washington, DC: Government Printing Office.

American Federationist. Various issues.

American Labor Legislation Review. Various issues.

Employment Service News. Various issues.

Perspective. Various issues.

The Rockefeller Foundation. November 1987. *From Welfare to Work: Minority Female Single Parent Program.* New York: Rockefeller Foundation.

Ellwood, David T., and Mary Jo Bane. 1984. "The Impact of AFDC on Family Structure and Living Arrangements." Grant 92A-82, Department of Health and Human Services, Washington, DC.

Gueron, Judith M. 1987. *Reforming Welfare With Work.* Ford Foundation Project on Social Welfare and the American Future, Occasional Paper 2. New York: Ford Foundation.

Nightingale, Demetra Smith, and Lynn C. Burbridge. 1987. *The Status of State Work-Welfare Programs in 1986: Implications for Welfare Reform.* Washington, DC: The Urban Institute Research Paper.

Theses

Finegold, David. 1992. "The Low-Skill Equilibrium: An Institutional Analysis of Britain's Education and Training Failure." D.Phil. diss., Oxford University.

Robertson, David Brian. 1981. "Politics and Labor Markets." Ph.D. diss., Indiana University.

Worcester, Kenton W. 1990. "From Tripartitism to the Enterprise Culture: The Trade Unions, Training Policy, and the Thatcher Government, 1979–1988." Ph.D. diss., Columbia University.

Other Published Primary Sources

International Labour Organization. 1952. *National Employment Services: Great Britain.* Geneva: ILO.

International Labour Organization. 1955. *National Employment Services: United States.* Geneva: ILO.

Organization for Economic Cooperation and Development. 1965. *The Public Employment Services and Management.* Geneva: OECD.

Organization for Economic Cooperation and Development. 1966. *The Public Employment Services and Management.* Paris: OECD.

Organization for Economic Cooperation and Development. 1970. *Manpower Policy in the United Kingdom.* Paris: OECD.

Organization for Economic Cooperation and Development. 1984. *The Public Employment Service in a Changing Market.* Paris: OECD.

Secondary Sources

Abramovitz, M., and F. F. Piven. 1993. "Scapegoating Women on Welfare," *New York Times*, 2 September: A23.

Adams, L. P. 1969. *The Public Employment Service in Transition, 1933–1968.* Ithaca, NY: Cornell University Press.

Ainley, P., and M. Corney. 1990. *Training for the Future.* Oxford: Cassell.

Albert, M. 1993. *Capitalism Against Capitalism.* London: Whurr Publishers.

Altmeyer, A. J. 1966. *The Formative Years of Social Security.* Madison, WI: University of Wisconsin Press.

Amenta, E., and Y. Zylan. 1991. "It Happened Here: Political Opportunity, the New Institutionalism and the Townsend Movement." *American Sociological Review* 56: 250–65.

Andersen, K. 1979. *The Creation of a Democratic Majority, 1928–1936.* Chicago: University of Chicago Press.

Anderson, D., ed. 1980. *The Ignorance of Social Intervention.* London: Croom Helm.

Anderson, D., D. Marsland, and J. Lait. 1981. *Breaking the Spell of the Welfare State.* London: Social Affairs Unit.

Ashton, D., and G. Lowe, eds. 1991. *Making Their Way.* Milton Keynes: Open University Press.

Atkinson, A. B. 1990. "Income Maintenance for the Unemployed in Britain and the Response to High Unemployment" *Ethics* 100: 569–85.

Atkinson, R., L. C. Odencrantz, and B. Deming. 1940. *Public Employment Service in the United States.* Chicago: Committee on Public Administration of the Social Science Research Council.

Bagguley, P. 1992. "Protest, Acquiescence and the Unemployed: A Comparative Analysis of the 1930s and 1980s." *British Journal of Sociology* 43: 443–61

Bailey, S. K. 1950. *Congress Makes a Law.* New York: Vintage Books.

Bailyn, B. 1967. *The Ideological Origins of the American Revolution.* Cambridge, MA: Harvard University Press.

Baker, P. 1984. "The Domestication of Politics: Women and American Political Society, 1780–1920." *American Historical Review* 89: 620–47.

Baldwin, P. 1990. *The Politics of Social Solidarity.* Cambridge and New York: Cambridge University Press.

Balogh, B. 1988. "Securing Support: The Emergence of the Social Security Board as a Political Actor, 1935–1939." In D. T. Critchlow and E. W. Hawley, eds., *Federal Social Policy*, pp. 55–78. University Park, PA: Pennsylvania State University Press.

Bane, M. J. 1988. "Politics and Policies of the Feminization of Poverty." In M. Weir, A. Orloff, and T. Skocpol, eds., *The Politics of Social Policy in the United States*, pp. 381–96. Princeton, NJ: Princeton University Press.

Barber, W. J. 1985. *From New Era to New Deal.* Cambridge and New York: Cambridge University Press.

Barry, N. 1990. *Welfare.* Milton Keynes: Open University Press.

Baum, E. 1991. "When the Witch Doctors Agree: The Family Support Act and Social Science Research." *Journal of Policy Analysis and Management* 10: 619–30.

Bawden, D. L., and J. L. Palmer. 1984. "Social Policy: Challenging the Welfare State." In J. L. Palmer and I. V. Sawhill, eds., *The Reagan Record*, pp. 177–215. Cambridge, MA: Ballinger Publishing Co.

Beenstein, M., and Associates. 1987. *Work, Welfare and Taxation*. London: Allen and Unwin.

Bellamy, R. 1992. *Liberalism and Modern Society*. Oxford: Polity.

Bentley, M. 1977. *The Liberal Mind, 1914–29*. Cambridge: Cambridge University Press.

———. 1987. *The Climax of Liberal Politics*. London and New York: Edward Arnold.

Berkowitz, E. 1984. "Changing the Meaning of Welfare Reform." In J. C. Weicher, ed., *Maintaining the Safety Net*, pp. 23–42. Washington, DC: American Enterprise Institute.

Berkowitz, E., and K. McQuaid. 1980. *Creating the Welfare State*. New York: Praeger.

Berryman, S. 1992. "Apprenticeship as a Paradigm of Learning." In William T. Grant Foundation, *Youth Apprenticeship in America*. Washington, DC: William T. Grant Foundation.

Besharov, D. A., and A. J. Quin. 1987. "Not All Female-Headed Families Are Created Equal." *The Public Interest*, no 89: 48–56.

Beveridge, W. H. 1914. "Seventeenth-century Labour Exchange." *The Economic Journal* 24: 371–76.

———. 1930. *Unemployment*. London and New York: Longmans, Green and Co.

———. 1960. *Full Employment in a Free Society*, 2d ed. London: Allen and Unwin, 1960; originally published in 1944.

Blank, S. 1973. *Industry and Government in Britain: The Federation of British Industry, 1945–65*. Farnborough: Saxon House Co.; and Lexington, MA: D. C. Heath and Co.

Blankenburg, E. 1978. "Comparing the Incomparable—A Study of Employment Agencies in Five Countries." In G. W. England, ed., *Organizational Functioning in a Cross-Cultural Perspective*. Kent, OH: Kent State University.

Block, F., and J., Noakes. 1988. "The Politics of New-Style Workfare." *Socialist Review* 18: 31–58.

Block, F., R. A. Cloward, B. Ehrenreich, and F. F. Piven. 1987. *The Mean Season*. New York: Pantheon Books.

Bowles, N. P. Forthcoming. "'Playing the Old Record': The Presidency and the Politics of Fiscal Disorder." In R. Maidment and J. Thurber, eds., *The Politics of Relative Decline*. Oxford: Polity Press.

Brackman, H., et al. 1988. "Wedded to the Welfare State." In J. Jenson, et al., eds., *Feminization of the Labour Force*, pp. 214–30. Oxford: Polity Press.

Brady, D. W. 1988. *Critical Elections and Congressional Policy Making*. Stanford, CA: Stanford University Press.

Brehm, C. T., and T. R. Saving. 1964. "The Demand for General Assistance Payments." *American Economic Review* 54: 1002–18.

Brenner, J., and M. Ramas. 1984. "Rethinking Women's Oppression." *New Left Review*, no. 144: 33–71.

Bridges, A. 1986. "Becoming American: The Working Classes in the United

States before the Civil War." In I. Katznelson and A. Zolberg, eds., *Working-Class Formation,* pp. 157–96. Princeton, NJ: Princeton University Press.

Brock, W. R. 1984. *Investigation and Responsibility: Public Responsibility in the United States, 1865–1900.* Cambridge and New York: Cambridge University Press.

———. 1988. *Welfare, Democracy and the New Deal.* Cambridge and New York: Cambridge University Press.

Burstein, P. 1985. *Discrimination, Jobs, and Politics: The Struggle for Equal Employment Opportunity in the United States since the New Deal.* Chicago: University of Chicago Press.

Chegwidden, T. S., and G. Myrddin-Evans. 1934. *The Employment Exchange System in Great Britain.* London: Macmillan.

Collins, R. M. 1981. *The Business Response to Keynes, 1929–1964.* New York: Columbia University Press.

Constantine, S. 1992. *Lloyd George.* London and New York: Routledge.

Corina, J. 1975. "Planning and the British Labour Market: Incomes and Industrial Training." In Jack Hayward and Michael Watson, eds., *Planning, Politics and Public Policy,* pp. 177–201. Cambridge and New York: Cambridge University Press.

Craig, F. W. S. 1975. *British General Election Manifestoes, 1900–1974.* London: Macmillan.

Crewe, I. 1991. "Labor Force Change, Working Class Decline and the Labor Vote: Social and Electoral Trends in Postwar Britain." In F. F. Piven, ed., *Labor Parties in Postindustrial Societies,* pp. 20–46. Oxford: Polity.

Crosland, C. A. R. 1956. *The Future of Socialism.* London: Cape.

Daniel, W. W. 1990. *The Unemployed Flow.* London: Policy Studies Institute.

Danzinger, S., and D. Weinberg, eds. 1986. *Fighting Poverty: What Works and What Doesn't.* Cambridge, MA: Harvard University Press.

Danzinger, S., R. Haveman, and R. Plotnick. 1981. "How Income Transfers Affect Work, Savings, and the Income Distribution." *Journal of Economic Literature* 19: 975–1028.

Davison, R. C. 1938. *British Unemployment Policy.* London: Longmans, Green and Co.

Deacon, A. 1976. *In Search of the Scrounger.* London: Macmillan.

Deakin, S., and F. Wilkinson. 1991. "Labour Law, Social Security, and Economic Inequality." *Cambridge Journal of Economics* 15: 125–48.

de Schweinitz, K. 1943. *England's Road to Social Security.* Philadelphia: University of Pennsylvania Press.

de Swaan, A. 1988. *In Care of the State.* Oxford: Polity Press.

Dixon, J., and R. P. Scheurell, eds. 1989. *Social Welfare in Developed Market Economies.* London and New York: Routledge.

Domhoff, G. William. 1992. "The Death of State Autonomy Theory: A Review of Skocpol's *Protecting Soldiers and Mothers.*" *Critical Sociology* 19: 103–16.

Douglas, P., and A. Director. 1931. *The Problem of Unemployment.* New York: Macmillan.

Edsall, T. B., and M. D. Edsall. 1992. *Chain Reaction.* New York: W. W. Norton.

Elbaum, B. 1989. "Why Apprenticeship Persisted in Britain but Not in the United States." *Journal of Economic History* 49: 337–49.

Elbaum, B. 1991. "The Persistence of the Apprenticeship in Britain and its Decline in the United States." In H. Gospell, ed., *Industrial Training and Technological Innovation.* London: Routledge.

Ellwood, D. T. 1988. *Poor Support.* New York: Basic Books.

Erickson, C. 1957. *American Industry and the European Immigrant, 1860–1884.* Cambridge, MA: Harvard University Press.

Esping-Andersen, G. 1985. *Politics against Markets.* Princeton, NJ: Princeton University Press.

———. 1990. *The Three Worlds of Welfare Capitalism.* Oxford: Polity Press.

Evans, P., D. Rueschmeyer, and T. Skocpol, eds. 1984. *Bringing the State Back In.* Cambridge and New York: Cambridge University Press.

Fenno, R. 1989. *The Making of a Senator: J. Dan Quayle.* Washington, DC: Congressional Quarterly Press.

Finegold, D. 1991. "Institutional Incentives and Skill Creation: Preconditions for a High-Skill Equilibrium." In Paul Ryan, ed., *International Comparisons of Vocational Education and Training for Intermediate Skills,* pp. 93–116. London: Falmer Press.

———. 1993. "Making Apprenticeships Work." *Rand Issue Paper,* no 1: 1–6

Finegold, D., and D. Soskice. 1988. "The Failure of Training in Britain: Analysis and Prescription." *Oxford Review of Economic Policy* 4: 21–51.

Finn, D. 1987. *Training without jobs.* London: Macmillan.

Foner, P. S. 1981. *Organized Labor and the Black Worker, 1619–1981.* New York: International Publishers.

Forman, C. 1978. *Industrial Town: Self-Portrait of St Helens in the 1920s.* London: Cameron and Taylor in association with David Charles.

Fraser, S. 1992. *Labor Will Rule: Sidney Hillman.* New York: Basic Books.

Freeden, M. 1978. *The New Liberalism.* Oxford: Oxford University Press.

———. 1986. *Liberalism Divided: A study in British Political Thought, 1914–39.* Oxford: Oxford University Press.

Galambos, L., ed. 1987. *The New American State.* Baltimore, MD: Johns Hopkins University Press.

Galenson, W. 1960. *The CIO Challenge to the AFL.* Cambridge, MA: Harvard University Press.

Garraty, J. A. 1978. *Unemployment in History.* New York: Harper & Row.

Garrett, G. 1993. "The Politics of Structural Change: Swedish Social Democracy and Thatcherism in Comparative Perspective." *Comparative Political Studies* 25: 521–47.

Gilder, G. 1981. *Wealth and Poverty.* New York: Basic Books.

Gilder, G., et al. 1987. "Welfare's `New Consensus.'" *The Public Interest,* no. 89: 20–35.

Ginsburg, H. 1983. *Full Employment and Public Policy: The United States and Sweden.* Lexington, MA: Lexington Books.

Glennerster, H., and J. Midgley, eds. 1991. *The Radical Right and the Welfare*

State. Hemel Hempstead: Harvester Wheatsheaf.

Goldfield, M. 1987. *The Decline of Organized Labor in the United States.* Chicago: University of Chicago Press.

Goodin, R. E. 1985. "Self-Reliance versus the Welfare State." *Journal of Social Policy* 14: 25–47.

Gordon, L. 1992. "Social Insurance and Public Assistance: The Influence of Gender in Welfare Thought in the United States, 1890–1935." *American Historical Review* 97: 19–54.

Gotbaum, B. 1993. "When Workfare Is Just Make-Work." *New York Times,* 4 September.

Grant, W., and D. Marsh. 1977. *The CBI.* London: Hodder and Stoughton.

Gray, J. 1991. *Liberalism.* London: Routledge.

Grossman, J. 1973. *The Department of Labor.* New York: Praeger.

Gueron, J. M., and E. Pauly. 1991. *From Welfare to Work.* New York: Russell Sage Foundation.

Haber, W., and D. H. Kruger. 1964. *The Role of the United States Employment Services in a Changing Economy.* Kalamazoo, MI: W. E. Upjohn Institute for Employment Research.

Hall, P. A.. 1986. *Governing the Economy.* New York: Oxford University Press.

Hall, P. A., ed. 1989. *The Political Power of Economic Ideas.* Princeton, NJ: Princeton University Press.

Harris, J. 1972. *Unemployment and Politics.* Oxford: Clarendon Press.

―――. 1977. *William Beveridge.* Oxford: Clarendon Press.

Harris, R., and A. Seldon. 1987. *Welfare without the State.* London: IEA.

Hartz, L. 1955. *The Liberal Tradition in America.* New York: Harcourt, Brace and World.

Haskins, R. 1991. "Congress Writes Law: Research and Welfare Reform." *Journal of Policy Analysis and Management* 10: 613–18.

Hattam, V. C. 1993. *Labor Visions and State Power.* Princeton, NJ: Princeton University Press.

Haveman, R. H. 1987. *Poverty Policy and Poverty Research.* Madison, WI: University of Wisconsin Press.

Hayek, F. 1960. *The Constitution of Liberty.* London: Routledge, Kegan and Paul.

Heclo, H. 1974. *Modern Social Policies in Britain and Sweden.* New Haven, CT: Yale University Press.

―――. 1986. "General Welfare and Two American Political Traditions." *Political Science Quarterly* 101: 179–96.

Heclo, H., and H. Madsen. 1987. *Policy and Politics in Sweden.* Philadelphia, PA: Temple University Press.

Hill, M. 1982. "Unemployment and Government Manpower Policy." In B. Showler and A. Sinfield, eds., *The Workless State—Studies in Unemployment,* pp. 89–121. Oxford: Martin Robertson.

―――. 1990. *Social Security Policy in Britain.* Aldershot: Edward Elgar.

Himmelfarb, G. 1984. *The Idea of Poverty.* London: Faber.

Hoover, K., and R. Plant. 1989. *Conservative Capitalism.* London: Routledge.

Horowitz, R. L. 1978. *Political Ideologies of Organized Law.* New Brunswick, NJ: Transaction Books.

Jackman, R., C. Pissarides, and S. Savouri. 1990. "Labour Market Policies and Unemployment in the OECD." *Economic Policy* 5: 449–90.

Janoski, T. 1990. *The Political Economy of Unemployment.* Berkeley: University of California Press.

Jencks, C. 1992. *Rethinking Social Policy.* Cambridge, MA: Harvard University Press.

Jencks, C., and P. E. Peterson, eds. 1991. *The Urban Underclass.* Washington, DC: Brookings Institution.

Jenkins, R. 1954. *Mr Balfour's Poodle.* London: Heinemann.

Jephcott, A. P. 1953. *Rising Twenty.* London: Macmillan.

Jones, B. L. 1972. "The Role of Keynesians in Wartime Policy and Postwar Planning, 1940–46." *American Economic Review* 62: 125–33.

Joseph, A. 1993. "The Solidarity of Skilled Workers: Creating a Logic of Particularism." *Journal of Historical Sociology* 6: 288–310.

Kalecki, M. 1943. "Political Aspects of Full Employment." *The Political Quarterly* 14: 322–30.

Katz, M. 1986. *In the Shadow of the Poorhouse.* New York: Basic Books.

———, ed. 1993. *The Underclass Debate.* Princeton, NJ: Princeton University Press.

Katznelson, I. 1981. *City Trenches.* New York: Pantheon Books.

———. 1985. "Working-Class Formation and the State: Nineteenth-Century England in American Perspective." In P. Evans et al., eds., *Bringing the State Back In,* pp. 257–84. Cambridge and New York: Cambridge University Press.

Katznelson, I., and B. Pietrykowski. 1991. "Rebuilding the American State: Evidence from the 1940s." *Studies in American Political Development* 5: 301–39.

Kaus, M. 1986. "The Work Ethic State." *The New Republic,* 7 July.

Keeler, J. T. S. 1993. "Opening the Window for Reforms." *Comparative Political Studies* 25: 433–86.

Kellogg, R. 1933. *The United States Employment Service.* Chicago: University of Chicago Press.

King, D. S. 1987a. "The State and the Social Structures of Welfare." *Theory and Society* 16: 841–68.

———. 1987b. *The New Right: Politics, Markets and Citizenship.* London: Macmillan; and Chicago: Dorsey.

———. 1991. "Citizenship as Obligation in the United States: Title II of the Family Support Act of 1988." In U. Vogel and M. Moran, eds., *The Frontiers of Citizenship,* pp. 1–31. London: Macmillan.

———. 1992. "The Establishment of Work-Welfare Programs in the United States and Britain: Politics, Ideas, and Institutions." In S. Steinmo, K. Thelen, and F. Longstreth, eds., *Structuring Politics: Historical Institutionalism in Comparative Analysis,* pp. 217–50. Cambridge and New York: Cambridge University Press.

———. 1993a. "The Conservatives and Training Policy: From a Tripartite to a

Neoliberal Regime." *Political Studies* 41: 214–35.

―――-. 1993b. "'The Longest Road to Equality': The Politics of Institutional Desegregation under Truman." *Journal of Historical Sociology* 6: 119–63.

―――. 1993c. "Government Beyond Whitehall: Local Government and Urban Politics." In P. Dunleavy, G. Peele, A. Gamble, and I. Holliday, eds., *Developments in British Politics 4*, pp. 196–218. London: Macmillan.

―――. 1993d. "Sectionalism and Welfare Policy in the United States: The Failure of President Carter's Initiatives." Mimeo. St. John's College, Oxford.

King, D. S., and B. Rothstein. 1993. "Institutional Choices and Labour Market Policy: A British-Swedish Comparison." *Comparative Political Studies* 26: 147–77.

―――. 1994. "Government Legitimacy and the Labour Market: A Comparative Analysis of Employment Exchanges." *Public Administration* 72: 289–306.

King, D. S., and J. Waldron. 1988. "Citizenship, Social Citizenship, and the Defence of Welfare Provision." *British Journal of Political Science* 18: 415–43.

King, D. S., and H. Ward. 1992. "Working for Benefits: Rational Choice and the Rise of Work-Welfare Programmes." *Political Studies* 40: 479–97.

King, D. S., and M. Wickham-Jones. 1990. "Social Democracy and Rational Workers." *British Journal of Political Science* 20: 387–413.

Korpi, W. 1983. *The Democratic Class Struggle*. London: Routledge, Kegan and Paul.

―――. 1989. "Power, Politics, and State Autonomy in the Development of Social Citizenship: Social Rights during Sickness in Eighteen OECD Countries since 1930." *American Sociological Review* 54: 309–28.

Lane, C. 1989. *Management and Labour in Europe*. London: Edward Elgar.

Lee, D. 1989. "The Transformation of Training and the Transformation of Work in Britain." In S. Wood, ed., *The Transformation of Work?*, pp. 156–70. London: Allen and Unwin.

Lee, D., D. Marsden, P. Rickman, and J. Duncombe. 1990. *Scheming for Youth*. Milton Keynes: Open University Press.

Lemann, N. 1991. *The Promised Land*. New York: Knopf.

Lescohier, D. 1919. *The Labor Market*. New York: Macmillan.

Leuchtenburg, W. E. 1963. *Franklin D. Roosevelt and the New Deal, 1932–1940*. New York: Harper and Row.

Levine, L. 1969. *The Public Employment Service in Social and Economic Policy*. Paris: OECD.

Levitan, S. A., and I. Shapiro. 1987. *Working but Poor*. Baltimore, MD: Johns Hopkins University Press.

Lewis, J. 1992. "Gender and the Development of Welfare Regimes." *Journal of European Social Policy* 3: 159–73.

Lister, R. 1990. "Women, Economic Dependency, and Citizenship." *Journal of Social Policy* 19: 445–67.

―――. 1993. "Tracing the Contours of Women's Citizenship." *Policy and Politics* 21: 3–16.

Longstreth, F. H. 1988. "From Corporatism to Dualism? Thatcherism and the

Climacteric of British Trade Unions in the 1980s." *Political Studies* 36: 413–32.

Louchheim, K., ed. 1983. *The Making of the New Deal: The Insiders Speak.* Cambridge, MA: Harvard University Press.

Lowe, R. 1986. *Adjusting to Democracy.* Oxford: Clarendon Press.

McCoy, D. R., and R. T. Ruetten. 1973. *Quest and Response.* Lawrence, KS: University Press of Kansas.

MacInnes, J. 1987. *Thatcherism at Work.* Milton Keynes: Open University Press.

McKibbin, R. 1974. *The Evolution of the Labour Party, 1910–1924.* Oxford: Clarendon Press.

———. 1990. "The Social Psychology of Unemployment in Inter-war Britain." In R. McKibbin, *The Ideologies of Class,* pp. 228–58. Oxford: Clarendon Press.

Mangum, G. 1968. *MDTA: Foundation of Federal Manpower Policy.* Baltimore, MD: Johns Hopkins University Press.

Mangum, G., and J. Walsh. 1973. *A Decade of Manpower Development and Training.* Salt Lake City, UT: Olympus.

March, J., and J. Olsen. 1984. "The New Institutionalism: Organizational Factors in Political Life." *American Political Science Review* 78: 734–49.

Marks, G. 1989. "Variations in Union Political Activity in the United States, Britain, and Germany from the Nineteenth Century." *Comparative Politics* 22: 81–104.

Marmor, T. R., J. L. Mashaw, and P. Harvey. 1990. *America's Misunderstood Welfare State.* New York: Basic Books.

Marshall, F. R., and V. Briggs. 1967. *The Negro and Apprenticeships.* Baltimore, MD: Johns Hopkins University Press.

Marshall, T. H. 1964. *Class, Citizenship and Social Development.* New York: Doubleday.

Martin, A. 1973. *The Politics of Economic Policy in the United States.* London and Beverly Hills: Sage.

Mead, L. M. 1985. *Beyond Entitlement.* New York: Free Press.

———. 1991. "The New Politics of the New Poverty." *The Public Interest* 103: 3–20.

———. 1992. *The New Politics of Poverty.* New York: Basic Books.

Meehan, E. M. 1985. *Women's Rights at Work.* London: Macmillan Publishers.

Milgrom, P., and J. Roberts. 1992. *Economics, Organization, and Management.* Englewood Cliffs, NJ: Prentice-Hall.

Miller, D. 1989. *Market, State and Community.* Oxford: Clarendon Press.

Minford, P., and P. Ashton. 1991. "The Poverty Trap and the Laffer Curve—What Can the GHS Tell Us?" *Oxford Economic Papers* 43: 245–79.

Minkin, L. 1991. *The Contentious Alliance: Trade Unions and the Labour Party.* Edinburgh: Edinburgh University Press.

Moffitt, R. 1992. "Incentive Effects of the U.S. Welfare System: A Review." *Journal of Economic Literature* 30: 1–16.

Moon, J. D. 1988. "The Moral Basis of the Democratic Welfare State." In A. Gutmann, ed., *Democracy and the Welfare State,* pp. 20–44. Princeton, NJ: Princeton University Press.

Morley, F. 1981. *Freedom and Federalism.* Indianapolis, IN: Liberty Press; originally published, 1959.

Moynihan, D. P. 1973. *The Politics of a Guaranteed Income: The Nixon Administration and the Family Assistance Plan.* New York: Random House.

Mucciaroni, G. 1990. *The Political Failure of Employment Policy, 1945–1982.* Pittsburgh, PA: University of Pittsburgh Press.

Mukherjee, S. 1972. *Making Labour Markets Work.* London: P.E.P.

Murray, C. 1984. *Losing Ground.* New York: Basic Books.

———. 1985. "The Great Society: An Exchange." *The New Republic,* 8 April.

———. 1987. "In Search of the Working Poor." *The Public Interest,* no. 89: 3–19.

Murray, C., et al. 1990. *The Emerging British Underclass.* London: IEA.

Musgrave, R. S. 1991. *Workfare: A Marginal Employment Subsidy for Private and Public Sectors.* Cherster-le-Street, Durham: The City Printing Works.

Nathan, R. P., F. Doolittle, and Associates. 1987. *Reagan and the States.* Princeton, NJ: Princeton University Press.

Nathan, R. P. 1993. *Turning Promises Into Performance: The Management Challenge of Implementing Workfare.* Washington, DC: Twentieth Century Fund.

Nichols, T. 1986. *The British Worker Question.* London: Routledge, Kegan and Paul.

Nordlinger, E. A. 1981. *On the Autonomy of the Democratic State.* Cambridge, MA: Harvard University Press.

Northrup, H., and R. L. Rowen, eds. 1965. *The Negro and Employment Opportunity: Problems and Practices.* Ann Arbor, MI: Bureau of Industrial Relations.

Nourse, E. G. 1947. "The Employment Act of 1946 and a System of National Bookkeeping." *American Economic Review Papers and Proceedings* 37: 21–30.

Novak, M., et al. 1987. *The New Consensus on Family and Welfare.* Washington, DC: American Enterprise Institute for Public Policy Research.

Oliver, W. H. 1958. "The Labour Exchange Phase of the Co-operative Movement." *Oxford Economic Papers* 10: 355–76.

Ollson, S. 1989. "Sweden." In J. Dixon and R. Scheurel, eds., *Social Welfare in Developed Market Economies.* London: Routledge.

Olson, M. 1965. *The Logic of Collective Action.* Cambridge, MA: Harvard University Press.

Orloff, A. S. 1993a. *The Politics of Pensions.* Madison, WI: University of Wisconsin Press.

———. 1993b. "Gender and the Social Rights of Citizenship: The Comparative Analysis of Gender Relations and Welfare States." *American Sociological Review* 58: 303–28.

Orloff, A. S., and T. Skocpol. 1984. "Why Not Equal Protection? Explaining the Politics of Public Social Spending in Britain, 1900–1911, and the United States, 1880s–1920." *American Sociological Review* 49: 726–50.

Page, B., and R. Y. Shapiro. 1992. *The Rational Public.* Chicago: University of Chicago Press.

Parker, H. 1982. *The Moral Hazards of Social Benefits.* London: Institute of Economic Affairs.

Pateman, C. 1988. "The Patriarchal Welfare State." In A. Gutmann, ed., *Democracy and the Welfare State,* pp. 231–60. Princeton, NJ: Princeton University Press.

Patterson, J. T. 1981. *America's Struggle Against Poverty, 1900–1980.* Cambridge, MA: Harvard University Press.

Peele, G. 1984. *Revival and Reaction.* Oxford: Clarendon Press.

Perry, P. J. C. 1976. *The Evolution of British Manpower Policy.* London: Eyre and Spottiswoode.

Peterson, P. E., and M. C. Rom. 1990. *Welfare Magnets.* Washington, DC: Brookings.

Phelan, C. 1989. *William Green.* Albany, NY: State University of New York Press.

Pierson, C. 1991. *Beyond the Welfare State?* Oxford: Polity.

Piore, M., and C. Sabel. 1984. *The Second Industrial Divide.* New York: Basic Books.

Piven, F. F. 1993. "Review of T. Skocpol *Protecting Soldiers and Mothers.*" *American Political Science Review* 87: 790–91.

Piven, F. F., and R. Cloward. 1971. *Regulating the Poor: The Functions of Public Welfare.* New York: Random House.

———. 1979. *Poor People's Movements: Why They Succeed, How They Fail.* New York: Vintage.

Plant, R., and N. Barry. 1990. *Citizenship and Rights in Thatcher's Britain: Two Views.* London: Institute of Economic Affairs.

Polanyi, K. 1944. *The Great Transformation.* Boston: Beacon Books.

Polenberg, R. 1966. *Reorganizing Roosevelt's Government: The Controversy over Executive Reorganization, 1936–1939.* Cambridge, MA: Harvard University Press.

Pollard, S. 1982. *The Wasting of the British Economy.* London: Croom Helm.

———. 1983. *The Development of the British Economy, 1914–1980,* 3d ed. London: Edward Arnold.

Pontusson, J. 1988. *Swedish Social Democracy and British Labour.* Ithaca, NY: Cornell Studies in International Affairs Western Societies Program.

———. 1992. *The Limits of Social Democracy.* Ithaca, NY: Cornell University Press.

Przeworski, A. 1985. *Capitalism and Social Democracy.* Cambridge and New York: Cambridge University Press.

Quadagno, J. 1988. "From Old-Age Assistance to Supplemental Security Income: The Political Economy of Relief in the South, 1935–1972." In M. Weir et al., eds., *The Politics of Social Policy in the United States,* pp. 235–64. Princeton, NJ: Princeton University Press.

———. 1990. "Race, Class, and Gender in the U.S. Welfare State: Nixon's Failed Family Assistance Plan." *American Sociological Review* 50: 11–28.

Ragin, C. 1987. *The Comparative Method.* Berkeley: University of California Press.

Redford, E. S., and M. Blissett. 1981. *Organizing the Executive Branch: The Johnson Presidency.* Chicago: University of Chicago Press.

Robertson, D. B. 1988. "Policy Entrepreneurs and Policy Divergence: J. R. Commons and W. H. Beveridge." *Polity* 20: 504–31.

———. 1989. "The Bias of American Federalism: The Limits of Welfare-State Development in the Progressive Era." *Journal of Policy History* 1: 261–91.

Roche, M. 1992. *Rethinking Citizenship.* Oxford: Polity.

Roediger, D. 1991. *The Wages of Whiteness.* London: Verso.

Rothstein, B. 1990. "Marxism, Institutional Analysis, and Working-Class Power." *Politics and Society* 18: 317–45.

Rueschmeyer, D., E. H. Stephens, and J. D. Stephens. 1992. *Capitalist Development and Democracy.* Oxford: Polity; and Chicago: University of Chicago Press.

Ruggie, M. 1984. *The State and Working Women.* Princeton, NJ: Princeton University Press

Ruttenberg, S. H., and J. Gutchess. 1970. *The Federal-State Employment Service: A Critique.* Baltimore, MD: Johns Hopkins University Press.

Sapiro, V. 1986. "The Gender Basis of American Social Policy." *Political Science Quarterly* 101: 221–38.

Sautter, U. 1991. *Three Cheers for the Unemployed.* Cambridge and New York: Cambridge University Press.

Sawhill, I. V. 1988. "Poverty and the Underclass." In I. Sawhill, ed., *Challenge to Leadership,* pp. 215–52. Washington, DC: Urban Institute.

Schattschneider, E. E. 1960. *The Semi-sovereign People.* New York: Holt, Rinehart and Winston.

Schlozman, K. L., and S. Verba. 1979. *Injury to Insult: Unemployment, Class, and Political Responses.* Cambridge, MA: Harvard University Press.

Schorr, A. L. 1986. *Common Decency.* New Haven, CT: Yale University Press.

Schwartz, J. E. 1988. *America's Hidden Success.* New York: W. W. Norton.

Segalman, R., and D. Marsland. 1989. *Cradle to Grave.* London: Macmillan.

Seldon, A. 1981. *Whither the Welfare State.* London: Institute of Economic Affairs.

Seymour, J. B. 1928. *The British Employment Exchange.* London: P. S. King and Sons.

Sheldrake, J., and S. Vickerstaff. 1987. *The History of Industrial Training in Britain.* Aldershot: Avebury.

Shonfield, A. 1965. *Modern Capitalism.* Oxford: Oxford University Press.

Showler, B. 1973. *Onto a Comprehensive Employment Service.* London: Fabian Research Series 309.

———. 1976. *The Public Employment Service.* London: Longman.

Sigelman, L., and S. Welch. 1991. *Black Americans' Views of Racial Equality.* Cambridge and New York: Cambridge University Press.

Skildelsky, R. 1992. *John Maynard Keynes: The Economist as Saviour, 1920–1937.* London: Macmillan.

Sklar, S. K. 1993. "The Historical Foundations of Women's Power in the Creation of the American Welfare State, 1890–1930." In S. Koven and S. Michel, eds., *Mothers of a New World: Maternalist Politics and the Origins of Welfare States,* pp. 33–54. London: Routledge.

Skocpol, T. 1985. "Bringing the State Back In." In P. B. Evans, D. Rueschemeyer, and T. Skocpol, eds., *Bringing the State Back In,* pp. 1–37.

Cambridge and New York: Cambridge University Press.

———. 1992. *Protecting Soldiers and Mothers.* Cambridge, MA: Harvard University Press.

Skocpol, T., and J. Ikenberry. 1983. "The Political Formation of the American Welfare State." *Comparative Social Research* 6: 87–148.

Skocpol, T., and G. Ritter. 1991. "Gender and the Origins of Modern Social Policy in Britain and the United States." *Studies in American Political Development* 5: 36–93.

Skowronek, S. 1982. *Building a New American State.* Cambridge and New York: Cambridge University Press.

Smith, R. M. 1993. "Beyond Tocqueville, Myrdal, and Hartz: The Multiple Traditions in America." *American Political Science Review* 87: 549–66.

Sorge, A., and M. Warner. 1980. "Manpower Training, Manufacturing Organization, and Workplace Relations in Great Britain and West Germany." *British Journal of Industrial Relations* 18: 318–33.

Spence, C. C. 1985. *The Salvation Army Farm Colonies.* Tucson: University of Arizona Press.

Stedman Jones, G. 1971. *Outcast London.* Oxford: Oxford University Press.

Stein, H. 1969. *The Fiscal Revolution in America.* Chicago: University of Chicago Press.

Steinmo, S. 1989. "Political Institutions and Tax Policy in the United States, Sweden, and Britain." *World Politics* 41: 500–535.

Steinmo, S., K. Thelen, and F. H. Longstreth, eds. 1992. *Structuring Politics: Historical Institutionalism in Comparative Analysis.* Cambridge and New York: Cambridge University Press.

Stephens, J. D. 1979. *The Transition from Capitalism to Socialism.* London: Macmillan.

Sundquist, J. L. 1983. *The Dynamics of the Party System.* Washington, DC: Brookings Institute.

Sullivan, S. 1984. "Employment versus Training in Federal Manpower Programs." In J. C. Weicher, ed., *Maintaining the Safety Net,* pp. 154–66. Washington, DC: American Enterprise Institute.

Swenson, P. 1991. "Bringing Capital Back In, or Social Democracy Reconsidered: Employer Power, Cross-Class Alliances, and Centralization of Industrial Relations in Denmark and Sweden." *World Politics* 43: 513–44.

Tawney, R. H. 1979. *The American Labor Movement and Other Essays.* Brighton: Harvester.

Taylor, R. 1993. *The Trade Union Question in British Politics, 1945–1992.* Oxford: Blackwell.

Thelen, K., and S. Steinmo. 1992. "Historical Institutionalism in Comparative Politics." In S. Steinmo, K. Thelen, and F. Longstreth, eds., *Structuring Politics,* pp. 1–32. Cambridge and New York: Cambridge University Press.

Therborn, G. 1986. *Why Some Peoples Are More Unemployed Than Others.* London: Verso.

Tilly, L. A., and J. W. Scott, eds. 1978. *Women, Work, and Family.* New York and London: Routledge.

Tomlinson, J. 1987. *Employment Policy: The Crucial Years, 1939–1955.* Oxford: Clarendon Press.

Tonge, J. 1993. "Training and Enterprise Councils: The Privatisation of Britain's Unemployment Problem?" *Capital and Class* 51: 9–16.

Ulman, L. 1968. "Collective Bargaining and Industrial Efficiency." In R. E. Caves and L. Krause, eds., *Britain's Economic Prospects.* London: Allen and Unwin.

Vickerstaff, S. 1985. "Industrial Training in Britain: The Dilemma of a Neo-corporatist Policy." In A. Cawson, ed., *Organized Interests and the State,* pp. 45–64. London and Beverly Hills: Sage.

Vincent, A., and R. Plant. 1984. *Philosophy, Politics and Citizenship.* Oxford: Blackwell.

Ware, A., ed. 1989. *Charities and Government.* Manchester: Manchester University Press.

Weir, M. 1988. "The Federal Government and Unemployment: The Frustration of Policy Innovations from the New Deal to the Great Society." In M. Weir, A. Orloff, and T. Skocpol, eds., *The Politics of Social Policy in the United States,* pp. 149–90. Princeton, NJ: Princeton University Press.

———. 1989. "Ideas and Politics: The Acceptance of Keynesianism in Britain and the United States." In P. A. Hall, ed., *The Political Power of Economic Ideas,* pp. 53–86. Princeton, NJ: Princeton University Press.

———. 1992. *Politics and Jobs.* Princeton, NJ: Princeton University Press.

Wikeley, N. 1989. "Unemployment Benefit, the State, and the Labour Market." *Journal of Law and Society* 16: 291–309.

Wilensky, H. 1976. *The New Corporatism, Centralization and the Welfare State.* London: Sage.

Wilson, J. Q. 1985. "The Rediscovery of Character: Private Virtue and Public Policy." *The Pubic Interest* 81: 3–16.

Wilson, W. J. 1987. *The Truly Disadvantaged.* Chicago: University of Chicago Press.

Wiseman, M. 1987. "How Workfare Really Works." *The Public Interest,* no. 89: 36–47.

———. 1988. "Workfare and Welfare Reform." In Harrell R. Rodgers, ed., *Beyond Welfare,* pp. 14–38. New York: M. E. Sharpe.

Witte, E. E. 1963. *The Development of the Social Security Act.* Madison, WI: University of Wisconsin Press.

Wolkinson, B. 1973. *Unions and the EEOC: A Study of Administrative Failure.* Lexington, MA: Lexington Books.

Wood, G. 1969. *The Creation of the American Republic, 1776–1787.* New York: Norton.

Zeitlin, J. 1980. "The Emergence of Shop Steward Organization and Job Control in the British Car Industry." *History Workshop Journal* 10: 119–37.

INDEX

Abramovitz, M., 292n. 168
Advisory Committee on Equal Opportunity in
    Apprenticeships and Training (U.S.). *See*
    U.S. Department of Labor
Aid to Families with Dependent Children
    (AFDC), 4, 13, 16, 140, 181, 253n. 86;
    Family Support Act, 175–76; Omnibus
    Budget Reconciliation Act, 186–87; Social
    Security Act of 1935, 181–82; Work
    Incentive Program (WIN), 140
Ainley, P., 264n. 46, 269n. 104
Albert, M., 231n. 64
Altman, R., 244n. 223
Altmeyer, Arthur, 54, 56, 57, 65, 73; merger
    of USES and unemployment insurance,
    56–58, 63, 65, 244n. 224, 245nn. 226, 237,
    248n. 264
American Federation of Labor–Congress of
    Industrial Organization (AFL–CIO), 3;
    and active labor market policy, 117, 136,
    208; AFL and CIO traditions, 8, 227n. 32;
    annual conferences, 243n. 196; differences
    of interests from black Americans,
    100–101; discrimination on apprentice-
    ships, 146; and discrimination against
    black Americans, 9–10, 146–47, 228n. 43,
    258n. 182, 259n. 183; and founding of
    labor exchanges, 8, 33, 49–52, 62, 242n.
    194; and funding of USES, 121; and
    Hoover veto, 243n. 209; membership,
    228n. 36; objection to postwar decentral-
    ization, 94, 256n. 153; opposition to
    Philadelphia Plan, 267n. 77, 295n. 20; and
    passage of Wagner-Peyser Act, 26, 49–52,
    242n. 192; voluntarism, 62, 248n. 261
American Federation of State, County, and
    Municipal Employees, 188, 286n. 97
American Liberty League, 53
American Public Welfare Association, 197;
    Family Support Act JOBS program, 291n.
    152

American Society for Training and
    Development, 295n. 21
American Vocational Association, 117; voca-
    tional training, 270n. 128
Andersen, K., 229n. 53
Anderson, Digby, 278n. 6
Apprenticeships, 10, 127. *See also* U.S.
    Bureau of Apprenticeship and Training;
    Training and manpower policy; National
    Association for the Advancement of
    Colored People
Ashby, Peter, 292n. 158
Ashton, P., 226n. 20
Askwith, G. R., 45
Asquith, Herbert, 12, 24
Association of British Chambers of
    Commerce, 210, 288n. 115; workforce
    skills, 210
Atkinson, A. B., 278n. 12, 281n. 44
Atkinson, R. C., 101, 237n. 82, 244n. 220
Attlee, Clement, 178

Bagguley, P., 225n. 12
Bailey, S. K., 262n. 15
Bailyn, B., 230n. 55
Baldwin, P., 224n. 4, 225n. 8
Balfour, Arthur, 25, 232n. 4
Banbury, Sir Frederick, 232n. 8
Bane, Mary Jo, 280n. 35
Barber, W. J., 243n. 214
Barkin, S., 113–14, 259n. 196, 262n. 4
Barnett, R. M., 266n. 66
Baron, L. D. A., 250n. 34, 253n. 84
Barry, N., 230n. 56, 281n. 47, 282n. 50, 296n.
    28
Bartlett, Alan, 288n. 115, 292n. 161
Baum, Erica, 279n. 23, 286n. 101
Beall, Senator Glenn, 142
Beckett, Margaret, 285n. 84
Bellamy, R., 230n. 55
Bendick, Marc, 276n. 211, 291n. 146

Bentley, M., 232nn. 4,12
Berkowitz, E. D., 229n. 50, 244n. 218
Berryman, S., 295n. 22
Beveridge, William: advocacy of labor
    exchanges, 4, 12, 21, 23, 25, 33, 41,
    60–61, 63, 226n. 17, 231n. 2, 232n. 5,
    232n. 11, 233n. 16, 233n. 20, 233n. 23,
    237n. 88, 240n. 137; criticism of
    exchanges, 92, 248n. 263, 255n. 139;
    objections to labor exchanges and strikes,
    41, 233n. 26, 240n. 139; objections to
    labor exchanges and wage rates, 45–46;
    and post-1945 welfare state, 11, 12, 16,
    178; and 1942 Report, 16, 178, 213, 281n.
    45
Beveridge Report of 1942, 281n. 45. *See*
    William Beveridge
Bingham, Senator Hiram, 235n. 60
Bjornaraa, B., 223n. 13, 231n. 2
Black Americans: and apprenticeships, 9–10,
    126–28; attitudes toward welfare, 281n.
    41; discrimination in apprenticeships,
    146–48; discrimination against by unions,
    9–10, 228n. 43; and discrimination in
    USES, 266n. 66; and New Deal electoral
    coalition, 13, 62; and Roosevelt's
    Committee on Fair Employment Practices,
    9; and segregated U.S. Employment
    Service, 98–101, 124–26, 258nn. 173, 182,
    259n. 183; and trades unions, 3, 8; and
    unemployment, 4. *See also* National
    Association for the Advancement of
    Colored People
Blair, Tony, 292nn. 162, 164
Blank, S., 255n. 142, 262n. 14, 268n. 90
Blanton, Congressman Thomas, 235n. 60
Blissett, M., 266n. 63
Board of Trade (Britain), xii, 24, 33, 35, 78,
    237n. 88
Booth, Charles, xiii–xiv
Booth, P., 244n. 223
Bowles, N. P., 263n. 24
Boyd-Carpenter, Lord, 175
Brackman, H., 280n. 35
Brady, D. W., 257n. 163
Brenner, J., 228n. 37
Brewster, Senator Daniel, 142
Briggs, V., 229n. 45
Brock, Bill, 160
Brock, M., 224n. 2
Brownlow Report. *See* President's Committee
    on Administrative Management
Burbridge, Lynn, 280n. 31

Bureau of Employment Security (U.S.). *See*
    U.S. Employment Service (USES)
Burke, Vee, 279n. 21
Burstein, P., 229n. 45
Butler, Arthur, 256n. 151
Buxton, Sydney, 39, 48

Califano, Joseph A., 124, 265n. 61
Callaghan, James, 293n. 5
Campbell-Bannerman, Sir Henry, 20
Carey, Sarah, 153, 275n. 192
Carter, President Jimmy, 158, 266n. 61
Castle, Governor Michael, 196
Caves, R. E., 267n. 84
Cellar, Congressman Emanuel, 235n. 54
Chegwidden, T. S., 252nn. 59, 66
Churchill, Winston, president of Board of
    Trade, xii, 212, 213
—and employers, 35–38, 47–49, 204
—and Labour Exchanges Act of 1909, 19–26,
    33–46
—and trades unionists, 35–46, 47–49, 204;
    labor exchanges and strikes, 41–43; labor
    exchanges and wage rates, 43–46, 241n.
    167; representation of union members,
    38–40
—and unemployed, 61
—and unemployment insurance, 24–25
—and welfare programs, 11
—and work tests, 36, 61
Civilian Conservation Corps, 60, 247n. 258.
    See also New Deal
Civil Rights Act of 1964 (U.S.), 126; Title VI,
    126, 127; and War on Poverty, 143
Civil Works Administration, 31. *See also* New
    Deal
Clark, Robert, 101
Class. *See* Labor movement theory
Clinton, Governor Bill, 188; welfare reform,
    188, 286n. 99
Clinton, President Bill, 212, 277n. 226; train-
    ing proposals, 277n. 226, 295n. 22; wel-
    fare reform proposals, 200–201
Cloward, Richard, 52, 225n. 12, 244n. 217
Cohen, Malcolm S., 276n. 209
Collins, R. M., 229n. 48, 244n. 217, 262n. 15
Colm, Gerhard, 101
Committee of Inquiry into Exchanges, 1920
    (Britain), 79–80
Committee on Fair Employment Practices, 9
Community Action program (Britain), 292n.
    156. *See also* Work-welfare
Community Work Experience Program (U.S.),

174. *See also* Work-welfare

Comprehensive Employment Training Act of 1973 (U.S.). *See* Work-welfare, and training policy

Confederation of British Industry (formerly Federation of British Industry), 93; and Employment Training program, 190–91; and National Economic Development Council, 268n. 90; and training policy, 131, 162, 190–91, 270n. 122; and workforce skills, 190, 210, 284n. 76, 288nn. 109, 110, 295n. 24

Conservative Party, 6, 86, 87, 224n. 14, 229n. 52; and electoral support, 151, 161–62, 185, 205–6, 276n. 215, 294n. 17; and industrial training boards, 269n. 114, 277n. 216; and Manpower Services Commission, 150–52, 162, 168–69; John Moore and welfare state, 179–80; No Turning Back group, 180, 282n. 53; and social security, 253n. 82, 254nn. 97, 99, 281n. 44; and trades unions, 151–52; and training policy, 129, 161–62, 209, 267n. 85, 276n. 215, 277n. 216, 295n. 19; and unemployment, 93; and welfare state, 179–80, 211, 282n. 51; and White Paper on Employment Policy, 1944, 114–15, 170, 254n. 104, 262n. 9; and work-welfare programs, 168–73, 199, 202, 211

Corina, John, 268n. 100

Corney, M., 264n. 46, 269n. 104

Council of Economic Advisers, 77, 263n. 24, 266n. 61; and active labor market policy, 116–17, 142; and Keynesianism, 116–17; and Edwin Nourse, 263n. 24; and training, 116; and USES, 142

Cousins, Frank, 268n. 96

Craig, F. W. S., 269n. 114

Crewe, Ivor, 293n. 6

Crosland, Anthony, 114, 262n. 9

Cushman, Edward, 251n. 46

Danzinger, Sheldon, 283n. 60

Davis, John C., 116

Deacon, Alan, 80, 252n. 64, 253n. 73

Deakin, S., 278n. 12

Deming, B., 237n. 82, 244n. 220

Democratic Party, 17; electoral support, 11, 206–8, 210–11. *See also* New Deal electoral coalition

Department of Employment (Britain; formerly Department of Employment and Productivity), 184, 264nn. 31, 35, 39, 40,

269n. 115; and Employment Training program, 184, 270n. 124, 289n. 127; plan for Employment Service, 1972, 264n. 35, 264n. 36, 265n. 51; proposals for training, 269n. 105, 270n. 120, 278n. 3, 279n. 14; Training and Enterprise Councils, 288n. 111, 288n. 116, 289nn. 121, 122, 123, 292n. 160. *See also* Manpower Services Commission

Department of Employment and Productivity (Britain), 86; and Manpower Services Commission, 120–21; report on employment service, 86–87, 103–5, 264n. 40; reorganization of employment service, 118–20, 248n. 4; role of employment service, 254n. 101, 260nn. 199, 206, 207. *See also* Department of Employment

de Schweinitz, K., 224n. 2

Dimock, Marshall E., 57–58

Dirksen, Congressman Everett M., 96, 257n. 166

Dixon, J., 231n. 63

Doak, William, 50–52, 243n. 202, 243n. 205; reorganization of employment service, 246n. 255

Dole, Elizabeth, 160–61, 276n. 212

Domhoff, G. William, 282n. 55

Dukakis, Governor Michael, 187; Massachusetts ET, 187, 198

Dungan, Ralph, 142

Dunlop, John, 264n. 26

Economic Opportunity Act of 1964 (U.S.). *See* Johnson, President Lyndon B.

Edsall, Mary, 275n. 202, 294n. 8

Edsall, Thomas, 275n. 202, 294n. 8

Egham Labour Exchange, 41

Eisenhower, President Dwight D., 108, 125; and segregated USES, 125

Elbaum, B., 267n. 86, 294n. 11

Ellwood, David T., 284n. 69

Emery, James, 52

Employer organizations, 10–11, 35–38; American Liberty League, 53; hostility to labor exchanges in Britain, 37–38; hostility to labor exchanges in the U.S., 52–53; and labor exchanges, 10, 33, 36–38; Report of the National Employers' Committee for Improvement of the State Employment Service, 1972, 275n. 203; and USES, 154, 161. *See also* Association of British Chambers of Commerce; Confederation of British Industry;

Employer organizations (*continued*)
National Alliance of Business (U.S.); U.S.
Chamber of Commerce; and U.S. National
Association of Manufacturers (NAM)
Employment Act of 1946 (U.S.), 10, 115–17,
164, 262n. 15; and Kennedy administra-
tion, 133
Employment Act of 1989 (Britain), 168–73.
See also Work-welfare
Employment Action (Britain), 199–200. *See
also* Work-welfare
Employment Exchanges. *See* Labor
Exchanges
Employment and Training Act of 1948
(Britain), 74, 103, 114
Employment Service (Britain), 118–21, 265n.
54; and Department of Employment,
118–19; and Manpower Services
Commission, 265n. 51; renamed
Employment Service Agency, 120–21;
responsibilities of, 120–21
Employment Service Agency (Britain). *See*
Employment Service, and Manpower
Services Commission
Employment Training program of 1988
(Britain), 133, 168; Department of
Employment, 270n. 124; founding of, 133
Engineering Employers' Association (Britain),
35, 37; hostility toward labor exchanges,
37–38
Enterprise Allowance Scheme (Britain), 192.
See also Training and manpower policy;
Work-welfare
Erskine, General Groves, 263n. 22
Esping-Andersen, G., 224nn. 3, 5, 225n. 8,
231n. 63
Evans, P., 227n. 22, 296n. 33
Ewing, Oscar, 259n. 196

Fair Employment Practice Committee. *See*
President's Committee on Fair
Employment Practice (FEPC)
Fallon, Congressman George, 142
Family Support Act of 1988 (U.S.), 173–77,
186–90, 193–97, 279n. 25, 290n. 135,
292n. 169; antecedents, 140, 159, 163,
279n. 21, 280n. 33; enactment, 173–77,
211; and Job Training Partnership Act,
193–97, 290n. 138; participation rate
requirements, 196–97, 290n. 135, 293nn.
171, 172; work requirements, 174. *See
also* Work-welfare

Fechner, Robert, 60, 247nn. 258, 259
Federal Advisory Council of USES, 30, 55–56
Federalism, and work-welfare, 13, 210–11
Federal Security Agency, 57, 99. *See also*
Social Security Board
Federation of British Industry. *See*
Confederation of British Industry
Federation of Engineering and Ship-Building
Trades, 2n. 12
Field, Frank M.P., 199, 292n. 159
Finegold, David, 18, 231n. 65, 231n. 66, 267n.
80, 267n. 82, 268n. 93, 270n. 118
Finn, Dan, 265n. 54, 279n. 19, 289n. 126,
289n. 128
Fitzgerald (National Apprenticeship) Act of
1937 (U.S.), 273n. 169. *See also* U.S.
Bureau of Apprenticeship and Training
Fogarty, Congressman John, 89, 122–23
Foner, P. S., 228nn. 33, 41
Forman, C., 223n. 9
Fowler, Norman, 193, 284n. 78, 289n. 132
Fraser, S., 243n. 210
Freeden, Michael, 12–13, 230n. 57, 230n. 58,
232n. 12
Fry, George, 25
Full Employment Bill. *See* Employment Act
of 1989 (Britain)
Full Employment UK, 199, 292n. 158
Fulton Report (Britain), 269n. 108

Galenson, W., 225n. 11
Garrett, G., 278n. 4
"Genuinely seeking work," 79, 279n. 15,
289n. 127. *See also* Work-welfare
Germany: labor colonies, 238n. 105; labor
exchange system, xiv, 22, 36, 41, 43,
232n. 6, 239n. 118, 241n. 168; training
policy, 164–65, 267n. 86, 292n. 161, 296n.
27
Gibson, John, 251n. 46
Gilder, G., 230n. 56, 284n. 69
Gilens, Martin, 281n. 41
Ginsburg, H., 293n. 4
Ginzberg, Eli, 264n. 26
Glazer, N., 284n. 69
Glennerster, H., 278n. 5
Goldberg, Arthur, 70, 136, 270nn. 125, 126,
271n. 132; in Kennedy administration,
136, 157–58
Goldfield, M., 228n. 36, 248n. 260
Gompers, Samuel (AFL founder), 8
Goodin, R., 230n. 56

Goodwin, Robert, 67, 70, 83, 88, 94, 95, 100, 101, 111, 253n. 86, 257n. 160; and discrimination in USES, 266n. 67; and employment policy, 116, 259n. 195; and ICESA, 272n. 150; and segregated USES, 124
Gospell, H., 267n. 84
Graham, Congressman George, 235n. 60
Grant, W., 255n. 142, 262n. 14
Gray, J., 230n. 55
Great Society, 6, 77, 136. *See also* Johnson, President Lyndon B.
Great Society programs, 141–46; Apprenticeship Information Centers, 145, 146–47; Conceptual Model approach, 139; employability development program, 139; Human Resources Development program, 139, 145–46; Work Incentive Program, 148–49, 155
Green, Paula, 285n. 85
Green, William, 8, 50, 51, 52, 58, 97, 243n. 212, 256n. 153, 258n. 171
Greenberg, Mark, 291n. 148
Grossman, J., 266n. 63
Gueron, Judith, 286n. 102
Gutchess, J., 271n. 143
Gutmann, A., 281n. 43

Haber, William, 264n. 26
Hagen, Jan L., 291n. 152, 293n. 172
Hall, P., 115, 227n. 22, 262nn. 5, 7, 14, 15, 267n. 80, 296n. 30
Hardie, Keir, 33, 237n. 86
Harris, J., 224n. 1, 226n. 15, 240n. 140
Harris, R., 281n. 44
Harrison, S., 243n. 215
Hartz, L., 230n. 55
Harvey, P., 279n. 22
Haskins, Ron, 279n. 23, 286n. 101
Hattam, V. C., 227n. 30, 243n. 200, 294n. 14
Haveman, Robert, 283n. 60
Hayek, F. A., 281n. 47
Headstart, 182
Healey, Denis, 132
Heartwell, William, 274n. 190
Heclo, H., 230n. 56, 230n. 61, 284n. 73, 296n. 33
Henderson, Fred, 37
Hillman, Sydney, 52
Himmelfarb, G., 227nn. 21, 28
Historical Institutionalism, 5–14, 212–14; and state-centric theory, 5–7

Hodgson, James, 70, 283n. 61
Holland, Sir Geoffrey, 192, 289nn. 121, 124
Hoover, President Herbert, 26, 28; and labor exchanges, 50–52
Hoover, K., 278n. 5
Hopkins, Harry, 53
Horowitz, R. L., 248n. 261
Hunt, David, 180
Hutton, Alfred, 21

Ikenberry, John, 282n. 55, 283n. 58
Industrial Relations Act of 1971 (Britain), 131
Industrial Training Act of 1964 (Britain), 113, 130
Industrial Training Boards (Britain), 93, 130; Central Training Council, 130; and Conservative Party, 269n. 114; organization of boards, 130, 268n. 100; and TUC, 269n. 106, 270n. 120
Institute of Economic Affairs, 170. *See also* Liberalism
International Association of Personnel in Employment Security, 94
International Labour Organisation, 82, 92, 251n. 42, 253n. 80, 253n. 83, 254n. 98, 255n. 137, 255n. 140
Interstate Conference on Employment Security Agencies (ICESA), 15, 66, 84, 91, 107, 110, 156–57, 204, 265n. 59; criticism of, by 1971 National Urban Coalition study, 157; and decentralization of USES, 94–98, 256n. 145, 256n. 151; and Department of Labor, 272n. 150; funding of ICESA, 123, 265n. 59; and funding of USES, 122; ICESA 1989 study of Job Service, 276n. 211; and labor market policy, 141–42, 291n. 146; political strength in Congress, 122–23, 156–57, 204, 256n. 147; response to 1971 National Urban Coalition study, 153–54, 274n. 190

Janoski, T., 164, 242n. 192, 249n. 9, 256n. 151, 265n. 58, 270n. 128, 277n. 225, 286n. 101, 294n. 11
Jencks, C., 279n. 29, 280n. 35, 284n. 69
Jenkins, R., 232n. 4
Jensen, J., 280n. 35
Jephcott, Pearl, xiii, 223n. 10
Jobcentres (Britain), 118–19, 121, 150, 192, 265n. 52, 289n. 126; and Conservatives, 165, 291n. 154; Manpower Services Commission study, 265n. 52; Rayner

Jobcentres (*continued*)
  review, 192, 289n. 125; 1978 report on
  Jobcentres, 121, 264n. 37, 265nn. 50, 52,
  53
Job Creation Programme. *See* Manpower
  Services Commission
Job Training Partnership Act of 1982 (U.S.).
  See Training and manpower policy, in
  U.S.
Johnson, Senator Hiram, 235n. 54
Johnson, President Lyndon B., 116, 121, 162,
  181, 266n. 61, 271n. 135
—and civil rights, 162
—Great Society, 136, 137–41, 162;
  Apprenticeship Information Centers, 145,
  146–47; Economic Opportunity Act of
  1964, 137, 139–40, 181–82; Headstart,
  182; Model Cities Program of 1967, 137;
  Neighborhood Youth Corps, 139;
  Operation Mainstream, 139; principal pro-
  grams, 138; Public Service Careers, 139;
  Work Incentive Program, 140–41, 148–49
—Great Society and USES, 141–46
—and New Deal electoral coalition, 162
—and private employment agencies, 142,
  272n. 153
—and segregation in USES, 124
—War on Poverty, 136, 143, 181–82, 286n.
  101; and Manpower Demonstration and
  Training Act, 143; and USES, 143, 144
Joint Board of the Parliamentary Committee
  of the TUC, the General Federation of
  Trade Unions and the Labour Party, 34.
  See also Trades Union Congress
Jones, B. L., 254n. 90, 256n. 143
Joseph, A., 227n. 32
Jowell, R., 281n. 44

Kalecki, M., 223n. 5, 244n. 216
Katz, M. B., 224n. 2, 279n. 28
Katznelson, I., 95, 227n. 30, 229n. 48, 257nn.
  158, 159, 258n. 168, 264n. 25
Kean, Governor Thomas, 194, 195
Keeler, J. T. S., 235n. 48, 278n. 4
Keenan, E. L., 244n. 223
Kellogg, Ruth, 59, 231n. 2, 246n. 255, 247n.
  256
Kennedy, President John F., 108, 121, 142;
  and economic policy, 116, 270n. 126;
  Labor Day address of 1961, 135; and man-
  power policy, 133, 144, 157–58; and seg-
  regation in USES, 124; and USES, 142,
  144, 273n. 159

Kenyon, Senator William, 27, 235n. 53
Kerr, Clark, 264n. 26
Keynes, J. M., 229n. 46
Keynesianism, 74, 92, 113, 148; and Kennedy
  administration, 133–35; and labor
  exchanges, 74–77, 117–18, 260n. 206; and
  labor market policy, 148–49; and macroeconomic policy, 113–17, 163–64, 205,
  262n. 3, 263nn. 16, 23
Keyserling, Leon, 116; oral history, 263n. 22
King, Desmond S., 223n. 2, 226n. 18, 231n.
  62, 231n. 63, 258n. 177, 262n. 12, 264n.
  46, 271n. 146, 278n. 5, 279n. 18, 283n. 58,
  284n. 78, 285n. 91, 288n. 111, 288n. 119,
  293n. 2, 293n. 6, 294n. 10, 296n. 28
Kingsley, Donald, 75, 251n. 47, 257n. 160,
  259n. 195
Knights of Labor (U.S.), 9
Korpi, W., 224n. 4, 225n. 6

Labor, as a commodity, xii, xiv
Labor colonies. *See* Report on Agencies and
  Methods for Dealing with the Unemployed
  (1893)
Labor Exchanges:
—association with unemployed and unskilled,
  6–7, 204–5
—attitude of employers, 37, 46, 71–72
—attitude of trades unions, 34–36, 38–46,
  47–49
—attitude of trades unions in Britain: labor
  exchanges and strikes, 41–43; labor
  exchanges and wage rates, 43–46; representation of union members, 38–40
—attitude of trades unions in U.S., 49–52
—compulsory registration, 252n. 68, 291n.
  154
—criticisms of exchanges, 233n. 26
—defined, xii–xiii
—founding of, 6–14; in Britain, 19–26, 231n.
  2; in U.S., 26–33
—integration of placement and unemployment
  insurance: in Britain, 19–20, 22–23; in
  U.S., 53–60
—and Keynesianism, 74–77, 92, 251n. 56,
  259n. 191, 265n. 54
—labor exchanges in Sweden, 259n. 196
—liberal origins of, 12–13, 20–24, 60–64
—national regulation and placement, 85–91
—placement record of: in Britain, 66–67; in
  general, 109–11; in U.S., 67–72
—and private employment services, 29, 250n.
  28

—processing of unemployed, xiv
—and the Second World War, 72–78
—and separation of placement and benefit, 102–9; in Britain, 118–21; in U.S., 121–28
—and work-tests, 22–23, 36, 61, 78–85, 252n. 63
—work-tests and placement, 78–85, 92
—and work-welfare programs, 174–75. *See also* Labour Exchanges Act (1909); U.S. Employment Service (USES); Employment Service (Britain)
Labor market, xiv–xv; and government intervention, 1
Labor market policy. *See* Training and manpower policy; Work-welfare
Labor movement theory, 1–5, 224n. 4, 225n. 13
Labour Exchanges Act (1909), 12, 19, 33, 78, 93, 103, 104, 234nn. 31, 32, 34, 35
—administrative arrangements, 234n. 40
—advisory committees, 38–43
—amendment of, 103
—negotiations with employers, 35, 36–38
—negotiations with trades unions, 35–46, 47–49; labor exchanges and strikes, 41–43, 239n. 118; labor exchanges and wage rates, 43–46; representation of union members, 38–40, 239n. 125
—passage of, in Parliament, 19–26
—and work-welfare, 104
Labour Party, 15; Commission on Social Justice, 296n. 32; electoral support, 11–12, 87, 161–62, 205–6; and labor exchanges, 105; and trades unions, 209–10; and training, 130, 161–62, 268n. 92, 268n. 94, 292n. 162; and unemployment, 284n. 75; and welfare state, 178–79; work-welfare, 198, 289n. 134, 292nn. 162, 163
La Dame, Mary, 245n. 235
LaGuardia, Congressman Fiorello, 235n. 53
Lait, J., 278n. 6
Lane, Christel, 268n. 87
Layard, Richard, 292n. 159
Lee Associates (U.S.), 142
Lemann, Nicholas, 271n. 134, 271n. 138, 284n. 69
Leslie, John W., 266n. 68
Leuchtenburg, W. E., 53, 181, 244n. 219, 283n. 57
Levine, Louis, 144, 273n. 161
Lewis, J., 228n. 40
Liberalism: defined, xii, 12, 223n. 7; neoliberalism, 162; New Right interest groups,

169–70; New Right and work-welfare, 162, 165, 167–73, 211, 282n. 50; work-welfare and liberal tradition in Britain and in U.S., 177–84, 281n. 47
Lilley, Peter, 282n. 54
Lister, Ruth, 223n. 3, 281n. 43
Llewellyn-Smith, Hubert, 39, 45, 46
Lloyd George, David, 11, 12, 20
Local Enterprise Councils (Britain). *See* Training and manpower policy; Work-welfare
Long, David A., 293n. 171
Long, Senator Russell, 148
Longstreth, F. H., 227n. 22, 278nn. 5, 8
Lovell, Malcolm, Jr., 182, 273n. 168, 275nn. 191, 192; and National Urban Coalition study, 153–54, 275n. 192
Lowe, R., 81, 252nn. 60, 65, 253nn. 77, 79
Lurie, Irene, 291n. 152, 293n. 172

McCoy, D. R., 257n. 164
McKibbin, R., 80–81, 227n. 23, 253nn. 74, 78, 260n. 198, 294n. 16
McNutt, Paul, 73
McQuaid, K., 229n. 50, 244n. 218
Madsen, H., 230n. 61
Mangum, Garth, 273n. 163
Manpower Administration (U.S.). *See* U.S. Department of Labor, Manpower Development and Training Act of 1962
Manpower Demonstration Research Corporation (U.S.), 189, 286n. 102, 287nn. 103, 104, 105
Manpower Development and Training Act of 1962 (U.S.), 77, 108, 113, 163, 272n. 156, 277n. 218; and focus on welfare recipients, 144–45; and Kennedy administration, 133–35; Keynesianism and manpower policy, 135–36; skills crisis, 136–37; and USES, 144–46; U.S. Employment Service Task Force 1965 recommendations, 141–43
Manpower policy. *See* Apprenticeships; Manpower Services Commission (Britain); Training and manpower policy; U.S. Department of Labor; U.S. Employment Service Task Force, 1965; Work-welfare
Manpower Services Commission (Britain), 18, 92, 104, 115, 130, 205, 265n. 47, 268n. 98, 269n. 113
—budget, 132–33
—chairmen, 270n. 123
—under Conservatives, 168–73

Manpower Services Commission (*continued*)
—definition of roles, 265n. 51
—establishment of, 120–21, 131, 150–51,
    269nn. 104, 109, 111, 116, 270n. 117
—and Jobcentres, 265n. 52
—programs: Job Creation Programme, 121;
    Job Training Scheme, 185, 285n. 82;
    Youth Opportunities Programme, 169;
    Youth Training, 133, 170, 172, 200, 285n.
    84; Work Experience Programme, 120–21
—Rayner review, 289n. 125
—renamed Training Commission, 151
—renamed Training Agency, 151
—training proposals, 205, 270n. 119, 278n. 3
—tripartite organization, 131–32, 269nn. 110,
    111
—and unemployment, 150–52, 165–66
March, J., 227n. 22
Marks, G., 227n. 30
Marmor, T. R., 279n. 22
Marsh, D., 255n. 142, 262n. 14
Marshall, F. R., 229n. 45
Marshall, T. H., 223n. 2, 296n. 28
Marshaw, J. L., 279n. 22
Marsland, D., 278n. 6
Martin, Andrew, 270n. 127
Maude, Francis, 199
Meacher, Michael, 289n. 134
Mead, Senator James, 58, 246n. 252
Mead, Lawrence, 176, 230n. 56, 281nn. 37,
    39, 296n. 29
Meehan, E., 228n. 39
Midgley, J., 278n. 5
Milgrom, P., 261n. 229
Miller, David, 296n. 28
Mills, Congressman Wilbur, 89, 123, 257n.
    165
Minford, P., 226n. 20
Ministry of Labour (Britain), 75, 78, 80, 81,
    93, 115, 251n. 43, 260n. 206; Employment
    and Insurance Department, 78; training
    proposals, 268n. 93
Minkin, L., 277n. 217
Mishel, Lawrence, 281n. 40
Mitchell, Clarence (NAACP), 100, 258n. 175
Mitchell, James (U.S. Secretary of Labor),
    108, 266n. 68
Mitchell, William (U.S. Attorney General),
    51, 125
Moffit, R., 226n. 20
Moore, John, 179–80, 282nn. 48, 52
Moran, M., 283n. 58
Mosses, W., TUC delegate, 7, 47, 238nn. 100,

107
Moyers, Bill, 266n. 61
Moynihan, Senator Daniel Patrick, 13, 230n.
    59, 277n. 221; Family Support Act of
    1988, 175, 189, 196, 207
Mucciaroni, G., 163, 164, 264n. 27, 265n. 60,
    277n. 220, 293n. 1
Mukherjee, Santosh, 268n. 107
Murray, Charles, 176, 279n. 29, 281n. 38,
    283n. 60, 284n. 69
Myrddin-Evans, G., 252nn. 59, 66

Nathan, Richard, 283n. 65, 292n. 169
National Alliance of Business (U.S.), 194; and
    workforce skills, 210, 290n. 141, 295nn.
    21, 23
National Assistance Board (Britain), 85, 86
National Association for Advancement of
    Colored People (NAACP), 10, 15, 66, 93,
    162, 225n. 10, 229n. 44; and discrimina-
    tion in apprenticeships, 146–48, 273n.
    170, 274nn. 173, 175; and discrimination
    in USES, 266n. 70; and postwar decentral-
    ization of USES, 258n. 178; segregation in
    Washington USES, 100, 258nn. 174, 175;
    and the U.S. Employment Service,
    98–101, 258nn. 173, 178, 179, 181, 189
National Economic Development Council
    (Britain), 129–30, 184, 262n. 6, 268nn. 90,
    91; and employers, 268n. 90
National Governors' Association, 175, 279n.
    28, 286n. 98; Family Support Act of 1988,
    175, 188–89; welfare reform, 286n. 99
National Insurance Act of 1911 (Britain), 20,
    78
National Insurance Act of 1946 (Britain), 82
National Joint Advisory Council (Britain), 93
National Labor Relations Act (U.S.), 50, 53
National League of Women Voters (U.S.), 26,
    29
National and Local Government Officers'
    Association (Britain), 184
National Planning Association (U.S.), Labor
    Committee, 84, 93, 95, 254n. 91, 256n.
    143, 257n. 161
National Re-employment Service (U.S.),
    30–31
National Resources Planning Board (U.S.),
    117, 263n. 16
National Union of Public Employees (Britain),
    184
National Urban Coalition and the Lawyers'
    Committee for Civil Rights Under Law,

1971 study of the USES, 128, 152–53, 249n. 27, 267n. 78, 271n. 139, 274nn. 176, 178, 180, 275nn. 193, 200, 206; and apprenticeships, 274n. 174; and ICESA, 157; Office of Economic Opportunity, 137
National Urban League (U.S.), 187–88, 286n. 96
National Women's Trade Union League of America, 29
Neoliberalism. *See* Liberalism
New Deal, 13, 26, 31, 52–53, 59–60, 244n. 219; Civil Works Administration, 31, 53; Civilian Conservation Corps, 60, 247n. 258; Committee on Economic Security, 180–81; Public Works Board, 31; Social Security Act of 1935, 180
New Deal electoral coalition, 11, 13, 162–63, 206–8
New Liberalism: defined, 12; and labor exchanges, 21, 60; and work-welfare, 12
New Poor Law (1834). *See* Poor Law
New Right, 162, 165, 167, 169–73, 177–78, 211, 281n. 47. *See also* Liberalism
Next Steps reforms (Britain), 289n. 129
Nichols, T., 270n. 121
Nightingale, Demetra, 280n. 31
Nixon, President Richard, 70, 183, 277n. 221; family assistance plan, 208, 271n. 146, 277n. 221, 283n. 66; reform of USES, 160
Nolan, Congressman John, 27, 235n. 53
Northrup, H., 229n. 45
Notification of Vacancies Order of 1952 (Britain), 92
Novak, M., 281n. 37, 283n. 60
Nourse, Edwin, 116–17, 263n. 24; role of Council of Economic Advisers, 263n. 24

Odencrantz, L. C., 237n. 82, 244n. 220
Office of Economic Opportunity (U.S.), 137; community action agencies, 143; and Great Society, 137; and U.S. Department of Labor, 137–38, 143; and USES, 142; Welfare Administration, 139. *See also* Johnson, President Lyndon B.
Office of War Mobilization and Reconversion (U.S.), 116
Old Age Pensions Act of 1908 (Britain), 11
Olsen, J., 227n. 22
Olson, Mancur, 48, 242n. 189
Olsson, S., 231n. 63
Omnibus Budget Reconciliation Act of 1981 (U.S.), 186, 216, 280n. 30. *See also* Reagan, President Ronald

Organisation for Economic Cooperation and Development, 82, 103, 113, 250n. 34, 259n. 196, 262n. 4, 269n. 108
Orloff, A. S., 224n. 3, 228n. 40, 230n. 60, 282n. 55, 292n. 168

Page, B., 229n. 49, 281n. 41
Painter, Joseph M.P., 20, 232n. 6
Palmer, Gladys L., 30, 231n. 2, 236n. 70, 236n. 78
Parker, H., 278n. 6
Parliamentary Committee of the TUC. *See* Trades Union Congress (TUC)
Pateman, C., 281n. 43
Patterson, J. T., 271n. 138
Patterson, Orlanda, 176, 281n. 40
Peele, G., 284n. 69
Perkins, Frances, 26, 30, 31, 54–60, 235n. 51; and merger of USES with unemployment insurance, 54–60, 245n. 237; and Wagner-Peyser Act, 26–33, 62, 236n. 79
Perry, P. J. C., 267n. 82
Persons, Frank, 30, 31, 32, 54–60, 90, 246n. 254; conception of USES's role, 31–32, 236n. 69; opposition to integration of U.S. Employment Service and unemployment insurance, 54–60, 245n. 228, 248n. 262; resignation as director of USES, 54, 60, 247nn. 257, 258, 259
Peterson, P., 279n. 29
Phelan, C., 228n. 34, 243nn. 200, 212
Philadelphia plan, 267n. 77, 295n. 20. *See also* American Federation of Labor–Congress of Industrial Organization (AFL–CIO)
Philpot, John, 292n. 159
Pierson, C., 225n. 8, 281n. 43
Pietrykowski, B., 95, 229n. 48, 257nn. 158, 159, 258n. 168, 264n. 25
Piore, M., 225n. 9
Piven, Frances Fox, 52, 225n. 12, 244n. 217, 282n. 55, 292n. 168
Placement policy. *See* Labor Exchanges; U.S. Employment Service (USES)
Plant, R., 230n. 56, 278n. 5, 282n. 50, 296n. 28
Plotnick, Robert, 283n. 60
Polanyi, Karl, xii, 223n. 4, 227n. 21
Polenberg, R., 246n. 241
Pollard, Sidney, 268n. 88
Pontusson, J., 225n. 6, 294n. 15
Poor Law, 4, 7, 22–23, 224n. 2; and New Poor Law of 1834, 4–5, 227n. 28

Poor Law Commissioners. *See* Royal
    Commission on the Poor Laws
Portillo, Michael, 171
Powell, Oscar, 59
President's Committee on Administrative
    Management (Brownlow Report), 57, 101
President's Committee on Economic Security
    (U.S.), 180–81, 206, 213, 282n. 56
President's Committee on Fair Employment
    Practice (FEPC), 228n. 43, 257n. 164
Preston, Steve, 265n. 54, 289n. 126
Private employment services, 29
Private Industry Councils (U.S.). *See* Training
    and manpower policy
Public Employment System. *See* Labor
    Exchanges

Quadagno, Jill, 14, 208, 230n. 60, 294n. 13

Ragan, C. C., 224n. 15
Ramas, M., 228n. 37
Rayner, Sir Derek, 192, 289n. 125
Reagan, Governor Ronald, 182–83; welfare
    reform in California, 182–83, 283nn. 62,
    65, 67
Reagan, President Ronald, 158, 183–84, 198,
    212, 284n. 70; Family Support Act of
    1988, 173–74, 183–84, 188–89, 193–97,
    198, 207, 211; New Federalism program,
    160; Omnibus Budget Reconciliation Act
    of 1981 and workfare, 186, 280nn. 32, 33,
    34; reform of USES, 160; State of the
    Union address, 1986, 183
Redford, E. S., 266n. 63
Redundancy Payments Act of 1965 (Britain),
    86
Redwood, John, 180
Reich, Robert, 277n. 226; Clinton administra-
    tion training proposals, 277n. 226
Report on Agencies and Methods for Dealing
    with the Unemployed (1893), 1, 223n. 3,
    224n. 1, 226n. 14, 227nn. 27, 29, 231n. 2;
    labor colonies, 238n. 105
Report of the National Employers' Committee
    for Improvement of the State Employment
    Service, 1972, 275n. 203
Republican Party, 6, 206–11
Restart interview (Britain), 171–73, 285n. 86.
    See also Work-welfare
Ritter, G., 228n. 40
Roberts, J., 261n. 229
Robertson, D. B., 242n. 192, 243n. 215, 273n.
    163, 274n. 179

Roche, M., 223n. 2
Roediger, D., 226n. 19, 228n. 41
Roosevelt, President Franklin D., 13, 27,
    57–60, 61, 101, 212; and economic policy,
    263n. 17; mandate, 235n. 48; merger of
    USES and unemployment insurance,
    58–60, 247n. 259; and New Deal, 26, 31,
    52–53, 59, 229n. 46; and Social Security
    Act of 1935, 180; and Wagner-Peyser Act,
    27, 63
Rothstein, B., 231nn. 62, 63, 262n. 12
Rown, R. L., 229n. 45
Royal Commission on Labour (1892),
    xiii–xiv.
Royal Commission on the Poor Laws, 20–21,
    213, 232nn. 3, 13, 233n. 17; Minority
    Report, 226n. 17; Poor Law
    Commissioners, 21, 24
Royal Commission on Unemployment
    Insurance, 1932, 80, 252n. 70
Rueschmeyer, D., 227nn. 22, 31, 229n. 53,
    296n. 33
Ruetten, R. T., 257n. 164
Ruggie, M., 225n. 13
Ruttenberg, Stanley H., 152, 271nn. 137, 143;
    oral history, 271n. 137, 274n. 185
Ryan, P., 231n. 65

Sabel, C., 225n. 9
Sautter, U., 213n. 2
Sawhill, I., 279n. 29
Schattschneider, E. E., 296n. 31
Scheurell, R., 231n. 63
Schlozman, K. L., 277n. 2
Schorr, A. L., 296n. 28
Schultz, George, 141, 160, 266n. 65, 267n. 77.
    See also U.S. Employment Service Task
    Force of 1965
Schultze, Charles, 124, 266nn. 61, 62
Schwartz, John, 283n. 60
Schwellenbach, Lewis, 97, 256n. 153, 258n.
    171, 259n. 186, 266nn. 66, 67
Scott, J. W., 228n. 40
Scott, Nicholas, 167, 175
Segalman, R., 278n. 6
Seldon, A., 278n. 6, 281n. 44
Servicemen's Readjustment Act of 1944
    (U.S.), 108
Seymour, J. B., 80, 237n. 87, 252n. 68
Sexton, J., 43
Shackleton, D. J., 35, 41, 44–47, 241n. 168
Shapiro, R. Y., 229n. 49, 281n. 41
Sheldrake, John, 267n. 82, 269nn. 101, 112

Shephard, Gillian, 198, 291n. 154
Sherwood, Kay E., 293n. 171
Ship-Building Employers' Federation (Britain), 35, 37; hostility toward labor exchanges, 37–38
Shonfield, A., 113, 114, 231n. 64, 261n. 1, 262n. 2, 262n. 6, 267n. 81, 268n. 88, 268n. 89
Showler, Brian, 67, 105–6, 248n. 1, 252n. 69, 254n. 100, 261nn. 209, 210, 262n. 4
Siciliana, Rocco C., 67, 68–69
Siemans, Alexander, 37, 41
Sigelman, L., 229n. 49
Simon, Jacqueline, 281n. 40
Skildesky, R., 229n. 46
Skocpol, T., 224n. 3, 227n. 22, 228n. 40, 230n. 60, 282n. 55, 296n. 33
Slichter, S. H., 243n. 209
Smith, Harold, 57, 59
Smith, R. M., 230n. 56
Social Affairs Unit, 170. See also Liberalism
Social democracy: in Sweden, 224n. 5; and work-welfare, 6, 293n. 4
Social Security Act of 1935 (U.S.), 10, 14, 16, 53, 55, 164, 180–81; contributory-noncontributory distinction, 16, 164, 206, 252n. 62; and U.S. Employment Service, 53–60
Social Security Act of 1985 (Britain), 171. See also Work-welfare
Social Security Act of 1988 (Britain), 168, 169–73. See also Work-welfare
Social Security Act of 1989 (Britain), 168, 169–73. See also Work-welfare
Social Security Board, 53, 63, 65; Federal Security Agency, 57, 99, 101, 257n. 159; and integration with U.S. Employment Service, 53–60
Soloman, Carmen D., 279n. 21
Sorge, A., 268n. 97
Soskice, David, 18, 231nn. 65, 66, 267n. 82, 270n. 118
South Central Metropolitan Employment Exchanges (Britain), 25
Speenhamland System, 4
State centric theory. See Historical Institutionalism
Stedman-Jones, Gareth, 7, 226nn. 15, 16, 227n. 25
Stein, H., 256n. 143, 262n. 15, 270n. 127
Steinmo, S., 227n. 22, 278n. 5, 296n. 30
Stephens, E. H., 227n. 31, 229n. 53
Stephens, John, 2, 17, 224n. 4, 225n. 6, 227n. 31, 229n. 53

Stevens, David W., 276n. 209
Stewart, Charles, 68
Stratton, Cay, 169
Sundquist, J. L., 229n. 53
Sweden, 92, 224n. 5; labor exchanges in, 103, 259n. 196; and work-welfare, 230n. 61
Swenson, P., 225n. 7

Tawney, R. H., 31
Taylor, David, 289n. 126
Taylor, Paul, 281n. 42
Tebbit, Norman, 278n. 3
Thatcher, Margaret, 180, 198, 212
Thelen, K., 227n. 22, 278n. 5, 296n. 30
Theories of welfare, 1–14. See also Historical Institutionalism; Labor movement theory
Thomas, Robert, 67–70, 88, 89, 90, 91, 110
Thomas Report (U.S.), 67, 69, 87–91, 110, 148, 254n. 105, 261n. 212; and Congress, 122–23; recommendations, 106–8
Thorne, Will, 34
Tilly, L. A., 228n. 40
Todd, Ron, 185
Tomlinson, J., 262n. 8
Tonge, Jon, 288nn. 111, 118
Tories. See Conservative Party
Trades unions:
—craft tradition, 2–3, 46, 225n. 9
—and founding of labor exchanges, 7–10, 34–36, 38–46
—and founding of labor exchanges in Britain, 38–47; labor exchanges and strikes, 41–43; labor exchanges and wage rates, 43–46; representation of union members, 38–40
—and founding of labor exchanges in U.S., 49–52
—skilled and unskilled workers, 7–8, 47
—and training, 267n. 84
—union-operated labor exchanges, 3, 226n. 14
—and women workers, 8–9
Trades Union Congress (TUC), 33, 93
—and Conservative Party, 151–52
—discussion of labor exchanges at annual conferences, 47–48, 237nn. 91, 95, 242n. 187
—and founding of labor exchanges, 33, 47–49; labor exchanges and strikes, 41–43; labor exchanges and wage rates, 43–46; representation of union members, 38–40
—and industrial training boards, 130, 268n.

Trade Unions Congress (*continued*)
95, 269nn. 96, 106, 270n. 120
—and Labour Party, 208–9
—and Manpower Services Commission,
150–51, 162, 184
—opposition to Employment Training,
184–85, 198
—Parliamentary Committee of the TUC, 22,
35, 61, 253n. 71
—and training policy, 150–51, 162, 269n.
106, 284n. 76, 285n. 83
—and unemployment insurance, 80, 253n. 71
—and voluntarist training, 129–30
—and work-welfare programs, 169, 184–85
Trafton, George, 51
Training Agency (Britain). *See* Manpower
Services Commission
Training and Enterprise Councils (Britain),
184, 190–92, 288nn. 111, 116, 289nn. 121,
123, 124, 292n. 160. *See also* Training and
manpower policy; Work-welfare
Training and manpower policy, 17–18,
149–61
—active labor market policy, 113–14, 161–66,
272n. 156
—in Britain, 118–21, 150–52, 251n. 41, 268n.
93; and employers, 270n. 122;
Employment Action, 199–200; Enterprise
Allowance Scheme, 192; Local Enterprise
Councils, 184; persistent problems, 270n.
121; Training and Enterprise Councils,
184, 190–92, 288nn. 111, 112, 116, 289nn.
121, 122, 123, 124, 292n. 160; voluntarist
tradition, 128–29, 151–52, 267n. 80, 276n.
215; Youth Training, 200
—failure of training policy, 161–66
—in Germany, 129, 164–65, 268n. 86, 292n.
161, 296n. 27
—social democratic programs, 293n. 4
—as unemployment measures, 149–50,
165–66
—in United States, 121–28, 152–61, 263n. 22,
267nn. 75, 84; Comprehensive
Employment and Training Act of 1973,
155, 163; "creaming off" problem, 158,
275n. 205; Family Support Act of 1988
JOBS program, 163; Job Training
Partnership Act of 1982, 159, 163,
194–97, 290nn. 141, 142, 291nn. 143,
144; JTPA and private industry councils,
184, 284n. 74; principal manpower programs, 273n. 166; skills crisis, 136–37;
and unemployment, 272n. 156
—(U.S.) Manpower Development and

Training Act of 1962, 77, 108, 113, 163,
272n. 156, 277n. 218; and focus on wel-
fare recipients, 144–45; Kennedy adminis-
tration, 133–35; Keynesianism and man-
power policy, 135–36; skills crisis, 136–37
Training and Retraining Administration
(U.S.), 263n. 22
Training Commission (Britain). *See*
Manpower Services Commission
Transport and General Workers' Union, 184
Treasury (Britain), 81
Truman, Harry S., 62, 94, 116, 257nn. 164,
166; and training policy, 263n. 22

Ulman, L., 267n. 84
Unemployed, defined, 3–5; growth in number,
87; threat posed by unemployed, 242n.
190. *See also* Work-welfare
Unemployed Workmen Act of 1905 (Britain),
21, 33, 237n. 95; Employment Exchange
Committee of the Central (Unemployed)
Body of London, 41, 42, 234n. 33
Unemployment Insurance, Britain: and labor
exchanges, 24–25, 78–83. *See also* Work-
welfare; Labor Exchanges
Unemployment Insurance Act of 1930
(Britain), 79
Unemployment policy. *See* Work-welfare
Unemployment Unit (Britain), 186, 279nn. 15,
16, 285n. 79
United States, and labor movement theory,
2–3
U.S. Bureau of Apprenticeship and Training,
126–28, 146–48; AFL–CIO and appren-
ticeships, 126; Apprenticeship Information
Centers, 145; discrimination in apprentice-
ships, 146–48; exclusion of black
American workers, 10; Fitzgerald
(National Apprenticeship) Act of 1937,
273n. 169; National Joint Pattern
Apprenticeship Standards and Policy
Statements, 147; segregated programs,
126–27; and USES, 142, 145
U.S. Chamber of Commerce, 52, 95, 229n. 46;
and founding of labor exchanges, 52–53;
support for manpower policy, 136, 210;
workforce skills, 210, 295n. 21
U.S. Conference of Mayors, 194–95, 290n.
142
U.S. Congress: Congressman John Fogarty,
89; Congressman Wilbur Mills, 89; decentralization of USES, 93–98; Office of
Technology Assessment, 267n. 75; oversight of USES, 87, 89, 91, 204, 211; pas-

sage of Family Support Act of 1988,
173–77; passage of Wagner-Peyser Act
(1935), 26–33, 49–53; Report of the
Special Committee on Unemployment
Problems, 1960, 264n. 28; welfare reform
hearings, 286n. 100

U.S. Department of Health, Education and
Welfare, 143; and Great Society programs,
143; and manpower policy, 143

U.S. Department of Labor, 28, 29, 90, 97, 101,
117, 146
—administrative history of, 266n. 74, 267n.
76, 271n. 145
—Advisory Committee on Employment
Service Research, 272n. 158
—Advisory Committee on Equal Opportunity
in Apprenticeships and Training, 1963,
147, 274n. 177
—Apprenticeship Information Centers, 145
—Coordinating Committee on Manpower
Research, 273n. 167
—1989 ICESA study of Job Service, 276n.
211
—Manpower Administration, 146, 152
—Manpower Development and Training Act
of 1962, 77, 108, 113, 163, 272n. 156,
277n. 218; and focus on welfare recipients, 144–45; Kennedy administration,
133–35; Keynesianism and manpower policy, 135–36; skills crisis, 136–37
—manpower policy report, 108–9, 271nn.
131, 133
—Office of Economic Opportunity, 137
—Office of Equal Opportunity in Manpower
Programs, 126–27, 148
—Oral History of Unemployment Insurance
project, 244n. 223
—principal manpower programs, 273n. 166,
277n. 218; "creaming off" problem, 275n.
205
—Proposed Full Employment Act of 1961,
136
—reorganization of department, 259nn. 186,
187
—response to National Urban Coalition study,
153–54
—Report of the National Employers'
Committee for Improvement of the State
Employment Service, 1972, 275n. 203
—report on the USES, 117
—review of U.S. Employment Service, 274n.
189
—Training and Employment Service, 124
—Work Incentive Program (WIN), 140–41

U.S. Employment Service (USES):
—black employees in USES, 267n. 76
—Briefing Paper on the Public Employment
Service, 1990, 276n. 213
—budget and funding, 95, 122–23, 265n. 58
—Bureau of Employment Security, 99, 123,
125, 142, 154, 259n. 194, 261n. 223
—and Comprehensive Employment and
Training Act, 155
—and computerization, 271n. 143
—Congressional oversight, 87, 89, 91
—consultants' report on USES, 1959, 264n.
29, 271n. 130
—counseling work, 251n. 54
—and discrimination, 266nn. 66, 70, 71
—and employers, 154
—Federal Advisory Council, 30, 55–56, 73,
107, 236n. 71, 261nn. 216, 220, 271nn.
131, 133, 272n. 157
—federalization of, 15, 72–74, 256n. 145
—federal regulation of USES, 87–91
—founding, 26–33
—and 1977 General Accounting Office report,
156
—and Great Society programs, 141–46;
Apprenticeship Information Centers, 145,
146–47; Conceptual Model approach, 139;
employability development program, 139;
Human Resources Development program,
139, 145–46; Work Incentive Program,
148–49, 155
—integration with unemployment compensation, 53–60, 244nn. 220, 223, 245nn. 235,
237
—and Job Training Partnership Act, 159
—merger with National Reemployment
Service, 30–31
—Office of National Contracts, 147;
Apprenticeship and Journeymen Outreach
Programs, 147
—placement record, 67–72, 109–11
—politicization, 246n. 255
—postwar decentralization, 93–98, 110, 256n.
145, 257nn. 157, 166, 258n. 178, 259nn.
184, 185
—principal claimants, 107
—and private employment agencies, 142,
250n. 28, 272nn. 152, 153
—processing of job seekers, 32
—reform of USES under President Bush,
160–61
—reform of USES under President Nixon, 160
—reform of USES under President Reagan,
160

U.S. Employment Service (*continued*)
—response to the National Urban Coalition
  study, 153–55, 274n. 190, 275nn. 191, 192
—and Second World War, 72–77
—segregation in USES offices, 98–101,
  117–18, 124–28, 258nn. 173, 179, 181,
  182, 259n. 183
—separation of placement and benefit work,
  106–9, 152–57
—state advisory councils, 33, 154–55, 237n.
  82
—statement on postwar role, 76–77, 251nn.
  50, 56, 257n. 161, 259n. 191
—Thomas Report, 67–70, 87–91
—and unemployment compensation work-
  test, 83–85, 244n. 223, 248n. 264, 253n.
  86, 261n. 219. *See also* Interstate
  Conference on Employment Security
  Agencies; Labor Exchanges
U.S. Employment Service Task Force of 1965,
  70, 96–97, 109, 249n. 24, 252n. 58, 254n.
  89, 266n. 65, 272nn. 149, 151, 154; recommendations, 124, 141–43, 258n. 170,
  261nn. 227, 228, 266n. 64; support in
  Johnson White House, 266n. 62; USES
  and labor market policy, 141–43
U.S. General Accounting Office, 70; criticisms of USES, 70, 72, 249n. 22, 250n.
  28; 1977 report on USES, 155–56, 275n.
  195; 1986 Report of USES, 266n. 62;
  1987 report on work incentive programs,
  187–88
U.S. National Association of Manufacturers
  (NAM), 10; and founding of labor
  exchanges, 52–53; and funding of USES,
  122; support for manpower policy, 136,
  210; workforce skills, 210
U.S. Training and Employment Service. *See*
  U.S. Department of Labor

Verba, S., 277n. 2
Veterans' Readjustment Assistance Act of
  1952 (U.S.), 108
Vickerstaff, Sarah, 267n. 82, 269nn. 101, 112
Vogel, U., 283n. 58

Wagner, Senator Robert F., 23; and advocacy
  of labor exchanges, 27–29, 61–62, 235n.
  49; and Hoover veto of labor exchanges,
  50–52, 243n. 210; and postwar economic
  policy, 116
Wagner-Peyser Act (1933), 10, 88, 122, 144,

155, 211; administration of work-tests, 62;
  details of legislation, 29–30; Federal
  Advisory Council, 30; funding of USES,
  122; passage of, in Congress, 26–33,
  49–53, 243n. 213; and manpower policy,
  144–45; and National Re-employment
  Service, 30–31; and New Deal, 63; and
  organized labor, 49–52
Waldron, J., 223n. 2, 296n. 28
Walsh, John, 273n. 163
War Manpower Commission (U.S.), 62, 65,
  72–73, 75–76, 90; and postwar role of
  USES, 75–76, 102, 250n. 39, 251n. 50,
  254n. 93, 257n. 161; and U.S.
  Employment Service, 72–74
Ward, H., 226n. 18, 279n. 18
Warner, M., 268n. 97
War on Poverty. *See* Johnson, President
  Lyndon B., Great Society
Webb, Sydney and Beatrice, 12, 226n. 17
Weinberg, Daniel, 283n. 60
Weir, M., 163, 230n. 60, 235n. 58, 262nn. 5,
  15, 264n. 26, 265n. 60, 270n. 127, 275n.
  194, 277nn. 220, 222, 280n. 35, 293n. 3
Welch, S., 229n. 49
Welfare dependency. *See* Work-welfare
Welfare policy. *See* Work-welfare
Welfare state, xi–xvi; and social rights of citi-
  zenship, xi; theories of welfare policy,
  1–14. *See also* Work-welfare
White, Walter, 99
White Paper on Employment Policy, 1944
  (Britain), 74, 92, 114, 129, 164, 170, 255n.
  135, 262nn. 8, 10, 11, 267n. 83, 278n. 7
Wickham-Jones, M., 293n. 6
Wikeley, N., 278n. 12
Wilkie, Alex, 42
Wilkinson, F., 278n. 12
Wilson, Harold, 130, 209, 268n. 92, 293n. 5
Wilson, Havelock M.P., 21
Wilson, James Q., 283n. 60
Wilson, Governor Pete, 202
Wilson, W. J., 279n. 29
Winship, Chris, 176, 281n. 40
Wirtz, Willard, 125–26, 136, 262n. 3, 265n.
  59, 266n. 71, 270n. 125, 271nn. 131, 135,
  272nn. 137, 150; Kennedy/Johnson
  administration, 136–37; and manpower
  policy, 144–45; and private employment
  agencies, 142
Wolkinson, B., 229n. 45
Wood, G., 230n. 55

Women workers, 9; and trades unions, 8–9; and labor exchanges, 9
Worcester, Kenton, 264n. 46
Work Experience Programme. *See* Manpower Services Commission
Workfare. *See* Work-welfare
Work Incentive Program (WIN). *See* Johnson, President Lyndon B.; Work-welfare
Work-tests. *See* Labor Exchanges; Work-welfare
Work-welfare:
—Clinton administration proposals, 200–201, 277n. 226
—defined, xi, xv–xvi
—institutionalization of work-welfare, 14–17, 65–66, 92–102, 229n. 52
—integration of benefits and placement, xiv–xv, 4, 14–16, 19, 65, 151, 204
—manpower policy and welfare recipients, 144–45
—and policy legacies, 14–15, 17–18, 61–64, 78–85, 92, 110–11, 118–20, 123, 197–202, 203–5
—political origins of, xii–xiii, 17–18, 205–11; in Britain, 33–46, 60–61, 205–6, 207–9; in United States, 47–53, 206–7, 209–10
—and social citizenship, 167–77
—social democratic programs, 293n. 4
—and training policy: in Britain, 118–21, 128–33, 150–52; in United States, 121–28, 133–41, 144–46, 152–56
—and underclass, 176–77, 279n. 29
—and welfare dependency, 158, 175–76, 183–84
—workfare, xv, 140–41, 174, 185, 186, 198–200, 279n. 16, 284n. 77, 292n. 155
—work-tests, 36, 61, 78–85, 92, 204, 252n. 64
—work-welfare and liberal tradition, 177–84; in Britain, 177–80, 192–93; in the United States, 180–84, 207
Work-welfare programs, 149–50, 167–77
Work-welfare programs in Great Britain, 220–22
—Community Action Programme, 292n. 156
—Employment Act of 1989, 168–73
—Employment Action, 199–200
—Employment Training Programme of 1988, 133, 165–66, 168–73, 180, 279n. 16; Local Enterprise Councils, 184; Training and Enterprise Councils, 184, 190–92, 288nn. 111, 116, 289nn. 121, 123, 124
—Enterprise Allowance Scheme, 192
—job-seeker's allowance, 170–71, 172, 200
—Restart interviews, 171, 172–73, 285n. 86
—Social Security Act of 1985, 171
—Social Security Act of 1988, 168–73
—Social Security Act of 1989, 168–73
Work-welfare programs in the United States, 53–60, 219–20
—Clinton administration proposals, 200–201, 277n. 226
—Community Work Experience Program, 174
—Comprehensive Employment and Training Act of 1973, 155, 158, 163, 193
—Demonstration programs, 216
—Family Support Act of 1988, 168, 173–77, 193–97, 198–202, 279n. 25, 290n. 135; antecedents, 140, 159, 163, 279n. 21, 280n. 33; enactment, 173–77, 211; and Job Training Partnership Act, 193–97, 290n. 138; participation rate requirements, 196–97, 290n. 135, 293nn. 171, 172; work requirements, 174
—ET, Massachusetts, 187, 271n. 142, 290n. 136, 291n. 153
—GAIN, California, 187, 196, 279n. 24, 287nn. 103, 105, 291nn. 149, 150, 151
—Healthfare, Maryland, 202
—Learnfare, Wisconsin, 202
—MOST, Michigan, 287n. 106
—Victory, Tennessee, 285n. 90
—Wedfare, New Jersey, 202
—WORK, Arkansas, 287nn. 103, 104
—Work Incentive Program (WIN), 140–41, 148–49, 155, 182–83

Young, (Lord) David, 133, 289n. 132
Youth Opportunities Programme. *See* Manpower Services Commission
Youth Training Programme. *See* Manpower Services Commission

Zeitlin, J., 267n. 84